T0304305

This is the first monograph dealing with any aspect of the experience of the Italian *petite bourgeoisie*. From the mid-1880s a shopkeeper movement developed in Milan, centred around a shopkeeper newspaper, a federation of shopkeeper trade associations and a shopkeeper bank. Initially the movement aligned itself with the Radicals in city politics, but in 1904 it was shopkeeper representatives who set in chain the sequence of events that led to the fall of the first Radical-Socialist administration within the city.

The author explains these events with reference to the business of shop-keeping itself. He analyses the trades, techniques, tax structure and topography of the Milanese retail sector. The study traces the history of the contest between shops and cooperatives, and the changing nature of the shopkeeper's relationship with his employees, and with his clientele.

Considerable emphasis is placed upon the politics of the shopkeeper movement. These are analysed in the context both of Italian history and of the debates over *petit-bourgeois* identity and autonomy which have become essential for our understanding of modern European history. In his final chapters the author confronts the crucial question of why it was the Milanese shopkeepers were to be found on the right in the years that led up the Fascist takeover in Italy.

Past and Present Publications

The political economy of shopkeeping in Milan 1886–1922

Past and Present Publications

General Editor: PAUL SLACK, *Exeter College, Oxford*

Past and Present Publications comprise books similar in character to the articles in the journal *Past and Present*. Whether the volumes in the series are collections of essays – some previously published, others new studies – or monographs, they encompass a wide variety of scholarly and original works primarily concerned with social, economic and cultural changes, and their causes and consequences. They will appeal to both specialists and non-specialists and will endeavour to communicate the results of historical and allied research in readable and lively form.

For a list of titles in Past and Present Publications, see end of book.

The political economy of shopkeeping in Milan 1886–1922

JONATHAN MORRIS

Lecturer in Modern European History
University College London

CAMBRIDGE
UNIVERSITY PRESS

CAMBRIDGE UNIVERSITY PRESS
Cambridge, New York, Melbourne, Madrid, Cape Town, Singapore, São Paulo

Cambridge University Press
The Edinburgh Building, Cambridge CB2 8RU, UK

Published in the United States of America by Cambridge University Press, New York

www.cambridge.org
Information on this title: www.cambridge.org/9780521391191

First published 1993
First paperback edition 2002

A catalogue record for this publication is available from the British Library

Library of Congress Cataloguing in Publication data
Morris, Jonathan.
The political economy of shopkeeping in Milan, 1886–1922 / Jonathan Morris.
         p.   cm. – (Past and present publications)
Includes bibliographical references (p.   ).
ISBN 0 521 39119 9
1. Retail trade – Government policy – Italy – Milan – History.   2. Milan (Italy) –
Commercial policy – History.   3. Milan (Italy) – Commerce – History.   4. Stores.
Retail – Italy – Milan – History.   5. Merchants – Italy – Milan – History.   I. Title.
HF5429.6.I82M556   1993
381'.1'094521–dc20   92–8745   CIP

ISBN 978-0-521-39119-1 hardback
ISBN 978-0-521-89384-8 paperback

Transferred to digital printing 2008

To Elizabeth, with love

Contents

Figures

Tables

Acknowledgements

When I presented my doctoral thesis, I was able to acknowledge the support I received from many quarters during my period of graduate study. In the interest of brevity, I shall confine this round of thanks to those who have assisted me in developing my work since then. I am glad that there is no need to make an exception to this in order to include Jonathan Steinberg, who still extends encouragement and advice with the same degree of enthusiasm that he did as my supervisor.

I would like to thank the Master and Fellows of Corpus Christi College, Cambridge, and the Department of History at University College London for providing me with the opportunity and the stimulus to continue my studies, as well as providing some financial assistance to that end. I would also like to thank the British Academy, the British School at Rome, Christ's College, Cambridge, the Council of Europe and the Italian Government for their generosity in supporting my research.

I have been fortunate enough to be asked to speak at the universities of Cambridge, Essex, Harvard, Oxford, Reading and Warwick, the European University Institute and the Fondazione Bagatti Valsecchi. On all of these occasions I benefited from the comments and suggestions of those present.

I am particularly grateful to Martin Brown, David Cannadine, Geoffrey Crossick, John Davis, Christopher Duggan, John Foot, Paul Ginsborg, Heinz-Gerhard Haupt, David Lavan, Bob Lumley, Adrian Lyttelton, Marco Meriggi, Cesare Mozzarelli, Lucy Riall, Rafaelle Romanelli, Marco Soresina, Cristina Stefanini and Louise Tilly, all of whom put their professional advice at my disposal, but none of whom is in anyway responsible for what follows.

I should like to thank Anne Morris and Caterina Paone for their heroic efforts with my English and Italian respectively. I am also grateful to Claudia Scott for all that she did for me in Milan. My three families, British, American and Italian, have been highly supportive of my efforts. Above all, however, I want to thank my parents Anne and Graham Morris for always having faith in me.

My wife, Elizabeth, has supported me in every possible way throughout the time that this book has taken to write. I dedicate it to her, with love.

Introduction: shopkeeping as a historical problem

The initial spark for this study came from a different set of shop-keepers in a different city from that with which it deals. In the mid-1980s I spent a year studying in Bologna, a city well known for the profusion of small shops under the porticoes of its historic centre, and in which the suburbs still host a far greater number of shops, bars and restaurants than similar cities in Britain and America.[1] The proprietors of these establishments were the first people I got to know in the city, and they good-humouredly assisted me in my struggle to learn Italian by engaging them in conversation whilst having my hair cut, buying my groceries or drinking my *cappuccino*. As an outsider I was very struck by the contrasts between the Italian small retailing sector and that in my own country, prompting a curiosity about the history of shopkeepers in Italy. To my surprise I found that no modern Italian scholar had investigated this stratum of society.[2]

In retrospect this does not appear so unusual. Even after the explosion of interest in social history in the 1960s, historians throughout Europe regarded the lower middle classes with sus-picion. Workers and peasants made more ideologically acceptable subjects for the practitioners of 'history from below' who tended to sneer at the *petit-bourgeois* values that theorists and psycho-historians suggested were indicative of inherently authoritarian, if

[1] The small shopkeeping sector in Italy is in decline, however, the victim of the supermarket habit and the chain retailer. Lonardi, 'Scompariranno centomila negozi'. (All notes and references are given as author plus short title; full details are given in the bibliography.)
[2] On the lack of literature on the Italian lower middle classes see Berezin, 'Created constituencies', p. 143. Rossano Zezzos did write the delightful *Vita della bottega* in 1942, but the subtitle, 'a sentimental guide to commerce', indicates the approach he adopted in this and several other works.

not Fascist, tendencies.[3] Mainstream historians utilised these stereotypes to bring Hitler and, crucially for the Italian case, Mussolini to power, but provided little of the context in which the actions of these strata could be understood.

This was especially the case for the 'old' lower middle class of shopkeepers and master artisans that has come to be known as the *petite bourgeoisie*. Indeed the inadequacies of this approach were highlighted by the repeated linkage of the 'old' and 'new' lower middle classes within a single group. The key to understanding these classes, it was argued, was the concept of status anxiety. Fearful of finding themselves squeezed into extinction between the interests of big business and organised labour, the lower middle classes were prepared to look beyond the political mainstream for a strategy to preserve their status. Arno Mayer, in an essay on the lower middle class (note the use of the singular), argued that

> in ... moments of extreme crisis ... the vague sense of negative commonality – of being neither bourgeois nor worker – is transformed into a political awareness or consciousness of economic, social and cultural identity. The economic incompatibilities and the status incongruities between the major occupational and professional segments of the lower middle class do not disappear, but in moments of soaring disequilibration, which bring existential issues to the fore, these internal strains and tensions become of lesser importance than the immediate conflicts with external economic and social forces.

At these moments a '*grande peur* of downward mobility ... is the root of the erratic and intermittently frenzied politicisation of the lower middle classes'.[4]

In many ways, however, Mayer's 1975 essay marked an important step forward in the analysis of the lower middle classes. An attack on Marxist determinism, it was intended as an injunction that the lower middle class should be studied 'on its own terms'.[5] In the mid-1970s several scholars published work predicated on concrete research into shopkeeper and artisan movements. Robert Gellately's study of the shopkeepers' movement, Shulamit Volkov's work on urban master artisans, and Heinrich Winkler's broad-canvas

---

[3] Nord, *Paris shopkeepers*, pp. 8–16 provides a good review of this and associated literature on the lower middle classes.
[4] Mayer, 'The lower middle class as a historical problem', p. 434.
[5] Ibid., p. 410.

interpretation of the politics of the *petite bourgeoisie* were all read-ings of the German situation that sought to explain support for Fascism through an analysis of the pre-war period.[6]

Two features of this period commanded particular attention. First, there was the fact that, in mid-century, artisans still voted liberal but had turned to the conservatives by the end of the century. Volkov's analysis of this phenomenon suggested an anomaly, however. Despite their support of liberal parties that advocated wider political participation, artisans were fearful of *laissez-faire* economics, and continued to be attached to the pre-industrial gild system. Their failure to adapt to new forms of production was accentuated by the onset of the great depression that reached its nadir in the 1890s. The institution of a wider franchise after unifi-cation, albeit in a restricted political system, encouraged artisans to advance their anti-modernist and backward-looking sentiments, until by the turn of the century they were associated with the extremist and anti-Semitic parties of the right.

Winkler and Gellately concentrated on the ways in which the parties of the right attempted to incorporate shopkeepers and master artisans into their bloc. Winkler argued for the development of *Mittelstandspolitik*, a series of measures of social protection, such as the re-establishment of gild organisations and discriminatory taxes against department stores and consumer cooperatives, by which the conservatives recruited the lower middle classes into their camp as a bulwark against the Socialists. This social protectionism, it was argued, caused the German shopkeepers and artisans to identify with the authoritarian conservatism of the final decades of the Empire and to regard the new Weimar Republic with suspicion. Thus the German *Mittelstand* were incorporated into the political system as adjuncts to an authoritarian, predominantly agrarian, conservatism which only survived as a result of the anachronistic political development of the nation.

These interpretations were criticised by the group of historians who participate in the international round tables on the *petite bourgeoisie* led by Geoffrey Crossick and Heinz-Gerhard Haupt.[7] In

---

[6] Gellately, *The politics of economic despair*. Volkov, *The rise of popular anti-modernism in Germany*. Winkler's work is usefully summarised in his article 'From social protectionism to national socialism'.

[7] For an account of one of these see Blackbourn, 'Economic crisis and the *petite bourgeoisie*'.

a collection of essays published in 1983, Crossick and Haupt argued that there was a 'regrettable' tendency for research on shopkeepers and artisans to focus too heavily on the political sphere, ignoring the social and economic context in which activity took place.[8] Where a trader's business was located, for instance, had a critical effect upon his relations with his clientele and on how he conducted his trade. In a working-class suburb his social status would be high and his economic power considerable, even if his actual business was not all that large. In a more mixed residential area the shopkeeper would find himself lower down the social scale, and might have to show deference to his 'betters' in order to retain their custom.[9] These kinds of consideration had considerable implications for the development of a *petit-bourgeois* identity.

In effect Crossick and Haupt called for a far more vigorous investigation of the *petite bourgeoisie* on its own terms. Instead of reading the history of *petit-bourgeois* organisations as that of the origins of Fascism, they sought to understand the reasons for the development of such associations in terms of their meaning to their members. One way of avoiding overly teleological interpretations was to concentrate exclusively on the pre-1914 period, as did all the essays in the published collection. Another was to recognise that 'at the level of national comparisons, similarities might be more striking than differences, especially in daily existence and experiences. The interesting contrasts might be less those amongst countries, and more the distinctions between types of town.'[10]

The value of city studies was proven by Philip Nord, a member of the round table, in his book on Parisian shopkeepers published in 1986.[11] This revealed the very different experiences of those retailers who had stores on the new avenues constructed by Haussmann and those left in the back-street arcades. It was the latter, under the influence of the deprivation wrought by the great depression, who set up shopkeeper organisations and allied themselves with that other section of society in decline, the displaced literary *boulevardiers*. The commercial environment created a fragmentation of interests and an autonomy of response that belied any deterministic notion of politics within the shopkeeper sector.

[8] Crossick and Haupt, 'Shopkeepers, master artisans and the historian', p. 6.
[9] On this see Blackbourn, 'Between resignation and volatility', p. 53. Vigne and Howkins, 'The small shopkeeper in industrial and market towns', pp. 194–5, 206.
[10] Crossick and Haupt, 'Shopkeepers, master artisans and the historian', p. 22.
[11] Nord, *Paris shopkeepers*.

The discovery of such concrete diversity within the *petite bourgeoisie* led the historians of the round table to reject the idea that this stratum proceeded along an inexorable path from left to right across the political spectrum. In Paris, for instance, members of the league of shopkeepers were prepared to support the far-right Nationalists and anti-Semites when these groups espoused shopkeeper concerns, but they were equally prepared to move back towards the conventional right when it appeared they would gain from doing so. Under certain circumstances, Nord claimed, it was possible to imagine the *petite bourgeoisie* finding allies not on the right but on the left.[12]

The explanatory power of *Mittelstandspolitik* was attacked from several directions. Its linkage to German particularities was undermined by the discovery that many governments, notably the Belgian, had made use of similar strategies to woo the *petite bourgeoisie*. Furthermore most of the measures governments introduced were of little real benefit to shopkeepers and master artisans; and traders, aware of this, continued to judge political programmes on their merits. In Germany, for instance, many small trade associations refused to support the conservatives' financial reforms of 1909 (which would have increased retailers' overheads) and switched their adherence to the liberal *Hansabund*.[13]

This flexibility was hailed as an indication of political autonomy. The *petite bourgeoisie* were neither incorporated into the conservative forces that sought to use them to bolster their own position, nor so excluded as to pose a threat to the system itself. Rather, they

[12] Nord raised the question of whether or not a form of revisionist Socialism that was more accommodating to the concept of private property might not have exercised some appeal on Parisian shopkeepers: *Paris shopkeepers*, pp. 16–17, 291, 431–2. Haupt, analysing the overall situation in France, states that the tendency to turn to the right should not be exaggerated and that although conflicts between workers and small capitalists became more violent at the énd of the nineteenth century many *petits bourgeois* who employed no outside labour found no problem in supporting the Socialists: 'The *petite bourgeoisie* in France', pp. 111–12. Blackbourn argues that, in Germany, shopkeepers in working-class areas often lived within the subculture of the labour movement, particularly the small publicans who were prominent in the SPD, and that many proprietors 'were actually refugees from the working class following depression or victimisation, who were locked firmly within the subculture of Social Democracy': Blackbourn, *Class, religion and local politics*, p. 185n, and 'Between resignation and volatility', pp. 53–5.
[13] On Germany see Blackbourn, 'The *Mittelstand* in German society and Politics' and 'Between resignation and volatility', pp. 50–3. On Belgium see Kurgan-van Hentenryk, 'A forgotten class', p. 129.

showed themselves prepared to turn to whatever political parties came closest to addressing their concerns, forming temporary alliances on the basis of specific policies. They were much more politically independent than earlier commentators have given them credit for.

Inevitably historians are now importing the round-table approach into the inter-war era. In 1990 Rudy Koshar edited a collection of essays on the politics and the lower middle classes in this period, and used his introductory essay to provide a typology of the political trajectories identified by the contributors.[14] These were support for political parties of the established centre or right, support for Fascist or Radical Nationalist parties, involvement with the left, and attempts to establish independent political parties of their own. The diversity of strategies again confirmed the political flexibility of these strata.

Such variety, however, can blind us to the fact that the first two trajectories were by far the most widely chosen, even in most of those states where others were available. This was not a purely post-war phenomenon. As Volkov observed when reviewing the Crossick and Haupt collection, the fact that a shift to the right was not predetermined does not mean that it did not take place.[15] It was not inexorable, it may not have been the product of authoritarianism or *Mittelstandspolitik*, but it still has to be explained.

This book reviews some of the questions raised by previous research within the Italian, and more specifically Milanese, context. The approach mirrors that of the round-table historians in that my primary aim was to analyse the emergence of a small-trader movement in Milan after 1885 through investigation of the social and commercial circumstances of shopkeeping in the city. The bulk of the book, a substantial revision of my 1989 thesis on the subject, concentrates on the first twenty years of the movement during which time a shopkeeper newspaper, federation and bank were all founded, and a variety of political positions were adopted culminating in an unsuccessful attempt at collaboration with the left.[16] I have added a chapter on the succeeding twenty years of the movement in order to explore further the vexed question of why shopkeepers ended up on the right in the post-war era.

[14] Koshar, 'On the politics of the splintered classes', in *Splintered Classes*, pp. 15–17.
[15] Volkov, 'Review of Crossick and Haupt, eds.', pp. 266–9.
[16] Morris, 'The political economy of shopkeeping in Milan'.

Italy provides a fruitful case study for the analysis of lower middle class politics. Industrialisation in the country that was to be the birthplace of European Fascism began even later than in Germany, but growth rates were extremely rapid, particularly in Milan. At the same time the political system of the country, and to a lesser extent the city, continued to be dominated by an agrarian and professional elite, primarily drawn from outside the industrial zone, whilst electoral and constitutional restrictions limited popular participation in politics.

There was a considerable separation between the 'legal' Italy of the elite political classes and the 'real Italy' that had evolved since unification. The *crisi del fine secolo* (end-of-century crisis) underlined this division, with a sequence of violent public-order disturbances culminating in the May events of 1898 in Milan when military rule was imposed on the city. In the aftermath of the crisis, Giolitti emerged as the dominant figure in Italian politics. His judicious use of *trasformismo*, the art of compromising with one's challengers in order to absorb them into one's coalition, and his understanding of the necessity for an appearance of state neutrality in disputes between capital and labour, apparently enabled him to reconcile 'legal' and 'real' Italy to each other through the management of a transition to mass politics.

These developments can be interpreted in several ways. One is to argue that Giolitti was able to achieve this feat by absorbing a weak commercial and industrial bourgeoisie into his political bloc, thus preserving power for the pre-industrial elites. Other scholars are far more wary of such characterisations of the Italian bourgeoisie, whether in terms of the way it employed its capital, the ways in which it affirmed its identity, and the political directions that it followed. They provide evidence of the development of a bourgeois identity through the growth of myriad associations, an identity that developed in tandem with, and sometimes in contradiction to, that being forged in the working-class institutions set up in industrialising areas within the country. In essence they argue that the bourgeoisie bought itself into the system, but not in order to play the part of liberal democratic revolutionaries.[17] Such readings are especially persuasive when applied to city politics in those

---

[17] For a review of these debates see Gozzazini, 'Borghesie italiane dell'Ottocento' and Meriggi, 'La borghesia italiana'.

centres in which industrial and commercial growth was most rapid.[18]

The history of the lower middle classes has hardly featured in these debates. Raffaele Romanelli has provided a study of town clerks throughout Italy, a unique group of public administrators whose social status varied considerably according to the council to which they were attached.[19] The experience of the *petite bourgeoisie* has yet to be analysed. Were they incorporated into the Giolittian bloc in an echo of the *Mittelstandspolitik* discerned by some scholars of the German Empire, were they an appendage of an industrial and commercial bourgeoisie that was formed within an urban setting, or did they develop their own identity as a borderline class between the bourgeoisie and the proletariat?

This study will address those questions, but before doing so it is necessary to clarify some points of methodology raised by an attempt to understand group politics in terms of class, identity and mobilisation.

If classes are to be defined in Marxist terms, that is by means of their relation to capital and labour within the framework of production and exchange of wealth, then any attempt to lump white-collar workers and small traders into a single lower middle class immediately falls in that the former are employees whilst the latter are self-employed, and, on occasion, employers. It has been suggested that the unique feature of the *petite bourgeoisie* lies in the fact that its livelihood is derived from working its own capital, that is both financing and working within the business.[20] As a working definition this is helpful, but both sides of the equation remain fraught with difficulty. Whose capital is employed in a shop when an individual retailer effectively survives on credit from his wholesaler?

---

[18] On Milan see Meriggi, 'Vita di circolo e rappresentanza civica' and Porro, 'Amministrazione e potere locale'.

[19] Romanelli, *Sulle carte interminate.* Since this introduction was written, a new study of white-collar workers in Milan has been published: Soresina, *Mezzemaniche e Signorine.*

[20] Bechhofer and Elliot have argued that 'though a good many [of the *petite bourgeoisie*] also become the employers of hired labour, the scale of that exploitation is typically very small and is an extension of, rather than a substitute for, their own labour' (Bechhofer and Elliott, 'Petty property', p. 183). See also their general discussion of the topic of the characteristics of the *petite bourgeoisie*, ibid., pp. 182–7. For a discussion of the structural difficulties of defining the *petite bourgeoisie* in Marxist terms see Crossick and Haupt, 'Shopkeepers, master artisans and the historian', pp. 6–10.

Should there be a distinction between labour which adds value to the product, and simply selling ready-made goods over the counter? And when does a proprietor graduate into the bourgeoisie? Working one's own capital would not preclude the employment of others to work alongside the proprietor, but does an employer's retreat from the counter or the workbench to handle the rest of the business signify the introduction of a division of labour sufficient to raise the proprietor into the next class up?

If it is difficult to define the *petite bourgeoisie* as a class 'in itself', it is also hard to see how it might be expected to act as a class 'for itself'. Master artisans and shopkeepers frequently had very diffferent interests: workshop owners accused retailers of stealing their markets by selling manufactured goods that had previously been brought from the producer, whilst shopkeepers resented artisans supplying department stores.[21] Many trades, such as baking, incorporated aspects of both production and retail, making it difficult to draw even a simple distinction between the interests of shopkeepers and workshop owners that might facilitate some form of sectorial consciousness. Trades such as grocery and pharmacy were often in direct confrontation with one another over which types of good each should be allowed to sell. Even within a single trade the interests of well-established retailers with several hands in their employ were very different from those of the one-man operations set up by retired workers. Ultimately all traders were in direct competition with one another.

A search for the creation of a compact *petit-bourgeois* identity is therefore almost certain to founder. What may be discerned, however, is the mobilisation of certain strata within the *petite bourgeoisie* as they identify common interests between them. These are likely to relate more to specific circumstances within the commercial environment in which they operate, than to a simple shared relation to capital and labour. Some form of mobilisation can be held to have occurred when there is a passage from, say, the existence of simple trade associations to the emergence of institutions representing the interests of several trades simultaneously – federations of such associations, journals targeted at a group of trades, rather than an individual activity, or simple campaign organisations supported by adherents from a variety of occupations, dedicated to the resolution of common problems.

[21] Blackbourn, 'The *Mittelstand* in German society and politics', p. 415.

The problem of identity is better approached by investigating groups who associated with each other because they felt they had similar needs within the commercial environment (that is, by taking account of their own definition of such interests), therefore, than by attempting to discern a class consciousness across the entire range of occupations that make up the *petite bourgeoisie*. The important questions become which groups associated with each other and why they did so, questions which can only be addressed through an understanding of a specific business environment. The local level is key here: small business tends to be locally orientated; small shop-keeping, almost by definition, is so.

Studying shopkeeper movements is not the same thing as studying shopkeeper identity, however. One must distinguish between leaders, members and sympathisers within such movements, and be aware of the diversity of meanings and motivations that par-ticipation in collective activity can indicate. Movements do not automatically become spokesmen for all shopkeepers: indeed their failures in this context are as important as their successes. Above all it is necessary to recall that individuals might have several 'identi-ties' formed on the basis of religious, family or neighbourhood affiliations, as well as occupational ones. The relative weight given to these identities might change as a result of circumstance – there is much evidence to suggest that this was the case as regards the political responses of Milanese shopkeepers.

It is the attempts to construct an occupational identity amongst Milanese shopkeepers that occupy the bulk of this book. The existence of a shopkeepers' newspaper, *L'Esercente*, is the key source for this analysis, but I have used it in accordance with the warnings delivered above. It is fortunate that this newspaper was a commercial venture which needed to sell copies amongst shop-keepers in order to survive, and was therefore obliged to print what it thought its readers would accept. More importantly the news-paper was in frequent dispute with the other main institutions of the movement, notably the shopkeepers' federation, with the result that the historian is offered two interpretations of the same situation, albeit that the alternative is sometimes wrapped in the excoriation of *L'Esercente*. Whenever I have been able to check reports of shop-keeper association meetings or statements in *L'Esercente* they have proved accurate; and I have naturally applied the discretion any critical historian should to those which cannot be verified. Political, commercial and trade association elections also provide substantial clues, particularly when the results provided a clear rebuke to the movement's leadership.

The history of the shopkeepers' movement cannot be approached without an understanding of the environment in which it evolved. The book begins, therefore, with an analysis of the business of shopkeeping in Milan.

1. The business of shopkeeping in Milan, 1859–1915

The first three chapters of this book investigate the historical context of retailing in the city, along with the business practices of small traders and their role in the local neighbourhood. By combining this context with an analysis of the differing fortunes of the various retail sectors, we can come to some conclusions about why it was that only certain trades, and only certain geographical sectors within those trades, were attracted to the idea of collective activity. First, though, it is necessary to outline the transformations in the Milanese economy during the post-unification era, and their effects on the shopkeeping business cycle.

THE MILANESE ECONOMY, 1859–1915

Between 1859 and 1915 the population of Milan nearly trebled, rising from 232,000 to 658,000, and the number of commercial enterprises registered in the city more than quadrupled. Milan was transformed into a centre of 'industrial capitalism' with over eight times as many financial operations and fifteen times as many engineering businesses. Immigrants arrived in large numbers, attracted by the employment prospects, and the number of registered enterprises renting out rooms or beds rose from 56 to 1,457.[1]

In the mid-nineteenth century the Milanese economy was dominated by the silk and textiles trade. The mills were located in the rural towns and villages of the Provincia, surrounding the city, but Milan was the trading and distribution centre for the industry. Within the city, small-scale artisan workshops produced consumer

---

[1] 'Curiosità statistche: esercenti in Milano dal 1859 al 1915', *Città di Milano*, December 1915, pp. 657–8. 'Milan 1880–1922: the city of industrial capitalism' is the title of an essay by Adrian Lyttelton.

goods for the local market.[2] By the 1870s the silk industry had fallen victim to cheaper Asian production and silkworm disease, but the cotton industry, producing primarily for the domestic market, experienced considerable growth, bolstered by granting of tariff protection in 1878.

This success provided the background to the industrial upsurge of the first eight years of the 1880s which was observed throughout northern Italy. Various explanations have been advanced for this phenomenon, but it is clear that Milan was one of its chief beneficiaries.[3] The most rapid expansion occurred in the engineering and chemical sectors, stimulated by both state orders and investment in agricultural machinery and fertilisers. Engineering firms built cars for the railway through the St. Gotthard pass, linking Milan to Switzerland and Central Europe, which was opened in July 1882. New companies such as Pirelli (chemicals) and the Società Edison (electricity) were founded.

The most important effect of the industrial spurt was demographic. The prosperity of the city attracted many migrants and its population rose from 299,008 in 1879 to 408,294 ten years later (see Fig. 1.1a–d).[4] In terms of the nature of production, however, Milan was still more a Paris than a Manchester. Large numbers of small workshops produced consumer articles for the fashion and luxury markets; the hat-making industry, for example, continued to use

[2] Della Peruta, 'Lavoro e fabbrica', pp. 223–34.
[3] Romeo argued that the acceleration between 1881 and 1887 was a consequence of a 'modernisation' of the Italian economy through infrastructural development and capital accumulation in the previous two decades: Gerschenkron and Romeo, 'The industrial development of Italy', p. 111. Gerschenkron, however, believed it was only a moment when 'the advantages of backwardness accumulate until they reach a certain high point', stimulated primarily by railway construction. When orders dried up 'the favourable moment was lost', ibid., p. 120. Later analysts, such as Fenoaltea, prefer a cyclical explanation ('Decollo, ciclo e intervento dello Stato', p. 109). Industry needed to renew its plant and machinery capacity, creating a demand to which the steel-making and engineering sectors responded; when refurbishment was completed, demand fell away until the late 1890s when this equipment was itself in need of renewal. There is a very useful critical analysis of these and other models of Italian development in Romano, 'Gli inizi del capitalismo italiano', pp. 17–28. He goes on to argue that whilst state demand stimulated the steel and shipbuilding industries through naval and railway orders, the growth in the engineering and chemical industries was partly explained by landowners finally investing in agricultural machinery and chemicals in an attempt to overcome the profound crisis in agriculture (ibid., p. 41).
[4] *Dati statistici*, 1905, p. 57.

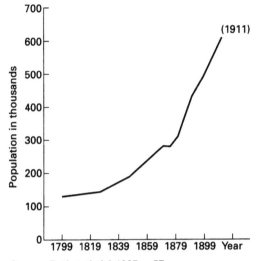

Source: Dati statistici, 1905, p.57

Fig. 1.1a '*Di fatto*' population of Milan, 1799–1911

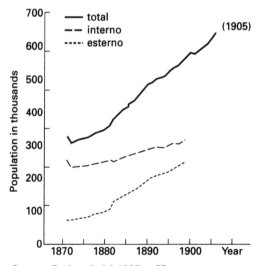

Source: Dati statistici, 1905, p.57

Fig. 1.1b '*Di fatto*' population of Milan, 1870–1905

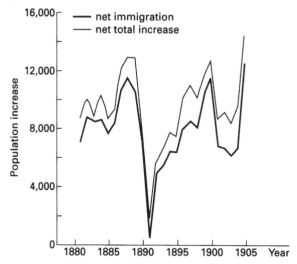

Source: *Dati statistici,* 1905, pp.54–5

Fig. 1.1c Population increase in Milan, 1881–1905

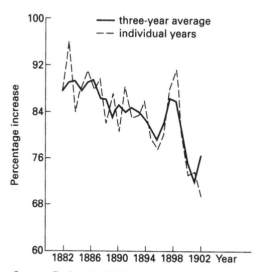

Source: *Dati statistici,* 1905, p.54

Fig. 1.1d Percentage population growth due to net immigration

traditional methods long after mechanised factory production had been introduced in nearby Monza.[5]

The fall in world prices badly affected agriculture in the later 1880s as overseas competitors undercut domestic producers of grain, rice and silk, aided by the return of the lira to gold convertibility in 1883. In July 1887, the government introduced a general tariff, artificially raising prices at a time when free market forces would have forced them down. A squabble between Crispi and the French led the two countries into a trade war which virtually closed off the French market to Lombardy's silk and dairy products between 1888 and 1892 and was not fully resolved until 1898. Milan's links to the French markets were now of little value and many of the city's leading merchants and industrialists entered into a fierce political struggle against the government.[6]

Growth was checked within the city as private demand failed to counterbalance a decline in government orders. Although the protective tariff was extended to some industries, for example textiles and iron and steel production, this placed other activities in even greater difficulties. The Italian engineering industry, a large part of which was situated in Milan, experienced a negative growth rate of 7.4% p.a. between 1888 and 1896 as the domestically manufactured steel the industry was forced to use was overpriced and of poor quality, making products uncompetitive abroad, at a time when the domestic market could not sustain the engineering sector.[7] In 1890 the Grondona and Elvetica engineering plants were forced to lay off workers, putting the blame for this on the (now privatised) rail companies for purchasing foreign stock.[8]

Depression extended over much of the city's economy as demonstrated by the returns for the *tassa esercizio e rivendita*, a municipal tax levied on all forms of commercial activities within the city according to their 'importance' (measured by a variety of instruments,

---

[5] Cocucci Deretta, 'I capellai monzesi', p. 162. Even Franco Della Peruta, who has emphasised the existence of some large units of production in the city prior to unification, accepts the comparisons of Milan and Paris made by the Milanese deputy Giuseppe Colombo in 1881. Della Peruta, 'Lavoro e fabbrica', pp. 238–9.

[6] This is recounted in Fonzi, *Crispi e lo 'Stato di Milano'*.

[7] Gerschenkron, *Economic backwardness in historical perspective*, p. 76.

[8] Tilly, 'The working class of Milan', p. 158. Tilly's unpublished thesis will be superseded in 1992 with the publication of her book *Politics and class in Milan, 1881–1901*.

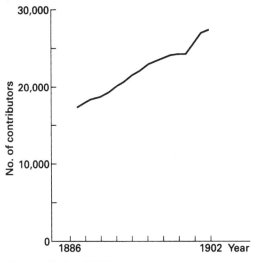

Source: Dati statistici

Fig. 1.2a *Tassa esercizio e rivendita* contributors, 1885–1902

chief of which was the size of their assets).[9] In the 1880s, the numbers of contributors and the amount of tax due rose at roughly equal rates (see Fig. 1.2a and b). Between 1889 and 1895 the annual revenue raised grew more slowly but the number of contributors

---

[9] The faculty to levy a *tassa di esercizio e rivendita* was granted under the *legge 11 agosto 1870 n5784 allegato O* and confirmed at n. 3 of article 164 of the *legge comunale e provinciale*. The tax was payable by all who exercised a profession (i.e. lawyer, doctor), any art, any form of commercial practice, a manufacturing business or retail operation of any sort on their own account. Firms, clubs and societies were also included, bar those of a purely political, educational or charitable nature. Those who sold state monopoly goods were exempt, however. The class to which each enterprise was assigned was calculated with reference to the nature and type of the enterprise, the number of rooms occupied and the rent payable upon them, the number of employees and, most importantly, the value of its assets. Each enterprise then paid the lump sum due in the category to which it was assigned. The very smallest enterprises were exempted. Those proprietors who owned several distinct establishments which all engaged in the same type of activity only paid the tax once (and were only counted once), although those who owned several diverse types of business were taxed (and counted) in each type. Thus though the graphical pattern is clear, the actual numbers given in the statistics cannot be taken to represent the exact number of *esercizi* in Milan. The regulations governing this part of the tax were changed by the *legge 23 gennaio 1902 n25* making the returns for 1903 onwards incompatible with those recorded previously. See Decastro, *La tassa di esercizio e rivendita.*

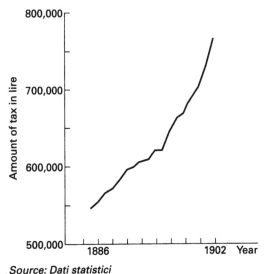

Source: Dati statistici

Fig. 1.2b Amount of *tassa esercizio e rivendita* due, 1885–1902

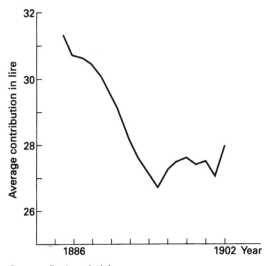

Source: Dati statistici

Fig. 1.2c Average contribution to *tassa esercizio e rivendita*, 1885–1902

was increasing faster than previously. In other words, individual assets were declining. The methods of assessment and payment of the tax make the returns a less than ideal tool for analysis, but the striking pattern shown in Fig. 1.2c is surely proof enough of a slump in the late 1880s and early 1890s.[10]

Milan suffered less than its agricultural hinterland, however, and continued to attract considerable immigration. The cotton industry was protected by the tariff, and enjoyed a period of counter-cyclical expansion between 1887 and 1895.[11] Although much of the French capital involved in industrial and commercial ventures in Italy was withdrawn, German banks moved in to fill the gap. These gravitated to Milan for cultural and geographical reasons. The Banca Commerciale Italiana, for example, was founded with German backing in the city in 1894. Gerschenkron has argued that the German banks were more used to making long-term investments in industry; for example, the Commerciale invested heavily in hydroelectricity.[12]

A restructuring of production also took place during the early 1890s. Large-scale manufacturing, though still far from the norm, grew significantly: in 1892, Sabbatini recorded seventy industrial establishments that employed over one hundred workers including the tannery Fratelli Gelli and the glove factory Francesco Maggioni. Firms also switched the emphasis of their activities. The Riva firm, for example, withdrew from the construction and importation of

[10] The figures themselves here are of very limited value, given both the method of assessment described above and the fact that all firms placed in one category paid the same tax. The top category paid only L. 300, despite including such concerns as the city transport company, a sum hardly in proportion to those levied on other concerns further down the scale. Furthermore the assessment of 'importance' left scope for abuse and the shopkeepers' journal *L'Esercente* claimed proprietors were forced to bargain with officials over the category they were placed in. The problem was compounded by the fact that half of the Commission appointed to assess the tax was nominated by the Chamber of Commerce, a body from which the *esercenti* had been excluded until 1888, and which remained an object of shopkeeper hostility for some time thereafter. See 'I nostri candidati alla Camera di Commercio', *L'Esercente*, 11 July 1889; 'La tassa d'esercizio', ibid., 19 August 1889.

[11] The boom ended in 1896 owing to a crisis of overproduction. Romano argued that this resembled the pattern of the English experience, and was evidence of the 'maturity' of the cotton industry. Romano, 'Gli inizi del capitalismo italiano', pp. 49–50.

[12] Gerschenkron, *Economic backwardness in historical perspective*, p. 88.

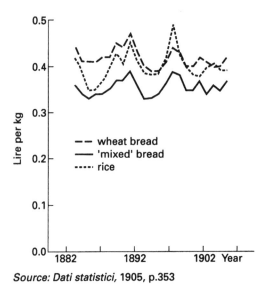

Source: Dati statistici, 1905, p.353

Fig. 1.3 Bread and rice prices, 1883–1905

agricultural machinery to concentrate on the production of hydraulic motors, especially turbines.[13]

In 1896 the business cycle began to pick up. The first beneficiaries of this were established firms, as shown by the *tassa esercizio e rivendita* returns. The growth in the number of businesses taxed after 1896 was not as fast as prior to that year, but the increased amount of tax received and hence the average contribution were certainly indicative of a recovery. Only after 1898 did the rate of increase in the number of enterprises recorded begin to take off, having presumably been restrained by the particular circumstances of 1897 and 1898.

These were years of rapid inflation, notably in grain and bread

---

[13] Sabbatini, *Notizie sulle condizioni industriali*, p. 410. Both the Fratelli Gelli and Gaetano Faninoni tanneries employed around 150 workers, whilst the glove factory had over 100 workers on the payroll. Della Peruta, 'Lavoro e fabbrica', p. 244. Louise Tilly used the data from the 1901 official census to demonstrate that most Milanese still worked in shops of fewer than ten employees, and that the garment-making and hygiene category employed the largest number of workers within the manufacturing sector. Tilly, 'I fatti di maggio', p. 133, and 'The working class of Milan', p. 270. For a case study of a successful engineering firm that sheds light on the whole industrialisation process see Bigatti, 'Commercianti e imprenditori'.

prices, because of a combination of harvest failure and the reduction in grain shipments from the New World caused by the Spanish American War (see Fig. 1.3).[14] In 1898 riots in the city led to heavy-handed intervention by the army and a brief period of military rule. These conditions are unlikely to have encouraged the foundation of new businesses, although one must also remember that, as the smallest enterprises were exempt from taxes, there would be a certain lag before new entrants showed up in the tax rolls. When they did arrive, paying the tax in the lower categories, average contribution was forced down between 1898 and 1901 (see Fig. 1.2c).

Improvements in the city's economic health were more apparent after 1898, the year in which the long-running trade dispute with France was finally settled, and in which the government abolished its own duty on grain. In September 1898 the city council extended the area in which it collected its own excise duty, the *dazio consumo*, to cover nearly all of the Comune di Milano (the Milanese administrative area). Until then a lighter *dazio* regime had applied in the city suburbs. The increase in revenue enabled the removal of the duty on many primary goods, thus reducing prices, whilst encouraging industry to move into the outlying *comuni* where the duty (to which construction materials were also subject) did not apply.

Succeeding years witnessed a remarkable upsurge in growth in the city, concurrent with what can best be described as the Milanese (and Italian) industrial 'take-off'. Italian industrial output increased by an astonishing annual average rate of 6.7% between 1898 and 1908, a period in which Milan was the leading industrial centre in the kingdom.[15] What factors were responsible for the city's achievement?

First, there was the advent of cheap energy in the form of hydroelectricity generated in the Alpine valleys to the north of the city, a welcome alternative to coal which had had to be imported from abroad.[16] This, in turn, stimulated the engineering sector.

[14] King and Okey, *Italy today*, 82. In Rome, too, although there was an appearance of economic recovery in 1897, rising prices held down levels of consumption and this, along with an increased tax burden, caused particular hardship to small traders. Bartoccini, *Roma nell'Ottocento*, p. 649.

[15] Gerschenkron, *Economic backwardness in historical perspective*, p. 75.

[16] The Paderno d'Adda power station, which came on stream in 1898, was the first to supply Milan with electricity generated this way, although the Santa Radegonda station had served the city since 1883.

Although much of the original investment and technology came from outside Italy, engineering firms played a leading role in developing electrically powered machinery, as well as in the construction of the generating equipment itself. Riva, for example, was chosen by the Berlin company, Siemens and Haske, to supply the turbines for the power stations at Castellamonte and Ruffoleno. Although they lost money on these particular projects, their involvement established them as the leading Italian firm in the field and led to many profitable contracts thereafter.[17]

Finally, the reinforcement of the city's financial domination by the influx of German capital must be recalled. The success of the Commerciale, which built up a network of branches throughout the country, was an important factor in persuading other banks to concentrate their activity in Milan. In 1896 the Banco Ambrosiano was founded in the city; two years later came the Società Bancaria Italiana. Moreover, after 1898, international trade increased sharply, particularly with Germany, and commercial houses and company representatives found the city to be the most logical place in which to locate.[18]

This phase of rapid growth was accompanied by profound changes in the nature of industrial production, occupational structure and work experience. Prompted by mechanisation and the increasing manufacture of industrial, rather than consumer, goods, manufacturing moved out of the workshop and into the factory. By 1901, 51% of the Milanese workforce was employed in manufacturing, as compared to 47% twenty years previously. Although there had been advances in techniques, the majority still worked in small shops or as a part of the 'putting-out' system and the biggest single sector was that of 'garment and hygiene workers' (seamstresses, glovemakers, hairdressers and the like).[19] Ten years later 'the majority

---

[17] Bigatti, 'Commercianti e imprenditori', pp. 97–8.
[18] Imports from Germany rose from an average of L. 156 million p.a. between 1891 and 1900 to L. 367 million p.a. in the succeeding decade, whilst exports rose from L. 172 million p.a. to L. 253 million p.a. Sapori, 'L'economia milanese', p. 871.
[19] These figures are derived from the censuses of 1881 and 1901 which were much more reliable for Milan than elsewhere in the kingdom because the city's full-time statisticians were allowed to analyse the data collected before it was sent to the Direzione Generale della Statistica in Rome. Correct classification is difficult, however, because the Italian language does not distinguish between workers and the self-employed in certain professions; a *macellaio*, for instance, can as easily be the proprietor of a butcher's shop or an employee within it. Tilly actually reworked the raw data given in the censuses by reclassifying them into new and

of Milanese were not working in numerous small establishments . . . they were in large shops'.[20] Of the active population 55% were now employed in manufacturing and 40% of those in heavy industry worked in shops of ten or more employees.[21] Even the nature of traditional industries had changed. Garment-making now used electrically powered sewing machines and was one of the activities in which large-scale manufacturing was most common.[22] The numbers of those employed in the metal and machine industries, and the average size of the plants they worked in, doubled between 1893 and 1911, until they accounted for 25% of the city's industrial workforce.[23]

The most intense period of growth was between 1900 and 1909, as is well demonstrated by the index of revenue from the *dazio* on construction materials shown in Fig. 1.4a. The protective tariff, cheap hydroelectricity and the extension of the rail and tram networks all provided further opportunities for expansion. Between 1904 and 1908 the demand for labour exceeded supply in many sectors of the manufacturing economy.[24] The earlier part of the spurt is somewhat harder to interpret. Near contemporary observers were convinced that Milan had suffered the same short recession that occurred in the rest of Europe, but historians can find little to indicate this.[25] There was a period of stasis between 1902 and 1904, particularly in terms of consumption (see Fig. 1.4b and c), which *Città di Milano*, the city's statistical journal, labelled a period of 'normal prosperity'. This has not subsequently been remarked on by historians but the period was one of labour unrest and might also

more relevant categories. Della Peruta makes the point that the survey of industrial workers conducted by the Società Umanitaria in 1903 confirmed the number and patterns of distribution recorded in the official census of 1901, with the exception of the garment-manufacture and domestic-service sectors in which numbers were far lower than those given in the census. *La popolazione di Milano . . . 1881*; *La popolazione di Milano . . . 1901*; Tilly, 'The working class in Milan', p. 107; Della Peruta, 'Lavoro e fabbrica', p. 248; Società Umanitaria, *Le condizioni generali della classe operaia.*

[20] Tilly, 'The working class of Milan', p. 84.   [21] Ibid., p. 107.

[22] Ibid., pp. 67–81.

[23] Ibid., p. 72.   [24] Ibid., p. 162.

[25] 'Uno sguardo retrospettivo', *Città di Milano*, July 1914, pp. 1–3. The journal refers quite specifically to a crisis in 1900; however, historians such as Tilly have concluded that 'the Italian economy and the Milanese showed little effect of the European downturn in the business cycle in 1900' but, rather, 'a characteristic resistance to cyclical effects associated with periods of rapid growth'. Tilly, 'The working class of Milan', p. 160.

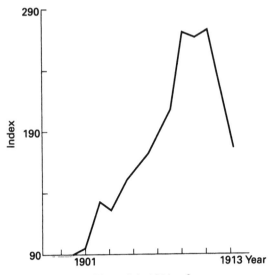

Source: Città di Milano, July 1914, p.2

Fig. 1.4a Index of *dazio consumo* revenues from construction materials, 1900–13

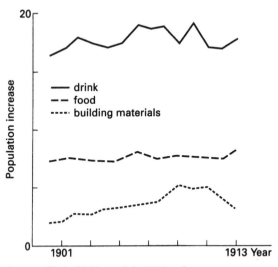

Source: Città di Milano, July 1914, p.2

Fig. 1.4b Index of *dazio consumo* revenues per capita, 1900–13

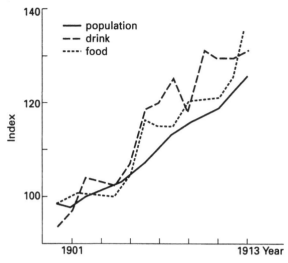

Source: *Città di Milano,* July 1914, p.2

Fig. 1.4c Index of *dazio consumo* revenues, 1900–13

have been a 'breather' between the strongest elements of the spurt between 1898 and 1901, and 1904 to 1908.

In 1907 a sharp recession occurred throughout Europe as a result of a cyclical crisis of overproduction, although recovery was swift thereafter. In Milan, though, the experience of response and recovery was more varied. Consumption figures suggest the crisis was felt immediately and that there was considerable fragility within the subsequent recovery (see Fig. 1.4a–c). In the construction trade, the crisis did not bite until 1909 but continued for a long time thereafter. The Lombard cotton industry became caught up on the European crisis of overproduction, whilst the silk industry had entered a phase of absolute decline. The metal and machine industries performed erratically: they seemed to have recovered from the crisis by 1909, yet the decline in railway orders led to layoffs in 1912 with the Libyan war providing some new stimulation thereafter. By 1911 labour supply outstripped demand in Milan, most notably in the construction, textiles and metallurgical industries.[26] If the punctual arrival of the 1907 crisis was indicative of Milan's integration into the wider economy, the fact that recovery from this setback was

[26] Ibid., p. 163.

more difficult than elsewhere in Europe suggests that elements of 'economic backwardness' persisted.[27]

The city's prosperity clearly had a strong influence on the most striking feature of Milanese history during this period, namely the remarkable rise in its population. During the first seventy years of the nineteenth century, the city's population rose from about 134,000 to 261,985 in 1871. In the following thirty years it nearly doubled to 491,460, whilst ten years later, in 1911, it stood at 602,236 (see Fig. 1.1a and b).[28] The major component of this increase was net immigration: between 1881 and 1901 this accounted for over 77% of the population increase in the city; in two years the proportion was over 90% (see Fig. 1.1d).[29]

Most historians claim that immigration followed the business cycle.[30] Certainly the 1888 and 1900 peaks in the numbers of immigrants would seem to confirm this, as would the trough of 1903. Both the rise in numbers between 1892 and 1897 and the fact that the levels of migration stayed high for several years after 1887 (regarded as the peak of the 1880s upswing), however, make it clear that the push factors forcing the immigrants from the countryside were at least as, if not more, important in determining levels of immigration, than the well-being of the city.

A different pattern is observed if the relative proportions of the net population increase accounted for by net immigration and net

[27] This raises the questions of when and to what extent the Milanese economy had been integrated into the predominant 'world' economy. The industrial growth spurt between 1880 and 1887 ran counter to the prevailing Kondratieff wave, and may indeed have been partly stimulated by the European deflation which lowered the prices of the raw material and capital needed by Italian industry. The turning of the cycle in 1896, however, was consistent with the general trend, though somewhat delayed, whilst the 1907 crisis struck immediately, unlike that of 1900 which, if it occurred in Milan at all, was more the result of the industrial conflicts between 1901 and 1903. This pattern would confirm Mandel's interpretation that long waves are more obvious in the economies of the leading capitalist countries and in world industrial output as a whole, and that the economies of individual countries attempting to catch up the industrialisation process might have rates of growth that varied significantly from those experienced overall. Mandel, *Long waves of capitalist development*, p. 2. See also Romano, 'L'industrializzazione nell'età giolittiana', p. 260.

[28] These figures are those for the '*di fatto*' population of the city (see n. 33 below) adjusted so as to include the population of the suburban area of the city which was a separate *comune* until 1873. Della Peruta, 'Lavoro e fabbrica', p. 232.

[29] *Dati statistici*, 1905, pp. 54–5.

[30] Tilly, 'The working class of Milan', pp. 172–4. Della Peruta, 'Lavoro e fabbrica', p. 258.

natural replacement are considered (see Fig. 1.1c–d). Immigration retains its dominant role but its share of the increase is gradually declining, bar a brief rally between the exceptional years of 1897 and 1900. The increasing importance of natural replacement may reflect a growth in confidence amongst the city's population, especially given the considerable growth in absolute numbers of net births after 1896 (see Fig. 1.1c). Also, more migrants settled in neighbouring *comuni* such as Sesto San Giovanni, partly because the *dazio* did not extend to them, partly because industry was increasingly locating there, a trend which became more pronounced as the new century continued.

It is, though, the sheer size of the population inflow that is important. Even in the early 1890s the proportion of the population increase accounted for by net immigration remained high despite the recession, fuelling resentment and fears in some quarters that immigrants were prejudicing the economic health of the city.

SHOPKEEPING AND THE BUSINESS CYCLE

Senator Alessandro Rossi summarised succinctly the importance of the business cycle to shopkeepers: 'the first thing(s) that an economic crisis hits are salaries and therefore bread'.[31] Employers, he argued, would always cut back on wages, rather than fail to meet their tax bills and risk prosecution and the possible confiscation of their property. A fall in wages would lead to a drop in disposable income and this would have an immediate effect on the consumption of basic goods such as bread.

Measuring consumption is an inexact science but the structure of the local excise tax in Milan (the *dazio consumo*) enables us to investigate Rossi's claim. The tax was essentially a duty levied on goods brought into the city for sale there. Until 1898 it covered many goods but was only applied directly to those items entering into the old city, the so-called *circondario interno*, more or less the area bounded by the Spanish walls. In the suburban *circondario esterno*, formerly an autonomous *comune*, which ringed the city, another method of assessment was used. In September 1898, however, the areas were united for *dazio* purposes, although the tariff was removed from many basic goods. A record of all goods

---

[31] Rossi 'Cerali e pane', p. 30.

entering the city was kept and the annual aggregate figures were given in the *Dati statistici* that the Comune published every year.[32] These also provide population figures for the city, although, when dealing with consumption in the *interno*, it should be remembered that many workers entered the zone during the day.[33] The higher prices caused by the *dazio* inhibited them from shopping there, however.

Fig. 1.5a–d shows a similar pattern of consumption *per capita* in the *interno* between 1880 and 1897, especially when three-year moving averages are constructed. There is a relative plateau of consumption during the first three quarters of the 1880s followed by a dramatic and virtually continuous fall thereafter. This mirrors the business cycle as a whole and confirms the immediate effect of the economic climate on the consumption levels of basic goods. One reason for this was the very high proportion of average family expenditure which was devoted to provisions, the largest part of it towards the acquisition of bread and pasta.[34] Indeed, consumption of other goods probably fell by a much greater proportion than that of cereal-based foods. Unfortunately, the figures are not accurate enough to investigate this hypothesis further.

The extension of the *dazio* belt in 1898 is as disappointing to the statistician as it was for the inhabitants of the *circondario esterno* at

---

[32] *Dati statistici*, 1884–1905. The figures are collected in Zaninelli, *I consumi a Milano nell'Ottocento*.

[33] The *Dati statistici* provide two sets of population data, the number of official residents in the city (*popolazione legale*) and the population actually found in the city on 31 December each year (*popolazione di fatto*). Both sets are broken down into the numbers resident in the *interno* and *esterno*. In calculating the consumption index the *popolazione di fatto* had been used as the base, as it makes some allowance for temporary residents who came into the city as a result of its cultural and commercial attraction. Even so, the figures make no allowance for those who worked in the city during the day but lived outside it, although the different *dazio* regime in the *interno* was a disincentive to consumption. Once again these considerations make the exactness of the figures open to question, which is why only the overall trend is analysed. Given that the numbers of day workers seem certain to have increased, it is striking that consumption indices, which ignored them altogether, should nevertheless have experienced a decline until 1897.

[34] Galletti claims that in both 1890 and 1914 provisions accounted for about 63% of weekly expenditure. In an earlier survey in 1878 the Società Archimede found that over half of a working-class family's food expenditure went on bread and rice alone. These figures are hardly conclusive, but non-quantitive sources also stress both the importance of food in the budget and the fact that bread and pasta accounted for the largest part of such expenditure. Galletti, 'I prezzi dei generi alimentari in Milano dal 1789 al 1918', cited in Zaninelli, *I consumi a Milano nell'Ottocento*, p. 109; Hunecke, *Classe operia e rivoluzione industriale*, p. 254.

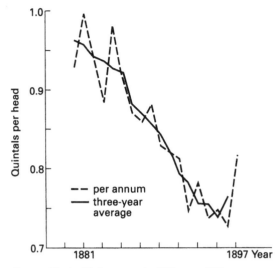

Source: Zaninelli, *I consumi a Milano,* p.123

Fig. 1.5a *Interno*: imports of flour and flour products (bread, pasta, etc.), 1880–97

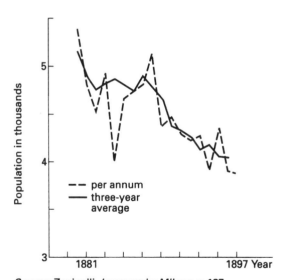

Source: Zaninelli, *I consumi a Milano,* p.137

Fig. 1.5b *Interno*: imports of fuel, wax and candles (*combustibili*), 1880–97

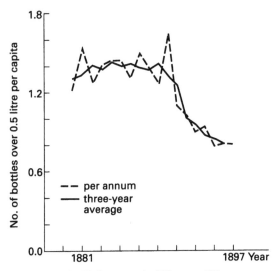

Source: Zaninelli, *I consumi a Milano,* p.130

Fig. 1.5c *Interno*: imports of wine and vinegar, 1880–97

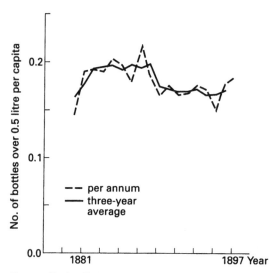

Source: Zaninelli, *I consumi a Milano,* p.130

Fig. 1.5d *Interno*: imports of alcohol and spirits, 1880–97

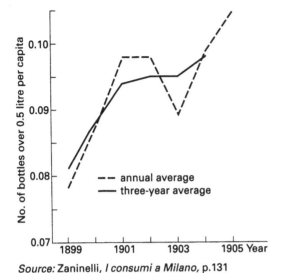

Source: Zaninelli, *I consumi a Milano,* p.131

Fig. 1.6 Imports of bottles of alcohol and spirits, 1899–1905

the time. At least, however, they gained some recompense in the removal of the *dazio* from many items! There is simply no continuity between the figures available for before and after 1898, an unfortunate circumstance which is compounded by the fact that we already know it to have been a pivotal year in the business cycle. The Comune published some general consumption statistics in 1914, whose reliability is probably greater when assessing drink than food, as all alcohol, including wine, carried the *dazio*, whilst many subsistence foods did not. It is, however, possible to calculate meat consumption, combining the figures for imported meat and that slaughtered within the city (this was previously impossible, owing to the fact that the distribution of the slaughtered meat between the two *circondari* was not known).[35] The results are shown in Fig. 1.4b–c and 1.6.

Once again consumption moves in line with the business cycle. There is a sharp rise into the new century, a short recession that

[35] Tilly calculated her index by working out the number of quintals of meat slaughtered in the Milan public slaughterhouse (using an average weight per carcass of 1.2 quintals) and adding the amount of freshly slaughtered meat brought into the city, reducing the amount given by 20% to allow for the bone. Tilly, 'The working class of Milan', pp. 253–5.

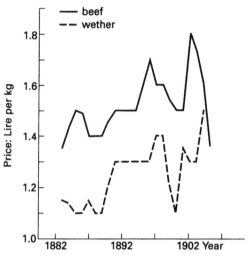

Source: *Dati statistici*, 1905, p.353

Fig. 1.7 Average annual meat prices, 1883–1905

bottoms out in 1903–4, followed by a steep recovery until around 1907, and variable behaviour thereafter. The initial stimulus for the rise in consumption came from the fall in prices when the *dazi* were altered in 1898 (see Fig. 1.3 and 1.7) and wage rises in the period 1899–1902. Between 1902 and 1904, however, employers clawed back some of these gains, forcing consumption down. This was particularly notable in the case of meat, which was only beginning to establish itself in the diet of the masses, with the trend being exacerbated by the rise in the price of wether (castrated ram) shown in Fig. 1.7.

Other indicators are more difficult to obtain. The original records of the bankruptcy courts are unavailable, for instance, and the only figures in existence refer to the bankruptcy trials conducted in the Milanese Court of Appeal, thus embracing all forms of business within roughly half of Lombardy. The figures for the number of bills of exchange protested in the court cover individual businessmen, limited companies and private individuals.[36] There appear to be no

---

[36] The records of the bankruptcy courts appear to exist only from 1938 onwards whilst the register of firms kept at the Chamber of Commerce does not cover the period prior to 1903 when a new bankruptcy law in effect made it impossible to

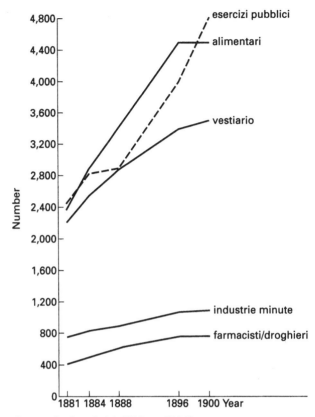

Source: *Dati statistici*, 1900, pp.266–7

Fig. 1.8a *Esercizi* in Milan (from *tassa esercizio e rivendita* rolls)

sources suitable for an investigation of rents or levels of capitalisation.

The tax records made available through the *Dati statistici* are also flawed as much relevant information is only given for selected years

trace small bankrupts in any case. See Cristofili and Degrada, 'L'archivio della cancelleria delle società commerciali di Milano', and 'L'archivio generale del Tribunale di Milano (sezione fallimentari)'. Aggregate statistics on bankruptcy and bills of exchange within the entire region under the jurisdiction of the Milanese tribunal (much larger than the city itself) may be found in the relevant editions of *Statistica giudiziaria civile e commerciale*. If anything these suggest that bankruptcies and unhonoured bills of exchange were indicative of greater business activity.

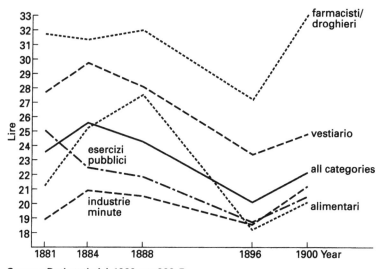

Source: *Dati statistici*, 1900, pp.266–7

Fig. 1.8b Average contribution per capita to *tassa esercizio e rivendita*

between 1881 and 1900. Fig. 1.8a shows the absolute number of *esercizi* entered on the rolls of the *tassa esercizio e rivendita* in these years. It is clear that the pattern of numerical growth varied dramatically between different types of enterprise during this period. Numbers rose very sharply in two categories: *alimentari* (food retailers such as butchers, bakers and greengrocers) and *esercizi pubblici* (all forms of eating and drinking establishments plus hotels and lodgings). The clothing sector (*vestiario*) grew at a somewhat slower rate, whilst the *industrie minute* (essentially artisan activities such as umbrella making, bric-à-brac selling and hairdressing) and the trades of pharmacy and grocery were much smaller in both numbers and growth rates. The difference between the categories was particularly pronounced between 1888 and 1896 when the *alimentari* and *esercizi pubblici* experienced much higher rates of growth than the others. The reason was surely that their ranks were swollen by enterprises set up by immigrants to the city.

These enterprises were not necessarily successful; indeed, quite the contrary. Fig. 1.8b shows that there was a universal decline in the average contribution of proprietors in all five of the categories in the period, but that it was particularly marked in the food sector.

Given our analysis of the business cycle in the city, it comes as no surprise to record a decline in average contribution in this period, but its severity in the food sector is indicative of too many enterprises competing in too small a market. An analysis of the ratio between the numbers of proprietors and assistants recorded in the censuses of 1881 and 1901 gives a similar result with a small overall increase in the ratio from 1.40 to 1.58 masking both the diminishing size of food retailing enterprises (consistent with the setting up of new small-scale operations in the sector) and the considerably larger ratio in the clothing and haberdashery sector occasioned by changes in both production and retailing techniques (see Table 2.4).

The business cycle within the shopkeeping sector, then, moved broadly in line with the city's economy as a whole; the severe depression of the early 1890s, the end-of-century recovery and the prosperity of the new century were all to be found in the retail sector. This chronology is vital to an understanding of the Milanese shopkeeper movement. The forces that determined this overall pattern had different effects on the various shopkeeping trades and their practitioners, however. In order to explain fully the effects of the changes in the Milanese economy on the shopkeeping trades, it is now necessary to analyse the business methods employed in the retail sector, and the background of the participants within it.

2. The context of shopkeeping: trades and techniques

This chapter is divided into two parts. The first considers the business of shopkeeping in the city as a whole, the practices and problems common to all small traders. The second provides a comparative analysis of the various trades that might be considered as part of the retail sector. Both are designed to assist with an assessment of the propensity of shopkeepers for collective action and to help understand what, and who, might be included in or excluded from a shopkeeper identity. Identity is clearly bound up with memory – the first section therefore begins with a brief examination of trade organisation prior to 1885.

THE CONTEXT OF SHOPKEEPING IN MILAN

In the thirteenth and fourteenth centuries Milan's trades and industries were organised into corporations. These functioned much as elsewhere, regulating standards within the profession and interceding in disputes between members and with the local authorities and the public. The notable features of the corporations were that the rights of members were not transferred automatically to their heirs, and the conditions of entry were the same for all candidates, irrespective of their family background.[1] This degree of 'openness' is striking. Even so the system was already in decline by the sixteenth century, as the autonomy of the corporations diminished whilst the powers of local government increased. There were frequent disputes

---

[1] Pagani, 'Alcune notizie sulle antiche corporazioni', pp. 893–4. A fine was paid both on entrance into the profession (as either apprentice or proprietor) and upon opening up a new shop. Employees were only permitted to commence trading at least a year after leaving their master and at a suitable distance from their old workplace. Zessos, *Storia dei macellai milanesi*, pp. 36–41.

between the corporations over who had the right to sell what, whilst higher bodies, such as a general chamber of merchants, acquired the legal powers that had once resided in individual corporations.[2]

By the eighteenth century the functioning of the corporative system was widely acknowledged as unsatisfactory, although the corporations governing the food provisioning trades retained more power than those in many other sectors. The chamber of merchants had become an elitist organisation from which many ordinary trades were excluded and 'trade discipline', supposed to be regulated by the corporative system, was, in fact, largely mediated through the hands of lawyers.

The malfunctioning of the existing system prepared the way for the modifications introduced by the Austrian administration in Milan during the reign of Joseph II. These culminated in the abolition of the corporations in 1787 and the foundation of the Chamber of Commerce (Camera di Commercio) in the same year. The Camera di Commercio was shorn of much of the legal autonomy of the old corporations and merchants' chambers, and was intended to be clearly subordinated to the government. Its role was increasingly that of an organisation of economic interests through which government and commerce could communicate, but the restrictions on membership, and more particularly on those allowed to stand or vote in elections to the chamber's council, meant that its personnel were not drawn from *petit-bourgeois* backgrounds, and the Chamber never represented the interests of small commerce. This continued to be true throughout the Napoleonic Cisalpine Republic and the restored Austrian administration of 1815–59 and even, as we shall see, during the first decades of Italian rule.[3]

The disappearance of the corporations in the 1780s, and their poor performance prior to suppression, helps explain why restoration was never an *esercenti* aspiration in Milan; an important contrast with the situation in Central Europe. A further factor was that several trades were able to form proprietors' associations to

---

2 A valuable guide to the performance of both the corporations and the Chamber of commerce is Mozzarelli, ed., *Economia e corporazioni*. See, in particular, Mainoni, 'La camera dei mercanti'; Cova, 'Interessi economici e impegni istituzionali', pp. 109–32; Trezzi, 'Governo del mercimonio e governo della città', pp. 133–53.

3 See Mozzarelli, 'La riforma politica del 1786'; Antonelli, 'Le camere di Commercio napoleoniche'; Meriggi, 'Dalla rappresentanza degli interessi alla legittimazione constituzionale'; Pagani, 'Alcune notizie sulle antiche corporazioni'; Lodolini, 'Le ultime corporazioni di arti e mestieri', p. 313.

control the market in their own interests in the immediate post-unification period. Milanese bread prices, for example, were fixed by the bakers' association, the Società Mutua Cooperativa fra i Proprietari Forno (usually abbreviated to the Mutua Proprietari Forno [sic]), which used its strength to maintain prices that benefited small proprietors rather than customers; whilst the pork butchers' Società fra i Proprietari Salsamentari negotiated new opening times for the public slaughterhouse and persuaded the local authorities to lower the dazio on small pigs when it became necessary to transport them from the south.[4] The strength of these association was the propensity of their members for collective cooperation: providing this was strong enough, there was no need for the compulsions of the old corporations. Opportunities for such cooperation were stronger in some trades than others, and it was these trades that would form the basis of the subsequent shopkeeper movement.

What was the attitude of shopkeepers to the risorgimento itself? Records suggest that small retailers played a part in the 'five days' of the 1848 insurrection, particularly those selling basic provision to the common people of the city. This is reflected by the comparatively high numbers of traders who were killed during the disturbances, although the overwhelming majority of those who died came from the labouring classes.[5] As vendors lived and worked in the same areas as their clients, it is no surprise to find some of them caught up in this activity.

It is more difficult to find reliable indications of shopkeeper sentiment during the unification process. In 1859, following the victory of the French and Piedmontese at Magenta, the Municipio proclaimed unity with Piedmont, whilst the swift withdrawal of the Austrians prevented a repetition of the five days. There was widespread approval of the overthrow of the Austrians, but there are no sources that can give us a deeper insight into the specific reaction of small traders to the risorgimento. When the shopkeeper newspaper, L'Esercente, appeared in 1886, it made much of the alleged patriotism of its readers during the risorgimento, aligning itself with the populism of Garibaldi and Mazzini, whilst suggesting that the Milanese establishment had been lukewarm in its support for unifi-

---

[4] Hunecke, Classe operaia e rivoluzione industriale, pp. 255–60; Società Proprietari Salsamentari, Venti anni di vita sociale, pp. 29–58.
[5] 'Registro Mortuario delle barricate in Milano', L'Italia del Popolo, 3 July 1848, reprinted in Cattaneo, L'insurrezione di Milano nel 1848, p. 211.

cation. The analysis suited the paper's editorial direction, but probably was not that inconsistent with the facts.

This raises questions about the shopkeepers' social background
and their interaction with their customers. Social historians have
often argued that the allegiances of shopkeepers tended to lie with
the residents of the quarter they worked in. Shops and bars were the
focus of neighbourhood social life, and their proprietors could not
avoid becoming well informed about the lifestyles and outlook of
their clients. Their awareness of the conditions of the area, therefore, led the small traders to sympathise with the inhabitants.[6]

These solidarities were reinforced by considerations of economic
self-interest. It was standard practice for shopkeepers, particularly
bakers, to allow their customers to buy goods on credit once they
had built up a reputation at the shop.[7] Customers' purchases were
recorded in a notebook, a *libretto*, and bills were paid at the same
time as wages or salaries were received. Credit was granted to all
classes; the well-off families who received home deliveries, the clerks
who were paid once a month and the workers who received their
wages either weekly or fortnightly. Few shopkeepers asked clients
for detailed references; indeed, some would grant credit to anyone
seen two or three times in the shop, in order to keep a new
customer.[8]

Likewise proprietors often extended credit beyond the usual
payment period, allowing those in difficulties (such as the
unemployed) to continue purchasing goods, despite their temporary
inability to pay. This was partly from genuine sympathy, partly
from a desire to keep the client and one day recoup part of the
existing debt. Eventually, however, shopkeepers were left with the
difficult decision of whether to close some accounts, thereby fore-
going the money owed, or to keep supplying the client in the hope of
recouping their investment should the debtor return to prosperity.
Either way the proprietor ended up paying the *dazio consumo* on
revenue that he had not actually received and he had to keep his
cash prices up in order to offset his debts on the credit accounts.[9]

---

[6] Crossick and Haupt, 'Shopkeepers, master artisans and the historian', pp. 18–20.
[7] According to Senator Alessandro Rossi 'it is the baker who acts as banker to the
common man'. Rossi, 'Macine e forni', p. 11.
[8] Zezzos, *Vita della bottega*, pp. 200–7.
[9] This point was made by Marmont, President of the Milanese Shopkeeper Federation in a speech on 19 May 1891 that was reprinted in *L'Esercente* under the title

His own living standards were squeezed, as what ready cash was available had first to be employed in paying the shop overheads, rent, wages and so forth.

It was a high-risk strategy but customers regarded *il fido* as a right, and it would have been commercial suicide for a shopkeeper to refuse credit when his competitors were granting it. Proprietors, therefore, repeatedly instanced the practice as evidence of their pivotal role in the local community, arguing that, as one shop-keepers' almanac put it, small traders 'offer the honest man the guarantee of bread for himself and his family in the long periods of unemployment which are as humiliating as they are undeserved'.[10]

Il fido featured prominently in the obligations that patrons believed fell on proprietors and vice versa. Customers believed they were entitled to credit as a right, just as they could expect to receive small gifts from the shopkeepers at Christmas, the so-called *regali natalizi*.[11] Traders were generally prepared to honour these obli-gations, but felt that acceptance of *il fido* and the *regali* imposed its own obligation on customers always to use the shop from which they had obtained these benefits. If shopkeepers were expected to make financial sacrifices in order to support the community during times of hardship, then customers would have to respect the traders' need to 'make a turn' on his merchandise, and accept the higher prices that resulted.

This was made more difficult by the fact that some shopkeepers still sold their wares by bargaining with the customer, so that the prices for which they sold the same item could vary dramatically. The proprietor had to guess the prices at which his competitors sold and, in the course of the verbal transaction, make it appear as if he were making a concession, whilst, in fact, still retaining his margin. No doubt the manner of negotiation was an important in retaining customers as the actual price agreed. Bargaining was a cause of distrust between customer and proprietor, between proprietors within the same trade, and with proprietors in other trades who sold at the fixed price (*prezzo fisso*). Customers correctly believed that proprietors tried to make them pay what they could afford rather

'L'agitazione contro i privilegi goduti dalle cooperative e la Federazione di Milano', 21 May 1891. See also 'Combattiamo il fido', ibid., 1 December 1895.

[10] *Il Prontuario*, p. 3.

[11] Typically bakers gave away *panettone*, a type of cake; grocers gave packets of nougat or mustard, delicatessens distributed salami cuts and licensees stood free drinks.

Table 2.1. *Marriages involving shopkeepers or their assistants in Milan, 1882–1900*

	Male shopkeepers	
Status of bride	Proportion of all brides (%)	
Worker	55.0	
Independent means	21.0	
Living at home	14.1	
Shopkeeper or assistant	7.0	
Clerk	1.4	
Other	1.4	
	Female shopkeepers	
Status of husband	Proportion of all husbands (%)	
Shopkeeper	41.6	
Worker	36.5	
Merchant, industrialist	9.8	
White-collar	7.6	
Independent means	2.0	
Master craftsman, jeweller	1.1	
Professional classes	0.5	
Other	0.8	

Source: Dati statistici 1882–1900; (see n. 16)

than a 'fair' price. This upset other shopkeepers who believed the practice undermined their attempts to demonstrate the value of the *esercenti* to society.

Further evidence of their utility, according to the shopkeepers, was that their profession represented an escape route from the ranks of the labouring poor. The *esercenti*, they argued, were former workers who now worked for themselves. No direct evidence exists to examine these claims, but an analysis of the marriages recorded in the *Dati statistici* (the annual handbook of statistics published by the Comune) indicates the strength of the links between shopkeepers and the labouring classes (see Table 2.1). Between 1882 and 1900, 55% of the brides chosen by male shopkeepers and shophands were women in working-class professions, whilst another 14.1% were without work and living at home. Over a fifth were property owners or in possession of a private income, however, suggesting that a prosperous shopkeeper might be regarded as a good catch.

Very few brides were shopkeepers or shop assistants themselves, reflecting the low numbers of women classified as such. Whilst the

Table 2.2. *Gender of shopkeeper proprietors in Milan in 1881 and 1901*

Category		1881			1901			Diff.
		Total	Female	%	Total	Female	%	
I	Food makers/vendors	1,825	595	32.6	2,868	836	29.1	−3.5
II	Food retailers	2,196	986	44.8	2,994	1,287	43.0	−1.8
III	Grocers, fuel sellers	761	156	20.4	1,103	258	23.4	+3.4
IV	Food/drink services	2,678	855	31.9	3,474	1,061	30.5	−1.4
V	Hotel	93	21	22.5	177	67	37.9	+16.5
VI	Hairdressing	424	12	2.8	626	16	2.6	−0.2
VII	Monopoly sellers	270	114	42.2	348	154	44.3	+2.1
VIII	Clothing, haberdashery	2,242	371	16.5	2,199	440	20.0	+3.5
TOTALS		10,489	3,110	29.7	13,789	4,119	29.9	+0.2

Source: Milan Censuses 1881, 1901. The figures are those given for *padroni* only (not *direttori*). For the composition of categories see n. 27.

statistics record 4,464 marriages involving male partners who were shopkeepers or shop assistants between 1882 and 1900, there were just 750 in which the female partner was placed in this category. Their husbands were usually involved in shopkeeping (41.6%) or working-class occupations (36.5%).

These figures are more indicative of the status of women involved in the retail trade than of the actual balance between male and female practitioners. As Table 2.2 shows, the census data of 1881 and 1901 suggest that nearly 30% of those proprietors involved in *esercenti* activities were women, and if the inevitably male-dominated trades of barber and shoemaker are removed from the data, this proportion rises to over 33%.[12] The trades in which women were most heavily represented, however, were the most precarious in terms of financial stability, often carried out from a barrow or stall, rather than a permanent shop. The census figures for 1881 show that the majority of poulterers, fishmongers, vegetable sellers and haberdashers were women. These trades generated little income, were often carried on in the street rather than the shop, and would often form part of a family economy in which a husband might be employed in other work.

In any case women faced a large number of legal barriers in

---

[12] See pp. 47–50 for an explanation of how these figures were obtained.

becoming recognised as shopkeepers or even as assistants. Married women were only allowed to act as traders (*commerciante*), if they had the permission of their husbands, or, if separated, that of the court, although this permission could be verbal or even tacit, so that when the wife was performing these functions and the husband had not registered an objection, permission was assumed. Separate permission had to be sought for the wife then to enter into a contract with an unlimited company because, according to one legal commentator, 'the husband, who might consider it convenient that the wife practises the trade, could have legitimate reasons for not permitting her to associate with third parties'.[13]

Wives who worked alongside their husbands in the shop, the most common working arrangement, were legally regarded as assistants, *commesse* rather than *commerciante*. Permission was also needed for married women to work as assistants, however, as this too involved the danger of contact with third parties.[14]

These legal restrictions reflect a widespread hostility towards women in business, even though the numbers involved were quite high. The general assumption was that women were generally minding the shop until their sons took over, particularly widows who, unsurprisingly, provided a large proportion of women proprietors. In fact these widows might control very large businesses – the Luraschi bakery, one of the five biggest in the city was for a long time run by the late proprietor's widow – but there was little recognition of their achievements, and women were not active in shopkeeper associations. Luraschi's son represented the firm in the bakers' association, just as in previous centuries women proprietors had sent male representatives to guild meetings.[15]

The marriage statistics would be more useful if they separated proprietors and assistants, yet their inclusion in the same category is itself indicative of the blurred perception of class distinctions in small-scale shopkeeping. This is not to argue that these distinctions did not exist, rather that both small shopkeepers themselves, and

[13] Milla, *Commercio e commercianti*, p. 77.
[14] On the legal position of women in retailing see Dompè, *Manuale del commerciante*, pp. 8–9; Milla, *Commercio e commercianti*, pp. 74–83, and *Commessi di commercio*, pp. 20–2.
[15] For a good example of the persistence of these patronising attitudes see Zezzos, *Vita della bottega*, p. 161. On women proprietors and the corporations Zezzos, *Storia dei macellai milanesi*, p. 41.

society generally, believed that the *esercenti* and the lower classes were closely linked to each other.[16]

The exception to this proves the rule. The retailers of up-market goods, such as jewellery, antiques and fashionable clothing, often shared the conservative opinions of their customers. Many of these retailers, particularly the proprietors of large-scale establishments in the city centre, are best described as merchant traders rather than shopkeepers, and it was probably these men who married into the better-off, propertied families, the *possidenti* and *benestanti*. The livelihood of these proprietors depended on selling to the well-off classes, giving them a considerable interest in the political protection of their customer base.

This relationship can be observed throughout Milan, although lower-class neighbourhoods might require very different forms of protection. A proprietor's fortunes were linked to the overall economic condition of an area; if his clients were badly off he was forced to grant them even more credit until an improvement in their fortunes enabled him to recover these debts. This reinforced the shopkeeper's interest in the condition of the neighbourhood, both as a resident and as a businessman.

Small traders had strong ties to their neighbourhood, but how many of them came from the community itself? Re-working the data obtained in the city censuses of 1881 and 1901 suggests that even in 1881, well before immigration rates hit their peaks, 59% of shopkeepers had been born outside the city itself, and this had risen to 69.2% by 1901.[17] Nearly all of these immigrants came from Lombardy, the majority from the Provincia di Milano itself. This was reflected in the shopkeepers' tolerance of new entrants into their trades.

Start-up capital for new enterprises nearly always came from private sources, usually personal and family savings, whilst most day-to-day business was financed through the short-term credit offered by bills of exchange. *L'Esercente* expressed resentment at the fact that a few classes monopolised credit to their own benefit so that large-scale speculation was served by banks of all sizes whilst

---

[16] The *Dati statistici* for each year contained tables which classified marriages within the city by the occupations of each of the spouses. The figures given in the text were derived from these and employ the same classifications as in the *Dati statistici* themselves: see *Dati statistici*, 1900, p. 43.

[17] See pp. 47–50 for an explanation of how these figures were obtained.

shopkeepers were forced to scratch around for credit flows which often dried up unexpectedly.[18]

Luigi Luzzatti, the father of the Italian cooperative movement, tried to resolve the problem through the institution of small cooperative banks, known as the *banche popolari*. Opening the Banca Popolare di Milano in 1865 Luzzatti spoke of the need to 'liberate the working classes through credit and savings' by making available 'to workmen, small traders, and small industrialists the bounteous springs of credit' from which, up until then, they 'could have availed themselves only in small measure'.[19]

Luzzatti also grouped shopkeepers and workers together, but his fulsome vision was not fulfilled. Small traders were as adept at keeping the workers from the *banche popolari* as the large speculators were in monopolising existing forms of credit. They also used their influence to discourage the banks from involving themselves in another element of Luzzatti's movement, the consumer cooperatives.[20] Much of the Banca Popolare's early activity consisted in discounting bills of exchange, but the institution could not meet all the shopkeepers' needs, and in later years *L'Esercente* suspected it too of having become too enamoured of big business although this did not prevent the journal from continuing to recommend candidates in the bank elections.[21]

Difficulties with commercial credit were known to small shopkeepers of all trades. Indeed there are striking similarities in the backgrounds and business methods of most proprietors, whilst the importance of their relationship with the local community was a constant factor in determining their wider outlook. These common experiences formed the basis for a potential *esercente* identity, but there were also many differences between the various trades, notably in the ways in which they responded to changes in the city's commercial environment, that affected the propensity for organisation amongst their practitioners.

---

[18] 'Una buona istituzione', *L'Esercente*, 17 September 1886.
[19] Quoted in Zezzos, *Milano e il suo commercio*, p. 272. See also 'Una buona istituzione', *L'Esercente*, 17 September 1886.
[20] King and Okey maintained that the small traders achieved this domination by making the banks adopt limited liability, although why this should have put off workmen is unclear (*Italy today*, p. 200–2).
[21] It is worth recording that only one of the recommended candidates was a shopkeeper, and even then a high-class haberdasher rather than a genuine *esercente*. 'La Banca Popolare ha bisogno degli esercenti', *L'Esercente*, 2 March 1890.

THE *ESERCENTI* TRADES

The key statistical sources for an investigation into the *esercenti* trades are the census records of 1881, 1901 and 1911, but the data are far from ideal.[22] To begin with, the choice of census day exercised a significant effect upon the results obtained. The 1911 census was performed on 10th June when many Milanese families had already left for their summer sojourn in the cool of the country-side, and, to make matters worse, the 10th was a Sunday on which, it may be assumed, many others had left the city on weekend excursions, or, in the case of many workers, gone to visit their families in the Provincia.[23] As many shopkeepers closed their businesses during the summer period, this makes the 1911 data particularly untrust-worthy, as does the fact that the analysis of the returns was performed by government statisticians in Rome rather than, as happened after the two preceding two censuses, by those of the Comune itself.

Secondly, there is the problem of classification. The censuses counted people, not businesses, so that employers who lived in the city but had their premises elsewhere, together with those who were passing through, were still included in the figures. It is improbable that these are the circumstances of many in the shopkeeping cate-gories, however; a much greater distortion might be expected from the fact that proprietors sometimes classified all of their family as *padroni*.[24] Day workers who left the city in the evening were not included, but in some of the *esercenti* professions, apprenticed assistants either lived on the premises or at the home of the employer.

The most pressing difficulty lies in the choice of categories employed by the censuses. In 1901 we find new categories, such as vendors of photographic equipment, and dealers in bicycles and cars, reflecting the rise of manufacturing and the opportunities it presented for new forms of retailing. In contrast, some of the more traditional activities, like the sale of cakes and refreshments, dis-appeared into more general 'catch-all' categories for wandering salesmen. These developments are illuminating in themselves, but as

---

[22] *La popolazione di Milano ... 1881; La popolazione di Milano ... 1901; La popola-zione di Milano ... 1911.*

[23] *La popolazione di Milano ... 1911*, p. 4.

[24] *La popolazione di Milano ... 1881*, p. 81.

both the large groups used to summarise the data collected and the individual sub-headings within them were changed with every census, immediate comparisons are rendered impossible.

The only way to solve this problem is to re-group the individual sub-headings in a more appropriate manner. Using the 1881 and 1901 censuses, I have distinguished nine categories to assist with an analysis of the different elements within the shopkeeping sector. The sub-headings employed in the census were themselves often different and the size and boundaries of the groups I have set up were determined partly by the need to accommodate such changes within one group. In the 1881 census, for example, poulterers and fishmongers were placed in separate sub-headings, whilst in 1901 one sub-heading covered both categories. Both trades involve simple food retailing (with little or no value added to the raw product) and I have therefore included them in my second grouping of trades of this sort. These groups reflect my own interpretations of the affinities between various shopkeeping activities, but, far more, they reflect the definitions and distinctions drawn by the *esercenti* themselves.

I have already discussed the difficulty in providing any watertight definition of small shopkeeper, small trader or even *petit bourgeois*.[25] To these problems of definition are added those created by the census data themselves; even after the re-grouping exercise many small traders cannot be adequately identified, particularly those who operated in the artisan trades of the *industrie minute* – leather-workers and cabinet makers, for example. It is therefore impossible to provide any meaningful estimate of the number of small traders in the city.

I would, however, argue that most of the professions whose practitioners readily identified themselves as *esercenti* are included in the groups I have delineated. In an article published in 1899, a contributor to *L'Esercente* claimed that the 'true *esercenti*' were the various types of pork butcher and delicatessen owner, bakers (both those who made bread themselves and those who simply sold it), grocers, butchers, dairy proprietors, owners of coffee shops and all forms of enterprise selling wines, beers and spirits, confectioners, pastry shops, greengrocers, innkeepers, 'pub' landlords, poulterers and fishmongers. Allied occupations, according to the article, were

[25] See pp. 8–10.

those of hotel-keeper, restaurateur, tobacconist, fuel seller and pharmacist. *L'Esercente* likewise stated that its intended audience was purely those who traded in *generi alimentari* (i.e. retail outlets and service enterprises dealing in food and drink), but in November 1900 the paper began using a new masthead which featured a list of trades at which it was targeted and this included both hotel-keepers and fuel sellers.[26]

Using these distinctions as our starting point we can turn to the 1901 census of the city's population for a rough indication of the numbers of proprietors who operated in *esercenti* professions. Proceeding from the smallest sub-headings we find that the total number of bakers, bread sellers; pasta makers, pastry makers, confectioners, pork butchers, delicatessen proprietors, butchers, tripe sellers; traders in dairy products; poulterers, fishmongers, greengrocers, grocers, proprietors of *trattorie, osterie* (i.e. popular eating and drinking establishments), bars, wine shops and liquor stores, vendors of roast, fried and other forms of prepared foods and coffee shop proprietors is 10,028 in 1901. If hotel-keepers and fuel sellers are added the total reaches 10,616, which with the addition of vendors of salt and tobacco (government monopolies) becomes 10,964. If the other related retail and services categories of barbers and hairdressers, shoemakers, traders in clothing, hosiery, underwear, etc., and haberdashers are also included the number rises to 13,789. Comparable figures derived from the 1881 census give 10,489 *esercenti* by the widest definition and 7,141 by the strictest.[27] These results are broken down into groups in Table 2.2.

[26] Simplicium, 'Gli Esercenti', *L'Esercente*, 3/4 December 1899, maintained that the '*veri esercenti*' were the Salumieri (comprendenti i pizzicagnoli ed i postai), Fornai (fabbriche e rivendite), Droghieri, Macellai, Lattivendoli, Caffettieri e Liquoristi, Confetterie e generi diversi, Offellieri, Fruttivedoli ed Erbivendoli, Trattori (vino, cucina ed alloggio), Osti (vino), Birrerie, Bottiglieri e Fissonetterie, Pollivendoli and *Pescivendoli*. According to the same article the *esercenti affini* were *Albergatori e Ristoranti, Tabaccai, Sostrai* and *Farmacisti*. For *L'Esercente*'s views on the definition of the *esercenti* see 'Il Programma dell'Esercente', 24 December 1899 and 'Un nuovo giornale commerciale', 8 April 1900.

[27] The groups are composed of the following census sub-headings:
Group 1: (1881) *Fornai e panettieri; Pastai e fabbricanti di ostie; Pasticcieri e confettieri; Pizzicagnoli e salsamentari; Macellai e trippaioli;* (1901) *Fornai, panettieri; Pastai, fabbricanti di galette e di biscotti; Fabbricanti di ostie; Pasticcieri, confettieri, fabbricanti di frutta candite; Fabbricanti di salumi e di conserve di carne, pizzicagnoli; Macellai, beccai, abbacchiari, trippaiuoli.*
Group 2: (1881) *Negozianti di formaggio; Lattivendoli; Pollivendoli e venditori di cacciagione; Pescivendoli; Erbivendoli e venditori di ghiaccio; Fruttivendoli e venditori di castagne;* (1901) *Negozianti di frutta, erbivendoli; Negozianti di burro e*

Table 2.3. *Numbers and nativity of shopkeeper 'padroni' in Milan 1881 and 1901*

Category		Numbers			% Immigrant		
		1881	1901	% In-crease	1881	1901	Diff-rence
I	Food makers/vendors	1,825	2,868	+ 57.2	61.2	69.0	+ 7.8
II	Food retailers	2,196	2,994	+ 36.3	57.8	67.8	+ 10.0
III	Grocers, fuel sellers	761	1,103	+ 44.9	55.8	60.3	+ 4.5
IV	Food/drink services	2,678	3,474	+ 29.7	61.5	75.0	+ 13.5
V	Hotel	93	177	+ 90.3	83.9	78.0	− 5.9
VI	Hairdressing	424	626	+ 47.6	64.6	79.2	+ 14.6
VII	Monopoly sellers	270	348	+ 28.9	47.8	55.1	+ 7.4
VIII	Clothing, haberdashery	2,242	2,199	− 0.02	55.9	65.4	+ 9.5
TOTALS		10,489	13,789	31.5	59.0	69.2	+ 10.2

Source: Milan Censuses 19881, 1901. The figures are those given for *padroni* only (not *direttori*). For composition of categories see n. 27.

> *formaggio; Lattivendoli; Pollivendoli, negozianti di uova, selvaggina, uccelli e pescivendoli.*
> Group 3: (1881) *Negozianti di legna d'ardere, carbone ecc; Droghieri e negozianti in coloniali;* (1901) *Negozianti di combustibili; Commercianti di prodotti chimici e medicinali, concimi artificiali, droghe, generi coloniali, petrolio, benzina, sapone, colori, vernici, fiammiferi, spugne, profumerie.*
> Group 4: (1881) *Trattori, osti, bettolieri, negozianti di vino ecc; Rosticcieri, friggitori e venditori di commestibili; Birrai, fabbricanti di birra gazose, seltz, ecc; Distillatori di alcool e liquoristi; Caffettieri;* (1901) *Negozianti di vino e liquori; Trattori, osti, rosticcieri, friggitori, cantinieri e vinai; Caffettieri, venditori di gelati, liquori, birra ed altre bevande.*
> Group 5: (1881) *Albergatori;* (1901) *Albergatori, locanderie.*
> Group 6: (1881) *Barbieri, parrucchieri, pettinatrici ecc;* (1901) *Barbieri, parrucchieri, lavoranti in capelli.*
> Group 7: (1881) *Rivenditori di sale e tabacchi;* (1901) *Tabbaccai.*
> Group 8: (1881) *Calzolai, zoccolai, ciabattini; Negozianti in filati e tessuti; Negozianti mercerie; Negozianti di biancheria, di guanti, calzatura, abiti, ecc;* (1901) *Calzolai, zoccolai, fabbricanti di pantofole, orlatrici di scarpe; Commercianti filati o tessuti, mercerie, cordami; commercianti abiti, biancheria, mode ed altri oggetti di vestario.* Although some trades are only nominated in the sub-headings once, I am reasonably confident that these were included in a more general sub-heading in the other census. The most problematic are Group 3, where the inclusion of *profumerie* in 1901 may have led to some overcounting, Group 5, where some of the institutions classified as *locanderie* in 1901 may have been included in the *Affitacamere e affitaletti* category in 1881 (although this same sub-heading is also used in 1901), and Group 6 where the inclusion of *pettinatrici* in 1881 but not in 1901 when they form a separate category is confusing. Examination of the figures, however, suggests that female *pettinatrici* employed as domestics or similar were not included in the 1881 sub-heading, as evidenced by the fact that only twelve female proprietors are recorded in 1881, compared to sixteen in the *Barbieri, parrucchieri* category in 1901 and the 266 women listed under a separate sub-heading as *pettinatrici* in 1901. *La popolazione di Milano . . . 1901.*

Again it must be stressed that these figures are purely indicative –
clearly some enterprises have been omitted, whilst counting all
proprietors active in a trade means including some who operated on
a very large scale indeed. As we shall see, however, the *esercenti*
trades were surprisingly resistant to penetration by large-scale oper-
atives, and generally respectful of the bigger operators within their
own sector. The figures also fit in with *L'Esercente*'s claims for the
size of the sector, and it should be pointed out that the approxi-
mately 14,000 proprietors of 1901 account for just under 47% of the
nearly 30,000 people over six years old whom the census classified as
industrial or commercial proprietors.[28] The data obtained from the
census figures are presented in Tables 2.2, 2.3, 2.4 and 2.5.

Category I (Food makers and vendors) contains those trades
which were involved in both the production and sale of food, such
as butchers and bakers. It is one of the largest categories in our
survey in terms of both employers and employees, and experienced
considerable growth in the period. The largest group of shopkeepers
within the category was that of the *salsamentari* and *pizzicagnoli*,
proprietors of small delicatessen shops who also prepared their own
cold meats, blood sausages and cheeses (the usual Italian term for
these shopkeepers is *salumieri*). They were followed by the bakers,
including the increasing numbers of *rivenditori*, proprietors who
simply sold bread manufactered elsewhere.[29] These trades offered
the easiest entrance into the category and by 1901 the census shows
that 75.1% of *salsamentari* and 77.5% of bakery proprietors had
been born outside the city. In 1879, there was a baker's oven for
every 998 inhabitants in Milan; by 1906 this ratio had fallen to

---

[28] The difficulty with *L'Esercente*'s occasional references to the size of the *esercenti*
population is that no indication is ever given of who is included in the figure
quoted. At times the paper referred to the numbers of *botteghe* or *bottegai*, that is
small shops (workshops, retail shops, in effect any small commercial space) or
small proprietors, to demonstrate the strength of this sector of society, at others it
concentrated on more narrow definitions of *esercenti* such as those employed in
this analysis, though never specifying where the boundaries were drawn. Perhaps
the most reliable of the figures provided by the newspaper are those for enfra-
chised *esercenti*. *L'Esercente* claimed there were 10,500 such voters in 1891
(shortly after a speaker at the Federation talked of 10,021 *bottegai* in Milano) and
12,500 in 1899. 'A campagna finita', *L'Esercente*, 25 June 1891; 'La Federazione
degli Esercenti di Milano e la guerra contro le cooperative di consumo', ibid., 31
May 1891.; 'Gli esercenti e i commercianti', ibid., 12/13 June 1899.

[29] The *Guide di Milano* published by Savallo listed seven *rivenditori* in 1885, but 129
in 1902, rising to 203 in 1906.

Table 2.4. *Employers and employees in the 'esercenti' sector in Milan in 1881 and 1901*

Category	Proprietors			Employees			No. of employees per employer		
	1881	1901	% In-crease	1881	1901	% In-crease	1881	1901	Diff-erence
I	1,825	2,897	+ 58.7	3,603	5,511	+ 44.9	1.97	1.90	− 0.9
II	2,196	2,994	+ 36.3	1,372	938	− 31.6	0.62	0.31	− 0.31
III	751	1,114	+ 48.3	603	1,256	+ 108.0	0.8	1.18	+ 0.38
IV	2,678	3,595	+ 34.2				0.96		
IV and V combined	2,771	3,772	+ 37.6	2,809	4,756	+ 69.3	1.01	1.26	+ 0.15
V	93	177	+ 90.3				2.59		
VI	424	634	+ 49.5	843	1,323	+ 56.9	1.99	2.09	+ 0.10
VII	270	348	+ 28.9	93	65	− 32.3	0.34	0.19	− 0.15
VIII	2,212	2,237	+ 1.3	5,343	8,250	+ 35.2	2.42	3.69	+ 1.27
All	10,449	13,996	+ 34.0	14,666	22,099	+ 0.57	1.40	1.58	+ 0.18

Source: Milan Census Records 1881, 1901. In the 1901 figures employers are calculated as *padroni* + *direttori* in order to give a closer approximation to the number of enterprises active in each sector. The categories are:

I	Food makers and vendors	V	Hotel
II	Food retailers	VI	Hairdressing
III	Grocers, fuel sellers	VII	Monopoly sellers
IV	Food and drink services	VIII	Clothing, haberdashery

See n. 27 for details of the composition of these groups.

1:866.[30] The same trades also experienced a decline in the mean number of employees in each shop, another indication that new small-scale enterprises were being set up. By contrast, only 42.4% of butchers were immigrants.

Food makers and vendors were at the top of the earnings hierarchy amongst shopkeepers, as Fig. 2.1, which illustrates the average taxable income per contributor to the *ricchezza mobile* tax in 1890, demonstrates. The prices they charged for their wares reflected the 'value' they had added to the goods by turning them into cuts, sausages or cakes. By agreeing a common price for this 'value', proprietor associations could assume a significant role in organising the market to the benefit of their members. Bread prices in the *circondario interno* were controlled by the *Mutua Proprietari Forno*. It kept them so high that even the 'liberal' local authorities

---

[30] 'Il pane', *Città di Milano*, July 1914, p. 4.

Table 2.5. *Age and nativity of shopkeeper employees in Milan in 1881 and 1901*

Category	Numbers			% Immigrant			% Aged under 20		
	1881	1901	% Increase	1881	1901	Difference	1881	1901	Difference
I	3,603	5,511	+44.9	75.7	75.8	+0.1	41.2	41.2	0
II	1,372	938	−31.6	61.2	67.6	+6.4	22.8	34.6	+11.8
III	603	1,256	+108.0	63.8	80.1	16.3	37.8	26.2	−11.6
IV V }	2,809	4,756	+69.3	75.1	79.6	+4.4	39.9	20.3	−19.6
VI	843	1,323	+56.9	71.6	84.9	13.3	24.3	68.1	43.8
VII	93	65	−32.2	49.4	70.8	21.4	22.6	29.2	+6.6
VIII	5,343	8,250	+35.2	57.9	66.8	+8.9	27.6	25.3	−2.3

Source: Milan Census Records 1881, 1901. In the 1901 figures employers are calculates as *padroni* + *direttori* in order to give a close approximation to the number of enterprises active in each sector. The categories are:

I	Food makers and vendors	V	Hotel
II	Food retailers	VI	Hairdressing
III	Grocers, fuel sellers	VII	Monopoly sellers
IV	Food and drink services	VIII	Clothing, haberdashery

See n. 27 for details of the composition of these groups.

of the 1860s had intervened to bring prices down in the interests of preserving order. As a result, the authorities retained the right to impose an official bread price in the suburbs after these were incorporated into the Comune in 1873.[31]

The opening of the public slaughterhouse in February 1863 completely changed the nature of the meat trade. All the butchers, tripe makers and cold-meat and blood-sausage makers were now obliged to slaughter their animals there, so that they immediately had a common interest in negotiating the best possible deal for themselves.[32] The Società fra i Proprietari Salsamentari was successfully relaunched in 1868, in response to a proposal to raise the charge for use of the slaughterhouse by the company that ran it, and although

[31] Hunecke, *Classe operaia e rivoluzione industriale*, pp. 255–60.
[32] The Municipio had awarded a contract to the Società del Pubblico Macello in which the Società agreed to build and run the slaughterhouse at its own expense, in return for the Municipio prohibiting the butchering of animals in any other location, in both the *interno* and *esterno*. Tripe makers were also only allowed to practise their art on the premises of the Macello, and the Società was obliged to furnish them with workshops on the premises. *Convenzione fra il Municipio di Milano e la Società del Pubblico Macello.*

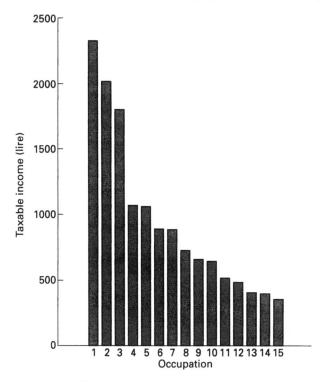

1 Pharmacists
2 Confectioners
3 Butchers
4 Jewellers
5 Bakers
6 *Salumieri*
7 Cafés
8 Grocers
9 Shoesellers
10 *Trattorie*
11 Hairdressers, umbrella sellers, etc
12 Bars, *osterie*, wineshops, etc
13 General stores
14 State-monopoly goods sellers
15 Fishmongers, greengrocers, poultry sellers

Source: Guida di Milano, publ. Savallo, 1892, p.35

Fig. 2.1 *Ricchezza mobile*: taxable income per contributor, 1890

it failed to avert this, it later succeeded in negotiating new opening times for the slaughterhouse. The Società also agreed bulk contracts for the sale of the blood and skins of the animal carcasses belonging to its members: another example of the benefits of association.[33]

Proprietors' associations in this category were stronger than in others, because individual traders perceived the greatest threat to themselves coming from external agents rather than their competitors. Collective action provided the best means for dealing with this threat as associations could work to insulate their members from the competitive environment.

Most of the artisan food retailers within Milan were protected by the fact that, unlike other trades, they were little affected by the rise of manufacturing. There were many attempts to industrialise bread production but they all failed, owing to consumer resistance to the final product. The small bakeries were able to produce twenty-five different types of *pane alla casalinga*, basic breads sold to the working classes, and thirty-six varieties of luxury, so-called Viennese, loaves.[34] Manufacturers could not match them in either quality or variety, so purchasers continued to pay the higher prices demanded by the bakers, despite the protests from the disadvantaged themselves, and from various administrations fearful of the consequences for public order.

Similarly the production of salamis and cold meats did not become an industry in Milan, in the way that happened in other cities such as Bologna. In fact, the only trade to be significantly altered by the rise of large-scale manufacturing was pasta making. Whereas the overall figures for this category suggest there were more small enterprises with fewer workers per proprietor, the reverse was true in the pasta-making sector, where there was a very limited growth in the numbers of proprietors, but a very substantial rise in the numbers of workers.[35]

---

[33] Another example of the benefits of association was the scheme introduced to enable breeders to insure their animals with the Società during an outbreak of a swine disease caught from couch grass in 1875. This preserved the supply of animals coming to market, thus benefiting both members and breeders. Società Proprietari Salsamentari, *Venti anni di vita sociale*, pp. 29–58.

[34] Società Mutua Proprietari Forno di Milano, *La panificazione privata e la panificazione municipalizzata*, p. 34.

[35] The censuses give sixty-two *padroni* under the heading of pasta makers and makers of holy wafers in 1881 and sixty-nine in 1901, but a rise from 118 to 340 employees within the category. The Savallo guides list forty-eight makers and vendors of pasta in 1885 and fifty-eight twenty years later.

Category II contains those whose income came purely from retailing food: greengrocers, fish and poultrymongers and vendors of dairy products. Although this is the second largest category of *padroni* within our classification by 1901, it is likely that the figures are a considerable underrepresentation of its size. This is because many of these traders were small producers, or the wives of small producers, who brought their own goods into the city and were as likely to have classified themselves as cultivators as vendors.[36]

These retailers operated on a much smaller scale than those in Category I. Indeed, many, particularly the greengrocers, did not have shops at all but sold from barrows in the streets (this poses another problem when using official figures as they may have been classified as wandering salesmen). In 1914 *Città di Milano* counted 1,303 greengrocers with shops, 274 with hand carts, 66 stallholders and 870 market traders in the city, excluding another 770 individuals whose enterprises were based on the wholesale market. There was a shop for every 471 citizens, a low figure even without considering the additional competition posed by those traders who didn't operate from a store.

These food retailers added little or no value to their merchandise, unlike the food makers of category I, and their incomes were correspondingly smaller. Naturally, they employed far fewer assistants, having neither a skill to offer them nor the money to pay them. The numbers of workers in this category actually fell considerably between the two censuses, although that of *padroni* rose. This should be interpreted as indicating both the precariousness of the trade and its attractiveness to those prepared to set up any kind of enterprise in order to survive. As Fig. 2.1 shows, these types of retailer were at the very bottom of the earnings hierarchy.

These trades in themselves, then, were not conducive to effective organisation, given their frailty and frequent lack of fixed premises. To this should be added the fact that this category contained a large number of female proprietors – well over 40%. In 1881 more women than men were poulterers, fishmongers and vegetable sellers. This again mitigated against collective action within the sector given the constraints on female participation in public associations.

Category III consists of retailers of basic goods, and in particular goods which were not necessarily consumables. Essentially this

---

[36] *La popolazione di Milano ... 1881*, p. 76.

group consists of grocers, vendors of 'colonial', i.e. imported, goods and fuel sellers, but the definitions employed by the sub-headings were very wide: the 1901 sub-heading was for traders in chemical and medicinal products, fertilisers, groceries, colonial articles, household oils for heating and lighting, soap, dyes, polishes, matches, sponges and perfumes. Unfortunately there is little reliable evidence to explain the fortunes of the group during the period, but it does seem that grocers increased considerably in both numbers and economic strength during the period; the numbers recorded in the Savallo commercial guides to the city more than doubled between 1886 and 1906, rising from 282 to 584.[37] This would mean that there were more potential customers for each grocer's shop than for the 643 bakers with ovens that the *Guida* recorded in 1906, however; an advantage that appears more pronounced when the further 204 *rivenditori* of bread are also taken into consideration.

Grocers' shops were certainly changing. As both production and preservative processes improved, there was an ever-increasing range of products which could be stocked and the first brand identities began to develop. As a result of this the grocers' original skills of preparation and confection became less important, so that, for example, the coupling, or at least advertising, of grocers' shops which also made chocolates decreased. Instead new, more commercial skills developed, such as that of using stock control systems, whilst it is possible that the grocery trade offered more opportunities for expansion through the acquisition of additional shops.

Category III also includes the fuel sellers, known as the *combustibili*. Coal and coke became more important in both commercial and domestic use, at the expense of wood. Most of the coke was obtained from the local gas company through an arrangement negotiated with the fuel sellers' association, and participation in this arrangement would require traders to have a reasonable amount of capital at their disposal. Again, the trade was relatively well organised because of the need to negotiate collectively with an outside agent, in this case the gas company.

That the average size of operations in both grocery and fuel selling grew larger is suggested by the rise in the average number of employees per employer from 0.8 to 1.18, a rate of increase only surpassed in the clothing sector, and one which contrasts with the

---

[37] *Guida di Milano*, publ. Savallo, 1885–1906.

decrease in the ratio found in category I. Potential prosperity might also be inferred from the relatively high level of native-born Milanese to be found amongst the *padroni* and the low proportion of women proprietors in this category; although, as Fig. 2.1 indicates, grocers still had not matched the extra earnings derived from the 'value added' profits of food makers and vendors in 1890. It is a shame similar figures do not exist for the 1900s.

Category IV embraces all those activities which involved the serving of food and drink to the public: bars, eating houses, cafés, hostelries and so forth. When combined with the hotels of Category V, they form most of what are described as the *esercizi pubblici*, that is, the service activities.

Category IV is the largest category and must have been very attractive to migrants as enterprises could easily be established on a family basis. The large number of immigrants amongst the *padroni* – 75% in 1901, the highest proportion amongst the four biggest categories – certainly bears this hypothesis out. There were relatively low barriers to entry into the sector, as the specialist (as opposed to business) skills required were few: it is easy to imagine establishments with the wife in the kitchen whilst the husband served at the bar. Such *esercizi* were seldom money spinners as the *ricchezza mobile* data demonstrates (see Fig. 2.1). Overcompetition was one of the chief causes of this: in 1914 *Città di Milano* estimated that there was an outlet serving alcohol for every 96 inhabitants.[38]

Why, then, is the overall rate of increase in the numbers of *esercizi* so low in this category (29.7%)? The *legge di pubblica sicurezza* decreed that all premises in which wine, beer, spirits and other types of drink were sold or consumed had to be licensed, and that when dealing with a licence request, 'the Giunta [local administration] will declare whether, in its opinion, in view of the existing number, it would be better to refuse to allow the opening of new *esercizi*'.[39] The wording of the law is indicative of the sentiments of hostility towards such establishments felt by many of those who believed themselves the keepers of public morality, and there is no doubt that this mitigated against a greater expansion of the sector.

There were many disincentives to association. Similar establishments were rivals in ways that were not fully replicated in other sectors – the physical environment created by a host and his or her

[38] Wine and liquor shops were also premises for consumption.
[39] *Legge di pubblica sicurezza*, Article 52. Reprinted in *Il Prontuario*, p. 77.

own personality were crucial points in attracting customers. On the other hand, although high-class restaurants were not in competition with low-class bars (*bettole*), they had little in common with them either. In 1887, for instance, the Milanese authorities refused to renew any of the licences for card playing granted to the *bettole* owners, and, as this was the most popular diversion amongst the lower orders at the time, many *bettole* were simply forced to close down.[40] The Mutua Associazione degli Osti, Trattori e Mercanti di Vino, one of the first trade associations to be founded in the post-unification period, took very little interest in the matter, however, seemingly finding this beneath its consideration. Licence holders were also unenthusiastic about wider shopkeeper federations as they believed that other enterprises, such as groceries and dairies, were competing with them by selling wine; a fact borne out by the *Città di Milano* figures.[41]

The fastest-growing elements amongst the *esercizi pubblici*, however, were the hotel keepers who form category V of our survey. The increasing dominance of Milan as a commercial and now industrial centre was the cause of this expansion. The growth or re-classification of lower-class hotels (*locanderie*) probably explains the big rise in the number of female proprietors between 1881 and 1901. It is difficult to think of hoteliers as part of the *esercente* sector, particularly when the *ricchezza mobile* figures show them to have earned nearly eight times as much as the proprietors of restaurants and eating houses. None the less, they did share the same workforce of cooks and waiters, a fact which assumed considerable importance during the strike amongst these workers in the 1900s.

Category VI comprises the barbers and hairdressers within the city. They frequently practised another trade in conjunction with their profession, justifying the inclusion of barbers amongst the *industrie minute* by the collectors of the *tassa esercizio* and *ricchezza mobile*.[42] These activities, which might include the making and sale of umbrellas and fans for example, were themselves subject to

---

[40] See pp. 111–12.
[41] Of the 6,218 outlets selling alcohol in Milan in 1914, 1,486 (23.9%) would not have been included in categories IV or V. These shops were mostly pharmacies, tobacconists, grocers, dairies, ice cream parlours and greengrocers. 'Il commercio delle bevande alcooliche in Milano', *Città di Milano*, September 1914, p. 2. For one hostile reaction to this see 'Un'esercente che fa sua l'idea della Federazione', *L'Esercente*, 29 April 1888.
[42] Società Umanitaria: Ufficio del Lavoro, *Scioperi, serrate*, pp. 108–9.

pressure from the growth of manufacturing industries and, perhaps most importantly, from the effects of the depression on purchasing habits. The effect of general economic health on the service sector can also be seen in the sharp boost in average per capita contribution to the *tassa esercizio* after 1896 amongst the *industrie minute* and the even greater growth rates recorded amongst the *esercizi pubblici*.

The census records reveal a substantial increase in the number of barber shop proprietors and their workers during his period, and likewise a considerable increase in the incidence of non-nativity amongst them. This may have been partly due to hairdressers moving in from the countryside, but, as 80% of proprietors were ex-apprentices, the most likely explanation is that the increase may be accounted for, in large part, by migrants learning the profession as workers and then setting up on their own. The native Milanese were unwilling to apprentice their sons into the trade, believing that better opportunities lay in other sectors.[43] The extreme youth of the workforce (over 68% were twenty or under according to the 1901 census) is further evidence of the rapidity with which the transition from *lavorante* and *padrone* was made, and also explains how it was that proprietors were able to afford their workers at all. It should be added, however, that the ratios of workers to *padroni* given by the censuses are misleading, as many workers would only be employed at weekends to cope with the rush.

The rapidity with which workers opened their own salons explains why the numbers of barbers competing with one another were so great. A vicious circle existed, as barbers were unable to pay their workers sufficient to retain them (those in the most down-at-heel areas were forced to pay more than they themselves earned), so workers set up shop for themselves and diluted individual market share yet further.[44] In such conditions, it was impossible for them to organise the market in their favour.

Category VII consists of the vendors of government monopoly goods, notably salt, tobacco and playing cards. The number were limited to roughly one concession holder per 2,000 inhabitants. The contracts to run these enterprises were usually awarded to those who had performed some form of state service and were now incapable of providing for themselves, such as ex-soldiers and

---

[43] Ibid., pp. 108–9.   [44] Ibid., pp. 108–9.

public-sector clerks who had no pensions, or to their widows or orphans. Only one concession could be held per *circondario*.[45]

These concessions were worth very little to their holders as their prime purpose was to make money for the state. Between 1881 and 1901, the number of employees in the sector actually declined (as was also the case with the food retailers of Category II, the only group of *padroni* which earned less than these vendors). The selection process, however, meant that native-born proprietors were in greater evidence in this category than elsewhere, whilst the increase in numbers was much slower, and the number of women proprietors (frequently widows) much greater.

The other group of retailers to be protected by the state was the pharmacists. Chemists had to pass an examination of competence to acquire the right to practise, and they then had to find an area in which the number of inhabitants was great enough to allow a new pharmacy to be opened without breaking government guarantees to existing pharmacists to restrict the numbers of practitioners within a certain zone (around one to 5,000 head of population).[46] This guaranteed them a reasonable income, particularly as legal restrictions also gave them a monopoly over the sale of many medicinal products. They were quick to defend any threats to this position, usually stemming from the grocers, and this, as well as their educated and privileged position, made it difficult for them to identify with the shopkeepers. Consequently they have not been included in any category.

Finally, Category VIII consists of clothing retailers together with haberdashers and shoemakers, but excluding tailors and seamstresses. This sector was most affected by the twin impacts of the growth of large-scale manufacturing and the beginning of department-store-style retailing. Hence there was only a very small rise in the numbers of *padroni* but a much more substantial one in the ranks of the workers. By the 1890s, for example, two shoemaking factories, Crema, Rovatti e C and Fratelli Zanotti, each employed 150 workers.[47] As the immigration statistics showed, cobblers were arriving in Milan in considerable numbers, but the choice they faced when they got there was often between enrolling as a worker or facing either underemployment or unemployment as an independent.

[45] *Il Prontuario*, pp. 101–2.   [46] Ibid., p. 6.
[47] Della Peruta, 'Lavoro e fabbrica', p. 244.

Clothing retailers were under pressure from some of the larger stores (including cooperatives) which hired their own workers to produce 'ready-made' garments they could sell. Meanwhile the advance of machine production brought about a switch from homework to shopwork. The slower rate of growth recorded in the *tassa esercizio* rolls for the *vestiario* sector, in which tailors and seamstresses were also recorded, suggests that these pressures told on those looking to set up new enterprises, but that this did not prevent many who had already acquired the skills from trying.

Haberdashers and clothiers all sold their wares by bargaining with the customer rather than quoting a fixed price. This made it difficult for proprietors to agree to cooperate and protect their markets and it also accounted for the unpopularity of these types of retailers with their peers. Furthermore, these trades included large numbers of female proprietors – in 1881, for example, the majority of haberdashers were women. Not surprisingly, then, the spirit of association within this category was weak, and few members became involved in wider shopkeeper movements.

It would be extremely useful to be able to analyse some of the other retailing enterprises in the city: those which did not deal in basic goods. It is impossible to combine the census categories to do this meaningfully, however, as many trades are to be found mixed with others of a completely different and, for our purposes, inappropriate character.[48] For what it is worth, looking at the census categories in individual years, it appears that more of these retailers, dealers in furniture, glass, ceramics and toys, bric-à-brac dealers, antiquarians, and so on, were born in the city. This accords with the fact that such shops were usually well-established enterprises catering for a reasonably affluent clientele, lower-class customers having little money for such items which, in any case, they were likely to have purchased in markets. These proprietors frequently did not sell at the *prezzo fisso* and played little role in shopkeeper associations.

Analysis of the various categories identified through the census records highlights the characteristics of individual trades that helped or hindered the process of association. Collective action was demonstrably easier in trades where 'value' was added to the goods

---

[48] Thus it is impossible to investigate bookshops as dealers were placed in the same category as publishing houses and newspaper owners because many publishing houses had their own bookstores on the premises.

being sold as this generated higher incomes and enabled traders to organise the market to their own benefit by agreeing prices and thus reducing competition. Those trades whose structures provided the opportunity for collective negotiation with 'outside' bodies – the bulk purchasing of coke by fuel sellers from the gas company for example – naturally had greater potential for association than those that did not. The trades in which these characteristics were most often to be found were those of the 'artisan' food retailers (butchers, bakers, etc.) of Category I and the grocers and fuel sellers of Category III.

Conversely trades which suffered from overcompetition had less potential for collective action and identity, especially if they were conducted in ways that provoked the distrust of other retailers (use of the bargaining system rather than the *prezzo fisso*, for instance), or if their practitioners were themselves distrustful of other retailers (the resentment felt by proprietors of *esercizi pubblici* for other shopkeepers selling alcohol). Those trades whose ability to organise their market was effectively undermined by mechanisation and the penetration of large-scale enterprise were clearly at a disadvantage when it came to collective activity. The social restrictions placed upon women meant that trades in which there were large number of women proprietors (usually, in any case, amongst the least profitable of *esercenti* activities) also had difficulties in organising effectively.

Unsurprisingly then, bakers, butchers, delicatessen proprietors, grocers, fuel sellers and, in later years, hoteliers, were the most prominent participants in the Milanese *esercenti* movement. There were also significant numbers of members from the licensed trade and the simple food retailers, but these trades were less well organised, had weaker identities, and provided few of the leading figures within the movement. Within Milan, and within the shopkeeper movement itself, the term *esercenti* was usually interpreted as meaning retailers of essential goods, particularly foodstuffs, as opposed to clothing and craft outlets, reflecting the very different nature of these trades in terms of the way that their business was conducted, and their weakness in the face of large-scale competition, as well as the nature of the articles sold.

What, though, could form part of a shopkeeper, as opposed to a trade, identity? We have already noted the universal problems arising from some business practices such as the granting of *il fido*, whilst the prevalence of non-native Milanese within the shopkeeping professions would prove important in later years. The context of retailing within the city was clearly related to the neighbourhood in which it was conducted, however, given the multiple linkages between patron and proprietor. Chapter 3 will further investigate these components of shopkeeper identity by introducing a spatial element into the analysis.

3. The economic geography of shopkeeping: the role of the dazio consumo

The decision of the newly installed Italian government to continue with the *dazio consumo* (that is, a locally imposed duty on retail goods of which a share was passed on to government) as a source of both municipal and central funding led to many distortions in the fiscal map of Italy.[1] Local administrations were divided into four types according to size with the most crucial difference being between those *comuni* under 8,000 inhabitants, which had to levy excise under the *aperto* ('open') system, and the three levels of *comuni chiusi* in which the tariffs differed but the method of operation remained the same. In the *chiuso* ('closed') system the *dazio* was paid on all items as they entered the municipality, whilst in the *aperto* zone the shopkeeper paid an annual subscription to the authorities, based on estimated turnover, and calculated on a lower set of tariffs.

In 1891, therefore, the 8.3 million people living in the *comuni chiusi* paid L. 181 million to the *dazio consumo* authorities, compared with the L. 31.8 million contributed by the 20.7 million people living in the *comuni aperti*. This imbalance was particularly striking when the respective figures from the share of this revenue passed on to the government are compared (L. 52.5 million from the inhabitants of the *chiuso* zones, L. 15 million from those living in the *aperto* districts), given that national government supplied the same service to each group.[2]

The discrepancy between payments to the local authority was more plausibly explained by the fact that the large urban authorities which made up the *comuni chiusi* supplied a far greater number of

---

[1] The measures which governed the operation of the *dazio comsumo* were the *legge 3 luglio 1864 n1827*, the *decreto 28 guigno 1866*, and the *legge 11 agosto 1870 n5784*.

[2] Dalla Volta, 'Il dazio consumo in Italia', pp. 996–7.

services to their residents than the mainly rural districts which constituted the *comuni aperti*. Cities which also administered rural zones at the edge of their boundaries often also recognised that there they did not provide the same range of services as to their urban inhabitants and created what were effectively *aperto* regimes within a so-called *circondario esterno*. Usually these were scarcely populated areas into which the city was only likely to expand in the distant future. In 1854 Turin had enlarged its borders to cover an area of 1,705 ha, of which 1,185 ha were employed in agriculture: even by 1903 only 62,000 people lived in the *esterno* compared to the 306,000 within the *zona chiusa*. The malaria belt around Rome formed a large part of the capital's *circondario esterno*.[3]

In Milan, however, the situation was very different. Since 1781 the belt of small villages and land surrounding the city had been a *comune* in its own right, bearing the name of the Corpi Santi. It became the most populous *comune* in the province after Milan itself; largely because it operated the *aperto* system. This made the area very attractive to industry and commerce as it was effectively possible to have a Milanese location, yet avoid the city's fiscal regime. The Corpi Santi developed into Milanese suburbs, creating an overwhelming financial problem for the local administration which had to provide urban-type services whilst operating an agriculturally orientated tax regime. The final solution to this problem was the admission of the Corpi Santi into the Comune of Milan as its *circondario esterno* in 1873, thus preserving the fiscal advantages that had helped stimulate the suburbs whilst passing the financial burden of administering them on to the inhabitants of the city; especially those who lived in the *interno*.

The *circondario interno* approximated to the area within the Spanish Walls of the city as shown in Fig. 3.1. The oldest part of the *circondario* was the area bounded by the *cerchia dei navigli* (canal belt) within which the houses of the nobility and bourgeoisie were to be found. Immediately after Milan's liberation from the Austrians, this area also contained a fair number of low-class and artisan dwellings but rising rents and slum clearances had forced many of these residents out by the 1880s. The zone between the *navigli* and the walls had a much greater lower-class component within its

[3] Einaudi, 'La riforma tributaria di una grande città', in *Cronache econimiche e politiche*, Vol. 2, p. 649. 'Consiglio comunale: discorso Mussi', *Il Secolo*, 4/5 April 1886.

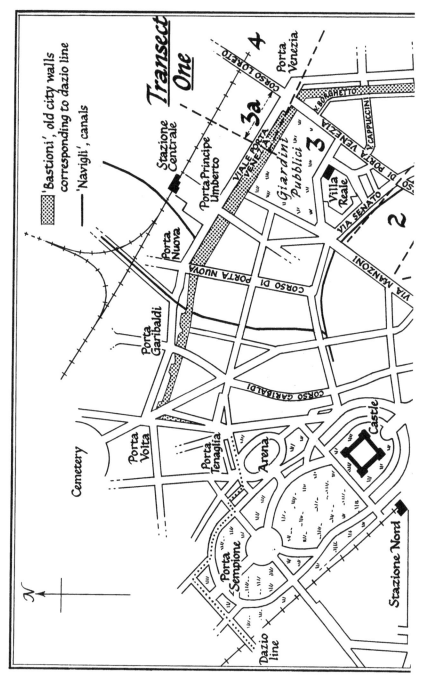

Fig. 3.1 Sketch map of Milan

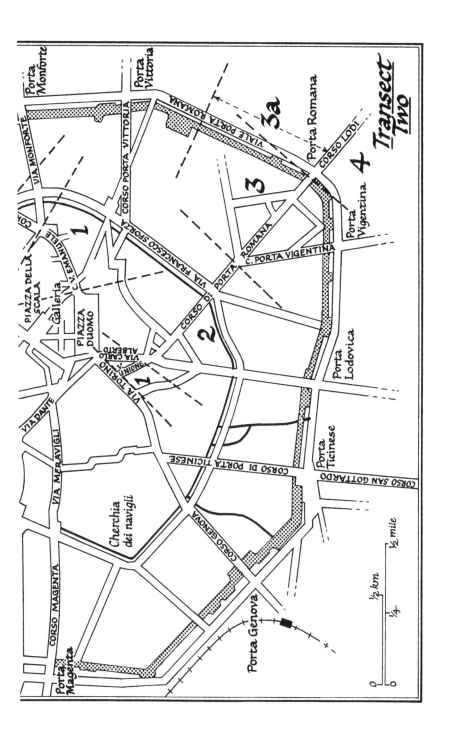

population. These people were directly linked to the wealthier elements through employment either as domestics or in the production of consumer articles for this market. Their politics were therefore more conservative than those of their peers in the *esterno*.[4]

The population of the *esterno* was largely lower class and contained a far higher proportion of immigrants than that of the *interno*. By 1901 the majority of the city's populations lived in the suburbs. The tax situation encouraged manufacturers to locate there, so the proportion of the population employed in industry in the *esterno* was significantly higher than in the *interno*. Not only were the prices of raw materials lower, it was also possible to pay lower wages, justified by the lower cost of living.[5] This situation was theoretically to everyone's advantage as the residents of the *interno* were notably averse to the encroachment of industry into the city centre.

The character of an area was reflected in its shops. As the city centre became progressively more upper class in character so its shops became increasingly resplendent. In the two decades that followed the liberation of the city the Corso Vittorio Emanuele became its leading shopping street, along with the Galleria which also bore the King's name and whose restaurants became very popular amongst the Milanese elite.[6] It was in these decades that antique shops were first opened in the city, concentrated in the quarter bounded by Via Monte Napoleone, Corso Venezia and Via Manzoni, nowadays the prime location for the international fashion and design houses.[7] Yet in the working-class areas, shopping itself was a relatively novel activity, and many purchases were still made at the market or from street barrows.

We can examine the differences between various zones and the shops within them by constructing two transects through the city. The data used comes from the commercial guides to the city issued by the Savallo publishing company between 1885 and 1890. These divided Milan into zones, each of which was then broken down into streets whose shops were listed by nature and proprietor. It would be foolish to claim that these are completely accurate; none the less

[4] See Lyttelton, 'Milan 1880–1922', pp. 250–6; Hunecke, *Classe operaia e rivoluzione industriale*, 107; Tilly, 'The working class of Milan', pp. 28, 413.
[5] Cattaneo, *Scritti economici*, Vol. 3, p. 429 (third letter of 7 September 1863).
[6] Fontana, 'La vita di strada', pp. 136–7; Zezzos, *Milano e il suo commercio*, p. 270.
[7] Schettini, 'L'antiquariato a Milano', p. 982.

the trend that emerges from them is sufficiently clear to be worthy of analysis if the defects in the data are always borne in mind.[8] The transects follow the main routes into the city as these are the most likely to have been accurately recorded. This does not give as rounded a picture as analysing complete zones, including back streets, but defining these zones would in itself have been arbitrary and maintaining them, in the light of changing guide layouts, more difficult. The aggregating of five years' worth of figures (the *Guida* for 1887 does not survive) reduces the importance of omissions in any one year and also makes some allowance for shops that might have opened but subsequently failed, as these count only once, whereas shops present throughout the period would have counted five times.

Some problems cannot be rectified, however. The *Guide* only identified shops, so that greengrocers selling from their barrows and newspaper vendors in their huts (*edicole*) cannot be included in the survey, whilst the *bettole* were not included after the 1887 incident (see pages 111–12). The descriptions used by the guides are also confusing. A *negoziante*, for example, could be either a wholesale merchant or a retailer. Where it was clear that a *negoziante di vino* (wine) or a *negoziante di stoffe* (fabrics) was only a merchant rather than a retailer, he has been excluded; doubtful cases remain (most *negozianti* in these two categories were retailers). An important exception to this rule was cheese merchants, *negozianti di formaggio*, as this title was often used to indicate wholesalers (half of those so

---

[8] *Guide di Milano*, publ. Savallo, 1885–90. The *Guide* are more accurate than one might expect. In August 1886 the police were ordered to produce a record of all the bakeries in the area under their supervision. The list compiled by the 5th division, responsible for the area around the Corso Porta Ticinese (a popular lower-class zone), records twenty-eight bakeries, twenty-seven of which appeared in the *Guida Savallo* that had been issued at the beginning of the year. It is possible that the bakery omitted was not open when the guide was published. This list may be found in the Archivio dello Stato di Milano (hereafter ASM). Fond. Questura, c. 45 f. 1, Scioperi, Disordini, Scioperi dei lavoranti fornai, 3/4 agosto 1886. Bardeaux stressed how much more accurate the Savallo guides were after 1885 describing them as 'a genuine commercial, topographical and industrial guide to the city, as well as to the province, infinitely better than the previous inventories for the wealth of information and for the clarity ... which renders any research into people or institutions extremely easy. Hence an extremely important work of great utility, an excellent means of advertising, still successfully published' (Bardeaux, *Catalogo delle guide di Milano*, p. 21). *L'Esercente* even maintained that the police passed their evenings selecting shopkeepers from the *Guide* at random and concocting charges against them. 'Contravvenzioni! a base di Guide Savallo', *L'Esercente*, 29 July 1888.

described were found next to the market on Corso San Gottardo): in this instance all these *negozianti* have been excluded so that some genuine retailers have almost certainly been omitted in the interests of consistency. There are also difficulties separating those engaged in the manufacturing and retailing functions, particularly as most artisan workshops performed both roles. Again the policy adopted was that those who could be identified as solely manufacturers, *fabbricanti*, were excluded, whilst all whose role was unclear were counted.

The different headings used by the guides make it impossible to maintain the categories employed to analyse the census data in chapter 1. Instead new alphabetical groupings were devised and these are listed below.

A Food retailers: bakers (inc. sales only), confectioners, pasta makers, general food products, dairy proprietors, butchers, pork butchers, delicatessen proprietors, poulterers

B Vendors of basic goods: grocers, tobacconists, fuel sellers

C *Esercizi pubblici*: licensed premises inc. basic eating houses (*trattorie*), wine and spirits shops

D Superior *esercizi pubblici*: hotels, restaurants, superior cafés

E Hairdressers

F Clothes, materials: traders in fashion garments, 'lady's' clothing, ready-made clothing, lingerie, knitwear, hosiery, materials, haberdashery

G Jewellery, antiques: goldsmiths, jewellers, watchmakers, bric-à-brac, toys, ceramics, table china, glass and crystalware, antiques

H Domestic, photo: domestic goods, ironmongers, photographers

I Furniture, stationery, leather goods: furniture traders, stationers, leather goods, furriers, saddlers

J Shoes: shoemakers, clogmakers[9]

---

[9] The descriptions used in the guides are:
  A Food retailers: *prestinai* (Milanese term for bakers), *offellerie* (Milanese for confectioners), *rivenditori di pane, pastai, prodotti alimentari, postai* (in Milan the *postai* were general food vendors who also made their own delicatessen specialities), *lattivendoli, pizzicagnoli, macellai, salsamentari* (Milanese for *salumieri*), *pollivendoli*.
  B Vendors of basic goods: *droghieri, tabaccai, legno e carbone*.
  C *Esercizi pubblici: trattorie, osterie, bar, fiaschetterie, vini toscani, negozianti di vino, bottigliere, liquoristi*.
  D Superior *esercizi pubblici: albergo, ristorante, caffè ristorante, caffè*.
  E Hairdressers: *parrucchieri, barbieri*.
  F Clothes, materials: *negozianti articoli di moda, moda e confezione per signora,*

The route of both transects may be traced in Fig. 3.1. The first runs along Corso Vittorio Emanuele and Corso Venezia, then passes into the *circondario esterno* through Porta Venezia to proceed up Corso Loreto, later renamed Corso Buenos Aires. Corso Vittorio Emanuele was one of the most prestigious shopping streets in Milan, whilst Corso Venezia led out to a more residential area, particularly after it crossed the *naviglio*, although this was still a well-to-do zone. Beyond the Porta, Corso Loreto was one of the most popular regions of the *esterno*, extending out quite considerably beyond the city.

The second route is somewhat different. Via Unione was a subsidiary road linking the Corso Porta Romana with Via Torino and not of as great importance as, say, Via Carlo Alberto; nonetheless, it was in the very heart of the city. The Corso Porta Romana itself was the centre of a popular quarter. Beyond the *naviglio* it was largely a lower-class residential area. Immediately outside the Porta itself was the chestnut market, beyond which Corso Lodi led out of the city, although the Corso was little developed in this period.

The profile of each zone along each of the transects can be investigated by comparing the density of shops in each zone, the patterns of proprietorship in each zone, and its 'retailing mix', that is the relative proportions of the different types of shop within each zone. The results of this analysis are given in Tables 3.1 and 3.2, and Fig. 3.2 and 3.3

Density has here been crudely defined as the aggregate number of shops recorded in the five years 1885–90 (the *Guida* for 1887 is missing) divided by five times the number of *palazzi* (blocks housing shops, offices and apartments) on the street. This ignores numerous factors, the size of the host block and the size of the shop being the most obvious ones, but it is probably the best rough measure available today. The density index declines sharply along the transects as one moves away from the city centre. Transect 2 shows this to be true even with respect to Via Unione and the head of Corso Porta Romana, despite the fact that Via Unione was a subsidiary

abiti confezionati, biancheria, maglieria, negozianti di stoffe, mercerie.
G Jewellery, antiques: *orefici e gioiellieri, bigiotterie, argentieri, orologiai, chincaglieri, giocattoli, ceramiche, porcellane da tavola, cristallerie, antiquari.*
H Domestic, photo: *utensili casalinghi, ferramenta, fotografi.*
I Furniture, stationery, leather goods: *negozianti di mobili, cartolai, cancelleria, valigiai, articoli da viaggio, pellicceria, sellai.*
J Shoes: *calzolai, zoccolai.*

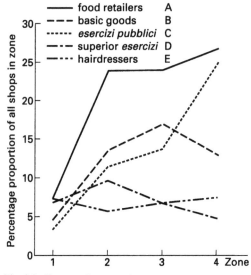

Fig. 3.2a Transect 1: categories A–E

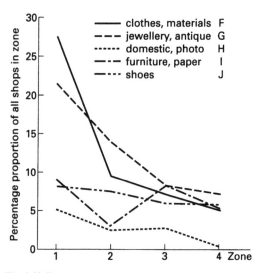

Fig. 3.2b Transect 1: categories F–J

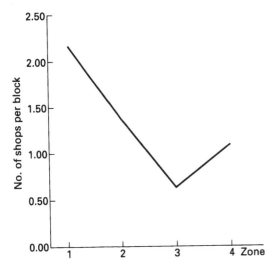

Fig. 3.2c Transect 1: density

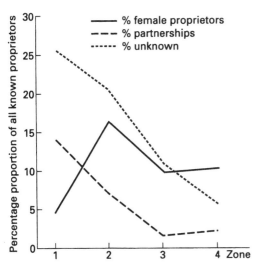

Fig. 3.2d Transect 1: forms of proprietorship

Table 3.1. *The pattern of retailing along Transect 1: The proportional distribution of various retailing activities within each zone*

Category	Zone 1	Zone 2	Zone 3	Zone 3a	Zone 4
A	7.2	23.9	24.0	19.0	26.7
B	4.4	13.4	16.9	14.0	12.8
C	3.2	11.4	13.7	32.2	25.0
D	6.7	9.5	6.6	4.1	4.5
E	7.2	5.5	6.6	9.1	7.3
F	27.7	9.5	7.1	1.7	5.1
G	21.5	13.9	8.2	9.1	7.1
H	5.1	2.5	2.7	0.0	0.4
I	9.0	3.0	8.2	3.3	5.3
J	8.1	7.5	6.0	7.4	5.8
% of female proprietors	4.4	16.4	9.8	5.8	10.2
% Proportion of partnerships	13.9	7.0	1.6	6.6	2.3
% Proprietorships unidentifiable	25.6	20.4	10.9	0.0	5.5
Aggregate no. of shops	443	201	183	121	532
No. of blocks	40	30	60	9	100
Density	2.17	1.34	0.61	2.69	1.06

Source: Compiled from *Guide di Milano* 1885–90 (except 1887). The figures represent the number of enterprises in each category within the zone as a percentage of all outlets.

route. Location in the central business zone was of fundamental importance in certain types of retailing, notably that of 'high-order goods', i.e. products purchased infrequently because of their expensive or luxury nature, just as conventional central-place theory would lead us to expect.[10]

There is an important difference between the two transects, however. Shop density along Transect 1 is actually lower in Zone 3 than in Zone 4, whereas the reverse is true along Transect 2 where density declines continuously. Transect 1 Zone 3, that is the Corso Venezia between Via Senato and the Porta, was a well-to-do residential area whose inhabitants were likely to use the central shops for their own purchases and have their basic goods delivered to

---

[10] For an introduction to central place theory see Bradford and Kent, *Human geography*, pp. 5–85.

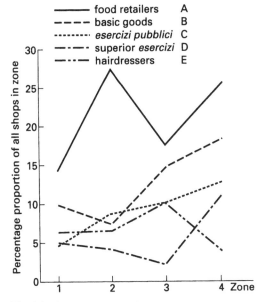

Fig. 3.3a Transect 2: categories A–E

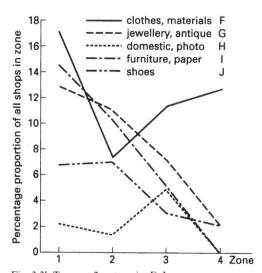

Fig. 3.3b Transect 2: categories F–J

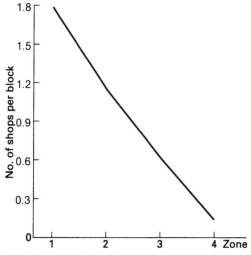

Fig. 3.3c Transect 2: density

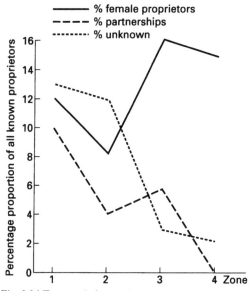

Fig. 3.3d Transect 2: forms of proprietorship

Table 3.2. *The pattern of retailing along Transect 2: the proportional distribution of various retailing activities within each zone*

Category	Zone 1	Zone 2	Zone 3	Zone 3a	Zone 4
A	16.7	32.3	20.6	29.6	29.8
B	11.5	8.5	17.0	13.9	21.3
C	5.2	10.1	11.8	34.5	14.9
D	5.7	4.7	2.3	1.1	12.8
E	7.3	7.4	11.8	6.4	4.3
F	17.2	7.4	11.4	3.4	12.8
G	13.0	11.0	7.2	1.5	2.1
H	2.1	1.3	4.9	1.5	0.0
I	14.6	10.3	5.2	5.2	0.0
J	6.8	7.0	7.8	3.0	2.1
% of female proprietors	12.0	8.1	16.0	8.6	14.9
% Proportion of partnerships	9.9	4.0	5.6	0.4	0.0
% Proprietorships unknown	13.0	11.9	2.9	4.9	2.1
Aggregate no. of shops	192	446	306	267	47
No. of blocks	22	80	102	72	68
Density	1.75	1.12	0.60	0.74	0.14

Source: Compiled from *Guide di Milano* 1885–90 (except 1887). The figures represent the number of enterprises in each category within the zone as a percentage of all outlets.

them. Zone 4, the suburban area on Corso Loreto, had a much lower-class profile, however, and its residents took advantage of the cheaper prices in their neighbourhood resulting from its status as a *zona aperta*.[11]

Although the lower-class residents of the Corso Porta Romana in Zone 3 of Transect 2 also did more of their own shopping than those of the Corso Porta Venezia in Transect 1 Zone 3, the actual density of shops in both zones was much the same. This was because the residents of the Corso Porta Romana would cross into the *esterno* to make their purchases there. The shops they favoured were located around the edge of the city, however, so the shop density measured

---

[11] A sample of the housing blocks at the start of Via Cappuccini and Via Borghetto, residential streets which turn off the Corso Venezia as it runs through Zone 3, gives a density of 0.08, compared with the 0.61 of the Zone itself.

along the still-underdeveloped Corso Lodi (Zone 4) remained very low: a caution against reading too much into the figures that were obtained. The later growth of the city raised the density of Transect 2 Zone 4 over that of Transect 2 Zone 3 and, for that matter, of Transect 2 Zone 3 over that of Transect 1 Zone 3 by the 1900s (see Fig. 11.1c and d). Differences between the better and worse-off residential zones will be a recurrent feature of our analysis.

Forms of proprietorship also tell us something of the character of retailing within each zone. The guides identified proprietors by sex and as to whether or not they were partnerships. By aggregating each year's record of shops in each zone (i.e. so that a shop present for five years counts five times and one for one counts one) we can compare the relative proportions of each type of shop in each zone (i.e. the percentage proportion of shops held in partnership out of all shops within a zone). Unfortunately, a combination of their recording methods and the vagueness of certain points of commercial law makes it impossible to say if all the shops whose proprietors were not identified were, in fact, managed shops, although it is notable that the proportion of these unidentified shops declined consistently along both transects and was highest of all along the Corso Vittorio Emanuele.[12] The proportion of shops held in partnership also follows this trend, and may be more easily identi-

12 The problem arises because of the nature of the title of *ditta* which any proprietor could take for his business and which became his legal commercial signature. Nearly always this was his own name and many shopkeepers probably never went as far as to choose a *ditta* for themselves at all: there certainly does not seem to have been a requirement upon them to register one. The *ditta* could, however, be transferred either with or without the attendant business so that there is no guarantee when, for example, the entry Ditta Leopoldo Luraschi appears in the *Guide*, that this refers to a business owned by Leopoldo Luraschi; nor does this imply that it did not. The designation of a *ditta* therefore makes it impossible to identify the form of proprietorship in which the business is held. The Ditta Leopoldo Luraschi (a bakery), for instance, was run first by Leopoldo's widow, then by his son after his death. As a result the *ditte* have been counted in the ranks of the unidentifiable forms of proprietorship mentioned in the text. The fact that they bothered to register as *ditte* does suggest that they were something more than simple shops, but it clearly means that the number of shops whose forms of proprietorship could not be identified does not equate with the number of managed shops or shops held as companies. None the less, the proportion of 'unknowns' does fall away considerably with the distance from the centre, as the hold of the small shops becomes stronger. The figures for the two transects are:

Transect 1	Z1 25.6%	Z2 20.4%	Z3 10.9%	Z4 5.5%
Transect 2	Z1 13.0%	Z2 11.9%	Z3 2.9%	Z4 2.1%

The legal position with regard to *ditte* is explained in Barberis, *Sulla ditta, insegna e nome commerciale*.

fied from the *Guide*. One could argue that these forms of proprietorship follow the degree of 'seriousness' in retailing in each sector,
indicative of the desirability of the location and the degree to which
it was exploited. In this context it should also be noted that it was
only in the Corso Vittorio Emanuele that a significant majority of
partnerships were identified as not being between family members.[13]

Using the same method of five-year aggregation we can calculate
the proportion of shops belonging to each of the ten categories.
Shops selling high-order goods were attracted to the centre, as that
was where most of their customers, usually the affluent, lived; and
also where out-of-town clients would be most likely to come. In
view of the relatively infrequent rate at which individual clients
purchased such goods, a central location would remain the optimal
way for stores to make themselves accessible to the largest number
of customers. For that reason we find a sharp fall in the proportion
of the jewellers, crystal, bric-à-brac and antique shops of Category
G as we move further from the centre. Similarly, shops such as
ironmongers, which sold 'new' types of manufactured goods, for
example electrical gadgets such as doorbells and household utensils,
and also photographers' studios were more frequently found
towards the centre of the city. These types of enterprise are recorded
in Category H.

In Category F, clothing and materials, the same forces produce
somewhat different results. The city centre was the prime location
for clothes shops, and it was rare to find actual shops far from this
central location. There was also, naturally, a considerable number
of resident tailors and dressmakers, not included in these figures.
Lower-class districts did not support many clothes shops, but did
contain large numbers of haberdashers, suggesting that residents
either bought their clothes elsewhere (markets, the *provincia*) or

---

[13] On the Corso Vittorio Emanuele, sixty instances of shops held in recognisable
partnerships were recorded (remember this figure counts every shop each time it
appears in the *Guide*, but excludes unidentifiable companies or *ditte*) of which
twenty-eight were recognisably family partnerships. The only other zone in which
non-family partnerships predominate was Transect 1 Zone 3a, but as there were
only three instances of partnerships recorded, of which one was a family partnership, the figure is hardly significant. The figures for the sample group as a whole
along the two transects are 143 recognisable partnerships in 2,340 'shop instances'
of which ninety-five are recognisable family partnerships. Thus 6.11% of the 'shop
instances' recorded were recognisable partnerships of which 66.43% were family
partnerships. The sample is anything but random, of course, so nothing can be
assumed from this about the figures for the city as a whole.

bought the material for clothes and made them or had them made up. Note again the significant difference this makes between the third zones of the two transects, with the residential zone of Corso Porta Romana containing a much greater proportion of Category F shops than its equivalent in Corso Venezia.

The furniture sellers, stationers and vendors of fur and leather goods of Category I demonstrate this principle in reverse. This group usually sold their wares to the comfortably off so proceeding along Transect 2 we notice a continuous decline in their representation amongst shops as a whole, consistent with the increasingly lower-class nature of the transect. Along Transect 1, however, the figure for Category I reaches its peak in Zone 3, the better-off residential zone, which was also, presumably, a somewhat cheaper location than the city centre in which the stores selling the highest-order goods were to be found.

The hairdressers of Category E and shoesellers and cobblers of Category J retain a fairly constant level of representation across the transects. This was because the nature of their enterprises varied according to the area in which they were located. The luxury hairdressing salons of the city centre employed three or more workers and made as much of their money from the sale of toiletries and accessories as they did from haircutting itself. In the salons in the rest of the *interno* it was haircutting that provided the bulk of the income, but outside the walls the barber often had to combine his trade with tailoring to make ends meet, only employing hired help for the weekend rush.[14] Similarly, the city centre played host to shoeshops, whilst further out, the trade was increasingly that of the cobbler and, in the worst-off areas, the clogmaker.

Category D contains what have been termed 'superior *esercizi pubblici*', that is hotels, restaurants and cafés whose clientele were usually of a higher social background than the frequenters of the *esercizi* in Category C, the *trattorie*, *osterie* and *negozi di vino*. By and large, the proportion of superior establishments in an area falls with distance from the city centre, although, as Transect 1 suggests, they had to settle for locations near to the centre, rather than right in the heart of it. The increased proportion of superior *esercizi pubblici* recorded in Zone 4 of Transect 2 is to be treated with care owing to the small numbers of shops located there; none the less it is

---

[14] Società Umanitaria, *Scioperi, serrate*, p. 108.

an indication of a pattern observed elsewhere, as travellers entering the city or merchants coming to the markets held around the various *porte* would make use of these establishments.

The three categories which tend to increase their representation as one moves along the transects, are those which supplied the basic needs of life: the food retailers of Category A, the vendors of other necessities in Category B and the licensed premises of Category C. This trend would be even more pronounced if those concerns which we had to exclude because of the nature of the *Guide* – the *bettole* and the greengrocers – had been included. In 1885 the *Guida* recorded seven *bettole* in Zone 3 on the Corso Porta Romana. These enterprises sold low-order goods and therefore could survive on low thresholds, whilst a market of sorts existed everywhere for their wares. Certainly there were shops which came under these categories in the centre as well, but there they coexisted with other forms of store and were themselves of a very different character. The famous Hagy wine shop and the Rainoldi *salumeria*, both to be found on Corso Vittorio Emanuele, were far removed from the run-of-the-mill forms of such establishments to be found on the Corso Porta Romana.[15]

There is, however, one very important inconsistency in the pattern described above. In Zone 3 of Transect 2, that is the lower-class residential area of Corso Porta Romana beyond the *naviglio*, the proportion of food retailers (Category A) falls dramatically whilst that of *esercizi pubblici* (Category C) hardly increases. This distortion runs completely contrary to the trend which common sense and the pattern recorded along the rest of the transects would suggest: that these activities would become increasingly predominant in lower-class and residential areas. A similar though less pronounced distortion is seen in the affluent Zone 3 of Transect 1. Why?

The reason was straightforward: the *dazio consumo*. Every time an individual crossed the customs line, the *cinta daziaria*, into the city they were permitted to bring in a certain quantity of goods 'duty free'. Because of its status as a *zona aperta* prices were significantly lower in the *esterno*, so residents of the *interno* who lived near the *porte* were able to save money by crossing into the *esterno* in order to do their shopping. It has been estimated that a working-class

---

[15] Although Rainoldi moved to new premises during our period. See Fontana, 'La vita di strada', pp. 136–7.

family of four or five members would have saved 30–50 *centesimi* a day by making all their purchases in the suburbs, an amount equivalent to between a quarter and a third of the daily salary of a textile worker, or put another way, the cost of between 0.75 to 1.25 kg of bread.[16] Consequently a shop located immediately outside the *porte*, particularly on the roads that ran parallel to the customs line, was in a much more desirable position than one in the *interno* in the area near to the boundary. Shopkeepers whose premises were sited on the border of the *cinta daziaria* were known as *frontisti*.

This consideration can be introduced into the transect analysis. A small area which ran from the Porta Venezia along the edge of the Viale Porta Venezia has been examined for Transect 1, whilst a much longer survey of the Viale Porta Romana was undertaken for Transect 2. These areas are shown as Zone 3a on Fig. 3.1 and the results obtained from them are given in Tables 3.1 and 3.2 and Figs. 3.4 and 3.5.

The attractiveness of these locations close to the customs line immediately becomes apparent when one examines the density indices. The area nearest to the *porta* was the most attractive of all, as this was the most directly accessible from the interno. Hence the extremely high figure recorded in Transect 1, where Zone 3a runs along the Viale for nine blocks only. Even in the much larger Zone 3a in Transect 2, however, density was greater than in either the preceding or succeeding zone. The proportion of partnerships was much higher, in accordance with the 'degree-of-seriousness' hypothesis.

Esercizi pubblici, particularly those involved in the straight-forward sale of alcohol, and food retailers, particularly bakeries, were the predominant types of shop found in these locations. Between 1876 and 1898 there was a duty of 10.5 *centesimi* on a litre of wine in the *interno* and of 3.4 *centesimi* on a kilogram of bread made with mixed cereals (as opposed to pure wheat bread, a luxury product). Between 1885 and 1890 wine cost roughly 77 *centesimi* a litre and bread 35 *centesimi* a kilogram.[17]

The difference between the two transects is borne out by the character of these frontal zones. Along the prosperous Transect 1 only, the proportion of *esercizi pubblici* increased dramatically in

[16] Hunecke, *Classe operaia e rivoluzione industriale*, p. 247.
[17] Rough average annual prices calculated from Dati statistici, 1905, p. 353. A full list of *dazio consumo* tariffs can be found in ibid., Allegato D.

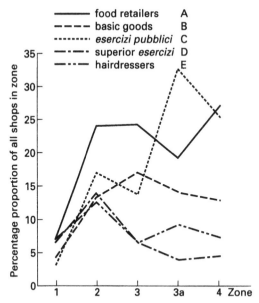

Fig. 3.4a Transect 1 with *frontisti*: categories A–E

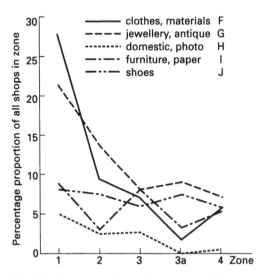

Fig. 3.4b Transect 1 with *frontisti*: categories F–J

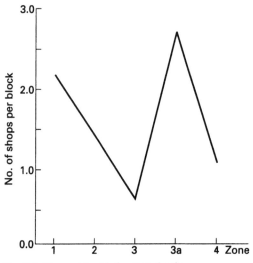

Fig. 3.4c Transect 1 with *frontisti*: density

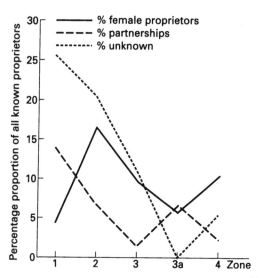

Fig. 3.4d Transect 1 with *frontisti*: forms of proprietorship

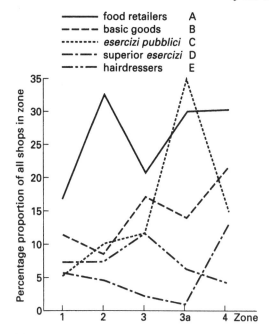

Fig. 3.5a Transect 2 with *frontisti*: categories A–E

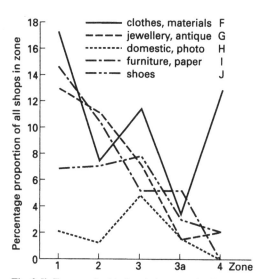

Fig. 3.5b Transect 2 with *frontisti*: categories F–J

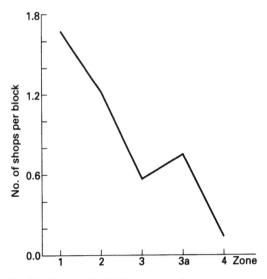

Fig. 3.5c Transect 2 with *frontisti*: density

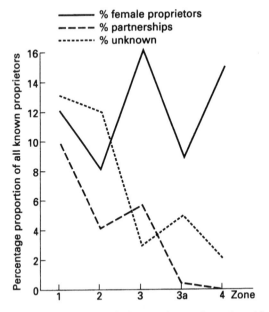

Fig. 3.5d Transect 2 with *frontisti*: forms of proprietorship

Zone 3a; indeed the proportion of food retailers actually fell. In Zone 3a of Transect 2 the proportions of both food retailers and *esercizi pubblici* rose significantly. One reason for this is the fact that Zone 3a in Transect 1 only encompasses the prime positions. Essentially, however, the difference is one of class. The prosperous residents of Corso Venezia were unlikely to bother to go beyond the *porta* to buy their bread, but wine was a different matter, a point reinforced by the fact that alcohol sold wholesale in the *esterno* paid no *dazio* at all (that is, the dealer himself was not assessed for any *dazio* contribution and therefore did not have to pass this on to the public in his price). Many well-to-do Milanesi were prepared to take advantage of this by buying 25 litres of wine, or 10 of alcohol and spirits (the legal definition of a wholesale transaction).[18]

The lower classes in the *esterno* also enjoyed the cheaper drink prices, both at home and in the *osterie* and *bettole*; but for them the price of food, especially bread, was just as important. This was why the residents of the lower half of the Corso Porta Romana went into the *esterno* to do their shopping, a fact which explains the low proportion of food retailers in Zone 3, and the much higher one along the Viale in Zone 3a. The suburbs were attractive to immigrants and to lower-class residents generally because the cost of living was significantly lower under the *aperto* regime, and this attraction was reinforced by the duty-free allowance which meant that those who worked in the city during the day could take in with them the cheaper foodstuffs they bought in the shops around their homes.

This further reinforced the strong neighbourhood ties between shopkeepers and their clients discussed previously.[19] The transects demonstrate the significant advantage the distortion caused by the *dazio* gave the *esercenti* of the *esterno*, particularly the *frontisti*. The preservation of the *circondario*'s fiscal structure was a primary concern for proprietors whose business was founded on it. Sympathy for their clientele, deriving from the 'daily soldarities' of day-to-day contact and intermarriage, was underpinned by the simple calculation that both customers, and the credit extended to them, would be lost to the shopkeepers should this local commercial environment be altered.

The analysis of the transects also indicates that retailers of basic

---

[18] *Il Prontuario*, p. 49.   [19] See pp. 39, 44.

essentials such as foodstuffs, fuel and drink (categories A to C), that is to say those identified in chapter 2 as having the most potential for association, became increasingly predominant amongst the shop-keeper community as distance from the city centre increased, particularly in the lower-class residential areas. Suburban bakers, butchers and grocers, for example, clearly had a collective interest in maintaining the *dazio* structure of the *esterno*; and this, given the relationships between patrons and proprietors within a neighbour-hood, could be explained in terms of the need to defend the interests of the lower-class suburban residents.

The success of the *frontisti*, however, was a direct consequence of their ability to take away trade from their peers in the belt of the *interno* between the *cerchia dei navigli* and the *cinta daziaria* (the customs line). This was most pronounced in the lower-class zones within this belt, such as that around the Corso Porta Romana. The *esercenti* of the *interno* might also be aligned to their lower-class customers through the ties of marriage, credit and simple day-to-day contact. What they could not be, however, was in sympathy with their colleagues in the *esterno* over the *dazio* system. Indeed some shopkeeper associations, such as that of the *salsamentari*, even maintained separate organisations for members in the *interno* and *esterno*.

The operation of the *dazio* system to the benefit of suburban retailers constituted the greatest barrier to the creation of a united shopkeeper movement within the city. Proprietors thought of them-selves first and foremost as members of a group defined by geog-raphy rather than by occupational activity. This was apparent from the moment the *esercenti* first entered Milanese politics as the analysis of these events in chapter 4 will demonstrate.

4. *The* esercenti *enter the political arena*

THE STRUCTURE OF MILANESE POLITICS, 1859–1890

Between 1859 and 1889 political power in Milan was largely exercised by members of the same wealthy elite which had been prominent in city administration under the Austrians. Their dominance was in large part a function of the highly restrictive income-based suffrage which meant that in the administrative elections of December 1867 only 9,973 citizens were registered to vote out of the city's population of 209,022 inhabitants.[1] Political organisation was very limited and most activity revolved around the various clubs and associations in which the electors were gathered.

These associations formed alliances to contest council elections which were held under a list system. There were eighty seats on the council, but sixteen of these were reserved for members of the opposition so, at a full council election, each contending list ran sixty-four candidates. Full elections were held every six years, but in the interim a portion of the council was renewed in what were known as partial or supplementary elections. The frequency of these varied in our period. Annual elections for one-fifth of the council seats were replaced by triennial elections for half the seats after the full election of 1895, and biennial elections for one-third of the seats were introduced in 1904. The councillors whose seats were to be contested were decided upon by lot. In all these partial elections one-fifth of the seats available were reserved for the minority list.

[1] Nasi, 'Da Beretta a Vigoni', p. 116. It should be remembered that the figures for the city's overall population given previously include women and children, whilst the franchise was, in any case, restricted to males over 25. This small electorate was rendered even more compact by the fact that only 4,237 of those registered to vote actually cast a ballot.

The most important of the political associations was the Associa-zione Costituzionale whose members were drawn from the ranks of the large agricultural landlords who lived in the city, many of whom came from the aristocracy. The prominence of these men in local politics led to their being described as the *consorteria lombarda*, the Lombard clique. Their mouthpiece was the newspaper *La Per-severanza*.

The group labelled themselves as 'Moderates', espousing an exclusive right-wing philosophy which, in national terms, placed them amongst the Destra, the primarily Northern Italian faction which governed Italy between 1860 and 1876. The political orienta-tion of the Destra can best be defined as a commitment to the creation of an economically liberal nation state in which there was to be free trade (internal and external), little government interven-tionism, and a balanced budget arrived at by the containment of expenditure on public works and the imposition of such taxes as were necessary. The Lombard parliamentarians were particularly keen on preserving as wide a sphere of action as possible for municipal, as opposed to national, government.[2]

This revealed much about the Milanese elite's attitude to politics and to the new Italian state. Prior to unification, Milan had been an occupied city, passing from Spanish rule to Austrian, then exper-iencing a period of effectively French rule during the Cisalpine republic, before returning to the Habsburg empire. As Giovanna Rosa has shown, the Milanese elite believed the foundations of their city's prosperity had been laid during the rule of Maria Theresa, and were further strengthened during the subsequent periods of French and Austrian rule, because the city's own administrative institutions were respected and preserved. City notables were left to get on with the business of administration whilst state politics (i.e. French and Austrian politics) were carried on elsewhere, without the involve-ment of the Milanese. As a result, Rosa suggests, the Milanese were not prepared to accept the validity of any project to build a strong central Italian state.[3]

[2] Rosa, *Il mito della capitale morale*, p. 173n. See also Vecchio, 'La classa politica milanese', pp. 273–81.

[3] Rosa, *Il mito della capitale morale*, pp. 108–10, 170–2. Rosa's work on the relation-ship between Rome and Milan and her debunking of the myth of Milan serving as the 'moral capital' of Italy, reads as a corrective to Fonzi's interpretation of the Milanese attitude in which he suggested that hostility to the South, rather than to the state *per se*, was the basis of the Milanese approach to national politics. Ibid.,

This opposition took several forms. At the national level Jacini, the best-known of the Lombard Moderates, called for greater regional autonomy, including the devolution of revenue-raising powers.[4] Most Milanese, however, continued to avoid involvement in state affairs. Political debate was centred on the best way to administer the city, and most Milanese parliamentary representatives limited themselves to defending their constituents' interests, rather than playing a role in national government. The much greater importance attached to city politics than to parliamentary activity remains constant throughout our period; and the attitude towards the state that this entailed can be observed throughout the political spectrum, even amongst the Milanese Socialists.

The Milanese elite was largely composed of aristocrats, landlords and merchants. Whilst some manufacturers were admitted into elite circles, they tended to be representatives of the small-scale luxury-goods industries that still predominated within the Milanese economy. The interests of the members of the *consorteria*, then, were not entirely homogenous; but they were sufficiently close for disputes to be resolved through trade-offs and temporary alliance building, without recourse to parties or even well-defined factions. The overall emphasis of their policies was on the preservation of social order and the promotion of their economic interests. As Hunecke's analysis of Milanese workers has shown, these concerns could have unfortunate consequences for those perceived to be challenging them.[5]

One threat to the social order came from the concentrations of workers occasioned by large-scale manufacturing industry, and this kind of economic activity and, indeed, its practitioners were looked on with suspicion as a consequence. It was Moderate policy to keep such enterprises out of the city, especially out of those areas near to the desirable housing of the city centre. The primacy of agriculture and a presumed symbiotic relationship between city and country-side remained at the heart of moderate thinking even in the 1880s.[6]

pp. 145–66; Fonzi, *Crispi e lo 'Stato di Milano'*, pp. XVI–XXVI. See also Rumi, 'La vocazione politica di Milano', pp. 17–22.
4 On Lombard parliamentary Moderatism see D'Angiolini, 'Il moderatismo lombardo e la politica italiana'; Ullrich, 'Il declino del liberalismo lombardo'; Vecchio, 'La classa politica milanese'.
5 Hunecke, *Classe operaia e rivoluzione industriale*. On the Moderates see Fonzi, *Crispi e lo 'Stato di Milano'*, pp. 111–18.
6 Rosa, *Il mito della capitale morale*, pp. 110–14.

Politics in Milan was changing, however. The act which annexed the Corpi Santi to the city in 1873 contained a clause enabling the suburbs to elect their own representatives to the city council. The limited franchise still only accorded the vote to the wealthiest members of the community, but the suburban elite was composed primarily of industrialists and professionals rather than nobles, land-owners and merchants. Felice Grondona and Gian Battista Pirelli, heads of the eponymous engineering and chemical companies, were two of the suburban councillors chosen. Whilst these men still described themselves as Moderates, they differed notably in outlook from the traditional *consorteria* which appeared to regard industry with some disdain.[7]

The position of the traditional Moderates was further eroded in 1882 when the parliamentary franchise was expanded. Whereas previously this had been limited to literate males over twenty-five who paid over L. 40 per annum in direct taxes, the vote was now given to all literate males over twenty-one who had completed a course of primary education or gained other qualifications or positions held to indicate this level of attainment (one such being the payment of L. 19.50 in direct taxes). The franchise was now based on literacy, rather than wealth, leading both to an initial doubling of the electorate to 40,342 and to its continued widening thereafter as literacy became more widespread amongst the lower classes.[8] The immediate result of this was that the Milanese Moderates lost all their seats in the parliamentary elections of that year to liberals who formed part of the opposition bloc known as the Democrats.

The Democrats embraced a range of views equally as wide as the Moderates. The bloc encompassed those liberal monarchists who probably regarded themselves as closest to Giolitti and Zanardelli of the parliamentary Sinistra Costituzionale, the radicals who aligned themselves with the poet and deputy Felice Cavallotti and the newspaper *Il Secolo*, and the early Republicans and Socialists (although the Republican and Socialist parties were not founded until the first half of the 1890s).[9] Again, however, it would be true to argue that many of the Milanese Democrats were not attracted to projects for building the Italian nation state, but, rather, concen-

---

[7] Nasi, 'Da Beretta a Vigoni', pp. 43–4.
[8] Ballini, *Le elezioni nella storia d'Italia*, pp. 93–9; Fonzi, *Crispi e lo 'Stato di Milano'*, p. 25.
[9] On the Democrats see Fonzi, *Crispi e lo 'Stato di Milano'*, pp. 153–60.

trated on the defence of their own immediate interests and those of their presumed supporters still excluded by the franchise.

The centre of their opposition within Milan was the Circolo Liberale Elettorale Suburbano which was 'founded for the defence of the guarantees that have been given to the *circondario esterno* by the Royal Decree of aggregation to the city, dated 8 June 1873, and of the relevant legal provisions'.[10] Most of its members, including the President, Giuseppe Mussi, were associated with the Radical party, although they frequently described themselves as liberals, and received electoral support from the Giolittian faction. Cavallotti, the parliamentary deputy, took pains to emphasise the anti-clerical and anti-socialist nature of radicalism, yet it was precisely the broad-church nature of the Democrats that accounted for their municipal success. The professionals, white-collar workers and small proprietors who provided the bulk of the Democrats' support were united not by ideology but by their commitment to defend the suburbs, particularly their status as a *zona aperta* within the *dazio consumo* regime.

The Moderates' failure at the 1882 parliamentary elections spurred on the development of a new tendency amongst the Moderates, sometimes called the *nuova destra*, or new right. Adherents of the tendency were more involved with industry and commerce and encompassed many of the suburban Moderates who had felt detached from the original *consorteria*. As businessmen they had a greater interest in politics at a national level, and it is easier to discern their influence upon Moderate parliamentary politics than on those of the Municipio. Nonetheless they remained opposed to the idea of a national project, a concern most readily observed in their objections to the burdens of high taxation. Their outlook was exemplified by the *Corriere della Sera* newspaper, their political organ and the first newspaper to break out of the local sphere. Pirelli was one of the paper's founding shareholders, although the figure most frequently identified with the *nuova destra* was Giuseppe Colombo, the engineer who built Europe's first electricity generating station in the city, and went on to become rector of the Polytechnic.[11]

[10] This description of itself was supplied by the *circolo* to the *Guida di Milano* published by Savallo.

[11] On the *nuovo destra* see Fonzi, *Crispi e lo 'Stato di Milano'*, pp. 118–35; Ulrich, 'Il declino del liberalismo lombardo', pp. 19–202; Vecchio, 'La classa politica milanese', pp. 281–5.

In 1886 Colombo was elected as the only Moderate representative amongst the city's six parliamentary deputies. In 1890 he ws joined by two colleagues and in 1892 the Moderates captured all four of the old city's parliamentary seats, whilst Mussi and Luigi Rossi became the first radicals to represent Milan in the Chamber of Deputies, having been elected in the two suburban constituencies. The expansion of the franchise had clearly made it impossible for the *consorteria* to command sufficient electoral muscle on its own, yet, by the same token, the expansion of the franchise frightened the city's bourgeoisie who feared that the newly enfranchised voters might lend their support to more extreme parties. The conservatives' tactic of broadening the Moderate bloc to incorporate tendencies such as the *nuova destra* was a successful response to these changes, and made sense in light of the concomitant developments in Milan's economic structure described in chapter 1. Potential conflicts between the different interest groups were further defused as agriculturalists and merchants joined with industrial leaders to support protectionism in 1887. Lombard deputies of all persuasions were highly prominent in the horse trading over tariffs that took place in the parliamentary chamber.[12]

Conflict was also avoided by the fact that the *nuova destra* exercised far more influence on parliamentary politics than it did at city level. It was at the national level that taxation and trade policies were decided and it was in these areas that government and business interests were most interconnected. The *consorteria*, with its disdain for national politics, was happy to allow the members of the *nuova destra* the political space to advance their opinions. At the municipal level, however, the *consorteria*'s dominance remained unchallenged until 1889. The crudest, and most fundamental, reason for this was that the franchise in local elections remained unchanged until this date. The *consorteria* faced no real threat to its position, negating the effect of the addition of the Corpi Santi by persuading the authorities to alter the structure of council by abolishing the separate section for the suburbs. Instead a single election was held across the whole of Milan, breaking the link between suburban citizens and their representatives. The architect of this scheme was Gaetano Negri, who became President of the Associazione Costituzionale in 1883 and was elected *sindaco* (mayor) the year after.

---

[12] D'Angiolini, 'Il moderatismo lombardo e la politica italiana', pp. 116–34.

Negri received his come-uppance in 1889 after the basis of the franchise in local elections was altered in much the same way as the parliamentary franchise had been in 1882. The electorate rose from around 25,000 to 42,000, and though only 21,131 of them voted in the municipal elections of November that year this was still a massive increase on the 8,610 who had turned out in January 1885. The Moderates' share of the vote fell sharply and Negri felt compelled to resign, whilst his successor, Count Belinzaghi, though a *consorteria* stalwart, felt obliged to appoint five Democrat councillors to his administration's Giunta (the executive body of councillors who ran the city administration).[13]

One of the chief causes of Negri's defeat was his attempt to tamper with the structure of the *dazio consumo* in the city in 1886. His attempts to shift more of the *dazio* burden onto the suburbs only served to reinforce the one clear division between the Moderate and Democrat blocs in the later 1880s, namely that the former served the interests of the city centre and the latter those of the suburbs. The Democrats knew that they could do little to challenge the Moderates' domination of city politics so long as the old franchise remained in place; indeed they did not even bother to contest the partial elections to the council in 1887 because of this. Instead they began organising for 1889, seeking to establish a presence amongst those potential supporters who would be admitted to the franchise in that year. By 1887 it was already clear that suburban shopkeepers would form one such group. A detailed analysis of the consequences of Negri's attempts to alter the *dazio consumo* regime will make this clear.

THE *MICCA* RIOTS OF 1886 AND THE MOBILISATION OF THE *ESERCENTI*

In January 1886, the city council (Consiglio Comunale) approved a new 'town plan' (*piano regolatore*) whose cost was estimated at L. 3,000,000.[14] In order to finance this, the Comune needed to increase its revenues, the major part of which came from the *dazio consumo*. The Giunta, mindful of the consequences for public order, did not dare to challenge the *esterno*'s *dazio* privileges, which were written into the Royal Decree that had sanctioned the addition of

---

[13] Fonzi, *Crispi e lo 'Stato di Milano'*, pp. 138–41; Nasi, 'Da Beretta a Vigoni', p. 116.
[14] Hunecke, *Classe operaia e rivoluzione industriale*, p. 263.

the Corpi Santi to the city in 1873. They did notice, however, that the amount of bread which workers were bringing with them into the city each day was considerably above the limit of half a kilogram established by the law.

The reason for this was that the Milanese bakers still used local measures, baking small loaves weighing half a *libbra* (about 400 grams), known as *micche*. The guards at the *dazio* line had therefore been under instructions to allow the workers to bring in a *libbra* of bread a day, that is two *micche* each.[15] On 15 March 1886 Mayor Negri, in conjunction with the new director of the *dazio* inspectorate, Pietro Gerli, ordered that the legal allowances were now to be strictly enforced, so that workers could bring in only one *micca* for their lunch and were forced to buy any additional *micche* from the bakeries in the *interno*.[16]

This provoked a violent response amongst the workers of the *esterno*. A price differential of 6 *centesimi* per *libbra* existed at that stage between the two *circondari* as bakers in the *interno* had raised their prices by 2 *centesimi* in response to an increase in the price of flour, but the prices in the *esterno* had remained unchanged as they were determined by level fixed by the Comune.[17] The day labourers felt that their privileges had been overturned, despite the theoretical legality of Negri's measures, and they took to throwing bread over the walls, or passing it through the *dazio* officials' legs.[18]

Suburban shopkeepers, especially bakers, were outraged by Negri's proposals. The adjustment to the 'duty-free' levels operating the two *circondari* significantly altered the commercial environment in which the small traders of the *esterno* had to operate. The incentives to suburban residents to shop locally, particularly in terms of the quantity of goods purchased, had been significantly reduced. Furthermore, according to *Il Secolo*, the working-class citizens of the *interno* no longer dared cross into the *esterno* to do their shopping for fear of being searched and turned back at the customs post. In any case, even if they did come over, they would make fewer purchases than before. As a result of these developments long-standing credit arrangements between patrons and proprietors were frequently broken. Many enterprises, not just the bakeries, suffered a loss of trade, and this forced proprietors to

[15] It appears that at one time even three *micche* were tolerated.
[16] 'La questione del pane e del dazio consumo', *Il Secolo*, 16–17 March 1886.
[17] Ibid.   [18] 'Per il pane', *Il Secolo*, 31 March–1 April 1886.

dismiss their staff. On 28 March, *Il Secolo* claimed that two hundred assistants had already been laid off.

The reaction to Negri's move served to highlight the contradictions of the small shopkeeping sector within Milan. Suburban small shopkeepers sought to protect their own interests and those of their worker clients, which, in this case, amounted to the same thing. They played a prominent role in the campaign of resistance organised by the political defenders of the suburbs, the Democratic bloc.[19] Shopkeepers in the *interno*, on the other hand, remained quiet, and may be presumed to have been in favour of Negri's reforms: the opposition campaign frequently stated that Negri was in league with the bakers in the *interno*. Zonal identity overrode occupational identity when the commercial environment itself was at stake. The Giunta's justification of its policy demonstrates how intent it was on exploiting these divisions between the two sets of *esercenti*. Negri issued a communication on 2 April in which he claimed:

> The truth is this: the Administration held it necessary, in the interests of all the city, to eliminate some abuses which benefit only one section of consumers and shopkeepers ... It is clear that the observance of this legislative provision tends to balance the conditions of the suburban workers with those of workers of the *interno*, and diminished the grave damage that the *esercenti* of this part of the city suffered owing to the abuse.[20]

The council treasurer, Vimercati, went further. His officials argued that income from the *dazio* had not risen in proportion with the population increase, because of the 'filtration' (*filtrazione*) of goods from the suburbs into the city, that cost the Comune L. 400,000 a year. These items were brought in by families crossing into the *interno* to do their shopping, and by the army of day workers who took their own food into the city with them. Vimercati told the Council that the outcry of the *esercenti* in the suburbs following the tightening of the restrictions was more than matched by the protests of the *esercenti* in the *interno* previously. He added that:

---

[19] This was confirmed in a memo written at the Prefettura on 2 April 1886. Prefettura di Milano No. 1253 Ogetti ... nuovi disordini 5¼ p.m. 2 April 1886 in ASM, Fond. Questura, c.45, f.1.

[20] Wallposter signed *Dal Palazzo del Comune, il 23 aprile 1886 Il Sindaco G Negri*. Copies in ASM's Fond. Questura, c.45, f.1.

We have a proof that filtration happens on a large scale in the fact that the *esercenti* in the *interno* of the city who have shops between the *porta* and the bridge over the *naviglio* ... are extremely scarce in number, and do poor business when they don't go bankrupt.[21]

The Democrats were also keen to demonstrate how the new restrictions benefited the Moderates' supporters. Reduced duty-free allowances raised the cost of living for those members of the working population who lived in the city centre but patronised the *frontisti*, forcing them to move to the suburbs: a phenomenon which pleased the bourgeois Moderate voters who lived in the city centre. *Il Secolo* argued that it was the smartly dressed citizens who took the tram back from the suburbs with contraband goods under their clothes who were really responsible for filtration.[22] On 31 March *Il Secolo* wrote 'Shopkeepers and workers are both harmed: why don't they unite to protest together?'[23]

The following morning, 1 April 1886, serious trouble occurred at the Porta Tenaglia when one of the *dazio* officials tried to arrest a man who had thrown a loaf into the crowd after being denied entry to the city. There were injuries on both sides and further arrests were made in the evening during a demonstration march into the city centre. Next morning there were outbreaks of violence at Porta Tenaglia (despite the presence of an infantry company at the gate) Porta Garibaldi and Porta Ticinese, and disturbances again took place in the city centre that night. Over the two days, 135 arrests were made, and on 3 April Negri announced that the old 800 gram limit would be restored.[24]

Of eighty-two people arrested during the demonstrations twelve can be identified as either shopkeepers or their assistants, although the majority of these were far more likely to have been employees rather than proprietors.[25] The wall posters that called the demon-

---

[21] 'Questione di dazio – Le dichiarazioni dell'assesore Vimercati', *Corriere della Sera*, 1–2 April 1886.

[22] 'Effetti del dazio consumo', *Il Secolo*, 28–9 March 1886. 'Contro il dazio consumo', ibid., 27–8 March 1886.

[23] 'Per il pane', *Il Secolo*, 31 March–1 April 1886.

[24] The events are fully documented in the records of the Questura which include relevant articles in the city newspapers. ASM, Fond. Questura, c.45, f.1, Scioperi, disordini, dazio consumo 1886.

[25] The Questura records contain several lists of people arrested during the demonstrations, but this is the only one which is both sufficiently large and sufficiently detailed to make any analysis possible. Altogether eighty-five names are given but

strators into the *piazza* made no mention of *esercenti* grievances, but confined themselves to stating the demands of the workers.[26] *Il Secolo* and the Democrats condemned the violence and appealed for the demonstrators to abandon it; but although the residents of the *esterno* were united in their opposition to Negri's alterations this bond was not as strong as liberal leaders liked to believe. Administrative politics were a middle-class pursuit; the masses were still excluded by the restricted franchise to which the shopkeepers were shortly to be admitted.

None the less the '*micca*' incident demonstrated that shopkeepers could be mobilised when their interests were threatened, as had been the case in the *esterno*. Democrat politicians were not slow to exploit this. In mid-May the Circolo Elettorale Suburbana ran eight candidates in the annual re-election to a fifth of the seats on the city council.[27] Of these, three were heads of shopkeeper organisations: Luigi Baroni, President of the Mutua Proprietari Forno, Alessandro Stabilini, President of the Società fra i Proprietari Salsamentari, and Cav. Pasquale Perelli Cippo, President of the Mutua Associazione degli Osti, Trattori e Mercanti di Vino. A fourth candidate was Luigi Gastel, a prominent pharmacist.[28] Baroni succeeded in being elected to the council.

These men were not simply shopkeepers; they were at the top of their respective professions and were all committed politicians. Baroni was the proprietor of one of the five largest bread and pasta-making establishments in the city, and might be better described as an industrialist. Significantly, his premises were in the *esterno*, outside Porta Magenta.[29] He was a committed Radical, just

the occupational status of three of these is unclear. Elenco nominativo degli individui che furono arrestati nella dimostrazione del giorno, I, II e IV aprile anno corrente, ASM, Fond. Questura, c.45, f.1.

[26] These can be found in ASM, Fond. Questura, c.45, f.1. On the workers' role in the *micca* riots see chapter 7 of the forthcoming book by Louise A. Tilly, *Politics and class in Milan, 1881–1901* (expected publication 1992), kindly made available to me by the author.

[27] In the spring of 1886, Negri succeeded in stage-managing the timing of the partial elections so they coincided with those of the city's parliamentary deputies. His intent was to unseat Mussi, who was standing in both elections, something he would have succeeded in doing had not one of the victors withdrawn, thus letting Mussi onto the Council. *Il Prontuario*, pp. 152–4; 'Le elezioni amministrative', *Il Secolo*, 15–16 May 1886; 'Cronaca milanese: elezioni amministrative', ibid., 17–18 May 1886; 'Cronaca milanese: Mussi fuori del consiglio', ibid., 18–19 May 1886.

[28] 'Le elezioni amministrative', *Il Secolo*, 15–16 May 1881.

[29] 'La Società di Macinazione e Panificazione', *L'Esercente*, 18 February 1887.

as Stabilini came from a well-established family of Republicans. His premises were in the *interno*, on Via Torino; indeed he was the head of the *interno* section of the *salsamentari* association. Nonetheless, his political convictions placed him firmly in the Democratic bloc. Perelli Cippo was also a well-known liberal, yet his attitude to shopkeeper affairs, as demonstrated in the *bettole* incident, was always rather aloof. Gastel was also politically active and had long sought to associate himself with shopkeepers, despite being a pharmacist, a profession somewhat removed from that of the *esercenti*. These men were attempting to exploit their retailing connections to further their own political careers, taking advantage of the new circumstances following the '*micca*' incident.

The most significant attempt to exploit this new mood came in August 1886 when the journalist named Annibale Rusca started a weekly newspaper called *L'Esercente*, which was directly targeted at the small shopkeeper. Although it disappeared during the last two months of 1886, apparently as a result of difficulties between Rusca and his financial backer, the paper was relaunched in January 1887, and by April 1888 it claimed to have between 4,000 and 5,000 subscribers.[30]

The list of initial backers of *L'Esercente* was a good guide to the nature of the shopkeeper movement at this time. Five of the eight candidates who had stood for the Circolo Elettorale Suburbano featured, including Mussi, Baroni, Stabilini and Gastel, whilst two more of these candidates, including Perelli Cippo, sank money into the journal's relaunch. The forty-six sponsors of the first edition comprised twenty-four bakers, five proprietors of *Esercizi pubblici*, five members of the professional, commercial and property-owning classes (generally prominent Democrat politicians), two *salsamentari*, a clockmaker, a pharmacist and five persons whose occupation cannot be traced.[31]

The heavy representation of bakers was due to several factors. The comparative wealth of the profession, notably amongst owners of large establishments such as Baroni's, and the fact that the nature of the trade endowed it with considerable potential for collective

[30] 'La Federazione degli Esercenti', *L'Esercente*, 8 April 1888.
[31] Occupations were traced through the *Guide Savallo*. The lists of backers are to be found in 'Elenco di coloro i quali hanno gentilmente aderito alla pubblicazione dell'Esercente', *L'Esercente*, 14 August 1886; 'Elenco degli Azionisti a fondo perduto del nostro giornale L'Esercente', ibid., 13 January 1887.

activity have already been discussed (see chapter 2, pp. 61–2). The role of the Mutua Cooperativa Forno, the leading trade association, with its already-established patterns of *esercenti* activity was clearly important. There were also two more immediate factors. One was the fact that the '*micca*' issue had revolved around the question of bread, the other that *L'Esercente* was launched the week after a strike of bakery workers.[32] Although serious divisions had arisen between the proprietors, some of whom supported the workers' demands, the strike was actually resolved by negotiation between the workers' and proprietors' associations. This experience probably confirmed the need for a proprietors' forum.

L'Esercente's success was indicative of an increasing consciousness amongst shopkeepers. In 1873 a similar newspaper, also called *L'Esercente*, had been published, funded by men of similar backgrounds to those involved in 1886.[33] Even the articles were largely on the same subjects: proposed tax reforms, the problems of the *dazio consumo*, the need to abolish the *regali natilizi* and reinvigorate the city festivals and fairs. Yet in 1873 the journal was an expensive failure and failed to see out the year, whilst Rusca's title rapidly established itself, and lived on in one form or another until 1934.

L'Esercente of 1873 was aimed at the shopkeepers of the *interno*. The actual incorporation of the Corpi Santi only took place at the end of the year, and though the newspaper covered *esercenti* activities in the suburbs it was of necessity primarily targeted at the far greater number of shopkeepers who lived in the city itself. Rusca's

[32] The strike itself took place between the 4 and 6 August, although it was first threatened on 31 July. A final accord was reached on 25 August, although there were many further difficulties over its implementation. The main issues were the number of holidays due to be accorded to the workers, and whether the running of the labour exchange should be in the hands of the workers' or proprietors' associations. The strike was covered in considerable detail in *Il Secolo* and *L'Esercente*, whilst further information may be found in ASM, Fond. Questura, c.45, f.1, Scioperi, disordini 1886, Lavoranti fornai.

[33] The journal was published between 16 January and 18 December 1873, with a special supplement announcing the suspension of the journal being published on 9 January 1874. This revealed losses of L. 1100.37 on an expenditure of L. 5059–80. One of those involved in the journal was l'Avv. Enrico Gastel, who remained prominent both in political life (as a Radical) and in the shopkeeper movement as adviser to both the Federation and the Mutua Proprietari Forno. He also subscribed money for the relaunch of Rusca's title in 1887. For the 1873 *L'Esercente* see ASM fond. Questura, c.116, and the copies of the journal held in the Biblioteca Nazionale Braidense.

L'Esercente, however, explicitly addressed itself to suburban shop-keepers, seeking to capitalise on the fears aroused by the '*micca*' incident. The dangers posed to the commercial environment by Negri's attempts to tamper with the structure of the *dazio consumo* had significantly raised the level of consciousness amongst suburban shopkeepers by simultaneously threatening their zonal and occu-pational interests.

The political character of the early editions of the 1886 *L'Eser-cente* was what might be expected from the list of its backers: that is to say, unambiguously pro-Democrat. Given the political structure of Milan, this was, in any case, the only credible position for an organ that sought to protect suburban interests. The imminent expansion of the franchise to include small traders undoubtedly made it easier for Rusca to attract financial support from leading Democrats, but it may also have helped him gather readers. There was now some point in the *esercenti* interesting themselves in poli-tics, another contrast with 1873.

The mobilisation of the small traders, then, occurred as a direct result of a threat to the local commercial environment that was analysed in chapters 2 and 3. It was a partial mobilisation in that it was confined to the suburbs, but it was a successful one. How then did the shopkeeper movement continue to grow once this threat had receded?

5. *Constructing the* esercenti *movement, 1886–1890*

Rusca's *L'Esercente* was launched to exploit the mobilisation of shopkeeper sentiment in 1886. The paper, however, along with all those who had an interest in the small traders, was conscious of the need to construct an *esercenti* movement that would reinforce shopkeeper identity, consolidating the opportunities that a conscious economic grouping presented. The crucial requirement was that ordinary *esercenti* be convinced of the value of such a movement within the context of their everyday business. Those involved in the *esercenti* movement were therefore obliged to create practical institutions which could demonstrate the utility of 'association' and 'class organisation'. At the same time they had also to foster a small-trader identity which recognised the zonal, i.e. suburban, preoccupations of those shopkeepers who had already been involved in collective action to defend their interests, whilst attempting to take account of the far broader concerns of small proprietors throughout the city.

THE INSTITUTIONAL BASIS OF THE *ESERCENTI* MOVEMENT

L'Esercente was the primary medium for the furtherance of the movement's message. Its early editions were full of exhortations to 'associate', and demonstrations of the need for permanent class organisation. In September 1888, for example, the paper advanced the importance of associations, arguing that just because previous generations of shopkeepers had not been organised was no reason to reject such organisations. 'When the president requests the reduction of a duty or whatever, it's as if 500 *esercenti* were speaking at the same time. The association working for the members, also works for all the class – One must be unfeeling and mean not to feel any obligation [to it].'[1]

At the same time, *L'Esercente* had to prove its own utility to its readership. The commercial information which the paper carried played an important part in its success, and at the beginning of 1889 it began publishing a commercial supplement on Thursdays which gave the price of butter established in the Milan market, information that was highly valuable to the delicatessen trade. The journal also published protestations of unpaid bills of exchange, enabling readers to check on the creditworthiness of prospective business contacts. A variety of free gifts and bargain-priced articles were also supplied, starting with a free book on card games (designed for use as a reference book by customers in the *osterie* and *bettole*) in 1888, and a series of humorous verses depicting the plight of the *esercenti* in the following year, whilst in 1890 the paper produced an almanac that acted as a practical guide to the business of shopkeeping.[2]

This activity was indicative of the success of the paper, as was the increasing frequency of its appearance. At first the paper was published weekly on Sundays, but the commercial supplement was added at the beginning of 1889 and in December 1890 the paper became a bi-weekly which also published two commercial supplements a week. In 1889 (the year of the franchise extension) *L'Esercente* also began its customary habit of appearing as a 'daily' in the run-up to the municipal elections.

As this suggests, *L'Esercente*'s main project was political. It was not enough to denounce the Moderate Giunta as an 'oligarchy of aristocratic banker leaders'; the point was to promote shopkeepers to a position in public life from which their voices could not be ignored.[3] To this end the paper devoted considerable energy to relaunching a General Federation of Milanese Shopkeepers (Federazione degli Esercenti) in 1888. This was structured as an association of shopkeeper associations, with the consequence that its leading lights included many of the same men who had put up the money for *L'Esercente* (although the paper and the Federation were financially independent of each other). L'Avv. Enrico Gastel, sponsor of the 1873 *L'Esercente*, provincial councillor and legal adviser to the Mutua Proprietari Forno, was the first secretary, and

[1] 'Così facevo mio padre', *L'Esercente*, 2 September 1888.   [2] *Il Prontuario*.
[3] 'I contratti daziari e il circondario esterno di Milano', *L'Esercente*, 2 June 1889.

Baroni, Stabilini and Luigi Gastel were all prominent participants. The Federation acted as a new forum for the Democrat shopkeeper politicians.

By the end of 1888, the Federation could claim 1,500 members, whilst attendances at general meetings averaged between 300 and 400.[4] The new institution was loaned premises by the Mutua Proprietari Forno which also joined its members *en bloc* to the Federation, collecting subscriptions to the two associations together.[5] Bakers provided nearly a third of the overall membership, including the first president, Francesco Rosio. Some 85% of the membership voted in the elections to the first Administrative Council, which were held in the thirteen sections for different trades in which a quota target of members had been reached. These sections were the usual *esercenti* trades connected with food and drink identified in chapter 2: haberdashers, shoemakers, barbers and clothes sellers only rarely joined as individual members.[6]

The Federation needed to fulfil a demonstrably useful role in order to overcome the shopkeeper 'apathy' it so often condemned and to justify its claim to be of vital importance to shopkeepers. Two advisory services were set up under the aegis of the Federation: one for the collection of credit payments, the other to provide legal advice to shopkeepers charged with contravening local regulations.

The Ufficio per l'Esazione dei Crediti maintained a list of names of those who had applied for credit from a shopkeeper and subsequently failed to meet their debts. The intention was that when a trader received a request for credit he would first check the client's name with the Ufficio and so avoid entanglement with habitual debtors. The service also took on the collection of bad debts on behalf of the *esercenti*. The onset of the economic depression imposed a severe strain on the bureau. In the year April 1889 to April 1890, 1,919 cases were referred to the Ufficio, of which 1,400 were for sums of less than L. 50. Whilst the remarkably high number

---

[4] Satisfaction was expressed when over 300 turned up to a general meeting on Maundy Thursday, which also clashed with a Buffalo Bill performance. 'L'Assemblea Generale della Federazione Esercenti di Milano', *L'Esercente*, 6 April 1890. The figures for membership come from 'Chi lavora', ibid., 8 July 1888.

[5] 'La riunione dei prestinai', ibid., 8 July 1888.

[6] The sections were hotel-keeper, café proprietors, grocers, milk vendors, butchers, landlords of licensed premises, general food stores, poultry sellers, bakers, delicatessen proprietors and tobacconists. 'Le elezioni della Federazione degli Esercenti', ibid., 25 November 1888; 'La chiusura dei conti', ibid., 30 December 1888.

Table 5.1. *Shopkeeper associations in Milan, 1885–1905*

Name	1885	1886	1887	1888	1889	1890	1891	1892	1893	1894	1895	1896	1897	1898	1899	1900	1901	1902	1903	1904	1905	
Proprietari Fornai	x	x	x	x	x	x	x	x	x	x	x	x	x	x	x	x	x	x	x	x	x	ms+c
Lattivendoli	x	x	x	x	x	x	x	x	x	x	x	x	x	x	x	x	x	x	x	x	x	a
Osti, Trattori e,																						
Mercanti di Vino	x	x	x	x	x	x	x	x	x	x	x	x	x	x	x	x	x	x	x	x	x	a
Salsamentari (interno)	x	x	x	x	x	x	x	x	x	x	x	x	x	x								a
Salsamentari (esterno)	x	x	x	x	x	x	x	x	x	x	x	x	x	x								a
Salsamentari															x	x	x	x	x	x	x	b
Banca Proprietari di Forno			x	x	x	x	x	x	x													b
Banca degli Esercenti										x	x	x	x	x	x	x	x	x	x	x	x	a
Droghieri		x[1]	x	x	x	x	x	x	x	x	x	x	x	x	x	x	x	x	x	x	x	a
Privativi (Monopolies)						x	x	x^c	x	x	x	x	x	x	x							a
Calzolai				x	x	x	x													x	x	a
Macellai[2]					x	x	x	x^3						x						x	x	a
Tabaccai													x	x	x	x	x	x	x	x	x	c
Pollivendoli												x	x	x	x	x	x	x	x	x	x	a
Postai										x	x	x	x	x	x	x	x	x	x	x	x	s
Commercianti in Combustibili												x	x	x	x	x	x	x	x	x	x	
Pasticcieri e Confetterii													x	x								a
Trippai													x	x								ms
Esercizi, Alberghi,																				x	x	a
Caffè-Ristoranti, etc.																						

Related organisations

Commercianti Erbaggi, Pollami, e Pesci	x	x	x	x	x	x	x	x	x	x	x	x	x	x	x	x	x	x	a
Rivenditori di Giornali	x	x	x	x	x	x	x	x	x	x	x	x	x	x	x	x	x	x	c
Farmacisti d'Italia	x	x	x	x	x	x	x	x	x	x	x	x	x	x	x	x	x	x	ms
Fabbricanti e Commercianti in Spiriti					x	x	x												a
Unione Lombarda fra i Negozianti di Vino							x	x	x	x	x	x	x	x	x	x	x	x	a

The letters indicate the type of association: a = simple association, b = bank, c = cooperative, ms = *mutuo soccorso* (Friendly Society).
1 Dormant between 1887 and 1890.
2 Although butchers' organisations appeared weak, the fact was that there were many commercial associations of butchers, including the Società Anonima del Nuovo Mercato Bestiame, which looked after their interests at the Pubblico Macello.
3 Dormant 1891–5.
Sources: Based on information taken from the *Guide di Milano* published by Savallo, *L'Esercente* and the records of the Questura. The sources for this work are far from ideal; the *Guide* are not available for some years, and are not always accurate whilst neither *L'Esercente* nor the Questura records contains systematic lists of such organisations.

of 1,250 accords for repayment were established, these tended to break down within the first few months and not one had yet resulted in the total extinction of the debt. Indeed, the sums reclaimed were hardly sufficient to pay for the personnel required to operate the office, especially as many shopkeepers themselves failed to pass on the appropriate fee to the office when a pact was concluded.[7]

The Ufficio di Consulenza Legale ran into difficulties arising from its overpopularity. During 1889/90, 150 settlements had been agreed with the authorities and a further 119 cases were in progress, yet the resources of the office were not sufficient to enable it to devote itself to all the instances referred to it. The difficulty was that the only way to raise more money was to increase membership, but more members would undoubtedly create further work. There was also the problem that some shopkeepers were too appreciative of belonging to an organisation which provided unlimited legal advice and debt collection for a subscription of L. 6 p.a.. In 1891 it was concluded that the Ufficio per l'Esazione dei Crediti would have to be closed, although shopkeepers could enter into their own negotiations with the Federation's lawyer for assistance in the retrival of debts. Meanwhile, the Ufficio di Consulenza Legale continued to provide advice and assist in the settlement of cases of shopkeepers in breach of the regulations.[8]

The momentum generated by *L'Esercente* and the Federation stimulated several other projects amongst the *esercenti*. New trade associations were formed amongst grocers in 1887, and monopoly sellers and shoemakers in 1888 (see Table 5.1). The strongest of the trade associations, the Mutua Proprietari Forno, sought to redress its members' problems in obtaining commercial credit. The Banca di Credito fra i Proprietari Forno ed Afini opened its doors on 3 January 1887, and on 31 March it had L. 217,417 of assets and a share of capital of L. 102,222. By 24 July 1888 assets had grown to L. 427,487.54 and share capital to L. 119,060. Thereafter, the bank began to suffer from trouble with bad debts, presumably connected to the decline in the business cycle. In February 1890 it was estimated that half of the debts would have to be written off and by the end of the year bank assets had fallen to L. 340,522.50. The following February the bank was forced to reduce its share capital and had to seek help from the Banca Popolare and the Cassa di Risparmio.

[7] 'L'Assemblea Generale della Federazione Esercenti di Milano', ibid., 6 April 1890.
[8] 'L'ufficio di consulenza legale e l'esazione dei crediti', ibid., 29 October 1891.

Even so it was still in a position to pay a dividend, and in 1894 it became a bank open to all shopkeepers.[9]

By 1890, then, the main institutions of the shopkeeper movement, *L'Esercente* and the Federation, were well established. They had succeeded in demonstrating their utility in terms of practical initiatives such as the two bureaux set up by the Federation, even if these came under strain with the onset of the depression. Indeed one problem that these bureaux encountered was that of overpopularity. High participation rates were encouraging, though, given that the movement was keen to demonstrate the practical advantage of speaking with a collective voice in the arena of public affairs.

THE POSITIONING OF THE *ESERCENTI* MOVEMENT, 1886–90

The *esercenti* movement faced a considerable problem in defining shopkeeper interests and identity. The suburban shopkeepers who had been mobilised in 1886 formed the great majority of those involved in the movement between 1886 and 1890 and were primarily concerned with defending their zonal interests. The leaders of the movement could not ignore this: *L'Esercente*, for example, had to reflect their views, if only to achieve the sales it needed to survive. Zonal interests could not be equated with occupational ones, however, as the split between the shopkeepers of the *interno* and *esterno* during the *micca* incident had already demonstrated. To develop the movement further, its leaders would have to construct an identity capable of bridging this zonal divide, one which could be shared by *esercenti* in the *interno* but which did not conflict with the suburban interests of the majority of the movement's adherents.

This meant that the issue of the *dazio consumo* had to be played down as much as possible: to reopen it would have prejudiced any chance of constructing a wider shopkeeper alliance. *L'Esercente* confined itself to occasional calls for the total abolition of the duty: a proposal acceptable to shopkeepers in both zones, but an impossible dream given that central government prescribed that a *dazio* system be set up and that it should receive a lump sum contribution

---

[9] Figures taken from the accounts of the Bank published in *L'Esercente* on 16 April 1887, 24 July 1888, 7 December 1890. See also 'La Banca dei Proprietari Forno', ibid., 27 February 1890; 'Banca Proprietari Forno', ibid., 22 February 1891.

(*canone*) from the resultant revenue. In any case, the city authorities could not afford to give up their major source of income.[10]

Instead the movement exploited that part of the *esercente* identity that was rooted in their prominent role within the neighbourhood. The links between the shopkeeper and the worker were frequently emphasised. The shopkeeper, through the extension of customer credit, enabled households to defer payment for goods until the arrival of the weekly wage packet, or, in the case of the unemployed, until their next job. The paternalistic relationship between the proprietor and his workers was recalled: the shopkeeper taught his apprentices the skills that they could later employ in their own business, whilst providing them with accommodation in his own home. The shop itself was the easiest escape route from the working class; indeed the *esercenti* 'at the end of the day are nothing else if not workers on the ascending scale of human progress'.[11]

It was the presumed affinity between shopkeepers and workers that led Rusca to write in 1887:

Milan must not be exclusively for the rich – The people and all the working classes must oppose the usurping aristocrats who work unceasingly to hold down the poor man and the *esercenti*, owing to the vanity of believing themselves to be called by destiny to govern the plebs because they were born counts or marquesses![12]

The links between shopkeepers and the working class were real enough, as the analysis of the marriage statistics demonstrated.[13] The *micca* affair had already seen shopkeepers acting as spokesmen for neighbourhood interests (although it is less clear that other residents accepted their playing this role). Rusca, however, was focusing on the shopkeepers' belief that they were opposed by a society from which they felt excluded. This resentment might equally be found amongst small traders catering to the lower orders in the *interno*, and was ubiquitous in the suburbs. The *esercenti* saw themselves and their customers as outsiders, their interests ignored by powerful, socially exclusive cliques.

The regulations on licensees and others who served the working

---

[10] This was still true after the government removed its own *dazio* on many items. The Democratic Giunta elected in 1899 found itself unable to abolish the *dazio*, much to the disappointment of many of its supporters. For the attitude of *L'Esercente* see 'Sull'abolizione del dazio consumo', 28 August 1886.

[11] 'Che penso io', *L'Esercente*, 22 January 1888.

[12] 'Esercenti ecco il momento', ibid., 7 May 1887.

[13] See Table 2.1, p. 41.

clases were a particular cause of resentment as these tended to reflect the paternalistic morality of the upper classes. As well as the restrictions on the granting of a licence, there were strict regulations concerning opening hours and the propriety of such premises. Niggling complaints abounded; for example, one landlord was accused of being in breach of the regulation that demanded that the premises be in darkness after closing time, after being found reading by candle-light.[14]

The refusal of the authorities to renew licences in 1887 for card-playing in the lower-class bars known as *bettole* highlighted these difficulties. Nearly 2,000 of the 2,600 or so licensed premises in Milan possessed such a licence. Although permission to open licensed premises was granted by the Giunta, the licence which permitted card-playing was granted by the police, representatives of the state. The Chief of Police, Santagostino, explained that the number of concessions was being reduced 'for reasons of morality and public order'.

> Every time the Questura has to decide on concessions it seeks to be generous in regard to those enterprises which offer the highest guarantees in terms of location, the class of person who frequents them and the importance of the concern. With regard then to premises of the worst class, accessible to the countryside or situated in peculiar localities, and frequented by low-class persons and people whose past offers no guarantees, where, finally, only wine or liquor are sold, the Police Chief must, of necessity, act on different criteria. He must proceed with much greater reluctance.

Indeed Santagostino believed that:

> the number of *osterie* and minor outlets for the sale of wine and liquor which spring up in our city is truly excessive, dangerous even, above all along some of the most popular main roads.[15]

Such attitudes served to force the *esercenti* and their clients closer together. 'For God's sake', wrote *L'Esercente*, 'one doesn't go to an

---

[14] The following week *L'Esercente* claimed that a host was fined for not having extinguished all the lights on his premises because he had left a devotional candle burning under a picture of a saint. Sadly the timing of this story does suggest it was one of the paper's parables designed to raise shopkeeper anger, rather than a true incident. 'Contravvenzioni! a base di Guide Savallo', *L'Esercente*, 29 July 1888; 'Une nuova licenza per gli osti', ibid., 5 August 1888.

[15] Extracts from an interview with Santagostino published in the *Corriere della Sera* and reproduced in *L'Esercente*. 'Il Corriere della Sera ed il giuoco delle carte', *L'Esercente*, 23 April 1887.

osteria to pray! Why shouldn't a regular have the right to enjoy the harmless pastime of a hand of cards?'[16]

The proprietors complained that it was in their own interests to make sure things did not get out of hand, and that it was unreasonable to take away their licences whilst those for the *trattorie* were happily reissued. *Bettole* were working-class haunts, frequently though far from exclusively found in the *esterno*, so when *L'Esercente* received a letter suggesting the whole affair was designed to make *bettole* proprietors apply for the more expensive *trattoria* licences it went out of its way to stress that the sympathetic correspondent was from the *interno*. None the less the issue touched on the divisions between the *esercenti* in the service sector. Indeed, when the policy was later reversed, some high-class establishments expressed disappointment, something which *L'Esercente* found difficult to understand as the paper was not yet aware of any recent social revolution that enabled workers to go and play cards in plush restaurants![17]

It was difficult to take action, as the problem was caused by the state authorities rather than the municipal ones. Thus, when a group of affected proprietors sent, first, a note of complaint and then a protest delegation to Negri, he simply expressed his sympathy and explained that he had nothing to do with the matter. Nor did Prina, head of the Committee set up to fight the issue, achieve much by standing in the municipal elections of 1887, failing even to attract the votes of the better-off enfranchised *esercenti*.[18]

A resolution of the situation was brought about in a most surprising manner. One act of the protest committee was to entrust the city's Democrat deputies with a memorandum of protest to be passed to the Minister of Public Order, Francesco Crispi. After some delay, he instructed the Questura to reverse its policy. *L'Esercente* presented this as proof of the utility of collective action. Victory had been achieved through the incessant campaign waged by the paper, which had alerted the deputies to the problem and

[16] 'Se vuole il permesso pel giuoco delle carte', *L'Esercente*, 18 March 1887.
[17] The letter is mentioned in 'Se vuole il permesso pel giuoco delle carte', ibid., 18 March 1887, the protests in 'Ancora il giuoco negli esercizi', ibid., 11 June 1887. As well as these articles, see 'La protesta degli esercenti al sindaco', ibid., 27 January 1887; 'L'istanza degli osti al Ministro Crispi', ibid., 23 April 1887.
[18] 'La risposta del Signor Sindaco alla Commissione degli Esercenti', ibid., 27 April 1887; 'La riunione degli esercenti ed i giornali', ibid., 7 May 1887; 'Abbiamo vinto', ibid., 15 May 1887.

kept the issue hot, whilst there would have been no Democratic deputies to take it up had not the voters elected them. 'Now do you understand the importance, the necessity, of going to vote?'[19]

Elitist attitudes also plagued the *esercenti* in their relations with the wider commercial community. The Chamber of Commerce was an excellent example of this. This body was legally obliged to admit all those engaged in commercial activity to membership, and to make representations on their behalf to the government. The government could also charge them with carrying out investigations into the effects of commercial policy in their cities.[20] The Milan Chamber however, was dominated by the Silk Producers Association and the protectionist Circolo Industriale Agricolo e Commerciale who kept the *esercenti* from playing an active role in the Chamber's affairs by preventing them from voting in elections up until 1889 (by employing the municipal franchise). This exclusion was particularly resented as it was the Camera di Commercio which nominated half of the members of the Commission that assessed the contribution to be paid by each enterprise to the *tassa esercizio e rivendita*.[21]

The difficulties small traders faced in obtaining commercial credit were also ascribed to exclusivity. *L'Esercente* wrote that whilst the class of big speculators was served by banks of all sizes, the shopkeepers were forced to scratch around for credit flows which often dried up unexpectedly. The reason for this, it argued,

> further to the tendency of some classes to monopolise credit to their own benefit, lies in the fact that the *esercenti* have never had any weight in public life ... and they, it's true to say, have never done anything to make themselves count, so that they have naturally come to be excluded as inferior citizens, from all Councils and forms of public administration.[22]

The attacks on elitism dovetailed well with the political project of many of the *esercenti* politicians. The social exclusivity of the Moderates made it easy for the paper to tar them with the elitist brush. Thus on 13 January 1887 *L'Esercente* pledged that they would not fail to:

[19] 'Il Ministro Crispi e gli esercenti di Milano', ibid., 21 May 1887.
[20] *Il Prontuario*, pp. 152–4, 141–5.
[21] 'Le elezioni imminenti', *L'Esercente*, 7 July 1889; 'I nostri candidati alla Camera di Commercio', ibid., 11 July 1889; 'La Federazione degli Esercenti e le elezioni commerciali', ibid., 4 December 1890.
[22] 'Une buona istituzione', ibid., 17 September 1886.

highlight the position of the shopkeeper created for him by our Giunta Municipale, which, as it's currently set up, favours the nobility, spares industry and comes down on the poor shopkeeper, paying little attention to his condition, and sometimes even contriving to distract him from his interests by, for example, placing the *esercenti* of the *interno* in conflict with those of the suburbs, as has happened in many circumstances which are not worth citing here, but which, however, can easily be recalled.[23]

It was true that the Moderates represented a social clique that had little time for small traders or the lower classes in general. On the other hand, the Giunta's difficulties should also be recognised. Milan was in severe need of extra finance, yet the legal limit on the *dazio* tariffs which could be charged in the *circondario interno* had already been reached.[24] This was the background to the two most important conflicts between the *esercenti* and the *municipio* between 1886 and 1890. These concerned the application of the regulations governing hygiene and the collection of the *dazio consumo* in the *esterno*. Breaches of these regulations were punished by fines that went into the coffers of the city council.

There were very high numbers of hygiene surveillance visits between 1885 and 1890 (see Table 5.2). Inspectors were able to enter premises and take samples at any time and did so with a frequency that upset the shopkeepers. The number of visits created an alarmist climate, undermining the relationship between patrons and proprietors by fuelling public suspicions of the latter.[25] In fact, the vast majority of those who were visited by the inspectors were found to have maintained their premises in perfect order, and the proportion of those in breach of regulations does not seem to have altered radically in the period. Offences arose more from ignorance of the restrictions, particularly the large number of regulations prescribing the types of instrument to be used for each function, than from dishonesty.[26]

[23] 'Sull'abolizone del dazio consumo', ibid., 28 August 1886.
[24] *Il Prontuario*, p. 7.
[25] 'Le contravvenzioni', *L'Esercente*, 19 August 1888.
[26] Admittedly these are only the figures for the first four months of selected years, a restriction imposed by the number to be processed in the time available. There is no particular reason to assume that these are in any way abnormal, however. The figures come from the Comune di Milano's monthly publication, the *Bollettino Demografico-Sanitario-Igienico-Metereologico*, 1885, 1888, 1890, 1895. See also *Il Prontuario*, p. 5.

Table 5.2. *The frequency of surveillance visits by local officials in Milan in the first four months of selected years*

	1885	1888	1890	1895
No. of visits	2,577	11,271	13,351	8,600
% in order	82.7	88.6	83.7	n/a
% irregular	17.3	11.3	16.3	n/a

Source: 'Visite effettuate agli esercizi dai Delegati di Mandamento' in *Bollettino Demografico-Sanitario-Igienico-Meteorologico* a cura del Comune di Milano 1885, 1888, 1890, 1895. See n.26.

The *esercenti* regarded the laws as too rigid and, in some cases, simply inappropriate. The definition of watered-down milk, for instance, was so strict that the degree of variation found in natural samples could lead to some of these being defined as adulterated.[27] The habit of the press of publishing the names of shopkeepers accused of contravening the standards particularly annoyed shop-keepers because the actual outcome of these cases was rarely reported, meaning that the public image of traders who were exon-erated was still badly damaged. This practice also contributed to the bad atmosphere surrounding hygiene, as the public were made aware of the number of charges made by the authorities (which, of course, was increasing), rather than the numbers of actual cases of proven fraudulence.

Tables 5.3a and 5.3b show the numbers of suspicious samples sent to the chemical laboratory by officials and private citizens (includ-ing shopkeepers themselves), and a breakdown of the results. The supposedly high levels of adulteration were clearly considerably exaggerated. Over half the samples, in every category examined, were found to be satisfactory, around 80% if wine, liquor and vinegar are ignored (and remember these were more likely to have been adulterated by their producers than their retailers).

These figures support *L'Esercente*'s case that the chief concern of the Municipio was keeping up appearances. They were not prepared to deal with 'the big fish', the wholesalers, and so turned on the retailers instead. Note the newspaper's implication that the Municipio was in league with big business to the detriment of the

---

[27] Furthermore, no account was taken of the need to skim milk in the summer in order to prevent it going sour too swiftly. 'I nostri lattivendoli', *L'Esercente*, 6 August 1887; 'Le contravvenzioni', ibid., 19 August 1888.

Table 5.3a. *Samples examined in the Milan Public Health Laboratory at the request of the municipal authorities*

Sample type	1885		1890		1895	
	Number	% satis-factory	Number	% satis-factory	Number	% satis-factory
Wine, liquor, vinegar	472	59.7	1,0452	80.7	2,077	56.7
Milk	0	0	416	87.3	423	82.7
Butter, cheese, sausage	4	0	187	100	138	92.8
Bread, flour, pasta	6	66.7	66	100	149	100

Source: Figures compiled from *Bollettino Demografico-Sanitario-Igienico-Meteoro-logico* a cura del Comune di Milano 1885, 1890, 1895.

Table 5.3b. *Samples examined in the Milan Public Health Laboratory at the request of private citizens*

Sample type	1885		1890		1895	
	Number	% satis-factory	Number	% satis-factory	Number	% satis-factory
Wine, liquor, vinegar	396	75.3	540	75.7	379	72.0
Milk	6	100	16	87.5	66	57.6
Butter, cheese, sausage	5	80	28	78.6	96	78.1
Bread, flour, pasta	13	92.3	27	92.6	20	100

Source: Figures compiled from *Bollettino Demografico-Sanitario-Igienico-Meteoro-logico* a cura del Comune di Milano 1885, 1890, 1895.

esercenti.[28] According to *L'Esercente*, when fraud did take place, it was the consequence of desperate competition between shop-keepers, which could best be controlled through strong trade associations.[29]

The Federation believed the issue demonstrated its utility in standing up to the authorities by using its political weight to protest

[28] 'Le contravvenzioni', ibid., 19 August 1888.
[29] 'Brutta china', ibid., 14 October 1888.

at the situation and through the practical assistance offered to individuals by the Ufficio di Consulenza Legale. Praising the Ufficio, Rosio said:

To explain myself in a few words, the presence of the police is sufficient for the thief not to risk reaching out his hand into his neighbour's pocket. From the day in which the Federation had the satisfaction of winning a significant number of cases against the authorities who were dishonestly carrying out their duty, the same authorities have been on their guard.

We must be implacable enemies of the unjust, oppressive, corrupt and cruel ways in which some functionaries interpret their duties.[30]

The opportunities provided for cruel interpretation of the *dazio consumo* regulations were even greater than those relating to the hygiene requirements. To avoid filtration, premises in the *esterno* were required to be devoid of any form of link to other property. Unless these conditions were satisfied, no trading could take place. A complex system governing warehousing, the branding of carcasses and the mode of payment of the *dazio* contribution placed the responsibility firmly on the shopkeeper to demonstrate he had abided by the law, by producing all the relevant receipts on request.[31] In addition to exercising their right to inspect premises, the *dazio* agents frequently stationed themselves outside the premises of '*frontisti*' in order to discourage people who might be tempted to purchase large quantities of goods and smuggle them into the *interno*. Even *Il Pungolo*, the most reactionary of the Milanese papers, condemned this as an odious form of espionage, and it was naturally resented by the traders themselves, especially when their livelihood depended on attracting custom from within the city.[32]

Pietro Gerli, the head of the *dazio* inspectorate, was under strict instructions from Mayor Negri to raise as much extra income as possible from the *esterno*, given that the burden on the *interno* could not be further increased. In 1885, Gerli succeeded in increasing the *dazio* yield by L. 170,000, yet the amount of money that had to be

[30] 'Riunione generale della Federazione Esercenti', ibid., 2 June 1889.
[31] These are described in *Il Prontuario*, pp. 51–66.
[32] Officials maintained that in the year that followed the introduction of this form of supervision the amount of meat legitimately imported into the city had risen by a fifth. 'L'Asses. Geppi che si giustifica', *L'Esercente*, 27 May 1888.

spent on the administration to do this meant a net increase of only L. 60,000 was achieved.[33] None the less his methods, designed to raise both the annual subscriptions paid by each trader and the income from fines imposed for breaching *dazio* regulations, caused considerable aggravation to the shopkeepers of the *circondario esterno*.

Gerli was particularly harsh during negotiations for new subscriptions. *L'Esercente* made a habit of publishing stories of his cruelty, such as his doubling of the *canone* for shops whose proprietors had recently died and left the business to their widows. Traders would be asked for exorbitant sums, sometimes equivalent to half their annual income, and were often forced to shut up shop. The paper frequently alleged that he and his staff were renowned for favouritism. Subsequent events proved that not all these stories were apocryphal.[34]

In 1888 and 1889 the shopkeepers' organisations attempted to make Gerli's conduct an issue during the council elections. In the partial elections of 1888 the *esercenti* were urged to overcome their usual apathy because:

> For the fear of losing a *lira* by leaving the shop for half an hour you lose a thousand *lire* by staying behind the counter, if not to stir yourself means approving the handiwork of the Giunta which has a faithful executioner in sig. Gerli to whom, from the moment you do not vote in protest against him, it will appear you are sincerely attached.[35]

The Democrats made little effort in the 1888 campaign, however, believing that the nature of the franchise gave them little chance of competing successfully. In the 1889 elections, though, the outcome was different. The Federation was allowed to nominate four individuals for inclusion on the Democratic list, whilst other members of the Federation also found places as a result of their political connections. Only one of the Federation candidates was elected – an industrialist rather than a genuine shopkeeper. None the less, the Moderates were significantly weakened and two of the councillors most intimately associated with the administration of the *dazio*

---

[33] *L'Esercente*, 18 June 1887, p. 134.

[34] A good selection of Gerli stories may be found in 'Gli osti chiudono', *L'Esercente*, 8 July 1888; 'Nel 1890', ibid., 5 November 1889.

[35] 'Il contegno della stampa liberale nella imminente lotta elettorale amministrativa', ibid., 8 June 1888.

consumo lost their seats. Negri was forced to hand over to Belin-zaghi, and his fall was held, in part, to be due to the links between himself and Gerli. *L'Esercente* proclaimed that the shopkeepers had achieved all they wanted from participation in the campaign and now looked forward to a Giunta that would do away with Gerli's regime.[36]

In fact it was the shopkeepers' movement itself that eventually dealt with Gerli. Whilst the Federation decided to investigate the possibility of taking on the negotiation of an overall figure for the *dazio canone*, and then redistributing this amongst the *esercenti* itself, in 1890 *L'Esercente* published a new series of reports of wrongdoings in the *dazio* service which gradually became a city scandal. Shopkeepers who faced ridiculously high *canone* demands from the *dazio* services had begun receiving visits from one 'Oliva' who offered to use his influence with the officials to try and reduce the figure, in return for a proportion of the sum saved. It gradually became clear that 'Oliva', far from being the mediator he claimed, was actually in league with the officials themselves. An inquiry was set up and Gerli was suspended, never to return.[37]

The Gerli affair highlighted many facets of the *esercente* identity which the shopkeeper movement had sought to develop. The defeats of both Negri and Gerli were useful demonstrations of the value of an *esercente* presence in politics, whilst individual traders had been able to use the Federation's legal advice bureau to defend themselves against the predations of both the *dazio* and hygiene inspectorates. Furthermore Gerli could be depicted as the agent of interfering, elitist and, above all, Moderate authorities who cared little for the small trader. This accorded well with the shopkeeper politicians' intent of positioning the *esercenti* firmly in the Democrat camp, and proclaiming their affinity with the equally excluded workers.

L'Esercente and the Federation could claim many significant achievements in this period. They had sustained the level of shop-keeper activity following the *micca* affair, and their campaigns

---

[36] See 'L'opinione di un reduce', ibid., 17 November 1889; 'Une bella notizia', ibid., 17 November 1889; 'Utili e perdite', ibid., 17 November 1889.

[37] 'L'Assemblea Generale della Federazione esercenti di Milano: I contratti daziari pel circondario esterno', ibid', 6 April 1890. Details of the 'Oliva' scandal can be found in 'I supposti raggiri di dazio consumo', ibid., 20 April 1890; 'Lebbra daziaria', ibid., 1 May 1890; 'Ancora e sempre dell'inchiesta daziaria', ibid., 8 June 1890; 'I brogli daziari', ibid., 19 June 1890; 'L'esito dell'inchiesta daziaria', ibid., 6 July 1890; 'O via lu o via mi!', ibid., 20 July 1889.

against the authorities over the *bettole*, the hygiene regulations and the *dazio consumo* inspectorate under Gerli demonstrated the utility of participation in public affairs as a counterpart to the practical assistance that could be rendered by institutions like the Federation's legal and credit bureaux. Yet whilst the movement had sought to foster a universal sense of shopkeeper identity as a response to the alleged oppression of shopkeepers by established (Moderate) society, it was still imperative that it avoid contradicting the zonal interests of the majority of its adherents: indeed the Gerli affair was still only of real significance to the shopkeepers of the *esterno*. As long as the *dazio* system remained, so too did the fundamental divide between the retailers in the two *circondario*. The *esercenti* movement simply avoided the issue in the hope that the authorities' experience in 1886 would force them to do the same. A shopkeeper identity could exist, but it had to be subordinated to the zonal solidarity that remained the fundamental expression of shopkeeper self-interest.

Furthermore the positioning of the *esercente* identity was already coming under stress. The problems arose not so much from the depiction of the *esercenti* as an excluded class, but rather from the much-vaunted alliance of shopkeepers and workers: again a largely suburban construction. The Democrat politicians of the Federation had laid great stress upon this, but at the beginning of the 1889 election campaign Rusca wrote an article in *L'Esercente* arguing that an accommodation between Democrats and Socialists was an 'impossible alliance'.[38] As well as accentuating the ideological incompatibility between Socialism and petty commerce, his argument played on the growing concern amongst shopkeepers that the newly enfranchised lower classes would give their votes to supporters of consumer cooperatives. Although *L'Esercente* eventually endorsed the two Socialists on the Democrat list, stressing that the crucial issue was that of the Moderates, many shopkeeper electors chose to vote for mixed lists, rather than follow the movement's guidelines.[39] The strains inherent in membership of the Democratic bloc would intensify during the depression years of the 1890s.

[38] 'Alleanze impossibili', ibid., 24 October 1889.
[39] Rosio, F., 'Un consiglio', *L'Esercente*, 3 November 1889; 'Gli esercenti e le elezioni amministrative', ibid., 4 November 1889; 'Leggete e giudicateli!', ibid., 7 November 1889.

6. *The* esercenti *and the depression,* 1890–1897

The economic slump between 1890 and 1896 produced an interesting paradox in the history of the Milanese *esercente* movement. The suffering wrought amongst individual proprietors created new opportunities for the shopkeeper movement and, above all, for the construction of shopkeeper identity. Adversity often breeds unity, but in the case of the *esercenti* there was a further paradox in that those factors on which they blamed their misfortunes, and that could only be combated by exercising the collective voice in the political sphere that the movement advocated, were not the root cause of the small traders' distress. Indeed, part of the movement's success arose precisely from its failure to address the most fundamental problem of shopkeeping in the period.

Chapter 1 illustrated the deep recession in the small retailing sector between 1889 and 1897.[1] Consumption fell as did real prices, although protectionist duties on agricultural produce sometimes forced shop prices upwards, accentuating the drop in demand and contributing to the demands for cheaper bread that fuelled the public disorders of 1898 (see Figs. 1.3 and 1.7). Indicative of the decline in economic activity was the fall in the volume of bills of exchange discounted by the Cassa di Risparmio delle Provincie Lombarde after 1892. These instruments were the primary source of operating capital and short-term credit available to small traders, and the fact that the proportion of those bills held by the Cassa di Risparmio which were not honoured on the date of expiry also rose dramatically between 1892 and 1896 suggests that *L'Esercente*'s

---

[1] See pp. 27–35.

unsubstantiated claims that the bankruptcy rate was rising during this period should be believed.[2]

There was widespread recognition that petty commerce was in severe difficulties. In 1893, for example, an anarchist wrote to *L'Esercente* to assure its readers that when his comrades sang:

let's stab the hated bourgeois we certainly couldn't consider the *esercenti*, who are certainly not thriving, as such, given the present economic conditions and the inclination of the big trader to absorb the small one. Today they are *esercenti*, tomorrow they become workers, because of the vicissitudes that petty commerce has to pass through.[3]

Many of the shopkeepers' problems resulted from outmoded business techniques. Small traders had difficulty monitoring their position as they lacked the necessary book-keeping skills and at best kept only a single register in which they noted each day's takings, and any financial commitments entered into.[4] *L'Esercente* pointed out that whilst a big wholesaler had time to occupy himself with such matters:

for the shopkeeper it's another kettle of fish. Many times he is alone in the shop with the wife, or with a shop-boy. Busy all day with grinding, slicing and wrapping. Hands sometimes wet, often soiled by goods that it is necessary to handle. He doesn't feel the need for registers. He keeps a proof sheet for small credits; recorded in such a way that only he understands them. His cash book is the drawer under the counter. He never writes letters, receives very few of them and even these he files together with bills paid or to pay. The memory keeps everything in order, and the business keeps going, if it keeps going.

Don't insist on saying that this system is risky; that it must lead to ruin. It is the system of nearly all shopkeepers, and it has never prevented, nor will it prevent, one who has had, or will have, the fortune to work in a shop with a good clientele, from making good money on it.[5]

The Commercial Code however, stated that a trader had to maintain three sets of books, an *inventario* (stock register), a *gior-*

[2] Bachi, 'Storia della Cassa di Risparmio delle Provincie Lombarde 1823–1923', pp. 198, 206; 'Proponimenti pel capo d'anno', *L'Esercente*, 1 January 1891. As explained previously, no exact figures for bankruptcies exist (see chapter 1, n. 36).

[3] Sperafico, G., 'La difesa di un anarchico', *L'Esercente*, 18 June 1893.

[4] Dompè, *Manuale del commerciante*, pp. 320–1.

[5] 'Il codice di commercio', *L'Esercente*, 4 October 1891.

nale (a daily record of all transactions) – both of which had to be certified by a magistrate – and a *copialettere* (a correspondence file). Shopkeepers whose businesses failed could be found guilty of 'simple bankruptcy', a criminal offence punishable by imprisonment, when these conditions had not been fulfilled.[6] Even if they avoided imprisonment the offenders were still not entitled to a suspension of the bankruptcy proceedings for a specified time period (*moratoria*) to negotiate an agreement (*concordato*) with their creditors for repayment of a certain amount of the debt. These provisions demonstrated the authorities' ignorance of the realities of petty commerce. Rising bankruptcy rates during the depression highlighted the problem, yet the government remained unmoved by vociferous demands from shopkeeper organisations that these unrealistic obligations should be removed from small traders.[7]

Whilst the *esercenti* ran the risk of imprisonment for bankruptcy, they were hindered in retrieving their debts by the fact that private citizens who failed to honour their debts could no longer be arrested. As the economic situation had deteriorated, the shopkeepers' habit of granting consumer credit (*il fido*) was an increasing liability.[8] By 1891 *L'Esercente* estimated that bakers (the most common creditors) were writing off over L. 150,000 a year in bad debts.[9] In the same year the newspaper told its readers that:

Cash sales are now a necessity imposed by the pressure of competition and the economic restraints. If the shopkeeper were certain not to be left damaged by credit, he could sell his goods at a lower price; he wouldn't be forced to make allowances in his modest budget for losses of 30 or even 40% for suspended or non-recuperable debts.

Cash sales would give the consumer cheap food; the bankruptcy register would be shorter and not as painful; in our opinion the measure is necessary in every respect.[10]

L'Esercente proposed that the Federation should organise a campaign amongst shopkeepers and wholesalers to eliminate credit over a six-month period. This could only have been achieved had the type of 'class consciousness' the *esercenti* movement sought to create

[6] Articles 856–60 of *Codice criminale*, reproduced in *Il Prontuario*, p. 72.
[7] In 1890, 1891 and 1892 a call for the reform of the law formed part of the electoral programme issued by the Federation and *L'Esercente*, a call repeated by the national small-business association in 1894.
[8] See pp. 39–40.   [9] 'Praticamente parlando', *L'Esercente*, 23 April 1891.
[10] 'Vendita per contanti', ibid., 6 September 1891.

already been established, however. The Federation would have needed to play a role similar to that of a highly disciplined trade union able to impose a 'closed shop' within petty commerce, so that customers who were denied credit by one proprietor would not be able to switch their customs to another trader who was not participating in the scheme. Participation rates in the Federation were too low, and proprietors' suspicions of their competitors too high, for this to be practicable. Credit sales continued unabated.

Similar problems were posed by the giving of Christmas gifts (*regali natalizi*). As well as the financial cost that these imposed, the shopkeeper had to spend a considerable amount of time on the preparation and packaging of the presents. Small-trader organisations argued that the custom was archaic; in a big city the clientele were unlikely to stay loyal to one shop just because the proprietor handed out small gifts once a year. New clients appeared in the shops, picked up their complimentary items and then took their custom elsewhere. The indiscriminate nature of the hand-out meant it fulfilled neither a commercial nor a charitable function. After all, rich clients had less need of Christmas presents than did the *esercenti* themselves.

In 1891 the Grocers' Society began a series of campaigns against the *regali*. Participants signed a pledge that they would not distribute gifts but make a contribution to charity instead (thus avoiding charges of meanness on the part of the public). The register was used in an attempt to convince other grocers that their peers would not steal their trade were they to renounce distributing gifts as well. The scheme began promisingly and was heralded as a breakthrough in terms of *esercenti* class action. Over the years, however, it was not a success. Members of the public, particularly lower-class customers, regarded the *regali* as a right rather than a privilege, the same attitude that prevented progress on the credit issue. Grocers in less-affluent areas such as Porta Genova and Porta Tenaglia felt unable to participate in the drive, fearing that they would lose many customers to any retailer who abstained from the scheme. The campaign was a failure in precisely those areas in which the retailers' margins were smallest.[11]

---

[11] 'Società dei Droghieri di Milano e Lombardia: assemblea generale', ibid., 17 September 1891; 'L'abolizione dei regali natalizi approvata', ibid., 20 September 1891; 'Società dei Droghieri: la vittoria del buon senso', ibid., 31 December 1891; 'Società dei Droghieri', ibid., 10 January 1892. Sporadic attempts to abolish the

Two aspects of these campaigns deserve particular mention. The first is the strains that were developing in the relationship between patron and proprietor. Customers' insistence that *il fido* and the *regali* were, in effect, acquired rights rather than privileges was the most important factor preventing proprietors from abandoning them. This was especially the case in the lower-class areas in which this affinity had been assumed to be at its most developed. The reassessment of the relationship between the *esercenti* and the workers that took place during the depression was, in part, predicated on this realisation.

The fact that campaigns such as that against the *regali natalizi* were now being initiated, however, was testimony to the increasing success of the *esercenti* movement. By 1890 *L'Esercente* claimed that fourteen small-trader organisations were in existence, with the butchers and bakers associations able to attract upwards of 300 participants to some of their meetings. The Grocers' Society was revived in that same year and virtually doubled its membership to reach 200 members by the beginning of 1892. Amongst other societies founded in this period were those catering for tobacconists in 1891, *postai* (a form of general-store owner) in 1895, and fuel sellers in 1896.[12] Details of the main shopkeeper associations are given in Table 5.1.

The appeal of these associations was based on the increasing recognition that collective action could produce beneficial results. Some organisations negotiated contracts on behalf of their members, the most notable example being the fuel sellers' association which bought coke in bulk from the gas corporation to redistribute amongst its members.[13] Many associations were divided

regali continued up until 1897, but met with little success because of the resistance of grocers in lower-class areas. 'L'assemblea generale della Società dei Droghieri', ibid., 1 April 1894; 'Società dei Droghieri di Milano e Lombardia', ibid., 16 May 1897.

12 'L'assemblea dei proprietari forno e la questione del lavoro diurno', ibid., 21 July 1889; 'I macellari in assemblea generale', ibid., 3 November 1889. 'L'assemblea generale della Federazione Esercenti di Milano', ibid., 6 April 1890; 'La Società dei Droghieri risorge', ibid., 28 October 1890; 'La nuova Società dei Tabacchi', ibid., 21 January 1892; 'I Droghieri in assemblea', ibid., 28 January 1892; 'La seduta dei Postai', ibid., 10 November 1895; 'L'associazione fra proprietari esercenti pasticcieri', ibid., 9 August 1896.

13 'L'assemblea generale della Società Droghieri di Lombardia', ibid., 17 May 1891; 'Ai signori Postai di Milano', ibid., 10 November 1895. For an account of the Società Commercianti in Combustibili's negotiations with Unione Gas see 'Una importante assemblea ... ', ibid., 8 April 1897. Relations between the two organisations were always strained and flared up again in subsequent years.

into *interno* and *esterno* sections, which, though reinforcing the importance of 'zonal' interests over 'class' ones, enabled the *esterno* sections to negotiate a lump-sum trade contribution with the *dazio consumo* authorities, which was then shared out on an equitable basis amongst the membership.[14]

The growth of these associations was both a cause and a consequence of the increasing success of the *esercenti* movement. The trade associations contributed to this by taking out bulk subscriptions to the Federation and, on occasion, to *L'Esercente* as well.[15] Meanwhile groups of Federation members whose trades did not possess their own organisations set up sections within the Federation. The number of individual members that the Federation claimed to include did not rise greatly over the years, being 1,200 in 1889 and 1,800 in 1896, but when *aderenti*, members of the various associations that subscribed to the Federation, were counted, the figure was close to 3,500 in 1892 and around 5,000 by 1899.[16] *L'Esercente*, meanwhile, regularly claimed a circulation of 5,000 plus from 1893 onwards, even if a substantial portion of these subscribers was always in arrears. The paper was obliged to move its offices four times between 1891 and 1894 in order to cope with this growth, ending up in a suite of rooms in Via Manzoni, a fashionable street in the city centre, where it also installed its own printing presses.[17]

[14] The Grocers' Society regularly undertook this task for its members in the *esterno*. See 'L'assemblea generale della Società Droghieri di Lombardia', ibid., 17 May 1891.

[15] In 1893 both of the *salumieri* associations joined their members to the Federation, as did the Grocers' Society. 'L'assemblea generale della Federazione degli Esercenti di Milano', *L'Esercente*, 20 April 1893. The Società Salumieri del Circondario Esterno took out a bulk subscription to *L'Esercente* for all its members in 1895. 'Società Esercenti solidali coll'Esercente', ibid., 2 May 1895.

[16] None of the various figures claimed are verifiable and the context in which they are cited is crucial. Marmont, a disgraced former President of the Federation, claimed that when he began the job in 1891 there were only 300 members but that the figure was 1,800 when he left. Yet the figures quoted by *L'Esercente* were of 1,200 members in 1889, 1,600 in 1890 and 1,250 in 1893. These, however, were usually wheeled out at election time and may have been partly designed to justify the number of nominations to the Democratic list allocated to the Federation. In 1893 the Federation's projected budget allowed for only 800 members. 'L'opinione di un reduce', ibid., 17 November 1889; 'I nostri candidati', ibid., 20 June 1890; 'Negozianti, sarti, calzolai', ibid., 12 June 1892; 'L'assemblea generale della Federazione', ibid., 20 April 1893; 'Il lavoro elettorale degli esercenti', ibid., 16 June 1893; 'Sempre sulle cause delle discordie fra gli esercenti milanese', ibid., 9 June 1898; 'Società che costituiscono la Federazione Esercenti e Commercianti', ibid., 21 May 1899.

[17] By 1893 these new supplements had 800 subscribers whilst the original commercial supplement now carried a considerable number of articles as well. In 1895

The movement's success reflected its achievements in defending *esercenti* interests in the depression. The movement failed to change the outmoded business methods common to petty commerce, but it did demonstrate the potential of collective action. Some grandiose schemes, such as that to build a *palazzo degli esercenti* to house the various associations, were flops, because they did not address a basic grievance of individual traders. On the other hand, successful practical initiatives were often coupled with efforts to generate a more political consciousness.

This was certainly the case in the movement's dealings with the Municipio. In 1892 the Comune decided to withdraw its grant to the traditional Lent carnival and support the race meeting held at San Siro instead. The decision was greeted with outrage by small traders who benefited from the number of outsiders who came into the city to see the spectacle and the extremely long hours they were permitted to keep during carnival week. The festival was especially popular amongst the lower classes, who also attended the Fiera di Porta Genova, organised by local shopkeepers, held at the same time.[18]

Unfortunately the traditional forms of behaviour associated with the carnival did not sit well with the new concepts of public decency. The floats were usually satirical depictions of the Giunta and other local dignitaries, and the crowd showed their appreciation of these by hurling sweets and coins at them, provoking a fair number of casualties each year.[19] Enthusiasm for the *carnevale* declined amongst the influential members of Milanese society and the

---

L'Esercente claimed it had 5,300 subscribers. When the paper was taken over by Giovanni Tadini in 1897 he first claimed it had a circulation of over 5,000 but later, when attacking the previous owners, that there were around 4,500 subscribers of whom 1,450 were in arrears. 'Il servizio speciale per i mercarti burro', ibid., 31 December 1891; 'La nuova Associazione degli Esercenti', ibid., 24 October 1895; 'Ai signori Associati e lettori', ibid., 10 October 1897; 'Ai signori Associati e lettori', ibid., 24 March 1898.

[18] For example in the week before Lent in 1885 the shops in the Piazza del Duomo remained open until midnight except for Wednesday when they stayed open until one, and Thursday and Saturday when they could stay open all night. A similar concession was granted to shops in the Porta Genova area. See ASM, Fond. Questura, c. 27, Carnevale 1885.

[19] The Questore (chief of police) banned one such float in 1884. Both the Carnevale and the Fiera required considerable policing, with twenty arrests per event being the norm. In 1885 every available police horse was deployed during the Carnevale. *La Lombardia*, 1 March 1884; ASM, Fond. Questura, c. 27, Carnevale 1885. See ASM, fond. Questura, c. 27, for general information on all the carnivals between 1884 and 1887.

Comune's decision to withdraw the grant was supported by many Democratic and Socialist councillors.

L'Esercente commented on the irony of the friends of the proletariat subsidising a sport organised by the nobility, and claimed the decision was taken because:

the carnival upsets disturbed people and councillors and creates the obstruction of many people on the streets greatly annoying the streetsweepers, the tramdrivers, and the state and local police. At San Siro, however, they can turn somersaults, amuse themselves, roll in the mud, bawl out, as no one hears. They can watch the horses run. They gamble, an extremely moral activity. The people can gallop out there to see the wealthy and amuse themselves, work themselves up over the big patriotic issues that come into play. The victory of an Italian horse over a French one means nothing to the rest of you? The honour of the nation is involved! The races are serious things whilst the carnival is for fools, and furthermore it is no longer consistent with modern times.[20]

The Federation stepped in to take over the running of the carnival, but, despite initial success in attracting a number of Milanese notables onto the committee, it lacked the financial resources necessary to organise so large an event. This honourable failure may have won the Federation some kudos amongst traders; it certainly generated considerable ill-will towards the Comune for ignoring the interests of petty commerce. The effects of the oversight were felt by the Municipio as well as shopkeepers themselves: Giunta reports admitted that one reason the money raised by the *dazio* was insufficient for the city's needs was that the *esercenti* had lost the extra trade such events created.[21]

The high levels of tax that governments maintained in order to finance the Italian adventures in Africa also antagonised the shopkeepers. *L'Esercente* regarded the increased income and property tax contributions demanded of many retailers in 1893 as a form of 'monetary conscription'.[22] Because these were based on estimates of the profitability of an individual's business, there were many who felt their incomes had been significantly overvalued. The Federation

---

[20] 'Il carnevalone milanese e i nostri consiglieri democratici', *L'Esercente*, 17 January 1892.
[21] 'I comitati dei divertimenti a convegno', ibid., 15 January 1893; 'Carnevale agonia', ibid., 3 March 1895; 'Le condizioni finanziarie del Comune di Milano e la cinta daziaria', ibid., 22 August 1897.
[22] 'Come agitarci', ibid., 12 September 1893.

set up a new office which offered advice to the *esercenti* and negotiated on their behalf with the authorities, whilst playing a part in
the campaign against the increases being conducted by the
Chamber of Commerce, thus combining the practical with the
political.[23]

The year 1893 was also the one in which an acute shortage of
small change developed in northern Italy. This was blamed on
poor management by the Government arising out of its over-
emphasis on military priorities. The Treasury appeared indifferent
to the situation, concerned only to limit its spending where possible. In one of its most impressive operations the Federation
began issuing its own bills of exchange which were accepted in
large numbers of shops, the Banca Popolare and even on the omni-
buses.[24] When the Government took remedial action the following
year, these *buoni* were successfully withdrawn and the holders
obtained their cash value. Over a million had been issued and of
those presented for reimbursement less than one in a thousand
proved forgeries.[25]

The issuing of the *buoni* had been carried out through the offices
of the Banca di Credito dei Proprietari Forno; the withdrawal was
administered by the Banca degli Esercenti into which the former,
with the aid of the Federation, had developed. In a sense the
existence of the bank was another comment on the general state of
the economy as it was hoped that the bank would provide credit to
small traders despite the prevailing high interest rates (caused by
government borrowing) which discouraged the larger banks and
savings institutes from investing in commerce.

The bank inherited a shaky position, made worse by in-fighting
amongst the new personnel and those who survived from the bakers'
bank. The value of the shares was reduced from L. 34 to L. 30 and
the reserves strengthened against probable losses, yet, surprisingly,
it made sufficient profit to warrant paying a dividend to its shareholders in its first year of operation. Two years later the share price
was raised by L. 3, and by 1898 the number of shareholders in the

---

[23] 'Gli accertamenti dei redditi e richezza mobile', ibid., 15 October 1897.
[24] 'Il credito', ibid., 1 June 1895; 'La protesta degli esercenti per la mancanza degli
spezzati metallici', ibid., 15 June 1893. See also Zezzos, *Milano e il suo commercio*,
p. 292.
[25] 'L'accorrere esagerato pel cambio dei buoni fiduciari', *L'Esercente*, 15 February
1894; 'Gli ultimi buoni fiduciari', ibid., 12 August 1894.

Table 6.1. *The progress of the Banca degli Esercenti, 1894–8*

Year	Shares No.	Members No.	Reserves L.	Net Profits L.	Capital L.
1894	4,374	741	1,512	5,003	131,190
1895	6,270	950	3,006	12,670	188,100
1896	9,360	1,197	16,012	24,817	286,800
1897	12,611	1,374	40,331	35,698	378,330
1898	13,774	1,454	61,162	35,025	413,220

Source: 'L'Assemblea della Banca Esercenti', *L'Esercente*, 16 October 1898.

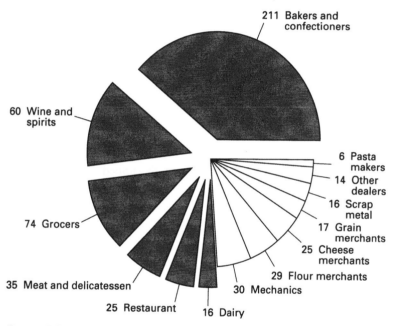

Source: *L'Esercente,* 9 February 1896

Fig. 6.1 Shareholders in the Banca degli Esercenti, 1896

bank had almost doubled from 741 to 1,454.[26] The bank's progress is shown in Table 6.1.

An analysis of 592 of the 950 shareholders in 1895 shows that the majority came from the more prosperous *esercenti* professions, particularly those of baker (reflecting the bank's previous existence) and grocer. In addition many were not true *esercenti*, but dealers and merchants on the fringes of shopkeeper activity (see Fig. 6.1). The bank appears to have been more a way for these men to raise more capital than a source of credit for the needy, as the pride it took in the low number of 'bad' loans it incurred suggests it was not keen to risk its capital. Indeed in 1898 it ceased making loans on trust altogether, reserving credit solely for shareholders, whilst taking measures to restrict the number of shares available.[27]

The relative success of the *esercenti* organisations in promoting themselves amongst the shopkeeper classes was reflected in their increasing political importance. At the Chamber of Commerce, for instance, the Circolo degli Interessi Industriali, Commerciali e Agricoli, which had been set up in June 1889 to exploit the new franchise, dominated elections to the Chamber's executive. The Federation, one of the Circolo's key supporters, nominated candidates to the Circolo's electoral list, enabling it to exercise a certain degree of influence within a body from which it had previously been effectively excluded.

At local and parliamentary elections the Federation drew up a list of candidates it supported, and this was publicised by *L'Esercente*, which appeared daily during the campaigns. Although the number of votes cast by *esercenti* was low, it was significant, given the poor turn-outs that characterised such elections. In the supplementary local elections of 1891, for instance, 1,000 *esercenti* voted for the *L'Esercente* list, 1,500 made their own selection and 8,000 did not vote (ascribed by the movement to a combination of indolence and retailers' desire not to offend sections of their clientele). Only 14,360 of an electorate of 43,096 bothered to cast their votes, however, meaning that 5,600 votes were sufficient to get elected.[28] This gave the *esercenti* movement considerable bargaining power during the

[26] 'Banca degli Esercenti', ibid., 24 May 1894; 'Un po' di cifre sul valore delle azioni della Banca degli Esercenti', ibid., 24 May 1894; 'La Banca degli Esercenti di Milano', ibid., 9 February 1896.

[27] 'Banca degli Esercenti', ibid., 20 October 1898.

[28] 'A campagna finita', ibid., 5 June 1891.

construction of electoral alliances, even if the overall numbers involved pointed to the limits of its achievements.

The movement's success was in contrast to that of its adherents. The *esercenti* institutions attempted to assist their members in overcoming the difficulties caused by the depression, but were far more circumspect when it came to dealing with the causes of the slump itself. The analysis of the *tassa esercizio e rivendita* records presented in chapter 1 concluded that the sharp rise in the numbers of *alimentari* (food retailers such as butchers, bakers and greengrocers) and *esercizi pubblici* (all forms of eating and drinking establishments plus hotels and lodgings) between 1888 and 1896 was indicative of the number of these enterprises that had been set up by immigrants to the city.[29] The severity of the decline in average tax contribution in the *alimentari* sector is indicative of too many enterprises competing in too small a market; that this was not so dramatic amongst the *esercizi pubblici* sector may perhaps be accounted for by the fact that this probably included the fast-growing and much more profitable businesses of hotel-keeping and room-letting.

Analysis of the census returns confirms this diagnosis. As Table 2.4 shows, the largest declines in the employer–employee ratio between 1881 and 1901 were recorded in the food making and food retailing categories I and II, whilst the highest percentage increase in the overall number of proprietors came in category 1: the leading *esercenti* category. Again this evidence suggests that large numbers of small concerns were being set up in this period.

The immigration statistics available for the city are not that helpful. Although all those who joined or left the citizenry were required to state their profession, this self-classification was a far from secure guide to the trade that immigrants would pursue within Milan and some respondents inevitably upgraded their status. Aggregating the figures for net immigration between 1885 and 1900 we find that the category '*esercenti e loro dipendenti*' (shopkeepers and their dependants) gained 4,463 male and 253 female members out of a total increase of 67,113 men and 63,798 women in the period. One in fifteen of the new net male entrants to the city were members of this shopkeeping category, an average of 279 entrants per year. The term *dipendenti* embraced shop-hands as well as family members, although the paucity of respondents in the female cate-

[29] P. 34.

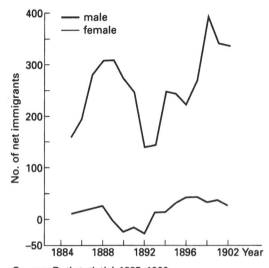

Source: Dati statistici, 1885–1900

Fig. 6.2 Net immigration: *esercenti e dipendenti*, 1884–1902

gory, in which the annual average gain was just sixteen, suggests many spouses simply classified themselves as housewives.

The pattern of net immigration amongst those who classified themselves as shopkeepers can be examined (see Fig. 6.2). Net *esercenti* immigration during the recovery years of the later 1890s was at a significantly higher level than during the previous peak of 1887 to 1889, suggesting shopkeeper migration was most responsive to the pull factor of an attractive business climate: the overall pattern of net immigration reveals peaks of similar value (see Fig. 1.1d). Furthermore, a considerably larger proportion of the shopkeeper immigrants moved to the city centre, where both opportunities and costs (because of the *dazio consumo*) were greater.[30] Even so, the peaks and troughs in the movement of the shopkeeper class coincide very closely with those of overall net immigration.[31]

These were far from being the only immigrants who might end up

---

[30] The exact figure for the shopkeepers was 38.6%, compared to 28.2% of the whole sample in the period 1885–97 (excluding 1894). After 1897 the boundaries of the *interno* were changed and the figures become meaningless.

[31] Unfortunately the categories of analysis the statisticians used were changed after 1900 so it is impossible to represent the pattern beyond this date.

in the *esercenti* sector. Newcomers possessed very limited financial resources and could never afford to be out of a job of some kind; but their preparedness to work for low pay and in poor conditions was resented by the better-organised sectors of the native labour force.[32] Workers sought to exclude immigrants from the workplace with the result that immigrants gravitated to the less well-organised small-scale workshops and to the service and retail sector. Those who could not find a job might well try setting up their own ventures to generate some sort of income. Retailing and services were attractive areas to enter because they required few special skills, could be run on a family basis, and could be continued even after the head of the household had found employment.

Immigrant shopkeepers were not a product of either a boom or bust era. As early as 1881, well before immigration rates hit their peaks, 59% of shopkeepers had been born outside the city itself, with native Milanese predominant only amongst the vendors of government monopoly goods whose positions were in the gift of the authorities. By 1901 the overall rate of non-nativity had risen to 69.2% and even a majority of the government monopoly concessionaries had been born outside the city (see Table 2.3). Nearly all of these immigrants came from Lombardy, the majority from the Provincia di Milano itself. The highest rates of all were recorded in the small *esercizi pubblici*: these required very few specialised skills and could be easily organised on a family basis.

The predominance of non-native proprietors helps account for one of the most remarkable features of shopkeeper politics in Milan, namely the lack of resentment against immigrants of any sort. This stance did not waver during the depression, even though the opening up of new enterprises diminished the existing retailers' market share without offering any real hope to the newcomers. In 1890 *L'Esercente* wrote:

> Commerce is going through difficult times. Many deluded individuals set themselves up as shopkeepers with little money, rich only in great hopes. After a few months trial they find themselves sorrowfully forced to shut up shop, without being aware that, through unfortunate delusions, they ruin themselves and horribly

---

[32] Tilly demonstrates that immigrant workers were less prone to take strike action than native workers and remained unemployed for shorter periods than them. Tilly, 'The working class of Milan', pp. 253, 141.

damage petty commerce. It's an ugly situation in which the
shopkeeper finds himself today.[33]

The paper suggested that when established traders were joined by
a new arrival:

instead of looking on him with irritation and resentment, why not
deem him worthy of a benevolent regard, why not remember that
you began like that and that at one time you would have cursed
your senior colleague if he were to have lowered prices to kill you
off.[34]

This tolerance extended beyond those proprietors who simply
came from the Provincia. There were not that many Jews in Milan,
but it is still a surprise to find a shopkeeper newspaper of the 1890s
condemning the public's hostility towards small traders by equating
it with the instinctive anti-Semitism of a previous age:

what centuries ago happened to the Hebrews now repeats itself
for the *esercenti*: After him, into him, he's a Jew.

Were they rogues, murderers, thieves, those sons of Israel? Eh!
but they were Jews. And one didn't reason beyond that . . .[35]

As an independent journal, whose income came entirely from
shopkeeper subscriptions, *L'Esercente* would hardly have printed
such advice had it not believed it to be a reflection of its readers'
views. The shared background of the majority of shopkeepers led
them to look favourably on immigrants and to ignore the fact that
the crisis of the early 1890s was primarily a function of the number
of competing enterprises within the trades. Whether this overcapa-
city was a function of the nature of petty commerce itself, or merely
a tendency that the 'invisible hand', in the form of the depression,
moved to correct, remains debatable. What seems clear is that the
esercenti were predisposed by their own backgrounds to ignore the
root of their problems and to seek solutions to them elsewhere.

Shopkeepers were very disturbed by the precariousness of their
position, however, despite their own inability to help themselves,
either by regulating the numbers of new entrants or by changing
their methods to come to terms with the problems of book-keeping
and consumer credit. Their own misfortunes united them in their

---

[33] 'Speriamo bene', *L'Esercente*, 1 January 1890.
[34] 'I piccoli esercenti', ibid., 9 October 1887.
[35] 'Respingiamo i rimproveri del signor Antoniotti', ibid., 8 April 1888. This is
remarkable when one considers the well-documented anti-Semitic attitudes of the
shopkeeper movement in other European cities. See, for example, Nord, *Paris
shopkeepers*, pp. 372–92.

distrust of other types of petty commerce. The fact that some of the advantages attributed to these forms of competition derived from their legal situation intensified shopkeeper hostility towards both the competitors themselves and the political classes who appeared to sanction this. This created a significant opportunity for the *esercenti* associations to strengthen their position by demonstrating their utility in campaigning against these 'privileges'. It was much easier to unite shopkeepers against a common external enemy than to persuade them to abandon the *regali natalizi* or *il fido*.

Street pedlars, private clubs, bankrupts selling off stock and consumer cooperatives, all enjoyed certain forms of tax exemption which the small shopkeeper did not. These could be abolished only by parliamentary legislation, enabling the *esercenti* movement to preach about the importance of large-scale shopkeeper associations which could make their voice heard in legislative circles. During the depression the protests about these privileges became much louder as parliamentary commissions and enquiries failed to lead to any action. *L'Esercente* reflected the gloom-laden mood of the times when it wrote that 'the government studies and the *esercente* dies'.[36]

Street traders had none of the overheads that came with running a shop and were able to avoid many of the taxes that fell on shop proprietors. They were able to avoid paying any form of *dazio* in the *esterno*, as they could not be registered to pay by *abbonamento*.[37] Shopkeepers also resented pedlars who sold cheap merchandise of poor quality, aware that the hygiene authorities would never catch them. Such low prices might prove too great a temptation for the poorer members of the small trader's clientele, especially those who were building up a debt on their *libretto*. Leaving their accounts unpaid, they attempted to subsist on the goods they could buy for cash from the *venditori*, parting the *esercente* from a customer, and, possibly, from the likelihood of ever recouping the accumulated debt.[38]

---

[36] 'Disagio economico', *L'Esercente*, 26 April 1891.

[37] The only time they could be held liable for the tax was when they took a stall at a fair, but this was not subject to the *tassa esercizio e rivendita*, a tax from which *venditori ambulanti* were exempt unless they spent more than a month in the same *comune*, a regulation which must have been difficult to administer. Comaron, 'I venditori ambulanti nei comuni aperti', *L'Esercente*, 5 August 1894; Decastro, *La tassa di esercizio e rivendita*, p. 15.

[38] 'Venditori ambulanti', *L'Esercente*, 27 May 1888; 'Il commercio ambulante', ibid., 24 December 1891; 'La concorrenza dei girovaghi agli esercenti', ibid., 11 February 1892.

Conflicts between street traders and shopkeepers pre-dated the depression. In 1887 *L'Esercente* described the wooden benches which vendors set up around Porta Ticinese and Porta Tenaglia as 'indecent' relics of a bygone era, although they were still the outlets most favoured by working-class shoppers. Was it fair that a retailer who had invested a not insignificant amount of capital into setting up an unobtrusive shop should be damaged by competition with those who only paid attention to their own interests and practised their trade between four badly connected tables in a poor state of repair, the paper asked?[39] *L'Esercente*'s complaints were carefully phrased to appeal to that part of influential opinion which was concerned with the 'respectability' of the city, and when the municipal authorities cleared the vendors away *L'Esercente* was swift to offer its congratulations.[40]

The Comune was not always responsive to these demands, however, arguing that street trading provided a lifeline for many country dwellers, such as those who sold their plucked chickens in the town. *L'Esercente*'s reaction to the authorities' rejection of a petition complaining about this trade that was presented to them by the poulterers of Porta Venezia in 1892 encapsulates the general feeling that shopkeeper interests were being ignored by the authorities.

That the Municipal Authorities should then act from sentimentalism seems too much to us. In essence it is a question of right. One pays for the stalls, the commercial taxes, the shop rents, in order to have the means to trade, and therefore the Comune that demands these is obliged to protect the interests of the taxpayer.[41]

The private clubs, the *circoli*, caused concern to the proprietors of *esercizi pubblici*. The *circoli* were for members only and had to pay the *dazio* on any food or drink they served, but they possessed significant advantages in terms of opening hours. Also they were not subject to the *ricchezza mobile* tax. Complaints about the *circoli* became much more frequent in the 1890s.[42]

[39] 'Pizzicagnoli e salumieri ambulanti', ibid., 11 February 1887.
[40] 'Baracche da salumiere', ibid., 11 March 1887.
[41] 'I ripetuti reclami dei pollivendoli di Porta Venezia', ibid., 3 October 1892.
[42] In 1895 the Società Generale fra i Negozianti e gli Industriali di Roma sent a petition to the Ministry of Agriculture and Commerce, requesting that a special tax be levied on the food and drink served in such *circoli*, a sentiment endorsed by the national association, the Confederazione Generale fra Industriali, Commercianti ed Esercenti, to which the Milanese Federation belonged (the growth of the

The *negozi di liquidazione* which opened for very short intervals were particularly resented by the *esercenti*. These were the medium through which traders who had taken the care to go bankrupt with all their books in perfect order sold off their stock to raise the money to pay off the often paltry obligations they contracted with their creditors during the *moratoria*. Traders were then able to slash their prices, as much tax legislation did not consider this form of activity. A swift turnover permitted them a substantial profit before terminating their activities.

Frequently these shops were not run by bankrupt traders themselves, but by intermediaries who bought up bankrupt stock, opened up in an abandoned shop and sold off the goods for a quick profit, often by public auction. The public were attracted in by men blowing trumpets in the street outside beforehand. By keeping on the move the proprietors of these bazaars or rag shops were able to escape a wide range of taxes which applied to other traders, notably those based on assets and income. Local shopkeepers complained bitterly of losing their trade to this *commercio girovago*.

Their protests were so intense that the Ministry of Agriculture, Industry and Commerce wrote to the Chambers of Commerce in 1894 to request further information on the extent of the problem and what strategies might be adopted.[43] Some Chambers of Commerce suggested a wide range of measures designed to ensure that these operations could no longer escape the attentions of the tax authorities.[44] The Milan Chamber of Commerce, however, stated

national business movement will be examined in chapter 8). 'L'agitazione degli esercenti contro i privilegi goduti dalle Cooperative di Consumo. Il V Congresso Commerciale Italiano a Venezia', *L'Esercente*, 13 October 1895.

[43] In an attempt to counter this problem the government had already given the Chambers of Commerce the power to impose special taxes on these sorts of traders, and in 1887 this had been strengthened to make such temporary establishments liable to the same Camera di Commercio taxes as the *esercenti* themselves. *Archivio della Camera di Commercio di Milano* (hereafter ACC), scat.73, Ministero di Agricoltura, Industria e Commercio, Sotto-segretariato di Stato Div. III Industria e Commercio, Sez. F, No. di protocollo 12447 della posizione XVIII.105, Oggetto: Norme per discplinare il commercio temporaneo, Rome, 1 September 1894.

[44] *L'Esercente* was sure that the first requirement was that the Municipio should only grant licences to trade to those who could produce a proof that they had already paid the Chamber of Commerce subscription. The Siena Chamber of Commerce replied that the answer was that these establishments should have to be notified to the Chamber of Commerce, the Commercial Court, the Weights and Measures tax authorities and the *tassa esercizio e rivendita* authorities and that special measures should be taken in order to ascertain the income of such operations and their

that, in its opinion, the bazaars, rag shops and so forth did no significant damage to the shopkeeper, and that there was no need to restrict their numbers. This was not another example of the Chamber of Commerce failing to represent the shopkeepers, who were now well represented in the institution; rather it was a reasoned response in the light of much hysteria elsewhere.[45] Street traders were not a true threat to the *esercenti*, something that *L'Esercente* admitted on occasion and on which the Ministry itself was clear.[46] Nor were the private clubs or the *negozi di liquidazione*.

Instead the campaigns against these insignificant competitors must be seen in the context of the *esercenti* response to the depression. Small traders were unable to alter their increasingly archaic methods and suffered from overfragmentation within their markets. Despite the excessive number of enterprises in the sector, however, new entrants continued to be tolerated, reflecting the non-native status of most city proprietors. The *esercenti* associations were able to offer some practical assistance during the crisis. However, the chief result of the depression was that shopkeeper resentments could be directed towards outside agencies, such as the government, that sanctioned privileges in the first place. Opposing these privileges necessitated greater shopkeeper participation in the political process, imparting greater momentum to the *esercenti* movement. The battle between the *esercenti* and the consumer cooperatives, which will be examined in the next chapter, bore this out.

liability for the *ricchezza mobile* tax. To this *L'Esercente* wanted to add provisions for the confiscation of goods and the levying of heavy fines in cases of infringement, plus some kind of restriction on street sellers as well. Poggero, 'Le giuste proteste degli esercenti contro il commercio girovago', *L'Esercente*, 31 January 1895; 'Ancora del commercio girovago', ibid., 25 November 1894.

[45] This was at a time when the *esercenti*-backed *circoli degli interessi* ..., including Federation representatives, held all the seats on the Chamber Committee. They added that a direct tax on such *esercizi* might be reasonable but it would be almost impossible to implement such a measure. ACC, scatt. 73, Camera di Commercio di Milano, Lettera No. 4375, Milan, 9 November 1894.

[46] 'I danni che arreca il commercio girovago', *L'Esercente*, 1 March 1896.

7. Shopkeepers, cooperatives and the politics of privilege

It was rare for an issue of *L'Esercente* not to contain an attack on the consumer cooperatives during the late 1880s and 1890s. These articles always complained about the tax concessions granted to the cooperatives, but a good deal of the resentment may be ascribed to the general regard in which shopkeepers held their competitors in this period. In fact the most successful cooperatives did not enjoy the privileges which the shopkeeper movement protested against so strongly. None the less the issue played a crucial role in realigning shopkeeper sympathies, a political shift resulting from a more developed perception of the *esercente*'s status in society. This chapter will examine first the nature of the privileges enjoyed by the consumer cooperatives and their influence on the competition between these institutions and the shopkeepers, before analysing the *esercenti* movement's campaign against these privileges and its influence on shopkeeper politics.

CONSUMER COOPERATIVES: PRIVILEGED COMPETITORS?

Most of the early consumer cooperatives were set up to benefit specific groups of workers, usually artisans and they often functioned under the auspices of friendly societies (Società di Mutuo Soccorso).[1] They cut out the *esercente* by buying in bulk and then distributing goods amongst the membership at prices which did not

---

[1] In 1865 the Magazzino Cooperativo dei Probi Pionieri (honest pioneers), later known as the Magazzino Cooperativo dell'Associazione Generale di Mutuo Soccorso degli Operai [workers] di Milano e Corpi Santi was founded in Milan; the following year the ribbon makers and garment workers set up their own cooperatives as well. Della Peruta, 'La società lombarda e la cooperazione', p. 13.

include the profit component charged in ordinary shops. The Socialists shunned these early cooperatives, believing that economic amelioration would obscure for longer the class contradictions that would eventually bring about the collapse of capitalism. The elite classes, however, welcomed the movement for precisely this reason. Liberals believed that cooperatives could help in the construction of a more integrated society whilst conservatives saw them as a means for furthering paternalism, and thus exerting 'social control'.[2]

This political consensus led to the concession of two tax privileges to the consumer cooperatives in the early 1870s. Smaller cooperatives were exempted from various stamp duties by the *leggi del 13 settembre 1874 nn.2076 e 2077* whilst Article 5, *Allegato L* of the *legge dell'11 agosto 1870, n.5784* which dealt with the *dazio consumo* stated that in the *comuni aperti*: 'Cooperative societies are not required to pay the *dazio* on goods which they supply and distribute amongst members for solely charitable ends, and which are consumed at the houses of those to whom the distribution is made'.[3]

L'Esercente later claimed that this exemption, by far the most important of the two, was introduced to rectify the fact that, in the countryside, the wealthy bought their wine wholesale and thus paid no duty on it, whereas the poor had to pay the *dazio* on their retail purchases. The predominantly rural nature of Italian society, and, at this stage, the cooperative movement, had led the legislators to forget the existence of the *frazioni aperte* in the cities.[4]

The battle against the first worker consumer cooperatives was already won by the later 1880s. With the onset of the depression, however, new working-class cooperatives appeared (see Tables 7.1 and 7.2). Generally speaking, these began promisingly and then faded away for lack of interest amongst members. Examples are the Sole Nascente and La Fontana consumer cooperatives.[5] Some, by no means all, of these cooperatives formed part of a political movement involved in the struggle for workers' emancipation. They

---

[2] Bonfante, 'La legislazione cooperativistica', pp. 191–4.
[3] Art.5, Legge 11 agosto 1870 n. 5784, Allegato L.
[4] 'Si domanda l'abrogazione dell'articolo 5 legge 1870', *L'Esercente*, 30 September 1894.
[5] The Sole Nascente (Rising Sun), founded in 1891, was stated to have 120 members in 1894, but by 1896 only fifty were turning up at meetings and the organisation folded in 1897. The same year saw the dissolution of the *La Fontana* cooperative (The Fountain) which had begun with seventy members in 1893, falling to fifty-three in 1896, and whose final demise was ascribed to lack of customers. For information on these cooperatives see ASM, fond Questura, f. 107, c. 18.6, c. 18.13.

Table 7.1. *Consumer cooperatives in Milan, 1885–1905*

Name	1885	1886	1887	1888	1889	1890	1891	1892	1893	1894	1895	1896	1897	1898	1899	1900	1901	1902	1903	1904	1905	
Suburbana	2	2	2	2	2	2	2	2	4	5	5	5	5	5	5	5	5	5	5	5	6	i
Impiegati e Professionisti	x	x	x	x	x	x	2	3	5	5	5	5	5	6	8	8	6	6	6	6	6	i
Ferroviaria	x	x	x	x	x	x	x	2	2	x	x	x	x	x	x	x	x	x	x	x	x	i
Corale	x	x	x	x	x																	?
Unione Cooperativa	x	x	x	x	x	2	3	3	5	6	22	26	28	28	28	28	28	28	28	28		i
Milanese				2	3	2														28		?
Magazzino Beneficio																						o
Figli di Lavoro					x	x	x	x	x	x	x	x										o
Sole Nascente						x	x	x	x	x	x	x										o
Figli del Progresso								x	x													o
Unione Militare								x					x	x								i
Combustibili									x	x	x	x	x	x	x							i
La Fontana										x	x	x	x	x	x	x	x	x	x	x		o
La Stella									x	x	x	2				(to Unione Cooperativa)						o
Porta Volta									x			x										o
Operai d'Arte e Mestiere									x													o
Leonardo da Vinci											x	x										?
Maddalena													x	x	x	x						?
Stabilimento Pirelli													x	x		x	x	x	x	x	x	o
Stabilimento Gadda																	x	x	x	x	x	o
Alle Rottole																		x	x	x	x	?
Operaia																	x	x	x			o
Ambrosiana																			x	x	3	c
Stabilimenti Erba																				x	x	o

Note: The numbers given represent the number of branches (including the principal store). The letters indicate the typical customer, o = worker, i = white-collar, c = catholic, ? = not certain.

Sources: *Guide di Milano*, publ. Savallo; Sabbatini, *Notizie sulle condizioni industriali*; ASM, fond Questura, c. 107 f. 18. Mellini, *Storia dell'Unione Cooperativa*; *Storia e sviluppo della Cooperativa Ferroviaria Suburbana 1881–1905*; Società Anonima Cooperativa di Consumo fra Impiegati e Professionisti, *Cenni Storico-statistici e statuto*; *Numero Unico della Società Anonima Cooperativa di Consumo fra Gli Addetti allo Stabilimento Pirelli e C.* The sources for this work are far from ideal, particularly the *Guide* which are not available for some years, and are not always accurate (although Savallo were keen supporters of the cooperative movement and likely to have been notified of most cooperative activity in the city).

Table 7.2. *Other cooperatives competing with the esercenti of Milan, 1885–1905*

Name	1885	1886	1887	1888	1889	1890	1891	1892	1893	1894	1895	1896	1897	1898	1899	1900	1901	1902	1903	1904	1905
Esercizi pubblici																					
Caffè-Ristorante		x	x			x	x	x	x	x	x	x	x	x	x	x	x	x	x	3	3
Cantina						x	x	2	2	3	6	6	6	6	6	6	6	7	7	7	7
Vinicola						x	x	x													
Osteria di Porta Venezia									x	x	x	x	x	x							
Trattoria Operai (stab. Bocconi e Rovatti)						x															
Osteria di Porta Volta													x	x							
Osteria Risveglio														x							
Ristorante per gli Operai														x							
Bakeries																					
Fabbricazione e Consumo di Pane			x																		
Panificio			x		x																
Panificio Operaio																					x
Pharmacies																					
Farmaceutica						x	x	2	2	2	2	2	3	3	3	3	3	4	4	5	5
Chimico Farmaceutica						x	x	x	x	x											
Farmaceutica Italiana																		x	x	x	x

Note: The numbers given represent the number of branches (including the principal store).

Sources: Guide di Milano, publ. Savallo; Sabattini, *Notizie sulle condizioni industriali;* ASM, fond. Questura, c. 107 f. 18.

became close to the Socialists who, under the influence of the reformist tendency, finally came to accept the legitimacy of certain forms of worker cooperative. Often these cooperatives were essentially political discussion groups with cooperatives attached, like the Figli del Progresso which combined a discussion group with a consumer cooperative selling basic provisions.[6]

Most of the early *esercenti* complaints against cooperative privileges were directed against the *dazio consumo* exemption under Article 5, for which these 'charitable' working-class consumer cooperatives qualified. Again, geography played its part in this. It was only in the *esterno* that cooperatives qualified for the exemption, and the suburbs were also the centre of the *esercenti* movement, many of whose members also catered to the 'needy' members of society who were the intended beneficiaries of the legislation.

Shopkeepers refused to accept that these cooperatives fulfilled a charitable purpose: *L'Esercente* was full of reports of societies which stocked luxury goods intended for well-off members who had been instrumental in setting up these 'charitable' organisations, rather than for the poor. This prevented small traders counterattacking by increasing their charges for 'luxury' items in order to subsidise the prices of their basic merchandise. The regulations governing the exemption were unenforceable: how could one check up if the goods bought were really consumed at the member's house? It was easy for a member to purchase goods for a non-member to consume, and as the individual member, rather than the society, was held responsible for such misdemeanours the cooperatives had no incentive to enforce the restrictions.[7]

The *esercenti* movement claimed that shopkeepers in competition with a cooperative were frequently paying a *dazio abbonamento* and a *ricchezza mobile* contribution, both of which were calculated on turnover before the cooperative set up in the vicinity. By virtue of the lower prices they were able to charge, cooperatives attracted customers without having to resort to the expense of marketing activities such as decorating their windows. Given the abject conditions of the *esterno* during the depression, it was only to be

---

[6] This folded in 1893 when the membership proved unable to meet the cooperative's liabilities, which were probably incurred as a result of the cooperative's habit of granting a credit of L. 5 to all its members, and L. 15 to any who were up-to-date with their accounts. The only record of this cooperative is in ASM, fond. Questura, f. 107, c. 18.11.

[7] See 'Cooperative che vendono ai non soci', *L'Esercente*, 7 January 1894.

expected that customers would purchase goods at the lowest price obtainable. The only fair thing to do would be to abolish all the privileges and let the cooperatives and retailers compete freely against each other.[8]

Fear of the cooperatives was as much social as economic. 'Cooperators', to use the word commonly employed to describe those involved in the movement, claimed that their institutions were necessary to protect the disadvantaged from *esercenti* dishonesty. Shopkeepers, they alleged, adulterated their goods, cheated their customers by using false weights and measures, and persistently overcharged for their merchandise. Conversely, members of consumer cooperatives paid reasonable prices for goods whose quality and quantity were always clearly indicated. Not only that; all goods were sold at the *prezzo fisso*, eliminating the natural suspicions that arose from bargaining for purchases.[9]

Shopkeepers were very sensitive to these insinuations. Their self-assumed position as spokesmen of the neighbourhood was already under threat from the franchise extension and the tensions over *il fido* and the *regali natalizi* caused by the depression. The seriousness with which *L'Esercente* viewed these attacks can be gauged from its own strictures to those *esercenti* who did not sell by *prezzo fisso*, primarily haberdashers and vendors of artisan goods. 'it is evident', wrote the journal, 'that a good proportion of consumers accept the cooperative principle, more to avoid the danger of being cheated ... in the shops, than because of a profound belief that they are saving, or, at the least, buying at cost price.'[10]

In the battle between shopkeepers and cooperatives for the minds of the workers, the *esercenti* emphasised the social and economic mobility that existed between their 'class' and that below it, and the effects on this were the cooperatives to triumph. Members of the lower classes had always been able to aspire to setting up their own small businesses, they argued, but should the cooperatives succeed then this form of upward mobility would cease and workers would be condemned to remain such all their lives. Furthermore many

[8] The shopkeeper movement's objections to the cooperatives were reiterated many times. Some of the best summaries of these may be found in the speeches made during the Federation's anti-cooperative propaganda drive in 1891, reprinted in the following issues of *L'Esercente*, 21 May, 28 May, 31 May, 7 June, 14 June 1891.

[9] See, for example, Società Anonima Cooperativa di Consumo fra Impiegati e Professionisti, *Cenni storico-statistico*, pp. 43–4.

[10] 'Qualche torto degli esercenti', *L'Esercente*, 8 June 1890.

would be unemployed as the cooperatives were far less labour intensive than the numerous small shops whose trade they would usurp.
Even those who were hired by the cooperatives would have no
chance of eventually taking over the business, unlike the assistants
trained in the *botteghe*. Therefore workers should think carefully
before taking advantage of the lower prices that the cooperatives
were able to offer because of the tax privileges they enjoyed.[11]

It seems unlikely that any of these considerations carried any
great weight with the lower-class customers of the day, just as it is to
be doubted that many were attracted to the cooperatives because of
their attempts to change society through the elimination of the
middleman. Shoppers patronised the stores that were most convenient for them. In this respect, *il fido*, though frequently an
important contributor in individual bankruptcies, proved to be the
sector's salvation.

Most working-class cooperatives did not grant *il fido* because they
wanted to make their members more responsible about their money.
In an attempt to fulfil their didactic role, the cooperatives argued
that to get into debt was irresponsible, if not wicked. Cooperatives
could not change the patterns of family life, however. Women, who
formed the most important part of any retailer's clientele, needed to
be able to defer payment until they received their weekly housekeep-
ing money from their partners. Whilst the depression intensified the
risks for shopkeepers who granted credit, it also made the demand
for it even greater, and proved the most effective way to retain
custom.

In compensation for the absence of consumer credit, the cooperatives tried to recruit members through low pricing. They sold their
goods at cost price, or as near as possible to this, rather than adopt
the 'English' system, of paying their members a dividend at the end
of a trading period.[12] Selling at cost enabled the cooperatives to
make the most of their price advantage over shopkeepers, par-

---

[11] See 'L'agitazione contro i privilegi goduti dalle cooperative e la Federazione di
Milano', *L'Esercente*, 21 May 1891.
[12] The 'English system' was so-called because it was first employed by the Rochdale
Pioneers. Data collected for the Ministry of Agriculture and Commerce in 1889
showed that of 153 consumer cooperatives, 137 sold at cost price, whilst of 120
stores for which information was available only fifty-four granted any form of
credit (and most of these were associated with railway employees). Data collected
for the Ministry of Agriculture and Commerce in March 1889. Reproduced in
Briganti, ed., *Il movimento cooperativo*, p. 154.

ticularly in the *esterno* where the exemption applied, but unless they were extremely skilled at administration the cooperatives cut too deeply into their margins, prejudicing their existence. Administration became even more difficult in those cases where credit was provided. Few of these operations were blessed with able directors capable of managing such precarious enterprises, with the consequence that most working-class cooperatives were short-lived and unsuccessful.[13] As early as 1892, a leading member of the Federation acknowledged that working-class consumer cooperatives posed little real threat to the shopkeeper, although this admission was soon lost amongst a further flurry of attacks on Article 5.[14]

Apart from the factory-based cooperatives set up around the turn of the century, the working-class consumer cooperatives set up during the 1890s failed to establish themselves securely. This was also true of most of the other forms of cooperative which posed a threat to the *esercenti*: those based on the *esercizi pubblici*, the bakeries and the pharmacies (see Table 7.2). It was the white-collar consumer cooperatives that catered to the clerks and supervisors (*impiegati*) such as the Cooperativa Ferroviaria Suburbana and the Unione Cooperativa which experienced most success in Milan in during the late 1880s and 1890s.

The Suburbana was the only white-collar cooperative which could realistically be said to enjoy privileges that were unavailable to the *esercenti*. It was a 'closed' cooperative whose members were all drawn from the ranks of suburban railway employees.[15] In accordance with its practice throughout Italy, the railway administration provided the cooperative with rent-free space for its shops and offices on railway premises, and granted it a 5% discount on freight charges for its food goods. The administration also gave the cooperative an initial loan, and placed a contract with it for over a thousand items of clothing a month.[16]

The Suburbana also claimed that it qualified for the *dazio* exemption. The city authorities contested this, arguing that cooperatives' members were not in need of charity. In 1885, after five years of

[13] Rota, *Ragioneria delle cooperative di consumo*, p. 11–13.
[14] Marmont, 'La ricchezza mobile sugli utili delle cooperative', *L'Esercente* 22 December 1892.
[15] For the history of the Cooperativa Suburbana see Società Anonima Cooperative Suburbana di Consumo, *Cenni storici e statistici*; Società Anonima Cooperativa Suburbana di Consumo, *Storia e sviluppo*.
[16] Degl'Innocenti, 'La cooperazione lombarda', p. 30.

court struggles, the Municipio won its case, but decided to negotiate a *dazio canone* with the cooperative which was significantly below what might have been expected had the organisation been treated in the same way as a similarly sized private retailer.[17]

The assistance afforded the Suburbana by both the railway and city administrations was unique. Both sets of privilege were hotly contested by the *esercenti*, who interpreted them as another indication of the lack of concern for shopkeepers amongst local and national government. The railway company was state-owned, yet the people, as owners, had certainly not been consulted about these concessions. Indeed, one section of the public, shopkeepers, had been seriously harmed by it.[18] One of the most important factors in the success of the Suburbana, however, was its ability to offer a limited amount of consumer credit to its members, arising from the facility with which defaulters could be traced within the company.[19]

The rest of the white-collar consumer cooperatives received no special legal privileges, yet still managed to establish themselves amongst their chosen clientele. The most successful of all was the Unione Cooperativa, established in 1886 by the Associazione Generale fra gl'Impiegati Civili di Milano, the general white-collar organisation in the city. Luigi Buffoli, its director, started the cooperative as an English-style operation trading in clothing. In 1886 the Unione was a one-room operation with 134 members and L. 1712 of subscribed capital. Four years later the cooperative employed 400 persons, had 3,412 members and was capitalised at L. 694,125.[20] During the 1890s branches opened all over Milan, transforming the Unione into the most important retail operation in the city.

The white-collar cooperatives were successful because they

---

[17] In 1880 the Municipio demanded L. 12,000 from the cooperative. The agreement reached in 1885 was for L. 3,000 p.a. Società Anonima Cooperativa Suburbana, *Storia e sviluppo*, p. 14.

[18] 'I privilegi delle cooperative', *L'Esercente*, 27 July 1890.

[19] This was the case with railway cooperatives throughout Italy. Briganti notes that railway cooperatives featured prominently amongst those cooperatives prepared to grant credit to their members in 1889 as the risks were not as great for these societies. In Milan members were given *buoni fiduciari* (credit notes) for up to L. 100 to spend in the cooperative's stores. Briganti, ed., *Il movimento cooperativo*, p. 154. Degl'Innocenti, 'La cooperazione lombarda', p. 31.

[20] For more information on Unione Cooperativa see Buffoli, *Lo sviluppo della cooperazione in Europa*; Caroleo, 'L'Unione Cooperativa di Luigi Buffoli'; Mellini, *Storia dell'Unione Cooperativa*.

responded more exactly to the needs of their clientele than did their working-class equivalents. The salaried lower middle classes were better able to appreciate the long-term savings that the 'English' system offered, not least because their relative security made it possible for them to plan this far in advance. From the cooperatives' point of view, it locked members into the system, and made administration and planning considerably easier, as did the fact that these salaried workers were better able to pay by cash. Along with the dividend system, the Unione's practices of selling to members and non-members alike and of opening membership to applicants from all backgrounds were gradually adopted by most of the other white-collar cooperatives in the city.

Significantly these cooperatives were most successful in those sectors where the *esercenti* were weakest, notably clothing. Much of their advantage came from more sophisticated sales techniques. Haberdashers displayed their goods in the window of the shop, so when customers entered they were forced to go straight to the counter and commence bargaining for the items they wished to purchase. In the Unione and other large cooperatives, merchandise was displayed throughout the store, and customers were allowed to stroll through the departments examining the goods and their prices without coming under pressure to buy from the assistants. As a result clients were more inclined to enter the store and make purchases on impulse.

These techniques were also familiar in the private department stores which some of the larger cooperatives closely resembled. Another stratagem, that of producing one's own goods or, failing this, buying direct from the producer rather than the wholesaler, was also copied from the department stores, and again served to lower the final price of the product. Both the Unione and the Suburbana had their own garment-making workshops, and the Unione moved into other areas such as upholstery and shoemaking.[21] These advanced capitalist techniques were consistent with cooperation because, as the Cooperativa di Consumo fra Impiegati e Professionisti explained, 'the highest purpose of cooperation ... is always that of moving as close as possible to direct production in

---

[21] The Impiegati e Professionisti began doing this with food products in 1889. Società Anonima Cooperativa di Consumo fra Impiegati e Professionisti, *Cenni storico-statistico*, p. 37.

order to offer better goods for consumption at a lower price'.[22] It was competitive advantage, rather than cooperative ideology, that accounted for these institutions' success.

This advantage did not derive from any special privilege, however. Shopkeeper associations frequently drew attention to the fact that cooperatives only paid their *ricchezza mobile* tax on the amount of profit declared in their published accounts, whilst the *esercenti* had to pay a sum determined by tax inspectors on the basis of the shop's expected performance during the following year. This meant that the cooperatives only ever paid the tax when they made a profit whilst the *esercenti*, having paid in advance, might, in fact, record a loss. It was difficult to regard this difference in procedure as a privilege, however; all public companies were assessed for *ricchezza mobile* in the same way, whilst the generally lax book-keeping methods used by the *esercenti* made it impossible for a similar method of assessment to be adopted in their case.[23]

The shopkeeper movement sought to impress the likely consequences of their support of these cooperatives upon the *impiegati* (the same tactic it adopted in resisting the working-class cooperatives).

What will become of our Milan and of the other cities when the *esercenti* have been suppressed? What will the landlords think when the large profit they derive from all the shops is taken from them? What will become of the beautiful city streets when all the shops, instead of presenting a splendid variety, a permanent exhibition of domestic and foreign commerce, will be closed as at a time of an epidemic and our beautiful evenings will not be gladdened by the thousands of lights which sparkle onto our roads today![24]

According to *L'Esercente* this would lead to a decline in the city's status and the major institutions which provided the clerks with their employment would hasten to leave the city.

The cooperators, however, argued that their institutions acted as a necessary brake on *esercenti* abuses, keeping prices down to an

---

[22] Ibid., p. 37.

[23] The shopkeepers' arguments are well set out in the *istanza* they presented to the Camera di Commercio in 1891. The government's rejection of this position delivered, ironically, by Colombo, appeared in *L'Esercente* two weeks later.

[24] Speech of L. Baroni reported in 'La Federazione degli Esercenti di Milano e la guerra contro le cooperative di consumo: la quarta riunione a Porta Genova', *L'Esercente*, 31 May 1891.

acceptable level. The official history of the Suburbana claimed the institution was founded 'to put a check on the boundless demands of the *esercenti* and set up a control on the prices of goods, prices which, because of their continual rise, were excessively burdening the already meagre budgets of the clerks in the railway service'.[25]

This infuriated the *esercenti*, who contrasted the security of an *impiegato*'s existence with the precariousness of their own. They were especially hostile to government clerks, as, under a law passed in 1864, a fifth of the salary of some state employees was paid directly into cooperative credit institutions nominated by the employee. These then granted him credit facilities at a much lower rate than those pertaining elsewhere. Because this portion of his salary was never in his hands it was impossible for the *impiegato*'s creditors to lay claim to it. The provision was particularly disliked in Rome, where most of those entitled to protection under the scheme were in residence. In 1892, however, the Unione Militare, one of the chief beneficiaries of state schemes of this sort, opened a branch in Milan, adding further spice to the local arguments.

The success of the white-collar consumer cooperatives further emphasised the need for a reassessment of the shopkeepers' social and political identity. Despite the shopkeepers' pleas, the *impiegati* patronised the cooperatives, allegedly at the expense of the *esercenti*. Meanwhile, according to *L'Esercente*, many of the government clerks were involved in the Socialist movement, even though the party stood for the overthrow of the state that provided its employees with such security.

The *esercenti* movement was unable to pinpoint any legal privileges that it could claim to be at the root of the white-collar cooperatives' success, because, with the exception of the concessions granted to the Suburbana, no real privileges existed. Instead the cooperatives sought to establish them, thus keeping the debate alive. Those that used the dividend system maintained that it was unjust that they paid the *ricchezza mobile* tax on their earnings, as these were actually savings which were restored to their owners through the dividend payment at the end of the year. From 1892 onwards all the Milanese cooperatives operating the 'English' system withheld the money demanded by the taxation authorities and supported legal actions bought by the Suburbana and the Unione to clarify the

---

[25] Società Anonima Cooperativa Suburbana di Consumo, *Cenni storici e statistici*, p. 11.

position. In 1895, the Court of Appeal ruled against them, arguing that as the cooperatives did not sell at cost price, they were still trying to make money in the same way as any other public company.[26] The defeat was a setback for the cooperatives, and in paying back the tax, several got themselves into financial difficulties.[27]

The *esercenti* movement likewise found the ruling problematic. The three-year campaign had enabled them to brand those white-collar cooperatives operating in the *interno* as unfair competitors, sheltering behind privileges, at the time when the movement was desperate for scapegoats on which to blame the depression. Now, however, it was impossible to argue that these cooperatives benefited from any legal privileges, as the shopkeeper organisations occasionally admitted.[28] From then on the *esercenti* movement was forced into more general accusations about the 'speculative' nature of the white-collar cooperatives and attempts to slur them by association with other, advantaged, cooperatives.

By 1895, though, the shopkeepers' fears of the white-collar cooperatives were gradually diminishing. Ironically this was because the two had now joined battle for the key market of working-class consumers of food and drink. In the 1890s the white-collar cooperatives, particularly the Unione Cooperativa, tried to reach the lower classes by expanding their food operations. The Unione opened its first food sections in 1891, and in 1895 it acquired the ovens of the defunct Massaia bakery, along with its sixteen outlets in the city.[29] It now had both the product and the distribution network with which to penetrate the working-class market, but failed to do so, even when, at the height of the grain crisis in 1898, it sold bread at 5 *centesimi* below the average price. The intent of the Unione was to 'help the less well-off classes and, at the same time, educate them in the moral system of buying with ready cash'.[30] The problem was that the lower classes did not want to be educated.

This was the cooperative movement's dilemma. Lower-class custom could only be won by granting *il fido* and selling at the

26 Società Anonima Cooperativa di Consumo fra Impiegati e Professionisti, *Cenni storico-statistico*, pp. 23–4.
27 Ibid. See also Società Anonima Cooperativa Suburbana di Consumo, *Cenni storici e statistici*, pp. 15–17.
28 'I cooperatori a congresso', *L'Esercente*, 27 October 1895.
29 See the accounts of Unione Cooperativa's activities during each financial year given in Mellini, *Storia dell'Unione Cooperativa*, especially pp. 21–46 (1890–6).
30 Ibid., p. 57.

lowest price possible. This would not have encouraged good habits amongst the membership, nor was it a sound basis for running a commercial enterprise. The Unione did not even necessarily stock the cheapest goods available, as shoppers had to learn the importance of quality over price. Buffoli repeatedly cited the old proverb 'he who spends more, spends less'.[31]

Small traders gradually realised that the refusal of the white-collar cooperatives to grant *il fido* and their stress on the quality of their products rendered them ineffective when competing for the crucial lower-class markets. In 1890, *L'Esercente* had been so panicked as to recommend that shopkeepers would have to unite into quasi-cooperatives themselves and even adopt some form of dividend payment.[32] By 1894, however, the newspaper was arguing that:

> There could be competition between a Bocconi establishment (department store) and the Unione, given the large size of both and their need to compete with each other, but Milanese commerce really has nothing at all to fear or be envious of. In a large number of shops one can make much better purchases, and at prices a good deal lower than those quoted by the *Unione*.[33]

Indeed, during the mid 1890s the cooperatives reported slower growth because of the increased competition from the *esercenti*.[34]

THE *ESERCENTI* MOVEMENT AND THE POLITICS OF PRIVILEGES

Consumer cooperatives, then, did not have the calamitous effect on petty commerce that the shopkeeper movement maintained. The power of the argument against the cooperatives was that it provided an explanation for the poor performance of the *esercenti* during the depression period, in the same way that the attacks on the pedlars, private clubs and *negozi di liquidazione* had done. The argument was rendered all the more forceful by the evident success of some of these cooperatives, notably those originally catering to white-collar

[31] Buffoli, *Lo sviluppo della cooperazione*, p. 27.
[32] 'Una cooperativa fra gli esercenti', *L'Esercente*, 11 May 1890; 'La cooperativa fra gli esercenti', ibid', 1 June 1890; 'Un giudizio sulle cooperative', ibid., 20 July 1890.
[33] 'La concorrenza alle cooperative', *L'Esercente*, 27 May 1894.
[34] Società Anonima Cooperativa di Consumo fra Impiegati e Professionisti, *Cenni storico-statistico*, p. 22.

workers such as Unione Cooperativa. The nature of their clientele
was important: it was not so much the suburban small traders who
were losing customers to the cooperatives as their peers from the
interno. By making the cooperatives the scapegoat for the depression, the *esercenti* movement was able to attract new members from
the city centre and work towards creating a shopkeeper identity
that bridged the *dazio* divide. In 1892, Berardo Marmont, a grocer,
became the first president of the Federation to hail from the
interno.

The movement emphasised that it was not the principle of
cooperation that it opposed, merely the privileges cooperatives
enjoyed. The campaign was not a call for regulation of competition
itself. This accorded with the shopkeepers' general disposition
towards unregulated trade, as demonstrated by their tolerance of
new entrants into the profession. The *esercenti* press was never
hostile towards the two Milanese department stores, Bocconi (the
precursor of 'La Rinascente') and Savonelli, even though these
shared many characteristics with the Unione Cooperativa. Ferdinando Bocconi, for instance, owed his prosperity to the lower-
middle-class customers who were allowed to browse unhindered
through the displays of ready-made clothing, checking the clearly
marked prices as they passed. These clothes were produced either
in Bocconi's own workshops or, like many other items sold in the
store, by artisans working in studios which the firm rented to
them.[35]

L'Esercente made light of the economies of scale enjoyed by the
big stores, arguing that the small trader also knew how to buy
wholesale, and that he might even have an advantage as his rent and
furnishing costs would be much lower, although it conceded that
only the shopkeeper with capital could exploit the advantages of
buying wholesale or direct from the producer. The paper ridiculed
the articles it reproduced from French journals denouncing department stores in the same terms as cooperatives, arguing that the
department stores were perfectly legitimate competitors, whom the
esercenti were happy to take on.[36]

[35] On Bocconi see Poggiali, *Ferdinando Bocconi*; Alfani, *Battaglie e vottorie*,
pp. 118–22; 'Una grande impresa industriale', *L'Illustrazione Italiana*, 4, 17
(1879), 270; Vaccari, 'Ferdinando Bocconi', pp. 270–8.
[36] 'I grandi magazzini e le cooperative', *L'Esercente*, 15 December 1892.

One article ended:

We desire equality of treatment. With every privilege abolished, petty commerce will willingly endeavour to struggle with the cooperatives, certain of beating them, private initiative, activity and intelligence being worth much more than any big bureau- cratic mechanism. As regards the department stores, no shop- keeper cares about them. They have existed for years and no shopkeeper has ever spent words on lamenting them. Rather they all aspire to expanding their own businesses and anyone would be extremely happy to succeed at it. Shopkeepers may envy the successful ones, but they would not cry injustice.[37]

Indeed Bocconi symbolised shopkeeper aspirations. Brought up in Lodi, in the Provincia, he came to Milan to run a market stall with his father and brother, graduated to a shop and, at the culmi- nation of a series of moves, arrived in the Piazza Duomo. It would have been difficult for Milanese shopkeepers to resent Bocconi when his early career so mirrored their own. Whilst consumer cooperatives were blamed for the nightmare of the depression, Bocconi's story provided a dream of salvation.

Privileges, then, not protection were to be the focus of the *eser- centi* campaign. This gave rise to the complication that the privileges enjoyed by the various forms of cooperative differed sharply, and in many cases were not particularly apparent. Article 5 was prominent in the campaign, as it was by far the clearest example of cooperative privilege, and also the easiest to attack. On the other hand none of the white-collar cooperatives benefited from this exemption. Indeed it was difficult to argue that these successful cooperatives had any privileges at all. The shopkeeper movement could only argue that the special concessions granted to the Suburbana and the cooper- atives' own refusal to pay the tax on their earnings between 1892 and 1895 amounted to unfair practices which appeared to have been sanctioned by government.

The achievement of the *esercenti* movement was to ensure that the debates on the privileges of working-class and white-collar cooper- atives were conducted in tandem. Most *esercenti* protests were worded in a way that minimised the differences between the various cooperatives and their situations, and stressed the woeful con- sequences for all small traders resulting from the unfair competition

[37] Ibid.

of the consumer cooperatives. This was an astute move; it made the much weaker case against white-collar cooperatives appear more plausible from the outside, and it also drew together two sets of shopkeepers whose *dazio* interests had so far divided them.

Furthermore any effective campaign against cooperative privileges had to be fought in the political arena, as the tax privileges against which the movement was protesting were determined at parliamentary level. This was a further benefit to the shopkeeper movement whose institutions were designed to speak with a collective voice. Both the Federation and *L'Esercente* argued that the campaign could only succeed by engendering a greater political consciousness amongst the shopkeepers that would best be expressed by adherence to the movement itself. Thus further concessions to the cooperatives were presented to the shopkeepers as an example of their weakness, whilst successes could be highlighted as demonstrations of the utility of association.

In 1890, for example, a provincial councillor, Moro, proposed that rural consumer cooperatives throughout the Provincia should be offered some form of financial assistance. Although this would have had little effect on shopkeepers in the city itself, *L'Esercente* launched into a tirade against the apathy of shopkeepers who failed to make their voices heard at election time, enabling this type of proposal to be passed.

What does this journal do every year at election time?

The answer is simple – It works with passion, with conviction, with heart, with faith, to protect the interests of the class it represents. – What does it achieve? – Little. – Why? – Because of the culpable indifference of the *esercenti* who, because of an inexplicable diffidence, or through mistaken regard and politeness for a special client, or because of absurd fears, or because they never, never ever, understand, that the ills complained of derive from their own carelessness, their extreme indifference, their lack of interest in anything that has to do with the public life of the country ...

At the next meeting of the Provincial Council we will see L. 50,000 voted for the setting up of consumer cooperatives, that is of institutions which intend destroying petty commerce.

No-one will oppose. Good Lord, fight progress, and the privileges and advantages of brotherhood! The only issue on which Moderates and Socialists find themselves in agreement. Freedom, gentlemen, complete freedom. The poor man has a right to cheap prices. The reactionaries agree with it – the stinking rich agree – naturally – there's nothing to lose. The Socialists have everything to gain. Who's paying? Commerce. Fine; long live privilege! The *esercenti* must disappear. The government knows it will ruin them, it has trapped them between two fires; between exorbitant taxes and the consumer cooperatives; but it's done well. When one is hungry doesn't one willingly and more easily, kill the kid which, like an ass, stays within rifle range? The *esercenti* provide good meat for the current appetite of the government, and since they've been standing with their hands in their pockets, it would have been a shame not to fleece them.[38]

The *esercenti* movement was well aware of the potential of the cooperative issue. In 1887 the Federation, prior even to its official relaunch, organised a petition to protest against the cooperatives' privileges. This proved a successful means of publicity, attracting around 3,000 signatories. It was noticeable, however, that the intensity of *esercenti* protests increased after 1890, the year in which Gerli was finally driven from office. The campaign against the *dazio* administrator had served to unite the suburban *esercenti*, capitalising on their increasingly politicised nature following the *micca* disturbances. Now the movement needed to broaden its appeal by offering a cause behind which all shopkeepers could unite, and which could be presented as relevant to their chief concern in the early 1890s, namely overcoming the effects of the depression.

The government's response to the petition, when it finally arrived, was extremely negative, virtually denying that such privileges existed.[39] This was indicative of the political consensus surrounding cooperation, now regarded not only as a method of social control but also as a potential vote winner amongst newly enfranchised electors. Most Democrats, who regarded these voters as their natural constituency, pronounced themselves friends of the cooperatives, as did a fair number of Moderates. The firmest supporter of the cooperatives was the Socialist party, founded in 1892 and courted by the Democratic bloc thereafter.

[38] 'Siate indolenti e perseverate!', *L'Esercente*, 17 April 1890.
[39] The government reply did not arrive until May 1888, after *L'Esercente* published an article suggesting that officials had used the petition for wrapping up slices of ham! 'La protesta degli esercenti per la disparità di trattamento: risposta del Ministero delle Finanze', *L'Esercente*, 19 February 1888; 'L'agitazione contro le cooperative: un po' di storia', ibid., 6 August 1891.

These developments created two major problems for the *esercenti*. Up until the franchise expansion they had claimed to be friends of the workers, to the workers themselves, and although there was no evidence to suggest that the workers recognised them as such there was likewise no way in which the lower classes could repudiate the claim. Now that some workers had the vote they were able to support their own political parties, notably the Socialists, whose opinion of the *esercenti* is best represented by *Critica Sociale*'s claim that: 'The grocer, the shopkeeper is an untrustworthy element by the very nature of his trade itself. His governing ideal is that of so much percent on sales.'[40]

Despite the failure of the worker cooperatives to woo trade away from the *esercenti*, many lower-class customers shared a similarly cynical view of the shopkeeper, as the relationship between patron and proprietor deteriorated during the depression years.

The further complication for the *esercenti* was that the other parties in the Democratic bloc increasingly favoured cooperatives in an attempt both to win worker votes for themselves, and to build a framework for cooperation with the worker parties. Radicals and Republicans, though sometimes concerned about the privileges granted to the consumer cooperatives, stopped short of calling for the repeal, as opposed to the reform, of Article 5.[41] This posed particular difficulties for the leaders of the Federation, many of whom were members of these parties and were keen to further their own political careers. Differences developed between the Federation and *L'Esercente* over the best way to make the *esercenti*'s voice heard, with the former advocating the compromise politics of membership of an electoral bloc, whilst the newspaper recommended a more unilateral approach.

L'Esercente's argument was straightforward; the shopkeeper movement had to turn itself into as powerful and coherent a public voice as possible:

If the apathy, indolence and obstinacy responsible for the lack of intervention in public affairs are to be the companions of the *esercenti* in the future as well, we must prepare to see this important class of industrious workers disappear, we must prepare to witness the ruin of thousands of families ... The party of the

---

[40] Reprinted as 'Un guidizio dei Socialisti sugli esercenti', ibid., 20 February 1895.
[41] 'La condotta dell'Esercente subordinata agli interessi della classe e del paese', ibid., 21 May 1895.

future (the Socialists), if it finds shopkeepers inactive, will take the upper hand and then the consumer cooperatives, the people's bakeries and other utopias will triumph – the victory will be brief, but the fearful period of anomaly will have scythed petty commerce down to its roots and you will be inexorably ruined.[42]

The tactical divisions between the Federation and *L'Esercente* first emerged during the parliamentary elections of November 1890. *L'Esercente*, ignoring the pro-Democratic Federation line, sought an undertaking from two Moderate candidates, Colombo and Ponti, that they would oppose cooperative privileges if elected to the house. In return, the journal carried them on its list in preference to the Democratic nominees for these constituencies. Both candidates were returned. *L'Esercente* trumpeted that now four of the six Milanese deputies were opposed to privilege, whilst some disgruntled elements of the Democratic bloc suggested the paper had been bribed.[43]

In succeeding months the newspaper waited for the day on which privileges would be denounced in the parliamentary chamber, but to no avail. Neither of the deputies was prepared to raise the matter, and both made it clear that they had been referring only to the special considerations granted to the Suburbana when they made their pledges. Nor did Colombo act when he was brought into the government. Ponti, meanwhile, was found to be involved with a rural consumer cooperative. *L'Esercente* was left to complain bitterly that it had been deceived, and that it would withdraw its support from them at the next election.[44] It appeared that both deputies were scared of isolating themselves in the face of the overwhelming support for cooperation.

The movement intensified its efforts in 1891, when the Federation organised a series of six propaganda meetings in various zones of the city. At each one, a member of the Federation's executive gave a keynote speech outlining cooperative privileges and the shopkeepers case against them. A common theme of these speeches was that the success of cooperatives was to be blamed on 'those who command' (i.e. the parliamentary classes who had granted the cooperatives their privileges), and on the *impiegati* who patronised them. A local propaganda committee was set up after each meeting.

---

[42] 'La minaccia dell'avvenire', ibid., 12 August 1888.
[43] 'Perchè non ci siamo astenuti', ibid., 30 November 1890.
[44] 'Il Milleottocentonovantuno', ibid., 31 December 1891.

L'Esercente trebled its print run, and copies were sent to commercial associations all over the country asking them to associate themselves with the struggle. There was a good response to this, whilst the meetings themselves brought the matter to public attention. Even so there were complaints that the rest of the press did not devote much coverage to the issue for fear of the political discourse it might produce.

The list of objections drawn up by the Federation during its 1891 campaign was adopted by the Milan Chamber of Commerce, in which the *esercenti* had begun to play a more significant role.[45] The Chamber sent the memorandum on the government; a further piece of publicity for the *esercenti* cause, and one which forced Colombo, now Minister of Finance, finally to address the subject of privileges in March 1892. In his reply, Colombo accepted that Article 5 'can give rise to abuses which damage the *esercenti*' and claimed that a new parliamentary measure was being drafted to define more clearly those societies entitled to the exemption. Meanwhile he dismissed the cooperatives' claim for special *ricchezza mobile* treatment, though he did the same to the *esercenti* complaint about shopkeepers having to pay an estimated contribution whilst that for cooperatives was based on their published accounts.[46]

The Federation now produced its own political platform which stressed the need for the abolition of privileges, the reform of the *dazio* system, avoidance of state regulation and reform of the bookkeeping requirements in the Codice di Commercio.[47] In November 1892, to avoid supporting a known advocate of cooperation, it ran its own candidate in one of the six parliamentary constituencies in the city. For a while the *esercenti* movement seemed in harmony, as a fortuitous combination of vote-bargaining and propaganda appeared to bring results. *L'Esercente* proclaimed that in the local elections of 1893 and 1894 it was only the workers' candidates who favoured cooperative privileges.[48]

The results of this activity gradually became visible in national political life. In 1893 the overall political consensus in favour of

---

[45] Later that year an *esercenti*-backed list, which included the abolition of the privileges as one of its goals, won every seat in the Camera.

[46] 'La risposta del ministro Colombo', *L'Esercente* 17 March 1892.

[47] 'L'assemblea generale di ieri della Federzazione degli Esercenti', ibid., 2 November 1892.

[48] 'Quale è la forza dei cooperatori?', ibid., 5 June 1893; 'Il lavoro degli esercenti nelle elezioni', ibid., 1894.

cooperation was such that two deputies, Villa and Roux, presented a bill to extend privileges to parliament, but the fact that the project encountered opposition from two of the Milanese deputies, Rossi (a Radical) and Ponti (a Moderate), was an indication of the success of the Milanese movement's campaign. The following year Ponti, despite having lost *L'Esercente*'e electoral support, went further and spoke in the house, condemning the privileges already in existence (including those relating to the *ricchezza mobile* tax). Sonnino, the new Finance Minister, concurred with Ponti that Article 5 had been abused by speculative organisations, i.e. non-charitable cooperatives, which sought its shelter.[49] From then on both he and Barazzuoli, the Minister for Agriculture and Commerce, repeatedly argued that a reform in the law was necessary to eliminate these 'speculative cooperatives'.[50] The cooperative movement itself even discussed the issue at conferences, and several leading cooperators, including Buffoli, went on record as being opposed to Article 5. The political consensus had begun to wear away.

This success was undermined, however, by the fact that these positive responses came from a national administration which was at loggerheads with a large part of the Milanese political community: the second Crispi administration of 1893. Its unpopularity derived from the high tax levels imposed to finance public works and colonial adventurism in Africa. Crispi's enthusiasm for raising Italy's standing in the world contrasted sharply with the attitude of most liberal Milanese (both *nuova destra* Moderates and Democrats) who had little time for national projects. Italy's tariff war with France and her involvement in the Triple Alliance that included Milan's former Austrian rulers were resented by Milanese businessmen who saw little profit to be made from the acquisition of colonies in Abyssinia.[51] The Federation argued that shopkeepers' best interests lay in participation in this Milanese bloc, even to the extent of supporting those of its candidates who favoured cooperative privileges (an analysis that suited the political aspirations of the Federation's leaders).

L'Esercente, however, refused to accept the necessity of supporting election candidates who came from parties that espoused

[49] 'Gli esercenti ricordati e difesi in Parlamento dall'On. Ponti', ibid., 15 March 1894.
[50] 'L'interessamento del Governo nella questione dei privilegi', ibid., 14 July 1895.
[51] For details see Fonzi, *Crispi e lo 'Stato di Milano'*.

policies the movement disagreed with, and opposed an administration whose ministers were beginning to show interest in the shopkeepers' grievances. Furthermore, whilst the Federation, along with most commercial opinion, believed that high taxes and high interest rates could be brought down simultaneously, Rusca argued that interest rates would only fall when the government balanced the budget through a combination of high taxation and reduced public spending.[52] Rusca maintained that Crispi, a strong man in Italian politics, was more likely than anybody else to implement the 'economies' necessary to redeem the situation. Again this analysis was not purely objective: Rusca began receiving money from the Crispi administration in November 1894.[53]

L'Esercente continued to lament the spending of money on Africa, the prime cause of the debt problem, though arguing that now they were there the Italians should conduct themselves with honour.[54] At least the Crispi government had managed to reduce interest rates from 18% by February 1895.[55] In effect Rusca's argument was that high taxes would have to be accepted as part of a budget-balancing manœuvre, so the prime *esercenti* priority was to ensure that none of the competitors was able to avoid these.

The disputes between Crispi and the 'State of Milan' and between *L'Esercente* and the Federation each came to a head in 1895 during the February local elections and the June parliamentary ones. The Federation formed part of the Democratic bloc at both elections, but *L'Esercente* abstained in the former (though in practice favouring the Crispian Moderate candidates) and directly supported Moderate candidates in the latter. The Federation claimed that it faced a stark choice between securing the election of several representatives by endorsing candidates whose views differed from its own, or taking a principled stand which would condemn all their candidates to defeat.[56] *L'Esercente*, however, rejected the idea that one could compromise over the question of privileges.[57] The

[52] 'Agli esercenti, agli amici, alla classe', *L'Esercente*, 3 January 1895.
[53] A full account of this is given in Fonzi, *Crispi e lo 'Stato di Milano'*, pp. 211–14.
[54] 'Di chi è la colpa', *L'Esercente*, 24 May 1894.
[55] 'Ci chiamono ministeriali', ibid., 17 February 1895.
[56] For example in the 1891 supplementary local elections cited above, the Federation drew up a list of four of its own candidates and eight Democrats who allegedly did not support cooperative privileges. As a result none of the *esercenti* candidates received the full support of the Democratic bloc and only one of them, Rosio, was elected. His success was due to the unexpected support of the *clericali*.
[57] 'Sempre nell'interesse vero degli esercenti', *L'Esercente*, 30 May 1895.

Federation, after all, was now supporting candidates who were active 'cooperators', one of whom was the same candidate against whom they had put up their own man in 1892. The *esercenti* movement experienced its first split after the Federation responded to *L'Esercente*'s ridiculing of its position by ceasing to provide the newspaper with information about its activities, and setting up its own paper, *La Voce degli Esercenti* ('The Shopkeeper's Voice').

Revealingly, *L'Esercente* appears to have been closer to shopkeeper opinion than the Federation. Both contemporary observers, such as the Socialist leader Filippo Turati, and subsequent historians, such as Fausto Fonzi, have singled out the shopkeeper vote as playing a crucial role in the success of the Crispian bloc at the administrative elections.[58] Clerical candidates who were also shopkeepers were particular beneficiaries. Meanwhile the Federation's own nominees, rejected by the Socialists, failed to get elected. In the national elections, however, anti-Crispi candidates were returned in every constituency, presumably because of the large numbers of Catholics who continued to observe the *non expedit* ordered by the Pope.[59]

The fact that *L'Esercente*, not the Federation, delivered the shopkeeper vote tells us much about the development of shopkeeper identity during the period. Shopkeepers were now using the cooperative issue as the basis for determining their allies and opponents within society. They resented high taxes (it would be stretching belief to imagine that they were as sanguine about them as Rusca contrived to be), but what irritated them most was that their competitors should enjoy any form of exemption from these, especially during a period of acute economic distress.[60]

The *esercenti* movement had succeeded in making cooperative privilege the key to small-trader identity, conquering the *dazio* divide. The Federation's mistake lay in not recognising what was partly their own achievement, and continuing to believe that the suburban origins of the movement, along with the shopkeepers'

[58] Fonzi, *Crispi e lo 'Stato di Milano'*, p. 383.
[59] For the campaigns generally, ibid., pp. 335–451. The foundation of the Associazione Cattolica degli Esercenti in Milano in 1895 was another indicator of increasing Catholic involvement in lay activity. Unfortunately no further documentation concerning the organisation has survived. *Statuto della Associazione Cattolica degli Esercenti in Milano*, 1895.
[60] 'Programma', *L'Esercente*, 14 August 1886; 'L'abbondanza di denaro', ibid., 2 September 1897.

perception of themselves as political outsiders, would lead the *esercenti* to gravitate towards the Democrats. Yet it was among the Democrats that many supporters of cooperative privileges were to be found, whilst the Socialists, with whom the Democrats were in alliance, refused even to support the Federation's own candidates for election, claiming they were representative of a class that would be inevitably be subsumed into the proletariat.

Rusca was more sensitive to the re-assessment of the shopkeepers' position in political society that the depression had provoked. The success of the white-collar cooperatives led shopkeepers to a particularly vitriolic dislike of the *impiegati*. Although workers continued to patronise small shops in preference to the cooperatives, their main reason for so doing was the attractiveness of the customer credit that shopkeepers felt obliged to provide for them, at considerable cost to their own financial security. It was probably through their role in ensuring the perpetuation of *il fido* that cooperative privileges contributed most directly to the decline in the fortunes of the *esercenti*.

Shopkeepers were also forced into a more realistic assessment of their relations with the working classes by the results of the franchise reform of 1889. Workers were able to exercise increasing political power in the city and did so through their own spokesmen, defending cooperative privilege and attacking the *esercenti*. The presumed affinity between patron and proprietor was seen to be just that. Although the *esercenti* were sufficiently powerful to put their protests against cooperation on the political agenda, it appeared to them that it was the workers who were now accepted in the political mainstream, their votes and parties courted by the democrats.

By 1895, then, shopkeepers' political responses were more conditioned by their occupational identity as small traders than by their zonal one as residents of the *interno* or *esterno*. This was a measure of the success of the *esercenti* movement, and one which had important consequences beyond Milan, as chapter 8 will make clear. This identity was still fragile, however, reliant on the local commercial environment, which still dictated that two types of shopkeeping should be practised in the *interno* and *esterno* zones, remaining unchanged. Chapter 9 examines the effects on the movement of new attempts to reform this environment between 1895 and 1899.

8. Milan and the national small-business movement, 1886–1898

The erosion of the parliamentary consensus surrounding cooperative privileges was a reflection of the growth of small-trader activity at both local and national level. The Milanese movement acted as an example to other local organisations, and played a key role in the development of a national small-business movement that attempted to deal directly with the government. By the later 1890s there were clear indications that national administrations accorded this lobby serious consideration.

When it first appeared in 1886 *L'Esercente* noted the existence of two strong shopkeeper associations, those of Genoa and Turin.[1] These were both prosperous trading cities with close contacts with other European economies, and, along with Milan, formed the points of the famous economic triangle which has always dominated commerce and industry in post-unification Italy. It was natural that these cities should be the first to spawn the same sorts of small-trader associations that had arisen in the nearby economies of France and Germany.

These associations inspired imitators in the smaller towns around them. In Piedmont, towns such as Biella, Moncalieri and Susa had their own *esercenti* organisations, associations in Sestri Ponente and Sampierdarena testified to the influence of the society at Genoa, whilst federations modelled on that in Milan were founded in nearby Lodi and Niguarda in 1890 and 1891 (see Table 8.1).[2] The difference between the Milanese shopkeepers' movement and those found in the other two 'triangle' cities was that it was able to spread

---

[1] In 1888 the journal claimed that the Genoa association was 1,500 members strong. 'I nemici della patria', *L'Esercente*, 10 June 188; 'Chi lavora', ibid., 8 July 1888.
[2] 'Una nuova Federazione degli Esercenti', ibid., 17 April 1890. See also letters published on 24 May 1891.

its message much further afield through the medium of the journal *L'Esercente*.

The newspaper highlighted issues which might draw the country's shopkeepers together – notably the privileges of the consumer cooperatives – and provided a model for the organisation of small traders through its description of the Milanese situation. Copies of *L'Esercente* reached other cities and, in the course of time, out-of-town subscriptions began. As the only stable shopkeeper journal, *L'Esercente* was well read in *esercenti* associations throughout the country and kept them informed about each other. Its primary focus remained Milan, however, so readers from out of town were much more familiar with shopkeeper activity in this city than in any other. This contributed significantly to the central role that the Milanese associations played in the national shopkeeper movement.

An early example of the importance of Milan was seen in the development of *esercenti* organisations in Pisa. The Federazione Pisana degli Esercenti set up in 1888 simply adopted the Milanese Federation's constitution and included a subscription to *L'Esercente* in its membership fee. It also sought to negotiate a deal with the journal allowing the Pisan members the same freedom to publish in its columns as was enjoyed by the Milanese adherents.[3]

In 1891 the Milanese movement set out to exploit its position to the full. The big campaign against cooperative privileges that the Federation had organised within the city was complemented by a trebling of *L'Esercente*'s print run, and extra copies recounting the Federation meetings were sent to associations of small traders and *camere di commercio* throughout the nation. Letters from shopkeepers in various centres who claimed to be about to set up their own local federations to combat these privileges were received by *L'Esercente* in response to this initiative.[4] The campaign established the cooperative question as the key issue facing the *esercenti*, and placed the Milanese organisations in the vanguard of the movement.

The stress laid on the cooperative issue was particularly important in bringing Rome into the fold of shopkeeper organisation. Roman traders were not so much concerned about the provisions of Article 5 as they were about state favouritism of the Unione Militare cooperative, but it was easy to unite these concerns in a 'catch-all'

[3] 'Gli esercenti di Pisa', ibid., 16 September 1888.
[4] See 'La spesa per la propaganda', ibid., 21 May 1891; letters published on 24 May 1891.

phrase such as '*Abassa i Privilegi!*' ('Down with Privileges!'), a slogan much favoured by *L'Esercente*.[5] Indeed, the journal succeeded in being appointed as the Rome Società fra Commercianti ed Industriali's official organ, a position it retained despite several interruptions during difficulties in the relationship. As the paper became more successful it opened an office in the capital and later began printing a separate edition there.[6] The Rome Association was one of the most active in the shopkeeper movement although *L'Esercente*'s claim that it had 3,500 members in 1893 may have been an exaggeration designed to shame more Milanese *esercenti* into joining the Federation.[7]

Milan's example was adopted by a considerable number of cities. In 1892 the Società fra Industriali e Commercianti of Vicenza wrote to *L'Esercente*, asking for advice on the best way to combat the privileges; in Livorno and La Spezia anti-privilege journals were set up in 1893, inspired by the Milan paper's success. The most successful of these was *Il Piccolo* of Cuneo. Even the more-established shopkeeper associations followed the Milanese lead; in 1892 the Turin Confederazione degli Esercenti organised meetings about privilege throughout Piedmont, whilst getting the Camera di Commercio to adopt an *istanza* on privileges that was sent to the government, the same strategy the Milanese Federation had employed a year previously.[8]

The growth in shopkeeper institutions was largely confined to northern Italy, reflecting the economic geography of the country, and Milan's own location within it (see Tables 8.1 and 8.2 and Fig. 8.1). In the south, however, shopkeeper activity tended to be more spontaneous. Here disputes with authority were often conducted by engaging in closures or lock-outs until the issue was negotiated. The official statistics on these forms of activity are dominated by southern and Sicilian towns; for example in Catania bakers closed down in 1878, 1880, 1882, 1884 and 1890 in pursuit of a better *calmiere* (officially controlled price), the worst of these

[5] According to Mussi most of the Roman *circondario esterno* was composed of the deserted marsh-fever zone. 'Consiglio communale: discorso Mussi', *Il Secolo*, 4–5 April 1886.

[6] 'L'Esercente a Roma', *L'Esercente*, 12 March 1893; 'L'Esercente a Roma', ibid., 25 October 1894.   [7] 'La Federazione degli Esercenti', ibid., 2 March 1893.

[8] 'Da Vicenza', ibid., 18 January 1892. 'Gli esercenti di Torino contro i privilegi', ibid., 17 March 1892. The Livorno journal was called *Il Movimento*, that in La Spezia *Il Nuovo Corriere*. 'Amici in Lissa', *L'Esercente*, 19 May 1893; 'Un nuovo giornale a difesa del piccolo commercio', ibid., 15 October 1893.

Table 8.1. *City associations attending national small-business congresses, 1893–8*

City	1893	1895	1898
Acqui*	x	x	x
Ancona	x	x	
Bari	x	x	x
Benevento	x	x	
Biella*	x	x	x
Brescia*	x	x	x
Brescia	x	x	
Carrara*	x	x	
Casale Monferrato	x	x	
Como	x	x	
Crema*	x	x	
Cremona*	x	x	
Cuneo*	x	x	x
Florence	x	x	x
Genoa*	x	x	x
Genoa*	x		
Lecco	x	x	
Lodi*	x	x	x
Marino	x	x	
Milan*	x	x	
Moncalieri*	x	x	x
Novara*	x	x	x
Padua	x	x	
Parma*	x	x	
Rivoli*	x	x	x
Rome	x	x	x
Rome	x	x	
Salerno	x	x	
San Daniele*	x	x	
Savona*	x	x	x
Sestri Ponente*	x	x	
Susa*	x	x	
Turin*	x	x	x
Treviso	x	x	
Udine	x	x	
Varallo Sesia	x	x	x
Venice*	x	x	x
Vicenza*	x	x	x

City	1893	1895	1898
Naples	x		
Novara	x		
Perugia	x		
Sampierdarena	x	x	
Torre Pellice	x		
Aosta			x
Bologna			x
Oleggio			x
Saluzzo			x
Spezia			x

Other associations mentioned in *L'Esercente*

Cantù (by 1888)
Pisa (1888)
Modena (1888)
Mantua (1893)
Livorno (1893)
Vigevano (by 1893)
Belluno (t)
Piacenza (t)
Stradella (t)
Lecco (1894)
Adria (t)
Monza (1894)
Boves (1895)
Pegli (1895)
Rovato (1896)
Sannazzaro (1897)
Intra (1899)
Busto Arsizio (1899)
Treviglio (1899)
Val Trompia (1899)

Key: t = tabacchi soc.
* 'esercenti' in title
dates in brackets are dates of first record
Source: L'Esercente, 16/11/83, 21/5/95, 28/8/98.

Table 8.2. *Closures and lock-outs in the 'esercenti' sector, 1871–93*

Year	City	Occupation	No.	Days Lost	Motive
1878	Pisa	Macellai	?	?	Local tax (N)
	Trapani	Fornai	25	25	To raise prices (U)
	Catania	Panettieri	4	12	Against *calmiere* (U)
1880	Catania	Panettieri	20	20	Against *calmiere* (N)
1881	Caserta	Panettieri	30	30	Against *calmiere* (N)
	Lecce	Fornai	24	100	Against *calmiere* (N)
	Livorno	Suburban	150	300	*Dazio consumo* (N)
1882	Catania	Fornai	75	525	Against *calmiere* (N)
	Verona	Calzolai	9	9	New factories (U)
1883	Catania	Macellai	5	10	Against *calmiere* (U)
1884	Ancona	Macellai	10	?	Local tax (U)
	Perugia (Prov.)	Vino	6	18	*Dazio consumo* (U)
	Catania	Fornai	36	324	Against *calmiere* (U)
	Catania (Prov.)	Pastai	13	117	Against *calmiere* (U)
1886	Catania	Macellai	70	?	Local tax (N)
1888	Catania	Macellai	70	490	Against *calmiere* (U)
1889	Gubbio	Vino	31	62	To raise prices (U)
	Casale Monferrato	Macellai	20	100	Local regulation (U)
1890	Catania	Macellai	53	1378	Against *calmiere* (N)
1891	Reggio Emilia	Fornai	3	12	*Dazio consumo* (N)
	Napoli (Prov.)	Macellai	22	110	Local tax (F)
	Bari	Panettieri	4	8	Falling prices (F)
	Taurisano	Fornai	24	148	Against *calmiere* (N)
	Caltanissetta (Prov.)	Macellai	?	?	Local tax (N)
	Butera	Pastai	4	4	Raise prices (F)
	Catania (Prov.)	Macellai	7	49	Raise prices (U)
1893	Cosenza (Prov. Calabria)	Macellai	9	90	Raise prices (U)
	Catania (Prov.)	Fornai	3	3	Against *calmiere* (U)
	Messina	Macellai	100	200	Local tax (N)

Key: U = Unfavourable exit, F = Favourable exit, N = Negotiated exit
Source: MAIC, *Statistica degli scioperi*, pp. 79–80 (1892), p. 42 (1894)

disputes involving the closure of seventy-five bakeries for a total of 525 shop days in 1882.[9]

[9] Ministero dell' Agricoltura, Industria e Commercio (hereafter MAIC), *Statistica degli scioperi ... dal 1884 al 1891*, pp. 79–80; MAIC, *Statistica degli scioperi ... 1892 e 1893*, p. 42. Butchers were also frequently in disputes with the authorities, and it is interesting to speculate on whether this might be connected with the well-documented *mafia* involvement in the trade. It should be recalled, however, that *mafia* activity has primarily been concentrated in the western half of the island, rather than the eastern provinces around Catania and Messina. See Schneider and Schneider, *Culture and political economy in western Sicily*, pp. 142, 183, 195.

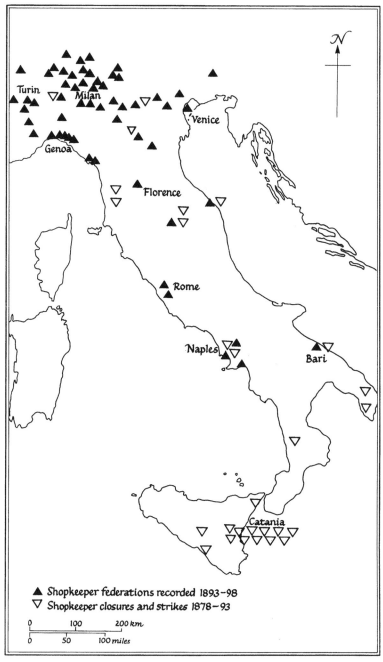

Fig. 8.1 Shopkeeper federations (1893–8) and shop closures (1873–93) in Italy

A few of these protests were resolved in the shopkeepers' favour and more ended in some form of compromise, but the majority were unsuccessful. The likelihood is that these failed because of traders breaking ranks or simply not participating in the first place, demonstrating the need for effective association. Shopkeeper 'strikes' appear to be a more primitive form of response to external threat, a hypothesis supported by their predominance in the south where mistrust of government and its processes was much greater. The strike was not unattractive to 'northern' shopkeepers *per se*; but although both Roman and Milanese associations fantasised about using it to protest against cooperative privileges, they readily acknowledged that it could never be properly enforced. They were, perhaps, more confident of influencing the authorities by acting as an organised interest group than their peers in the south.

As the new associations became more aware of each other via the pages of *L'Esercente* they sought each other's support for specific campaigns. In 1893 federations in Cuneo, Lodi, Udine, Crema, Vigevano, Genoa, Sestri Ponente and Turin all adhered to the Milanese protest over the scarcity of small change.[10] In the same year one Sig. Danieli of Vicenza organised a meeting in his home town to discuss the foundation of a Confederazione Generale fra Industriali, Commercianti ed Esercenti, a national congress of the small-business associations. Inevitably Milan was chosen as the venue for the inaugural Congress later in the year and the Federation acted as hosts for the event.

Thirty-eight associations were represented at the Congress from thirty-five towns and cities. Altogether these associations counted 8,519 members, demonstrating the importance of the Milanese Federation which probably accounted for at least a ninth of this total.[11] Yet Milan's leading position was also apparent in the greater militancy of its proposals. Many of the organisations in attendance were aimed not specifically at the shopkeeper, but at all forms of commercial activity. Their leaders were often local dignitaries who were also involved in business, rather than small traders pure and simple. They tended to have greater respect for govern-

---

[10] 'La protesta degli esercenti per la mancanza degli spezzati metallici', *L'Esercente*, 15 June 1893.

[11] 'Il Congresso della Confederazione Generale fra Industriali, Commercianti ed Escercenti', ibid., 16 November 1893; 'Il Congresso della Confederazione Generale fra Industriali, Commercianti ed Esercenti', ibid., 19 November 1893.

ment and its institutions and were unhesitating supporters of established liberal political positions.

This did not prevent full agreement on many issues, notably the need to abolish the *calmiere* and easy access to the *uffici d'analisi* (chemical laboratories) to enable *esercenti* to analyse suspect merchandise. The Congress disappointed the Milanese, however, in its cautious approach to the vexed questions of cooperative privileges and the *dazio consumo*. Milan urged for the complete abolition of both, but the Congress only called for the privileges to be limited to those 'closed' cooperatives selling essential goods to the poor (a restatement of the actual legal position), and a reform of the structure of the *dazio consumo* to allow for refunds on basic retail goods and raw materials.

L'Esercente did not hide its disappointment with both the motions passed at the Congress and the prevailing attitude of the delegates. It maintained that the resolution regarding cooperative privileges was naïve, as it was impossible to sustain a cooperative all of whose members were drawn from the poor, and it also appeared to recognise a right to which the journal objected. As for the *dazio*, the Congress, having appeared to agree that abolition was necessary, had drawn back and adopted a reformist half measure instead.

We awaited demonstrations of vigour from the Congress, we expected protests and injunctions addressed to the government, and instead, to everyone's satisfaction, we have found very good people, full of tact and regard, friends of authority, respectful and obedient subjects, ready even to go so far as to align themselves with the police in order to support the government in every event. We wanted the abolition of privileges but they soon voted that they remain as a consolation for the *esercenti*; if the humble desires of the delegates were to gain ground in the government we would have restrictions at the most. But let's be understood: if on occasion the provision were to upset someone, don't mention it, we will continue as at present. Above all we will respect the laws![12]

The prime example of this kind of delegate was the man elected President of the Congress, Marquis Carlo Ginori, a deputy from Florence. *L'Esercente* asked:

Is Hon. Ginori really the hot-blooded Achilles who will carry the

[12] 'La Confederazione Generale fra Industriali, Commercianti ed Esercenti', ibid., 19 November 1893.

dynamite of the *esercenti* into the Chamber of Deputies? . . . It doesn't seem so to look at him. To hear him even less.

Who remembers ever having heard him speak in the Chamber? Not us . . . The representatives of the Milanese associations knew even less about him than us . . . They know the Marquis is an industrialist in ceramics – we know his plates – not him . . .

As an industrialist and a Marquis he is undoubtedly a man worthy of much consideration and great respect, but what is it one expects from this meek, courteous, seemly man, this high-society gentleman, that he deal with the interests of shopkeepers in the Chamber? That he goes thoroughly into the privation in which the *esercenti* find themselves? Him, a multimillionaire? Oh, come on, one would have to be very naïve to hope for all that.[13]

None the less the Confederation succeeded in raising the profile of small business in national politics. At the end of the Congress a Giunta (central committee) was set up to monitor events and a report of the conference proceedings was presented to the government. This was done on 22 December when the Confederation Giunta met both Boselli, the Minister for Agriculture and Commerce, and, for half an hour, Crispi himself, the first time that ministers had had direct contact with any representatives of the *esercenti*.[14]

The Confederation continued to build up adherents and political weight in the succeeding years. Three more conferences were held in the next two years, at Florence in April 1894, Genoa in November 1894 and Venice in October 1895. By the end of this period many of the Milanese objections to the Confederation had been overcome. As had been the case in Milan itself, it had taken time for a genuine agenda to emerge. The Venice Congress voted for the abolition of the privileges granted to cooperatives under Article 5, opposed the insequestrability of stipends and elected Colombo, the Milanese Deputy and some time Minister, as its President, a man with far more political weight than Ginori.[15]

The example of the General Confederation led some forms of enterprise to organise their own national associations; a tobacconists' association, the Confederazione delle Società dei

[13] Ibid.
[14] 'Confederazione Generale delle Società Italiane fra Industriali, Commercianti ed Esercenti', *L'Esercente*, 31 December 1893.
[15] 'Il V Congresso Commerciale Italiano a Venezia', ibid., 10 October 1895.

Tabaccai in Italia, was founded in 1893 and held its first Congress in 1894, the same year that the association of manufacturers and traders of alcohol, the Associazioni Italiane dei Fabbricati e Commercianti in Alcool met for the first time in Milan (another meeting hosted by the Federation).[16] Meanwhile the General Confederation's increasing importance as a pressure group on government was testified to by its being granted a representative in the Consiglio Superiore of the Ministry of Agriculture, Industry and Commerce from 1896 onwards.[17]

Politically the Confederation did not depart much from its left liberal *laissez-faire* positions. It sought to influence individual deputies, not make political alliances, so divisive splits such as those in the Milanese *esercenti* movement were largely avoided. Crispianism held little attraction for the Confederation which criticised high tax levels and military adventurism, most notably at the Florence Congress of 1894, and continued to support free trade until 1898.[18] The fact that the delegates represented all kinds of small business, including those involved in international trade, not just small retailers, helps account for the solidity of these positions.

The Confederation's influence contributed to the growing attention paid to *esercenti* demands in the later 1890s. The most obvious example of this was the greater interest taken by government and parliament in the matter of cooperative privileges. It became commonplace to hear ministers affirm the need for strict regulation of the privileges granted to consumer cooperatives, a mood reflected in two pieces of legislation in 1897 which restricted the stamp duty exemptions to cooperatives which were run as friendly societies, and the Royal Decree of 27 February 1898 on the collection of the *dazio*

---

[16] There were around 200 delegates to the first conference of *tabaccai* representing societies from Turin, Vicenza, Venice, Como, Spezia, Modena, Udine, Brescia, Piacenza, Belluno, Stradella, Cremona, Lecco, Mantua, Adria and Florence. 'Confederazione delle Società dei Tabaccai in Italia', ibid., 31 December 1893; 'Il Congresso dei Tabacchi', ibid., 19 July 1884; 'Contro le minacce del monopolio sugli alcools', ibid., 26 August 1894.

[17] 'Il V. Congresso Commerciale Italiano a Venezia', ibid., 10 October 1895.

[18] Opposition to high taxes was particularly virulent in 1894 because Sonnino had unsuccessfully presented a scheme to parliament to increase them further. A resolution calling for salami manufacturers to be protected against American imports was passed at the Confederation's Turin congress in 1898. 'Le associazioni confederate a Congresso', ibid., 4 March 1894. 'Confederazione Generale fra Industriali, Commercianti ed Esercenti Italiani al Congresso di Firenze', ibid., 8 and 12 April 1894; 'Le ultime sedute del Congresso degli Esercenti a Torino', ibid., 1 September 1898.

consumo which restated unequivocally that the benefits of Article 5 applied solely to 'closed' cooperatives, and added a clause insisting that they be legally constituted under the provisions of the Codice di Commercio.[19]

Several parliamentary deputies could now be relied upon to bring up the interests of the *esercenti* in the Camera. Most of these had vociferous *esercenti* organisations in their constituencies; Santini and Mazza, for example, were two Roman deputies who regularly questioned the position of the Unione Militare. Although the Confederation did not succeed in its one-time aim of creating a 'commercial bloc' in parliament, it demonstrated political acumen in arguing that its various objections to the cooperatives were intertwined, so that opponents of one 'privilege' were persuaded to lend support to those fighting against another.

By the later 1890s, 'cooperators' were increasingly pressed to defend their privileges and they themselves differed on which were justifiable. The small-scale lower-class cooperatives were viewed with political suspicion (especially after the social unrest in May 1898 which led to many being closed down), and leading members of the cooperative movement, such as Buffoli and Luzzatti, pronounced themselves in favour of the abolition of Article 5.[20] The white-collar commercial societies were also under attack; indeed Fortis, the Minister for Industry and Commerce, was reported as believing that no self-styled 'cooperative' should be allowed to sell to non-members.[21] The Minister sent his greetings to the opening of the Confederation's Congress in 1898, and when the Giunta sent a report of their deliberations back to the Minister, expressing the hope he would pay them some attention, he swiftly cabled back that he would.[22] This ritual exchange of pleasantries confirmed that government now recognised small business as an interest group worth cultivating in the context of the political game.

[19] Bonfante, 'La legislazione cooperativistica', p. 202n. The full title of the Royal Decree was the Regolamento Generale per la Riscossione dei Dazi di Consumo.
[20] 'I cooperatori a congresso', *L'Esercente*, 27 October 1895.
[21] 'I privilegi delle cooperative in Parlamento', ibid., 22 December 1898.
[22] Full reports of the congress appear in the 28 August and 1 September 1898 editions of *L'Esercente*.

9. *The* allargamento *debate,*
1895–1897

During the last five years of the nineteenth century, both city and shopkeeper politics in Milan passed through their most turbulent phase since the flight of the Austrians in 1859. The municipality's search for a way to raise the revenue necessary to provide amenities for the city's burgeoning population, at a time when rapid inflation masked the beginnings of an economic recovery, lay at the root of the problem, and the system of the *interno* and *esterno* again came under threat. Milan's situation contributed to the 'end-of-century' crisis in which the legitimacy of Italy's existing political system was challenged by a combination of public disorder, economic distress and the development of viable political alternatives on the left. Disagreements over the best strategies to adopt in these circumstances led to the emergence of several divisions in the *esercenti* camp, reflected by the growth in shopkeeper splinter groups and news-sheets shown in Tables 9.1 and 9.2.

ESERCENTI POLITICS, 1895–6

The first of these disputes was that between the Federation and *L'Esercente*, which, it will be recalled, developed during the lead-up to the elections of 1895.[1] At the heart of the issue lay the question of the movement's political autonomy. The newspaper attacked the Federation as a nest of Republicans, asserting that it would never succeed in eliminating cooperative privileges whilst it remained so closely allied to the Democratic bloc. Rusca's preferred strategy of favouring whichever political actor seemed to offer the *esercenti* the most at a given time, however, led to *L'Esercente*'s flirtation with

[1] See pp. 161–3.

Table 9.1. *Shopkeeper political associations in Milan, 1885–1905*

Name	1885	1886	1887	1888	1889	1890	1891	1892	1893	1894	1895	1896	1897	1898	1899	1900	1901	1902	1903	1904	1905
Federazione Generale				x*	x	x	x	x	x	x	x	x	x	x		x	x	x	x	x	x
Cattolici											x	x	x	x							
Nuova Associazione Generale per gli Esercenti												x	x	x							
Associazione Generale del Commercio Milanese														x							
Associazione fra Commercianti, Esercenti ed Industriali																x	x	x	x	x	x

* Relaunched in 1888.

Sources: Based on information taken from the *Guide di Milano* published by Savallo, *L'Esercente* and the records of the Questura. The sources for this work are far from ideal; the *Guide* are not available for some years, and are not always accurate whilst neither *L'Esercente* nor the Questura records contains systematic lists of such organisations.

Table 9.2. *Shopkeeper news-sheets in Milan, 1885–1905*

Name	1885	1886	1887	1888	1889	1890	1891	1892	1893	1894	1895	1896	1897	1898	1899	1900	1901	1902	1903	1904	1905
L'Esercente	x	x	x	x	x	x	x	x	x	x	x	x	x	x	x	x	x	x	x	x	x
La Voce degli Esercenti[1]											x	x									
Il Contribuente[2]												x									
Il Piccolo Commercio[3]															x						
Il Contribuente Italiano[4]																x	x	x			
Milano del Popolo[5]																x	x	x			

[1] Merged with *L'Esercente*; 2 founded by Rusca and folded shortly thereafter; 3 later called *Il Messagero Commerciale* it had 800 subscribers when it was acquired by *L'Esercente* and absorbed into the journal; 4 Federation journal which folded in early 1900; 5 acquired and absorbed by *L'Esercente* in July 1900.
Sources: All this information comes from various editions of *L'Esercente*. See in particular 'Doverosa risposta ad Annibale Rusca', 5 July 1900; 'Milano del popolo', 29 July 1900.

Crispi, whose high taxes, colonial adventurism and domestic repression were anathema to liberal Democrats. In 1895 the Federation tired of Rusca's tirades and launched its own paper *La Voce degli Escercenti* ('The Shopkeepers' Voice'), to which Rusca replied by launching an alternative shopkeeper association, the Nuova Associazione Generale per gli Esercenti.

The major platform of the Nuova Associazione was that it would avoid links with any political parties. This was one of Rusca's main themes in his articles in *L'Esercente* (a somewhat hypocritical one since he was taking money from Crispi at the time). He proposed to put the newspaper at the service of the association, by allowing members to use its columns for their articles whenever they wished. Yet the truth was that the Association was Rusca's creation. The rest of the committee comprised men who had little or no record in shopkeeper politics, and the operation was run from *L'Esercente*'s offices in Via Manzoni.[2]

Nonetheless, by 6 November 1895, when the official inaugural meeting was held, the new association had some 627 members, around half the figure for individual membership of the Federation itself. This confirmed what the election results had already suggested, namely that the *esercenti* were more interested in opposing supposed threats to their trading activities, such as cooperative privileges, than they were in expressing neighbourhood solidarities. Indeed most of the members of the new association came from the suburbs, where these zonal loyalties had previously been strongest, and from where the Federation also drew the bulk of its membership.

Along with the Nuova Associazione, another new shopkeeper organisation was set up at this time, the Associazione Cattolica degli Esercenti in Milano, whose proposed statutes were issued in 1895, although the Association was not fully constituted until 29 May 1896, by which time it had some 500 adherents. One of those most committed to the setting up of the society was the Cardinal of Milan, Ferrari, one of the city's most important political operators and a keen supporter of the Moderates and Crispi.[3]

[2] A police report on the inaugural meeting can be found in ASM, fond. Questura, c.107, f.5. See also the reports in *L'Esercente* on 18 and 28 July, 24 October and 10 November 1895.
[3] Fonzi, *Crispi e lo 'Stato di Milano'*, p. 362n; Canavero, *Milano e la crisi del fine secolo*, p. 353.

Naturally, therefore, support for the Catholic Electors' Association, Associazione degli Elettori Cattolici, was written into the statutes of the organisation. So too, however, were a number of universal *esercenti* aspirations, most notably:

> to exercise the most practical and opportune methods to combat or render innocuous the privileges of the cooperative societies which are damaging to the *esercenti*.[4]

The statutes also provided for the support of professional schools, the setting up of a credit bank, and the provision of a range of legal and technical services.[5]

Little information is available concerning the Associazione Cattolica itself, and it is not clear if it survived beyond 1896 and the fall of Crispi. It was significant, however, because non-religious shopkeeper voters were prepared to vote for Catholic candidates if they shared the same small-business background; a crucial factor in the success of the clerical candidates in the local election of 1895.[6] *L'Esercente* reflected an important sentiment when it stated that it was easier to feel secure with the Catholics than with the Socialists as they were unlikely to run on to the streets calling for revolution.[7] Once in office the Catholic councillors returned this support by acting as shopkeepers over several issues, most notably the extension of the *cinta* to which suburban Catholic representatives were opposed.

The initial success of both these associations represented a further step in the process whereby shopkeepers gradually abandoned their original radical allegiances. By the end of 1896, however, both associations appear to have lost most of their relevance. This was a consequence of two events. The first was the announcement of a project to unify the *interno* and *esterno dazio* zones in November 1895, returning the suburban shopkeepers to a situation similar to that they had experienced in 1886, when the Commune and the Moderate 'establishment' had been perceived as a bigger threat to their interests than the cooperative movement.

---

[4] *Statuto della Associazione Cattolica degli Esercenti in Milano*, Art. 2k, p. 5.

[5] Two types of representative were elected to the executive, parochial ones to handle regional matters and trade representative to deal with technical problems.

[6] All four Catholic traders from the Clerico-Moderate list for the local elections of 1895 were elected. These were the bakers Bertani and Renoldi, the grocer Pizzali and the delicatessen-owner Maraschi. Fonzi, *Crispi e lo 'Stato di Milano'*, p. 372.

[7] 'Un altro pericolo', *L'Esercente*, 1 June 1895. See also 'La verità pura senza preconcetti', ibid., 24 March 1895, which explores the issue in greater depth.

Secondly, Rusca's advocacy of Crispi became extremely difficult to sustain as it became clear that the Sicilian statesman was more interested in ruling Ethiopia than in budget balancing. In October 1895 *L'Esercente* ran an article which was fiercely critical of the decision to use revenue raised by new taxes in order to finance the African escapade.[8] The shock of the defeat at Adowa in March 1896, greeted by demonstrations featuring both Moderate and Democratic speakers in Milan, settled the fate not only of the Crispi administration, but of the Nuova Associazione as well. Little more was heard of it, even in the pages of *L'Esercente*, although the journal was not reunited with *La Voce degli Esercenti* until the autumn of 1896.

The terms of this reunification should be made clear. The Federation bought Rusca out, taking over the newspaper's financial obligations and rehiring Rusca on an editor's salary. This compensated *L'Esercente* for the loss of Crispi's slush money, but cost Rusca the independence of the paper – even though he continued to stretch this to the limit for the remainder of his editorship.

THE DEBATE ON THE *DAZIO* EXTENSION, 1895–7

The enlargement of the *cinta daziaria* was first officially proposed in November 1895 when the councillor in charge of raising the city revenue, Domenico Ferrario, produced a proposal to increase the city's income by L. 1.5 million a year. This would be accomplished by the construction of a new wall embracing nearly all of the *esterno* to create a much larger *zona chiusa* in which the tariffs for a *comune chiuso* would apply. Indeed the revenue generated, according to Ferrario, would be so great that the tariffs on certain essential goods, notably bread and pasta, could be lifted.

Ferrario made his proposal because of the financial pressures building up on the city. The rapid population expansion in Milan, which continued throughout the depression years of the 1890s,[9] generated a demand for the provision of public services that coincided with a general European movement towards greater municipal intervention. One project that Ferrario had to finance, for instance, was the construction of a sewage network.

There was also the question of the government's attitude to

[8] 'Allegri!', ibid., 6 October 1895.   [9] See p. 26.

consider. In 1894 the government had removed its own *dazi* on flour, bread and pasta in the *comuni chiusi* but had allowed the *comuni* concerned to raise their *dazi* on these items to a level of half of the defunct government *dazi*. The government's actions were a response to the increasing agitation against the *dazi* throughout Italy caused by the high price of food, especially bread. This unrest had begun in the south, particularly Sicily, and gradually spread up the peninsula. It may have been that Ferrario believed that his plan to eliminate the tariffs on basic foodstuffs would persuade the government to forego its right to demand that any increase in the City's *dazio* revenues be matched by a proportionate increase in the *canone* due to it.[10]

Ferrario presented his proposals as being designed to remedy an injustice: the inhabitants of the *esterno*, he claimed, paid only L. 9.9 *per capita per annum* in *dazio consumo* contributions, whilst those in the *interno* paid L. 38.56. When both groups were paying for the same municipal services it hardly seemed fair that there should be such a gross disparity in the level at which they were taxed. Extending the *dazio* belt would right this iniquity, whilst the removal of the *dazio* on bread and other basic foods would protect the worse-off from any adverse consequences of the enlargement.

Both critics and supporters of Ferrario saw a wider political purpose, however. With the disappearance of the tax advantages of a suburban location, manufacturers would simply move their plant outside the city altogether. Immigrants would head for the new locations as would many current suburban residents. City-centre, Moderate-voting residents would be assured of living in an orderly unpolluted city.

Pietro Ceriani, the town clerk, for example, wrote a pamphlet in which he describes in nauseating detail the unhygienic habits of the peasantry who lived in the countryside around the city, where they ate the wrong types of food, drank poor-quality wine in the *osterie* where they spent most of their time, picked their noses and wore no underwear. If there were to be a massive extension of the *cinta* into the countryside, with a series of differential tax rings, then the city of Milan would be able to provide the basic services and education

---

[10] The 1894 law was the R. Decreto 21 febb. 1894 n.51. On this and the previous legislation regulating the relationship between the government and city *dazi*, see Dalla Volta, 'Il dazio consumo in Italia', p. 994–1001, which also explains the iniquity of the tax.

which were necessary to raise the standards of civilisation of such people. This was not an altruistic proposal; a particularly penal rate of tax was to be applied to the zone immediately outside the current *interno* in order, Ceriani euphemistically wrote, that those who lived in the city centre would be able to breathe healthier air.[11]

Most discussion of the Ferrario proposals concentrated upon the likely effects on industry and commerce in the suburbs, were the measures to go through. In 1895 the *esterno* contained roughly 43% of the city's population, 55% of its production units and 57% of its mechanical horsepower.[12] Manufacturers and landlords who had come to the suburbs because of the tax advantages available argued that they would lose the benefits of their enterprises' location, whilst residents would lose their jobs because plants would be forced to move outside the boundary of the new *cinta*. Critics also demonstrated that many of Ferrario's numerical assumptions were inaccurate and biased: in comparing *per capita* contributions, for instance, he made no allowances for the fact that a great deal of the *dazio* revenue raised in the *interno* came from sales to outsiders passing through the city, whilst the amount of revenue each individual worker paid in *dazio consumo* in the *esterno* was higher as residents who could afford to buy their goods wholesale paid no duty at all.[13]

For shopkeepers the proposals necessitated an assessment of priorities. The advantages of extension were obvious. The privileges granted to the cooperatives under Article 5 would become irrelevant as these applied solely in *comuni aperti*. The elimination of the *abbonamento* in the *esterno* would mean an end to the difficult business negotiation and the abuses that it could lead to under unscrupulous operators such as Gerli. The hated surveillance of shops conducted by the *dazio* inspectors in the *esterno* would cease,

[11] Ceriani, *Il Comune di Milano*.   [12] *Dati statistici*, 1905, p. 57.
[13] Other inaccuracies were caused by the fact that in calculating the amount of revenue likely to be raised by the project he had merely imputed the same spending levels to a family in the *esterno* that had been observed in the *interno*, whilst he had also assumed that the proportion of well-off to poor families would be the same in both zones! It was also argued that Ferrario had overestimated his needs and underestimated future revenues, in particular those from the trams. These arguments were obviously more hypothetical and it is worth recording that the Democratic administration which took over the city at the end of 1899 soon came to the conclusion that the remaining *dazi*, now applied over virtually the whole of the city, would have to stay. Snider, *Calcoli e commenti; Il comitato centrale contro l'allargamento*; 'L'agitazione per la riforma tributaria del Comune', *La Lombardia*, 25 November 1895; Canavero, *Milano e la crisi de fine secolo*, p. 400.

and there could be no more illicit sales of goods on which the *abbonamento* had not been paid. Finally a new set of customers would patronise the shops as the well-off would no longer be able to avoid paying the *dazio* by purchasing goods wholesale.[14]

Thus the extension of the *cinta* would eliminate at a stroke those perceived injustices against which the *esercenti* movement had campaigned almost since its inception, campaigns which had been intended to foster a collective shopkeeper 'consciousness' such that the group would be able to assert its political weight and authority to further its interests. Yet on the issue of the enlargement of the *dazio* belt, the movement split almost entirely down lines of zonal interest, to the point that none of the advantages listed above were significant in either the suburbanites' resistance to change or the city residents' enthusiasm for it.

The suburban shopkeepers believed that extension would take away their only advantage over their peers in the *interno*, and these peers hoped they were right. The most obvious effect of the extension of the *cinta* was that there would now be no economic reason for anyone to do their shopping in the suburbs in preference to the centre. Suburbanites who worked in the city would have no incentive to buy their food locally in the morning, and residents of the old *interno* would gain nothing by doing their shopping in the suburbs. The concept of the *frontisti* would be destroyed, a prospect which the shopkeepers of the *interno* viewed with delight.

The whole structure of the city, the suburbanites argued, would be changed. Commercial activity would decline uniformly with distance from the centre, producing a far stronger core-and-periphery effect like that found in other cities such as Rome. The suburbs would soon lose a substantial part of their population as many workers would follow industry out of the zone, whilst all the rich would leave now that their purchasing privileges (and in some cases their factories) had disappeared. Rusca claimed that a third of the suburban residents would leave. Rents would fall (severely damaging the interests of the landlords) but the decline in clientele and revenue would be much greater.[15]

[14] 'L'agitazione per la riforma tributaria del Comune', *La Lombardia*, 25 November 1895; 'Pro e contro l'allargamento della cinta daziaria di Milano', *L'Esercente*, 14 November 1895; 'La questione daziaria', ibid., 24 November 1895.
[15] 'Il grave problema dell'allargamento della cinta daziaria', *L'Esercente*, 10 November 1895; 'In difesa degli esercenti', ibid., 17 November 1895.

The difficulties that the *esercenti* movement would face in dealing with the issue became apparent at the first meeting the Federation held after the proposals were announced. The meeting was attended largely by suburban *esercenti* who, predictably enough, were opposed to the extension. A shopkeeper from the *interno*, however, made a speech welcoming the proposal because it would eliminate the *filtrazione* that he claimed was undermining many businesses in the centre. He argued that Paris was a city with a very extensive *cinta*, and yet industry still flourished there.

Suburban representatives disagreed with this, pointing out that in many foreign cities including Brussels and London there was no *dazio* system at all. Both of the leading Democrat politicians, Stabilini, the Republican pork butcher, and Baroni, the Radical bakers' leader, strongly attacked the proposals, although Stabilini had to admit that as the representative of the *salsamentari* of the *interno* he ought to welcome the proposal; it was only as a private citizen that he was opposed to it.

It was left to the milk seller Piovella to object to the way the meeting had degenerated into a dispute between the *esercenti* of the *interno* and *esterno* but the only practical measure that he could suggest to avoid this was the complete abolition of the *dazio consumo* and its replacement with some other form of direct tax. This, indeed, became the declared aim of both supporters and opponents of the Ferrario proposal; the question was whether or not the measures advocated in the proposition were, as their supporters claimed, a first practical step towards total abolition.

The climax of the meeting came when the President, Marmont, a grocer from the *interno*, was challenged to declare his position. He responded that as President of the Federation of the shopkeepers of both the *interno* and *esterno* he had to remain impartial in the matter; however, he did add that the dangers resulting from the extension were not as great as many maintained. This was correctly perceived as an indication of his support for the extension. Amid great acrimony the Federation passed a resolution calling on the Giunta to withdraw the proposed extension and study the best means to proceed to the total abolition of the *dazio consumo*.[16]

With the *esercenti* movement so divided, most shopkeeper

---

[16] 'Una tempestosa adunanza di esercenti', *La Lombardia*, 20 November 1895; 'L'Assemblea Generale della Federazione degli Esercenti', *L'Esercente*, 21 November 1895.

186 THE POLITICAL ECONOMY OF SHOPKEEPING IN MILAN

resistance to the planned extension of the *cinta* was channelled into the campaign mounted by the Circolo Liberale Electorale Suburbano. As with the *micca* affair almost ten years previously, the Circolo argued that the city was acting in its own interests as opposed to that of the ex-Corpi Santi, ignoring the undertaking given by the Comune to preserve an 'open' *dazio* regime in the suburbs at the time of unification.[17] The Circolo organised a series of meetings in each *rione* of the suburbs and at the end of each a committee for propaganda was set up to coordinate the campaign in the area. Above these a central committee with members drawn from various of the 'popular' organisations produced a counter-proposal to that mooted by Ferrario.

The purpose of the local committees was to give the opposition as broad a base as possible. In an attempt to attract more workers into the protest, Socialists were put on several of the *rione* committees, but the overwhelming majority of those involved in the campaign were from the middle and lower middle classes – shopkeepers, landlords and manufacturers whose businesses would be badly affected by the proposals, professionals and white-collar workers whose living standards would be. The committee for the *rione* of Porta Vitoria, Monforte and Venezia, for example, contained six property owners, five shopkeepers, one clerk and one master craftsman.[18]

Shopkeepers were once more brought into close contact with the suburban Democrat politicians who had been their first sponsors. Indeed many of those involved in the early campaign played important roles in the new one; Luigi Gastel, for instance, chaired the committee for the *rione* of Porta Volta, Tenaglia and Sempione. *Esercenti* leaders who were closely aligned to the Democratic bloc, such as Rosio, Baroni and Stabilini, were prominent at the protest meetings. With the Democrats providing the only clear opposition to the Ferrario proposals, Rusca's strictures against shopkeepers'

---

[17] This promise was repeated by subsequent mayors on several occasions. As late as 1894 Vigoni confirmed that the *dazio* division would be maintined in the *Resoconto morale della Giunta Municipale del Comune nelle annate 1892–1894*, p. 27. The various promises made to the suburbs and the 'legal' issue are examined in the report of *Il comitato centrale contro l'allargamento*, pp. 5–11.

[18] This information comes from a wall poster issued by the committee advertising a meeting to be held on 11 December 1895. The poster is amongst the collection of documents held in the Questura files concerning the campaign against the extension of the *cinta*. ASM, fond. Questura, c.57, f.1, (a) 1895, (b) 1897, (c) 1898.

movements having political links had been overtaken by events, with suburban shopkeepers returning to the Democratic fold.

In the face of the opposition to the proposals, the Giunta decided to appoint a Commission of nine members of the city council to review the project – the so-called Commisione dei Nove. One member was Marmont, deliberately chosen as a supporter of the proposal in a carefully balanced committee of whom four favoured the proposals, four did not and one was uncertain. His position highlighted the divisions in the shopkeeper movement and the Federation itself. *L'Esercente* frequently attacked Marmont over this issue and relations between Marmont and Rusca became very bitter.

Despite their differences the Commission succeeded in producing a report in October 1896 which recommended significant changes to the Giunta's plan, whilst advocating the extension of the *cinta*. The main difference was that the Commission wanted to abolish the *dazi* on a much wider range of basic goods, replacing the income lost through this by raising the levels of some of the existing local taxes, and most importantly, by introducing a new direct tax on family income. Furthermore they believed that the new area would have to be bounded by a line drawn on a map, rather than by a wall.

Marmont contributed a substantial article to the newly reunited *L'Esercente*, explaining the project. He argued that it represented the best possible outcome for shopkeepers as it simultaneously provided for the raising of enough revenue for the Municipio to meet its needs and the abolition of the *dazio consumo* on most of the basic items that the *esercenti* stocked. Also the new direct tax would correct the injustice of the poor paying a relatively harsher rate of tax than the well-off, as had been the case under the old system.[19]

The Giunta, however, rejected the Commission's proposals, apart from that not to build a physical barrier but merely have an administrative line. In the debate in the Council in early January 1897, the Mayor, Vigoni, stated that this was because the Giunta believed that substituting a direct tax for some of the *dazi* would create a more onerous tax burden on the populace. The unstated subtext to this position was that the Moderates had no intention of

[19] Marmont, B., 'La riforma tributaria e la tassa di famiglia', *L'Esercente*, 15 November 1896.

penalising their own supporters in the *interno* more than was necessary by introducing a direct tax in place of an indirect one.[20]

The council debate was notable for the contributions of those councillors who represented the small traders. Marmont argued that the Giunta had underestimated the likely yields from the *dazi* on wine and luxury meats, and proposed that they could take advantage of these to remove the *dazio* on raw sugar. As a grocer this would, of course, have been of considerable benefit to him. He also proposed, probably as a political move to retain favour within the Federation, that the *dazio* on pig carcasses be removed as these were primarily used to make lard for the poor. This was supported by the Catholic Councillor Maraschi, a pork butcher. The most obvious example of self-interest came from opponents of extension such as Baroni, however, when they opposed a suggestion that the poor could be protected by an extension of the *calmiere* on bread across the whole *dazio* area, should the *allargamento* go through. The protesters' first priority was to preserve shopkeeper standards of living, not those of suburban residents as a whole.[21]

In February 1897 the council adopted what was in essence Ferrario's original proposal, a belated tribute to its architect who had committed suicide in the interim.[22] Implementation, however, was made conditional on receipt of assurances that the government would not demand an increase in the *dazio canone* paid to it by the city. Legally the government was entitled to take such actions as it believed would protect its income from the city, although, arguably, not to prevent the reform or abolition of the Comune's own *dazio* system.[23] Many of the Giunta's opponents believed the government

[20] This opinion was shared by the well-known economist Luigi Einaudi who argued that the family tax would only be paid by those who couldn't afford to set up a legal residence in another *comune*, and would hit hardest those who were unable to hide the extent of their income, notably the *impiegati*. Einaudi, 'Imposta di famiglia o sul valor locativo (7 December 1896)', in *Cronache economiche e politiche*, Vol. 1, pp. 26–7.

[21] 'Il Consiglio Comunale ha approvato l'allargamento della linea daziaria e l'altre proposte Ferrario', *La Lombardia*, 8 January 1897.

[22] The measure pased despite opposition campaign organisers presenting a petition with over 25,000 signatures against it. Canavero, *Milano e la crisi fine secolo*, pp. 85–6.

[23] Article 1 of the *regolamento 25 agosto 1870 N. 5830*, explicitly stated that any change in a *comune*'s *cinta* had to be approved by the Minister of Finance. For an outline of the law regarding the *dazio consumo* at this time see Guidoti, L., 'Ragioni in sostegno all'abolizione del dazio consumo', *L'Esercente*, 23 January 1896.

would never agree to this. In fact, Finance Minister Branca presented a *progetto di legge* to the Chamber of Deputies in May 1897 which would have permitted the *comuni* to extend their customs area without the *canone governativo* being modified; however, this was lost when Parliament was adjourned for the summer. The Giunta's policy was in disarray and Vigoni was forced to promise that he would abandon the plans for the *allargamento*, in order to survive a vote of confidence.[24]

Whilst the *allargamento* itself was held up, the tensions created by it continued to dominate the *esercenti* movement. Opponents of the extension realised that some sort of reform was now inevitable and campaigned for the adoption of a direct tax as advocated by the Commissione dei Nove. To their consternation, Marmont, a member of the Commission, then supported the Giunta's proposals at the Consiglio Comunale. Meanwhile the two Vice-Presidents of the Federation, Baroni and Trezzi (leader of the pork butchers in the *esterno*), were using *L'Esercente* to publish notices urging members to sign the petition of protest.[25]

Marmont's actions were consistent with his individual situation as a trader in the *interno*, and it is clear that he did have a significant amount of support within the Federation from shopkeepers in similar positions. Yet the majority of members were still from the suburbs, and they were furious about his conduct. Rusca added his voice to the criticisms as it became clear that there was no official Federation line to which he had to adhere, arguing that Marmont was using the Federation as a vehicle for his private political opinions.

The internal conflicts at the Federation came to a surprising conclusion, however. 'Persons unknown' destroyed the Federation's books three days after the *allargamento* was passed; a committee which included Marmont's severest critics was set up to try to reassemble the information lost. The financial mismanagement it reported in late May was such that Marmont felt bound to tender his resignation. Shortly after this Marmont lost his position in the Grocers' Society as well.[26]

---

[24] The two councillors were De Angelli and Cornaggia who had always been hostile to the Ferrario scheme. Canavero, *Milano e la crisi fine secolo*, pp. 89–90.

[25] 'Per il referendum d'oggi', *L'Esercente*, 30 January 1897.

[26] 'Le dimissioni del sig. Rag. Marmont da Presidente della Federazione degli Esercenti', ibid., 27 May 1897; 'L'Associazione Droghieri di Milano chiamata

After a brief interval Baroni became President of the Federation. A prominent politician, a city councillor and leading member of the Circolo Liberale Elettorale Suburbano, his success was a further demonstration of the Democratic bloc's return to favour within the shopkeeper movement. It was impossible to maintain that the Federation should be a non-political organisation when the decision on whether to extend the *cinta* was to be made by politicians. With the Federation now firmly behind the Democrats and opposed to the *allargamento*, the major question was whether or not the Federation would retain the support of its members in the *interno*.

Some did put altruism above self-interest, but inevitably most were more interested in eliminating the perceived advantages of the suburban *esercenti*. In 1898 Marmont organised an Associazione Generale del Commercio Milanese to cater for these traders. This organisation was in favour of the extension of the *cinta*, regarding it as the only 'equitable' solution to the problem. Five hundred people attended its inaugural meeting at La Scala, and, although the Association claimed to be non-political, the very choice of venue indicated its pro-establishment leanings.[27] Whilst the Associazione attacked the Federation's partisanship, Baroni denounced the new organisation as that favoured by the 'establishment' papers *La Perseveranza* and the *Corriere della Sera*.

Further fragmentation within the *esercenti* movement was caused by the Federation's need to recoup the financial losses incurred as a result of Marmont's maladministration. The most attractive option open to it was to put *L'Esercente* up for sale. On 30 September 1897 Giovanni Tadini, who was already editor/proprietor of the agricultural journal *Il Corriere Agricolo*, assumed the same position at *L'Esercente*, once more making it completely independent of the Federation line. It was a condition of sale that Rusca would not set up any rival publications, but the former editor, with the encouragement of some dissident members of the Federation hierarchy, published various news-sheets, starting with *Il Contribuente* (The Taxpayer), in an attempt to retain influence within a movement he had nurtured since 1886. Tadini spent much of the succeeding three years engaged in various legal actions to silence Rusca, but none of

per un importante votazione', ibid., 27 June 1897; 'L'esito delle elezione alla Società Droghieri di Milano', ibid., 1 July 1897.
[27] 'Una nuova associazione d'esercenti', ibid., 28 April 1898.

the journals posed any threat to *L'Esercente*'s dominant market position.

The divisions within the *esercenti* movement around the end of 1897, then, were very different from those that existed two years previously. In the first half of the 1890s many more city-centre shopkeepers had participated in the movement, uniting with their suburban peers in the campaign against various forms of 'unfair' competition, particularly the legal 'privileges' of the consumer cooperatives. Disputes over the best political strategy to achieve these goals split the Federation and the Nuova Associazione, but both drew significant numbers of supporters from either side of the *dazio* line. By contrast, the division between the Associazione Generale and the Federation in September 1897 was rooted in economic geography. Traders in the *interno* sought to improve their local commercial environment, those in the *esterno* to defend theirs. The fact that the advantages that *allargamento* would bring in terms of cooperative privilege were so completely ignored by the suburban shopkeepers may be used as a further proof that these privileges were relatively insignificant in terms of their effect on *esercenti* enterprises, even if they had served a useful role in enabling the movement to foster a broader shopkeeper identity.

The zonal response to the *allargamento* debate reflected the paramount importance of business concerns in determining the political responses of the Milanese small traders. This was confirmed by the conduct of the *esercenti* during the crisis year at the end of the century. It does not follow, however, that occupational responses were put in abeyance: a shopkeeper identity continued to evolve in these years, ready to assume a central importance once the last great zonal conflict had been played out.

10. The end-of-century crisis and the enlargement of the dazio belt

After the fall of the Crispi government in 1896, a new administration was established under the leadership of Di Rudini. The new government was drawn almost entirely from the landed elite, and agrarian paternalism blinded it to the real nature of many of the urban, commercial and labour questions that confronted the country. The chasm between the 'legal' Italy of the state and the 'real' Italy of its citizens was the cause of the 'end-of-century' crisis whose most spectacular manifestation took place in Milan in 1898.

The government's most pressing problem was the rapid rise in bread prices and the public unrest which accompanied this. In 1897 just 23,891,000 quintals of grain were harvested in Italy, compared with figures between 31,798,000 and 39,920,000 for the previous five-year period. The shortfall had to be made up by imports, yet these were subject to a high protective tariff which the government was loath to reduce for fear of offending their supporters. Between them the *dazio* on grain and the *dazio consumo* accounted for around 40% of the price of bread.[1]

Bread prices rose sharply in Milan as elsewhere. The retail price of prime-quality bread in the *interno* was 30 *centesimi* per *libra* at the beginning of April 1897, 34 *centesimi* at the end of May, and 36 *centesimi* at the end of July, and it had reached 38 *centesimi* by January 1898.[2] Naturally these rises were resented and the Socialists organised a considerable number of public meetings amongst the city's workers to discuss ways of resolving the problem. The organisers of these meetings stressed that there was no point in workers taking their grievances on to the streets, reassuring at least one police official that there was little danger of unrest. On 23

[1] Candeloro, *La crisi di fine secolo e l'età giolittiana*, pp. 49–50.
[2] Canavero, *Milano e la crisi fine secolo*, p. 148.

January, however, mindful of the disturbances that had already occurred in other parts of Italy, the Prefect ordered that no further meetings should be permitted.[3]

There were two main thrusts to the Socialists' arguments. The first was that all the *dazi* on bread ought to be abolished. These accounted for half the price of grain which in itself made up two-thirds of the price of bread, and existed only to protect the traditional oppressors of the poor, the *latifondisti*. On this point they were supported by the whole of the Democratic bloc, which still remained committed to free trade.

The Socialists went further, however, arguing that the structure of bread production and distribution was at fault. Baking was undertaken by a large number of small individuals whose operations were both uneconomical and unhygienic, and who allowed the big producers to get away with charging higher prices for their goods than was necessary. The solution, according to the Socialists, was that cooperative bakeries, and above all municipal bakeries, be established to utilize all the economies of scale that came with large-scale production. These would also be more hygienic, provide better conditions for their workers, and could be trusted to pass on the lower prices to the consumer. The formerly struggling small bakers would be taken on as workers by the Municipio on a pensionable salary.[4]

Bakers did not accept this, arguing that rationalisation of the industry would lead to considerable unemployment amongst both bakers and workers, whilst those workers who did remain would have no prospect of ever becoming proprietors themselves. The administrative costs of the *forni municipali*, moreover, would eat up whatever economies of scale they might benefit from. Although some accepted that the profession was oversubscribed, particularly by new entrants who knew little about business, they were united in wanting to retain their independence, something the Socialists did

[3] See report from Section 6A to the Questore 'circa il rincaro del pane spirito pubblico', 18 January 1898, and the Prefect's banning order Prefettura di Milano, Gabinetto No. 176, 25 January 1898; risposta a nota 25 corr No. 326, Ogg: Agitazione pel rincaro del pane. ASM, fond. Questura, c. 52, f. 2a.

[4] For an exposition of these arguments see the handsheet produced by the Federazione Socialista Milanista, *Pane a buon mercato*, 1897, to be found in ASM, fond. Questura, c. 52, f. 2a, especially Dell'Avale, C., 'Molini e forni – il pane municipale'. One of the other articles included was by the noted Milanese journalist Paolo Valera, significantly recalling the riots of 1886.

not take into consideration. The bakers' usual defence, however, was to point out the overriding importance of the *dazi* on bread prices. The obvious solution to the problem was the reduction of these impositions, and they therefore looked to the government to move to the abolition of both the import tariff and the *dazio consumo*.[5]

The Di Rudini administration's apparent refusal to contemplate such a manœuvre reinforced the shopkeepers' impression that they were still discriminated against when it came to a clash between their interests and those of the landed sector. Branca, the Minister of Finance, had already introduced a proposal for a series of modifications to the tax system in 1897, including a restructuring of the *ricchezza mobile* to protect agricultural producers at the expense of commercial operators. Shopkeepers were strongly opposed to these proposals because their incomes were estimated in advance by the tax inspectors, a procedure designed to avoid the problems arising from the deficiencies in the book-keeping of the *esercenti*, but which invariably led to complaints that assessments were too high.

The Federazione degli Esercenti in association with the Chamber of Commerce protested vigorously about the proposals, as did other chambers throughout the country. Eventually Branca was forced to withdraw the project, whilst a committee to investigate individual assessments was set up. The Milan Prefect, concerned about the threat to public order from the various protests that had taken place, banned any further demonstrations once the committee had been established.[6]

The *esercenti*, then, were engaged in hostilities at both ends of the political spectrum in the inflationary years of 1897–8. Whilst the Socialists sought to threaten their independence through the policy of municipalisation, the government seemed content to shift the burden of the fiscal crisis onto the commercial sector, whilst protecting the interests of its landed supporters. Alienated from both sides,

---

[5] 'Ragionando sulla odierna questione del pane', *L'Esercente*, 12 September 1897; 'Società Generale tra i Negozianti e Industriali di Roma: in difesa dei fornai', ibid., 19 September 1897; 'Pane e Socialismo', ibid., 27 January 1898.

[6] The Questura records contain both the telegram from Prefect Winspeare ordering that no further demonstrations be allowed (12 October 1897) and a copy of a telegram sent by the Milanese Camera di Commercio to Di Rudini on 15 October 1897. ASM, fond. Questura, c. 53, f. 2a. For the shopkeeper viewpoint see the various articles in *L'Esercente* on 1 and 14 October 1897.

the *esercenti* could seek some solace, however, in the fact that the success of some of their protests again demonstrated their increasing weight within the political system.

Eventually, in January 1898, the Government bowed to the inevitable and introduced a bill which allowed for the reduction of the external *dazio* on grain from L. 75 to L. 50 a tonne. Although Milanese bakers reduced the price of bread the same day, the administration's action was largely interpreted as being too little too late. Originally due to last until 30 April, the *dazio* reduction had first to be extended until 15 July, and then, on 4 May, the tariff itself was temporarily suppressed as prices had been further driven upwards by the Spanish-American War.[7]

Branca also introduced a bill designed to encourage the *comuni* to remove their *dazio consumo* on flour and its products. Its principal effect was to commute the *dazio governativo* (government duties) into a fixed debt or *canone* to be paid by the *comuni* to the Government. The *comuni* could therefore design their own structure for the *dazio consumo*, allowing them to remove some duties altogether.

Furthermore Article 10 of this new *progetto di legge* permitted a *comune* to extend its *cinta*, provided it had reduced or eliminated its *dazio* on flour products, had applied all the permissible supertaxes on direct taxes, and had instituted various taxes including either a family or a property tax. In this case the state would be entitled to an increase in its *canone* equivalent to either a fifth or a tenth of the extra revenue raised, depending upon whether or not the *dazio comune* on flour products had been completely abolished. Although the article was ambiguously phrased, it did seem to offer a way out of the Giunta's dilemma, if they were prepared to overcome their objections to direct taxation. One commentator argued that the requirement to increase the government's contribution by a tenth could be avoided by making the *dazio* changes revenue neutral, and raising the extra revenue required through a combination of the two direct taxes.[8]

On the evening of 5 May, however, before the *progetto* became law, Socialist organisers were arrested outside the Pirelli factory

---

[7] Candeloro, *La crisi di fine secolo e l'età giolittiana*, pp. 50–1.
[8] The full text of the *progetto* and an analysis of its implications for Milan can be found in Gobbi, *Il nuovo progetto di legge sui dazi comunali e la riforma tributaria milanese*. His proposals for combining the family and property tax are found on pp. 19–31. A similar scheme is proposed in Vallardi, *Milan può abolire la cinta daziaria?*.

where they had been handing out leaflets advocating universal suffrage and the rights of workers to organise collectively. During the following day a group of protesters gathered outside the police station and troops dispersed them with gunfire, causing several fatalities. This caused demonstrations in the *piazza* that evening and disorders and strikes throughout the city during the next couple of days.[9]

The authorities over-reacted on a remarkable scale. Military rule was declared in the city and a division of troops under the command of Bava Beccaris was sent to quell the presumed revolt. Eighty people were killed, of whom just two were members of the security forces. Events took a tragicomic turn with the bombardment of a Cappucine monastery, alleged to be harbouring the rebels, whose only occupants turned out to be the friars and some beggars who were waiting for soup to be distributed!

The oppressive nature of this response was occasioned by the fact that the events in Milan were only the most dramatic of several incidents in Italian cities, whilst these themselves were the culmination of disorders which had been working up the peninsula during the last four years. The end-of-century crisis had reached its height, and with Florence, Livorno and Naples also under military rule the government embarked on a repressive crusade throughout Italy.

The authorities believed that the unrest was a product of the resentment fostered by high bread prices being manipulated by 'subversives' for their own ends. Consequently they responded by imprisoning those who were held to have 'inspired' the demonstrators (for example the Socialist Turati and the Republican De Andreis), and closing down such supposed organs of sedition as the newspapers *Il Secolo* and *L'Osservatore Cattolico*. Many worker organisations were closed down, including a large number of cooperatives, and even some of the lay Catholic organisations which had involved themselves in social activities were dissolved by order. It was a remarkable, frontal attack on the radical institutions.

Shopkeepers were alarmed by the effects of the disorder on city trade, and fearful that the workers had fallen under the spell of so-called subversives, notably the Socialists. The depression years

---

[9] Tilly, 'I fatti di maggio', analyses the social background to the May events whilst Canavero, *Milano e la crisi fine secolo*, is good on city politics in the period. Candeloro, *Storia dell'Italia moderna*, Vol. 7, pp. 49–60 examines the occurrences within the national context.

had already challenged the idea that shopkeepers could speak for their working-class customers, and what increasingly worried the *esercenti* movement was that the demands of the labour movement would undermine the status of shopkeepers themselves (the *esercenti* leaders were far quicker than the authorities to acknowledge that the disorders were motivated by more than the price of bread). Whilst recognising that there were valid reasons for discontent, *L'Esercente* defended the merits of the existing social system to the workers, emphasising the necessity for a social hierarchy as the basis of production and consumption.

One cannot change the world. – The rich will always be with us. Capital would no longer have any power if it were divided up as you would like.

All of us are aware of social inequalities and we understand very well that one could envy someone who is better off: but, then again, how could it be otherwise? The worker who yearns to become a lawyer does wrong. Everyone has his position in society and each position brings with it the duties inherent in one's own condition, then these duties taken together apply to everyone, and maintain the social order.[10]

This was the most explicit endorsement of social conservatism that *Esercente* had ever carried. It must be read as the product of a long process during which small traders had renounced their claims to speak for the workers, and come to accept that *esercenti* interests were best served within the existing social order, despite shopkeepers' continued resentments of those at the top of the social hierarchy. Though the *esercenti* were far from aligning themselves with the 'ruling elite', they recognised the utility of the society over which that elite presided for *esercenti* interests and sought to preserve it against the challenge of the 'subversive' ideologies whose success amongst the working class was the principal cause of the *esercenti*'s recognition that they could no longer claim to represent the aspirations of the people.[11]

The re-imposition of order after the events of May 1898 was welcomed, therefore, by the small traders. *L'Esercente* urged that people look favourably on the soldiers as guarantors of the citizens'

[10] 'A burrasca finita', *L'Esercente*, 15 May 1898.
[11] On the question of *esercenti* perceptions of the Milanese elite see Morris, 'I bottegai e il mondo Bagatti Valsecchi'.

security, despite their over-reaction.[12] Nor could the newspaper prevent itself from enjoying the new notoriety of the cooperatives, attacked by Moderate journals such as the *Corriere* which had previously lauded them. According to one headline the unrest had caused 'the fall of the consumer cooperatives and the revival of the *esercenti*'.[13] The dissolution of the board of the Cooperativa Suburbana for allegedly socialist tendencies was greeted with particular relish. Baroni, the President of the Federation, went as far as to support a vote of thanks to General Bava Beccaris passed by the city council, thereby arousing the fury of those of his Democrat colleagues who had not been forced into hiding, or imprisoned by the military tribunals.

The city authorities were also concerned to eliminate the supposed cause of the discontent.[14] On 7 May the Giunta suspended its *dazio consumo* on flour products. It also now had a considerable incentive to accept the terms of the *progetto* which became law on 14 July 1898.[15] By doing so it could convert the abolition of the *dazio consumo* on bread into a permanent state of affairs, and likewise eliminate the *dazi* on a range of other essential items. At the same time the *allargamento* would please its supporters, and it would be easy to get through the city council as many Democrats had gone into hiding to avoid the attentions of the military tribunals which had sentenced their colleagues to reclusion. For the Giunta these benefits outweighed the consideration that the government would still be entitled to claim 10% of the increased revenues, and that Moderates had always opposed the introduction of a further direct tax.

[12] For *L'Esercente*'s reaction to the events see *L'Esercente*, 12 and 15 May 1898.

[13] 'La caduta delle cooperative di consumo e la risurrezione degli esercenti', ibid., 2 June 1898.

[14] Tilly makes a useful analysis of the various contemporary explanations of the events. Her own conclusion is that 'violence can grow out of everyday politics, as movements take on an internal dynamism quite apart from the directions imposed on them by their leaders, a dynamism that is often shaped in response to official government reaction. What made the diffference in May 1898? On one hand tension and anxiety from months of unrest led to a determination to put a quick end to protest. On the other hand the workers were at the crest of a period of rapid growth of organisations, increased propaganda and mobilisation around issues such as the grain tariff, freedom of assembly and the right to strike. These differentiated the situation in 1898 from seemingly similar movements, and accounted to a large degree for the transformation of street demonstrations into a rebellion that transfixed the nation.' Tilly, 'I fatti di Maggio', p. 131.

[15] *Legge 14 luglio 1898 n. 302.*

In late July, the Giunta presented a new plan for an *allargamento* which bore much resemblance to that devised by the Commissione dei Nove. The direct property tax, the *valor locativo*, was included in this scheme for a symbolic (as opposed to a physical) *cinta* within which many of the *dazi* on essential goods, though not on meat or wine, were abolished. On the 28 July, with the city still under military rule, the proposal was approved by the Council and on 1 September 1898 the new, unified, customs area came into being.

The *allargamento* package introduced by the Giunta was close to that which the *esercenti* had regarded as the 'least bad' of the alternatives available. In early 1898 the Federation had explicitly called for the introduction of the *valor locativo* within a unified Milan whose *dazio consumo* would be organised on the basis of a *comune aperto*, and Vice-President Trasi devised his own scheme based on this premise. The preference for the tax derived from the fact that shops were exempt from it. Even so all the city councillors associated with the Federation opposed the plan when it came before the Council, as the *dazi* which remained would be much higher than those in existence in the *esterno*.[16]

Since 1895, when the *allargamento* issue had first been raised, the suburban *esercenti* had aligned themselves with the Democrats who had assumed their historical role as defenders of suburban and commercial interests. The 'establishment' interests who were in control at both local and national level had clearly favoured their own supporters, as was evident in both the *allargamento* proposals themselves and the government's failure to act promptly to cut the *dazi* on bread (particularly resented by the *esercenti* as it strengthened the Socialists demands for the municipalisation of the bakeries). This climate had enabled the Democrat politicians, notably Baroni, to take charge of the Federation and its political direction.

The extension of the *dazio* belt dramatically altered these circumstances. The main bone of contention between Marmont's dissident Associazione Generale and the Federation itself had disappeared: shopkeepers in the old *interno* and *esterno* zones were now united within the same commercial environment in that they operated under the same *dazio* system, and were subject to the same local and national regulations. Following the death of Marmont in October, the two bodies were reunited in early December 1898.[17] The ending

[16] 'La vivace seduta in Consiglio Comunale', *L'Esercente*, 25 August 1898.
[17] 'La conciliazione tra gli esercenti milanesi', ibid., 1 December 1898.

of the division between the city centre and the suburbs came at the same time as the process whereby the *esercenti* became convinced of the need to conserve the existing social structure reached its peak following the violence of the May events. Although neither of these developments necessarily implied a simple switch from the Democrat to the Moderate bloc, they clearly had considerable implications for the movement's future political alignments.

It would take time before these implications were fully understood, however. When the local government by-elections were held in June 1899, Baroni and the Federation fully supported the Democrats, although Baroni himself did not stand, so as not to cause embarrassment following his support of the vote of thanks to Bava Beccaris. To the Federation and its suburban followers the issue was simple: the Giunta had to be punished for its excessive taxation, for its handling of the period of military rule, and, above all, for the *allargamento* (which it was still hoped to repeal). *L'Esercente* also supported the Democratic list, making clear that its aim in doing so was not to make common cause with the Socialists and Republicans, but to provoke a crisis whereby the Giunta would lose its majority on the council and full elections would follow. At that point shopkeepers should determine the correct stance to take in the new circumstances created by the *allargamento*.[18]

L'Esercente's reservations concerning the Federation's position were shared by several shopkeeper leaders who were hostile to both the Socialists (owing to their support for 'municipalisation' and 'workers' rights') and the Republicans (who figured amongst the supporters of the consumer cooperatives). In May one of the Vice-Secretaries of the Federation, Meraviglia, wrote a letter to the *Corriere della Sera* denouncing the Federation as an organisation dominated by closet members of the two parties. The *Corriere*, a paper associated with the 'new' industrial wing of the Moderates, attacked the Federation and called on the *esercenti* to abandon its line. When a meeting of delegates to the Federation (as opposed to the ordinary members) was held, however, Baroni succeeded in winning a vote of confidence by seventy votes to five.[19]

---

[18] 'Agli esercenti e commercianti', ibid., 10–11 June 1899.

[19] Meraviglia's letter appeared in the *Corriere della Sera* of 18–19 May 1899 under the heading 'Gli esercenti, i socialisti e l'elezioni'. For the Federation's attitude see 'Le elezione amministrative; l'adunanza alla Federazione', *L'Esercente*, 25–6 May 1899.

At the elections themselves the Democrat list (including both Republicans and Socialists and known as the 'popular' list) scored an emphatic triumph over the Moderate one. Over 5,000 votes separated the last of the Democrats elected from the leading members of the Moderate list. All five Federation sponsored candidates won seats, and *L'Esercente* claimed that 7,500 of the 12,500 *esercenti* electors cast votes, at least 6,000 of them in favour of the Democrats (presumably the other 1,000 were city-centre traders or clerical voters).[20] Although the accuracy of these figures can be doubted, it is clear that the majority of the *esercenti* were little troubled by the width of the Democrat alliance at this stage. Even though the Giunta was not technically in a minority it could not ignore such a stunning defeat and general elections were called for 10 December – creating exactly the scenario that *L'Esercente* had hoped for.

The newspaper therefore launched its examination of the position of the *esercenti*. Tadini wrote eleven articles on the subject, all predicated on the premise that the cooperative issue remained the most important facing the *esercenti*. He argued that it was the big commercial consumer cooperatives which sold directly to the public that posed a threat to the *esercenti*, none more so than the Unione Cooperativa. These, he claimed, were primarily supported by the Moderates, whilst the Socialists and Radicals were more concerned with the fortunes of the small workers cooperatives which, once stripped of their privileges (as they effectively had been in Milan as a consequence of the *allargamento*), would pose little real threat to the small traders.

According to Tadini, the two major worries about the city authorities were that they would add yet more to the taxation burden on small business, and that they would protect the cooperatives. One could not necessarily distinguish the attitudes of the parties on these points by reference to their conduct over the

---

[20] The last of the candidates elected on the Democrat list was Edoardo Piovella, the milk seller, with 18,488 votes. The most successful candidate who features solely on the Moderate list was Pio Gavazzi with 13,407. Edoardo Porro, a Moderate but with additional endorsements, gained 14,255. *L'Esercente* gave the overall turnout as 32,857 out of 51,405, acknowledging that its estimate of *esercenti* turnout was arrived at by assuming that the proportion of the *esercenti* electorate casting its vote was in line with the overall pattern, and ratifying this through anecdotal observation. 'I risultati definitivi', *L'Esercente*, 15 June 1899; 'La grande vittoria della lista popolare. Gli esercenti e i commercianti', ibid., 12/13 June 1899.

allargamento and the period of military occupation, however. What was needed was a mass commercial movement, independent of parties, which would protect the interests of small traders alone. This would only cooperate with parties when they agreed to support a well-defined *esercenti* programme. Tadini's call for a form of political neutrality in 1899 began to look extremely like that of Rusca in 1895.[21]

Other shopkeeper leaders were also engaged in rethinking, particularly those associated with the old *interno* zone who had had little reason to support the Federation during its battle to save the *dazio* division, and were unlikely to be brought back into the fold by a backward-looking campaign to revive it, or at least punish the Moderates for its abolition. Even before the partial elections a group of dissidents headed by Perego, the head of the *salsamentari* in the *interno*, and Polli, the President of the Banca degli Esercenti, held a meeting in (significantly) the Teatro alla Scala at which they attacked the Federation line. They were joined at the meeting by two of the most prominent hoteliers in Milan, Bassano Clerici and Giuseppe Spatz, both well-known Moderate sympathisers and both businessmen in a different league from the average shopkeeper.[22]

At the end of October it became clear that the Federation intended to support the Democratic list wholeheartedly in the coming election. This provoked a variety of splits. The newly formed Associazione Salumiere (a product of the changed circumstances in that it was a fusion of the *interno* and *esterno* societies) voted by a narrow majority to break any link with the Federation. This followed a campaign by Perego who argued that the society needed to remain politically neutral. He was a prime mover in the foundation of an Associazione fra Commercianti, Esercenti ed Industriali which held its inaugural meeting on 27 November, attended by over 200 of the claimed 500 members.[23]

The Associazione claimed to be a non-political organisation whose only activity would consist in representing the economic interests of the classes it encompassed. Yet it was clearly recognisable as an offshoot of the Moderate party, a fact which also explained

---

[21] Tadini's articles, all entitled 'I Socialisti, i Moderati, i Radicali e le cooperative', appeared in *L'Esercente* between 31 August and 12 October 1898.
[22] 'L'assemblea dei "dissidenti" al teatro milanese', *L'Esercente*, 2–3 June 1899.
[23] 'Alla Società Salumiere', ibid., 26 October 1899; 'La nuova Associazione fra Commercianti, Esercenti ed Industriali', ibid., 9 November 1899.

the difference in personnel between this and other commercial associations. The council members were usually successful businessmen, at the head of large concerns in the heart of the city. There were few retailers, and even fewer plain *esercenti*.[24]

L'Esercente also disassociated itself from the Federation, claiming it had abandoned *esercenti* interests for the pursuit of pure politics – a charge Tadini was able to substantiate by pointing out that five of the six candidates recommended by the Federation were not shopkeepers at all. Furthermore the Federation's programme made no mention of the cooperative issue, presumably in order not to offend the Socialists whom Baroni had been attacking in anti-privilege speeches less than a year ago. The newspaper stated that it could not support an organisation which was doing nothing to raise public awareness of cooperative abuses, and therefore chose to recommend its own electoral list (essentially that of the Democrats, with Socialists and Federation candidates substituted by anti-cooperative Moderates).[25]

These criticisms were not entirely fair. As Baroni had pointed out, the Socialists were in favour of the closed workers cooperatives which Tadini himself had labelled as 'true cooperatives'.[26] The privileges they were entitled to under Article 5 had been lost with the *allargamento*. True the Federation programme did not make any references to cooperative privileges, but it was a coherent statement touching on many important aspects of shopkeeping activity.[27] For that matter the goals adopted by the Associazione fra Commercianti, Esercenti ed Industriali contained no mention of the cooperative issue.

Whatever the merits of Tadini's new thinking, he badly misjudged the mood of the majority of the *esercenti*. The full council elections of December 1899 witnessed the first clear victory of a Democrat list

---

[24] A full list of council members was published in 'La nuova Associazione fra Commercianti, Esercenti ed Industriali di Milano', ibid., 30 November 1899.

[25] 'Gli esercenti, i commercianti e le elezioni amministrativi', ibid., 3–4 December 1899.

[26] 'Alla Federazione L'Assemblea Generale', ibid., 2–3 June 1899.

[27] The programme included proposals for more severe regulation of *vendita ambulante*, for the Consiglio Comunale to work for a modification of the Public Health laws so that the supplier of a product, rather than the vendor, should take ultimate responsibility for its quality, for free or subsidised access to the municipal laboratories for the *esercenti*, for reform of the pharmaceutical service and for the enlargement of the public slaughterhouse. 'Postulati e candidati', *L'Esercente*, 5–6 December 1899.

in full council elections, and a Giunta composed of Radicals and Republicans was installed in office, resting on the support of the Socialists who, though an integral and influential part of the bloc, abstained from office-holding. The electorate still perceived the Moderates as discredited by the events of the previous two years, whilst the *esercenti*, particularly those from the suburbs, remained convinced of the need to reinstate the *dazio* division and punish those responsible for its abolition. All the Federation nominees were successful in winning seats on the council and Baroni was actually made a member of the Giunta itself. Of the eighteen candidates whom *L'Esercente* had supported in preference to members of the Democrat list, only six were elected, whilst the final indignity of coming last in the poll fell to Luigi Pozzi, a candidate sponsored by *L'Esercente* alone, who succeeded in gaining just 315 votes.[28]

How then should we understand the events of the end of the century in terms of their effect upon the small traders? Any interpretation must begin by recognising the still crucial importance of the local commercial environment in determining *esercenti* positions. Whilst shopkeepers were disturbed by the events of May 1898, and welcomed the restoration of order and even some of the ways in which this was carried out, they nevertheless identified the *dazio* alteration as the key issue in both the June and December elections of the following year. Suburban traders supported the Democrats because of their opposition to the *allargamento*, and were prepared to ignore their embrace of the Socialists. The Federation line not only was convenient for its political leaders, it also reflected the view of the majority of the membership who felt their commercial position had been undermined. Dissenters from this view were primarily shopkeepers from the old *interno* who, of course, stood to benefit from the *dazio* enlargement. Zonal interests and zonal identity still ruled.

The events of these years are also crucial to our understanding of shopkeeper political autonomy, particularly when viewed in con-

---

[28] Pozzi, President of the Catholic Shopkeepers Association, was originally to have been carried on the Catholic list, but lost this support and announced his retirement from the race on the eve of the election, well after the ballot papers were printed. It may be, therefore, that more voters supported *L'Esercente*'s list, but despite the paper's spirited attempts to claim this, the overall result was obviously disappointing to the newspaper which devoted an article to an explanation of just how significant 315 votes really were! '315 voti', *L'Esercente*, 14 December 1899.

junction with those surrounding the elections of 1895. During the earlier sets of elections, shopkeepers appeared to have moved away from the unconditional support of the Democrats, as advocated by the Federation, instead supporting the mixed list proposed by *L'Esercente*. In 1899, however, the process was reversed. In 1895 when the depression, rather than the *dazio*, seemed to pose the greatest threat to shopkeeper interests, the *esercenti* moved towards the centre, as they were not prepared to vote for men who supported the legal privileges extended to their competitors, the consumer cooperatives. In 1899, the suburban *esercenti* were much more vexed by the abolition of their *dazio* advantage than by the issue of cooperative privileges and voted accordingly.

This is suggestive of two types of political autonomy. First, the *esercenti* as a stratum did move back and forth across the political spectrum, lending their support to whichever set of politicians appeared most likely to pursue their interests. They were not incorporated into one electoral bloc, nor did they follow a simple progression from left to right. Second, the 'ordinary' *esercenti* demonstrated that they were capable of pursuing courses of action independently from their 'leadership'. In 1895 they effectively repudiated the Federation; in 1899 they largely ignored Tadini and *L'Esercente*. That there was competition between elements in the vanguard of the *esercenti* movement makes it easier for us to identify this expression of autonomy, but it cannot be held to diminish it.

What the *esercenti* did not have was a coherent, positive strategy of their own – something Tadini had highlighted in his calls for new thinking and his advocacy of a *partito economico* to represent commercial interests.[29] That such a party did not develop was a consequence of the fact that small traders were far better at defending themselves against specific threats – cooperative privileges, the *allargamento* – than they were in identifying programmes which they favoured. The suburban traders' reversion to the Democrats in 1899 was a case in point – it was essentially a posture of opposition, and, in effect, backward looking since the *dazio* belt had already been extended. When, early on in its tenure, the new administration conceded that there could be no reversal of the *allargamento*, the main justification for shopkeeper participation in the Democratic bloc disappeared. Thereafter, the Federation's city councillors

[29] See, for example, Tadini, G., 'Gli esercenti di fronte alle elezioni amministrative e ai partiti politici', *L'Esercente*, 29 October 1899.

found themselves largely occupied in a battle to prevent the enactment of their partners' programmes.

Tadini had correctly foreseen that the *allargamento* had created a new commercial environment in which shopkeepers would find it easier to think of themselves as forming a single occupational interest group. The mergers of those trade associations which had previously been organised in separate *interno* and *esterno* sections indicated the lack of importance of zonal interests in this new identity. Tadini was wrong, however, to believe that the cooperative issue would be the focal point of *esercenti* concerns, as it had been during the early 1890s. The campaign against cooperatives had always focused on their privileges rather than their existence *per se*, and was primarily a product of the fears generated by the depression. In the relatively prosperous years of the new century it was not competition that the *esercenti* feared, but the new forces of municipal interventionism and organised labour.

11. *Shopkeeping in the new century*

Milan marked the turn of the century with a fundamental change in both its government and its character. In January 1900 Giuseppe Mussi was formally sworn in as the new mayor of the city at the head of a Radical administration supported by the Republicans and Socialists who had made up the Democratic alliance in the elections of December 1899. For the next four years this coalition presided over a city whose economic and physical growth turned it into a true city of industrial capitalism: a fact confirmed by the 1901 census which, for the first time, recorded over half the city's workforce as employed in manufacturing.[1] Economic and political conflicts, particularly those involving class interests, assumed new forms: old alliances became outmoded.

The next three chapters examine the consequences of these developments for the *esercenti* movement. This chapter analyses changes in the business of shopkeeping at both local and national levels and their relation to the position of small business within the national political process. Chapter 12 focuses on the developments in labour relations within the *esercenti* sector, whilst chapter 13 analyses the effects of these changes on *esercenti* political activity in Milan in the first five years of a new century.

THE BUSINESS OF SHOPKEEPING

The early years of the new century were prosperous ones for the city of Milan and the retailers who served it. The economic resurgence of the city after 1897 has already been analysed in chapter 1, particularly in terms of the beneficial effects for shopkeepers of rising

---

[1] Tilly, 'The Working Class of Milan', p. 107.

consumption rates. Tax returns suggest that there were better returns to be made and there were certainly more traders making them. Only in the period between 1902 and 1904 when labour difficulties were at their peak were there any significant signs of a downturn.[2] The city's population continued to expand rapidly and by 1901 there were more people living in the old suburban zone than in the former *interno*.[3]

The effects of these phenomena on the retail trade can best be seen by comparing the density of shops along the two transects first analysed in chapter 3. Fig. 11.1 contrasts the results obtained along the two transects for the periods 1885 to 1890, and 1902 to 1906. Whereas between 1885 and 1890 the density of shops declined dramatically beyond the old city wall (Zone 4 in each case), it now remained high, indicative of the improved opportunities for shopkeeping in the suburbs. Indeed, the density of shops now matched that of many of the zones closer to the city centre, especially in Transect 1 where what had been Corso Loreto had now become the Corso Buenos Aires, the first large shopping street to develop in the suburbs.

The transect analysis suggests that any immediate disadvantages arising from the unification of the two *circondari* were offset by the growth of the suburbs. The old *frontisti* zones retained their high densities, indeed that for the zone around the Porta Romana rose significantly. Food retailers rather than *esercizi pubblici* now formed the largest single category of shops in the zones, however, as the relatively heavy duties on alcohol applied throughout the city. Density levels within the city centre were little changed: the creation of new shops would have required alterations to the existing structures.

The high densities recorded in the suburbs are probably indicative of the small nature of most of the enterprises. These shops continued to flourish as a result of various changes in the business of shopkeeping. A critical development was the rise in the number of outlets which sold fresh food manufactured off the premises. The number of stores selling bread baked off the premises rose dramatically, for instance, as new kneading machines which enabled bakeries to increase their output became more readily available (the

2 See p. 3.
3 Tilly, 'The Working Class of Milan', p. 42 calculated from data in Comune di Milano, *La popolazione di Milano ... 1901*.

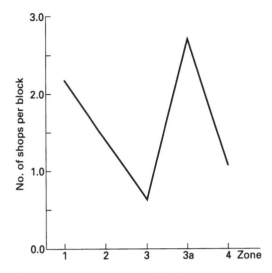

Fig. 11.1a Transect 1: density, 1885–90

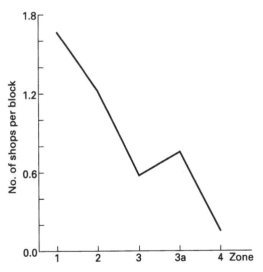

Fig. 11.1b Transect 2: density, 1885–90

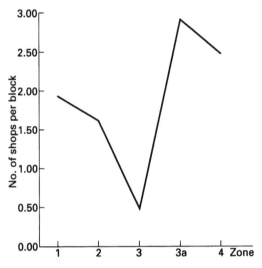

Fig. 11.1c Transect 1: density, 1902–6

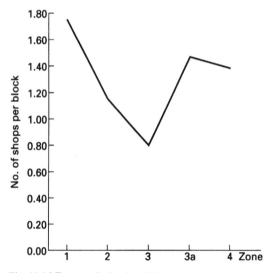

Fig. 11.1d Transect 2: density, 1902–6

Mutuo Proprietari Forno set up a technical section to evaluate these aids).[4] In 1885 the *Guida Savallo* recorded 298 bakeries and only seven *rivenditori di pane* (vendors of bread baked elsewhere). In 1906 the *Guida* listed 643 bakeries and 203 *rivenditori*.[5]

As manufacturers developed new products, so the opportunities for simple retailing increased. Shops began trading in gas and electrical appliances such as door bells and domestic lights. Bicycle stockists appeared in the city, along with phonograph and record shops. As has already been remarked upon, there was an increase in the number of manufactured 'branded' food products available.[6]

It was not only new products that became available – so too did new business machines. The most important of these was the cash register. This provided the means for a more efficient record of the state of the business as it could keep track of the overall sales of the enterprise, of what proportion of these were made by cash and what by credit, and of the relative attractiveness of the various items of stock. *L'Esercente* argued that registers were the best defence against bankruptcy as they enabled accurate bookkeeping. They also encouraged the elimination of *il fido* (and presumably the use of *prezzo fisso*), and might even be used to set up a dividend system similar to those of the cooperatives.

In addition the register reassured customers by eliminating arguments over price and payment, and allowed proprietors to spend less time supervising staff who were no longer exposed to the temptation of the petty cash drawer. The machine was particularly popular with the better-off clientele as they could now demand receipts from those servants they entrusted with making purchases on their behalf, thus preventing their employees from overcharging them and pocketing the difference.[7]

The increasing complexity of retailing led shopkeeper

---

[4] Browsing through the *Guide Savallo* gives a good sense of these developments, although, as explained previously, the figures derived from any analysis of this data would have to be treated with caution (see pp. 68–70). For one of the many reports on new machines for the food preparation industry see 'Macchine impastatrici', *L'Esercente*, 26 January 1902, which deals with the new kneading machine produced by the Fratelli Borgomainero of Milan. The Ufficio Tecnico per Notizie sulla Panificazione Meccanica within the Mutua Proprietari Forno is described in 'Ai soci della Mutua Proprietari Forno', ibid., 1 May 1903.

[5] *Guida di Milano*, publ. Savallo, 1885, 1906.   [6] p. 56.

[7] On the merits of registers see the National Cash Register Company advertisement in *L'Esercente*, 8 May 1903, and Tadini's article 'Le necessità amministrative degli esercenti e commercianti', ibid., 23 December 1904.

associations to recognise the need for some form of commercial training for those who wanted to succeed in the profession. The national congresses of small-trader federations repeatedly made this call, arguing that technical schools would raise the status of small commerce in the public eye by enabling shopkeepers to distinguish between adulterated and normal produce, to learn the principles of bookkeeping and to avoid being tricked and thereby tempted into deception themselves.[8] The Milanese dairymen's society set up such a school in 1898, offering instruction on both theoretical and practical matters to proprietors' sons and those workers who demonstrated 'zeal, enthusiasm and intelligence'.[9]

Although small shops prospered during the commercial upturn of the new century, the concomitant developments in the business of shopkeeping meant that the more successful *esercenti*, including most of the leadership of the movement, were increasingly involved in different activities from their peers. Conversely their contacts with those higher up the business hierarchy increased, and the feeling that shopkeepers were excluded from these echelons appears to have dissipated as *esercenti* representatives achieved prominence among the established commercial associations of the city. One result of this was that the city's more prestigious business organisations assisted with the development of commercial education intended for those entering retailing. In 1901, for example, the Associazione fra Commercianti, Industriali ed Esercenti set up a Scuola Practica di Commercio, which received a L. 1,000 subsidy from the Milanese Chamber of Commerce in 1902 and 1903. Altogether the Chamber subsidised some twenty schools in Milan, several of which were intended for those entering *esercenti* professions, emphasising its greater commitment to small business.[10]

The growing confidence and commercialism of the *esercenti* was

[8] 'Le ultime sedute del congresso degli esercenti a Torino', ibid., 1 September 1898; 'Le impressiono del congresso di Torino', ibid., 22 September 1898; 'I lavori del Congresso fra Commercianti ed Industriali a Roma', ibid., 12 June 1903; 'I lavori dell'ultima giornata del congresso', ibid., 14 June 1903.

[9] 'Il lavora delle Associazioni Milanese. La Scuola dei Lattivendoli', ibid., 29 September 1898.

[10] The Associazione school admitted twenty-eight pupils in its first year and fifty-one in its second. 'Prospetto riassuntivo del movimento degli alunni nelle scuole professionali e commerciali sussidiate dalla Camera di Commercio di Milano durante il periodo 1895–1903 e misura dei sussidi assegnati', *Atti della Camera di Commercio di Milano*, 1905; 'Per la scuola pratica di commercio', *L'Esercente*, 10 December 1901.

reflected in the increasing numbers of successful cooperative ventures established amongst them. Examples were the Società Milanese di Pastificio, founded by various bakers in 1902, the Società Cooperativa fra gli Esercenti per la Fabbricazione di Acque Gazose which supplied mineral water to bars and cafes, and a cooperative for the 'Protection of credit (*fido*) and recovery of debts' founded in 1903. For a stake of at least L. 50 this society disseminated commercial information, including the names of insolvent debtors, and provided legal assistance for the recovery of debts and the settlement of commercial disputes through arbitration.[11]

One of the most impressive organisations was the Cooperativa Vinicola, otherwise known as the Magazzini Cooperativi Vinicoli, established in 1900 amongst proprietors of *esercizi pubblici* such as *osterie* and *trattorie* to make collective wine purchases on their behalf. The cooperative could afford to negotiate direct with the vineyard and was thus able to obtain a significantly lower price for its shareholders than they would have got from the middleman. Furthermore they now did not have to have a cellar big enough to store all the wine they bought, and could buy wine on credit from the Magazzini to half the value of their shareholding. The financial arrangements were handled by the Banca degli Esercenti and the Vinicola was held up as a proof that the *esercenti* were capable of collaborating in a large collective venture.[12]

Several joint ventures were organised by the shopkeeper associations themselves. The most important of these operations in both commercial and political terms was the contract for the supply of school lunches won for individual shopkeepers by the bakery and delicatessen proprietors' associations in 1900. During the first two years of operation fifty bakers and sixty delicatessen owners were involved in the system which provided meals to forty municipal schools. These cold meals, consisting of salami or cheese with rolls and fortnightly chocolate, were supplied free to the poorest children whilst others could pay to have them if they wished.[13]

[11] *Guida di Milano*, publ. Savallo 1904, 1905; 'Per la tutela del fido ed il recupero dei crediti', *L'Esercente*, 29 August 1903.
[12] 'Osti e trattori', *L'Esercente*, 8 April 1900; 'I magazzeni cooperativi vinicoli', ibid., 6 September 1900; 'Società dei Magazzeni Generali Vinicoli', ibid., 20 September 1900.
[13] Apparently the numbers increased greatly when chocolate was included! Full details on the operation of the service may be found in Comune di Milano,

The service was a great success for the *esercenti* in both economic and political terms. In 1901–2 the bakers' collective income from the scheme amounted to L. 182,006.50. In the first year 1,343,590 meals were served and 2,014,655 in the second, yet only forty complaints were recorded. The bakers showed they could provide a more cost-effective service than the municipal bakery advocated by the Socialists which would have had to have closed down in summer and would have incurred considerable distribution costs.

The award of the contract was also a victory over a consortium of consumer cooperatives who failed either to win the initial contract or to match the *esercenti* tenders for the service in 1904 and 1905, despite apparently favourable treatment by the Council.[14] Indeed, during this phase of commercial resurgence, even the successful white-collar cooperatives were under pressure from the *esercenti*. The Cooperativa fra gli Impiegati e Professionisti, for example, took over the tram workers' consumer cooperative shops in 1899 but were forced to relinquish them in 1901 owing to the intensity of local competition. The same cooperative was involved in a fresh-meat venture with the Cooperativa Suburbana between 1902 and 1904 which also failed.[15] Even the Unione Cooperativa's sales of provisions and overall profits levelled off after 1900. The store's official history explains this by the fall in wine prices, but it must have also reflected the problem of greater shopkeeper competitiveness that was reported by other cooperatives.[16]

This competitive edge derived from the fact that customers attached greater importance to choice and convenience when shopping for provisions than they did to cost (especially when the cost benefits associated with purchasing from the cooperatives would only be passed on through the end of year dividend). When purchas-

---

Relazione sulla refezione scolastica distribuita nelle scuole comunali negli anni 1900–1 e 1901–2, 1903.

[14] The tenders came from Unione Cooperativa in 1904 and the Panificio Cooperativa Operaia in 1905. See 'La refezione scolastica e la vittoria degli esercenti', *L'Esercente*, 4 November 1900; 'Gli studi per un forno consorziale', ibid., 5 May 1904; 'Le cooperative e gli esercenti', *L'Esercente*, 13 May 1906.

[15] Società Anonima Cooperativa di Consumo fra Impiegati e Professionisti, *Cenni storico-statistici*, 1906, pp. 31–2, 36–8.

[16] Mellini, *Storia della Unione Cooperativa*, p. 34. According to *L'Esercente* the bakery operated by the Union was losing money owing to its failure to match the quality of both bread and service offered by the private bakeries. 'L'Unione Cooperativa di Milano', *L'Esercente*, 21 April 1904; 'Gli studi per un forno consorziale', ibid., 8 May 1904.

ing essentials, customers tend to buy little and often and were therefore more attracted by the proximity of a store than by its prices. The convenience of *il fido* played a key role in the retention of lower-class custom.[17] The *esercenti* also scored through the variety of products they made available – the cooperatives could only achieve considerable savings in cost by exploiting the economies of scale associated with the large-scale preparation or bulk purchasing of one or two varieties of a particular good.

These advantages had always been present, of course, so why did they only become readily apparent in the 1900s? One reason was that it was only then that the commercially minded cooperatives made their push into the provisioning sector, and discovered the strength of the forces ranged against them. In the 1890s the *esercenti*'s fear of the cooperative privileges was more a reflection of the depression than a consequence of these cooperatives' success in penetrating their markets. The extension of the *dazio* belt in 1898 eliminated all those privileges which had been the focus of shop-keeper resentment, effectively implementing *esercenti* calls for genuine competition. The commercial resurgence dispelled *esercenti* fears for their survival, and created the conditions in which, for the first time, *esercenti* joint ventures successfully competed against cooperatives in the manner which had long been urged on them by those concerned with building up *esercenti* consciousness.

The one form of consumer cooperative which did suceed in establishing itself in this period was that which drew its membership from the workforce of large single factories. As Table 7.1 shows, three such organisations were founded between 1900 and 1905, at the Pirelli, Erba and Gadda works. The Pirelli cooperative was the most successful of these, achieving aggregate sales of L. 1,000,000 within five years of its foundation. In this time it negotiated a contract to buy the entire production of a Piedmontese vineyard and opened a branch shop beyond the new *dazio* line, enabling it to pass on savings to the many workers who now lived outside the city altogether.[18]

Naturally, factory-based cooperatives were not popular with shopkeepers from the surrounding area. The convenience over cost equation no longer applied as the cooperatives had outlets at the

---

[17] See pp. 152–3.
[18] *Numero Unico della Società Anonima Cooperativa di Consumo fra gli addetti allo stabilimento Pirelli e C..*

workplace itself. It required relatively little effort to join such a cooperative, and there was even the possibility of persuading the management to pay part of the workers' wages in vouchers to be used at the cooperative. This was a much more effective method of tying-in custom than the shopkeeper's extension of customer credit, and when it was mooted at the time of the foundation of the Pirelli cooperative it provoked an outburst of protests from local shopkeepers that eventually caused Pirelli himself to scotch the proposal.

The success of the factory-based consumer cooperatives did not alter the fact that the nature of the rivalry between the cooperatives and the *esercenti* had changed. Following the *allargamento* 95% of the city was enclosed within the *zona chiusa* in which cooperatives enjoyed no fiscal privileges whatsoever. Disputes involving shopkeepers and cooperatives in the city between 1900 and 1905 had more to do with municipal contracts than with problems of competition. The *allargamento* had eliminated the legal basis for such complaints, and the improvement in the shopkeepers' commercial position dissipated the atmosphere of economic jealousy which nurtured them.

In fact a form of reconciliation between the *esercenti* and the white-collar commercial cooperatives took place, a consequence of the fact that both were simply unprivileged competitors in the same market, with shopkeeper cooperatives at times employing methods that paralleled those of organisations such as the Unione Cooperativa. This was certainly the perception of the National League of Cooperatives, a neo-Socialist working-class cooperative movement led by the Milanese Socialist deputy, Antonio Maffi. There was a striking similarity between the attacks of the National League on the Magazzini Cooperativi Vinicoli as a group of individuals adopting the forms of cooperation for commercial gain whilst remaining indifferent to its ideals, and the same organisation's castigation of the 'speculative' cooperation of Buffoli, the head of Unione Cooperativa.[19] Buffoli started to use the pages of *L'Esercente* to publish communications to his members, and even contributed articles (such as one denouncing Socialist calls for a municipal

[19] Lega Nazionale delle Cooperative Italiane, *Statistica delle Società Cooperative*, p. 171.

bakery) to the journal which had formerly described him as a 'class enemy'.[20]

In these new circumstances Tadini's initial attempts to put cooperatives back into the scapegoat role they had occupied in *esercenti* consciousness between 1890 and 1895 were simply inappropriate. The depression had lifted, privileges had disappeared and, most important of all, cooperatives were seen not to pose too great a threat to the *esercenti*. The elimination of the *dazio* division provided an opportunity to develop a shopkeeper consciousness throughout the city, yet the grievances on which the movement had previously sought to construct such an identity no longer existed. The business of shopkeeping in Milan had changed.

THE NATIONAL CONTEXT

It was not only at the local level that the business of shopkeeping had changed. It became clear during the new century that government itself was more concerned to pay attention to small-business grievances. The end-of-century crisis in Italy had convinced Liberal leaders such as Giolitti and Zanardelli that the state had to show itself more responsive to the needs of various elements in civil society in order to preserve its position: what Giolitti might have seen as an act of social *trasformismo*, the absorption of a potentially hostile group into a governing coalition. The expansion of the franchise, and the establishment of a Socialist basis amongst the working class of the northern cities made the *petite bourgeoisie* an obvious target for such an exercise, but one should be wary of overloading this with significance. What occurred was not so much the absorption of the small traders as the creation of an opportunity for small businessmen to exercise some political leverage within the system.

The reform of the bankruptcy laws provided the clearest indication of this. Under the old law many shopkeepers were found guilty of 'simple' bankruptcy because it was an offence not to be in possession of accurately maintained accounts.[21] Although it was possible to apply to the court for a moratorium in which to negotiate

---

[20] The Unione even began publishing communications to its members in the newspaper. Buffoli, L., 'La municipalizzazione del pane a Catania', *L'Esercente*, 17 March 1903; 'La gita dell'Unione Cooperativa', ibid., 12 June 1903.

[21] See p. 123.

Table 11.1. *Bankruptcies in Italy, 1896–9*

	1896	1897	1898	1899
Size of liabilities				
> L. 5,000	760	739	812	886
percentage	*33.0*	*33.1*	*34.3*	*36.3*
5–10,000	393	388	436	433
	17.1	*17.4*	*18.4*	*17.9*
10–20,000	423	403	420	411
	18.4	*18.0*	*17.7*	*17.0*
20–50,000	362	379	364	360
	15.7	*17.0*	*15.4*	*14.9*
50–100,000	151	146	156	149
	6.6	*6.5*	*6.6*	*6.2*
100–500,000	140	114	110	102
	6.0	*5.1*	*4.6*	*4.2*
500–1,000,000	11	8	15	15
	0.5	*0.4*	*0.6*	*0.6*
Unknown	57	47	52	53
	2.5	*2.1*	*2.2*	*2.2*

Source: Disegno di Legge presentato del ministro Gianturco nella seduta 21 Novembre 1900, *Senato del Regno n. 17, Legislatura XII*, 1, Sessione 1900, Documenti, disegni di Legge e Relazioni, p. 8.

an agreement with one's creditors once a judicial declaration of bankruptcy had been issued, many small traders' assets could not cover the court fees so that bankruptcy was inevitable. This occurred in around a quarter of all cases at the turn of the century, as shown in Table 11.1.

In 1900 the Minister of Justice, Gianturco, introduced a bill to replace the moratorium with a procedure to enter into negotiations for a *concordato preventivo* (preventative agreement) to be presented to the court before proceedings began. An agreement with creditors who held at least 75% of the debt between them would eliminate bankruptcy proceedings provided that the debtor was prepared to pay back 40% of what he owed.

The Minister went on to speak of how 'the widespread spectacle of bankruptcy trials, always for the irregular tenure or lack of commercial books, and of convictions often imposed on individuals guilty of nothing else other than being illiterate, is, in short, pitiable'.[22]

For a small trader, therefore, the procedure was made even easier. He had only to reach an agreement similar to a *concordato preventivo* with his creditors in front of a notary, and the proceedings against him would be dropped. Failure to maintain adequate records would no longer be a criminal offence for these *esercenti* and once they had fulfilled the terms of their agreement they would be able to re-enter business without there being any record of their previous failure.

Gianturco's proposals were generally well received. The 1902 congress of the Confederazione Generale fra Industriali, Commercianti ed Esercenti gave them an enthusiastic welcome as did Chambers of Commerce. Only the level of indebtedness below which the bankruptcy would be judged as a *piccolo fallimento* and was accorded these special provisions caused concern. Gianturco had suggested L. 10,000 which embraced around half the bankruptices which had occurred in recent years; critics argued that this was too high and, when the measure was passed in 1903, L. 5,000 was adopted as the limit and a court official, rather than a notary, was appointed to supervise operations.

The new procedures ran into problems, however, as debtors, protected by the lack of any requirement on them to produce documentary evidence of their situation, failed to reveal the extent of their indebtedness to the courts, and sometimes persuaded family and friendly creditors not to declare the sums they were owed so that the bankrupt could take advantage of the *piccolo fallimento* procedures.[23] As there was no legal requirement for these bankruptcies to be announced, many creditors never discovered that a *concordato* was being drawn up. Consequently it was still possible to use bankruptcy as a means of speculation, claiming to make a settlement of 40%, whilst actually paying back a much lower proportion of the outstanding debt.

---

[22] Disegno di legge presentato del ministro Gianturco nella seduta 21 Novembre 1900, *Atti Parliamentari* Senato del Regno n.17, Legislatura XII, 1., Sessione 1900, Documenti, disegni di Legge e Relazioni, p. 8.

[23] See Torquato, *Disposizione sul concordato preventivo*, and other reactions such as that of the Camera di Commercio di Bergamo in a letter to the Milanese Camera of 16 April 1902. ACC, scat. 124, f.4.

Surprisingly, perhaps, the small-business movement drew attention to these problems. The 1905 congress of the Confederazione Generale called for the limit to be lowered to liabilities of L. 2,000, and that the court officials, rather than the trader himself, be required to run the bankrupt's affairs until the conditions of the concordat had been fulfilled. *L'Esercente* urged that some form of bookkeeping requirement should now exist in order to protect creditors, later suggesting that any shopkeeper could practise simple bookkeeping with the aid of a cash register.[24]

This was a turnabout. During the depression years of the 1890s *L'Esercente* had frequently lamented the iniquity of bankruptcy legislation which placed so many burdens on the simple shopkeeper. Now the newspaper seemed more interested in the interests of other creditors, expecting the small trader to acquire the new skills commensurate with a more 'scientific' approach to retailing (at a time when the paper itself stated that only around 3,000 cash registers were in use in Italy).[25] Clearly the relative prosperity of those traders who had adapted best to the more commercial climate influenced the newspaper's attitudes, especially as these men were prominent in the *esercenti* movement.

The zeal with which the government had attempted to improve the bankruptcy situation suggested that small traders were beginning to be viewed as a legitimate interest group within the political game. Their greatest success came over matters such as bankruptcy reform when there were few competing interests to contend with, but other government actions reflected the shopkeepers' success in getting their views onto the political agenda.

The vexed question of cooperative privileges provides one example. As we have seen, these were of little consequence in Milan, following the *dazio allargamento*. At the national level, however, privileges continued to be a source of discontent amongst the *esercenti*.

There were already signs of a change in government attitudes towards cooperatives in the second half of the 1890s. Article 17 of

---

[24] The opinions of a good number of commercial associations on the functioning of the new law can be found in ACC, scat. 125, f.6. See also 'La cuccagna dei piccoli fallimenti', *L'Esercente*, 27 March 1904; 'La necessità amministrative degli esercenti e commercianti', ibid., 23 December 1904; 'Il Congresso Commerciale e Industriale a Venezia', ibid., 5 November 1905.

[25] 'Le necessità amministrative degli esercenti e commercianti', ibid., 23 December 1904.

the *legge daziaria 15 aprile 1897* and Articles 38, 39 and 123 of the *regolamento daziario 27 febbraio 1898* removed any ambiguity surrounding the provisions of the original 1870 law governing the exemption of consumer cooperatives from the *dazio consumo*. It was made quite clear that consumer cooperatives would enjoy no privileges whatsoever in the *zone chiuse* and that those in the *zone aperte* were to be divided into two types: those comprising only impoverished members, whose sales were confined to members themselves, and those which allowed sales to the public and admitted members of every class. The former were exepted from the *dazio consumo*, the latter were not.

Similarly the law of 11 July 1889 governing the granting of municipal contracts to cooperatives was strengthened by that of 9 June 1898 which specified that all members of the contracting cooperative had to be drawn from the needy, a condition the government enforced vigorously. As early as 1895 it disbarred 200 cooperatives from municipal work following an inquiry set up after 'cooperators' themselves had criticised 'speculative' organisations at their annual conference. The result of the strengthening of the law in 1898 was that all the Milanese cooperatives found themselves unable to claim the various privileges specified in the earlier law, with the result that they found it virtually impossible to tender successfully for municipal contracts, despite encouragement from the new radical *giunta* to do so.[26]

These changes were a clear response to the criticisms made by the *esercenti* of supposedly speculative cooperation. The National League of Cooperatives, in issuing a pamphlet rebutting the *esercenti* criticisms, made clear that it believed these were the key factor that had spurred the government to action. Again, this was an acknowledgement of the higher profile that small business had assumed in the political game, although the identification of cooperatives with subversion during the end of the century crisis was probably an equally important factor in the government's greater responsiveness to the small traders' criticisms.

By 1898, then, the government had moved to define cooperative privileges more strictly, to the point that the Milanese *allargamento* of that year rendered the question meaningless within the city. This was not the case elsewhere, however, most notably in Rome, where

---

[26] Lega Nazionale delle Cooperative Italiane, *Statistica delle Società Cooperative Italiane esistenti nel 1902*, p. XLVIII.

questions of cooperative privileges remained paramount owing to the government concessions to cooperatives whose membership came from public service. Shopkeeper hostility was focused upon the Unione Militare, a white-collar cooperative with military origins similar to those of Britain's Army and Navy Stores.[27] It was alleged that the Ministry of War had made favourable loans to the Unione at a time when it was financially unsound, and that it offered officers vouchers to buy uniforms at the Unione, thus assuring the cooperative of a clientele. The Roman *esercenti* feared that the proposed extension of the *insequestrabilità degli stipendi* would even further enhance the Unione's position.[28]

In 1900 the Società Generale fra Negozianti ed Industriali di Roma convened a large meeting of representatives from shopkeeper associations throughout Italy to attend to protest against privileges. This was cancelled at the last moment by the capital's police authorities and many felt they were pressurised into doing so by the government.[29] Following the cancellation, the Society organised a petition against cooperative grievances, dividing them into two types, fiscal (largely, with the exception of the *dazio* treatment, exemptions from some of the duties involved in setting up a commercial enterprise) and institutional (deriving from the different requirements placed on commercial and cooperative enterprises by the commercial law). The petition suggested that organisations which sold to third parties should be prevented from using the word cooperative in their name before reaching the root of the Roman *esercenti*'s grievances, namely the privileges accorded to the Unione Militare.

By enumerating cooperative privileges throughout the country, the Roman *esercenti* were able to organise a national campaign around their petition, culminating in a proposed demonstration against privileges in the capital in March 1902. Shopkeeper representatives were invited from all over Italy, but the march was again prohibited, this time on the direct orders of the Ministry of the

---

[27] On the Army and Navy Stores in Britain see Adburgham, *Shops and shopping*, pp. 215–18.

[28] The Memoriale was reproduced in *L'Esercente* on 10 and 27 October and 3 and 7 November 1901.

[29] 'Il Gran Comizio di Roma contro i privilegi delle Cooperative', *L'Esercente*, 22 March 1900; 'Il Gran Comizio di Roma contro i privilegi delle Cooperative', ibid., 25 March 1900; 'Il Gran Comizio di Roma contro i privilegi delle Cooperative', ibid., 29 March 1900.

Interior. The response of the shopkeepers was to close on two successive afternoons whilst *esercenti* leaders met briefly with the Interior Minister, Giolitti, who recommended them to present the petition for discussion in parliament.[30] This was duly done the following afternoon, and a debate was scheduled for 21 April.

The parliamentary debate produced no positive results one way or the other. Perhaps the most significant fact was that it had taken place at all, and that there were now deputies, such as Santini from Rome, who were prepared to take up the small-traders' cause. The conflict over the privileges issue demonstrated that shopkeepers could agitate successfully as a conspicuous interest group. The speed with which a debate to air shopkeeper grievances was scheduled contrasts sharply with the years the Milanese movement had spent waiting for its 'representatives' to raise the issue in parliament during the early 1890s, and the complete silence that greeted early petitions to ministers on the subject.[31] The banning of the demonstrations was a form of testimony to the shopkeepers' importance and if, as *L'Esercente* alleged, the reasoning behind this was that the government didn't want to suffer the embarrassment of the bourgeoisie taking to the streets to demonstrate against the proletariat, then this was further proof that shopkeepers were regarded as significant players within the political process.[32] It was from this time on that government ministers, along with telegrams of royal salute, began appearing at the Confederazione Nazionale's congresses.[33]

In Milan, though, the whole episode aroused what *L'Esercente* described as 'total indifference'.[34] None of the *esercenti* associations adhered to the petition, and there were no protests about the banning of the demonstration. A similar petition on the cooperative

---

[30] Other shopkeeper closures took place in Alessandria, Florence, Genoa and La Spezia, and the petition was supported by several shopkeeper associations in several other cities. 'L'agitazione contro le cooperative di consumo', *L'Esercente*, 23 March 1902.

[31] See p. 157 n.39.

[32] 'L'agitazione contro le cooperative di consumo', *L'Esercente*, 23 March 1902.

[33] The 1904 Naples conference was attended by Del Balzo, the under-secretary at the Ministry of Industry and Commerce and it received the offer of an address from Wollemberg, the Minister himself. The 1905 conference at Venice was sent a telegram of greeting from the King. 'Il Congresso dei Commercianti ed Industriali Italiani a Napoli', *L'Esercente*, 9 June 1904; 'Il Congresso Commerciale e Industriale a Venezia', ibid., 29 October 1905.

[34] 'L'agitazione contro le cooperative di consumo', *L'Esercente*, 23 March 1902.

issue, presented to parliament by twenty-six Chambers of Commerce, was not signed by the Milanese Camera di Commercio.[35] Following the parliamentary debate *L'Esercente* argued that the important thing now was not to waste time lamenting the failure to achieve anything on the cooperative issue but rather to bring other issues regarding small business into the public arena:

> Now that the die is cast, one shouldn't waste time on unimportant trifles. Instead it is incumbent on the influential men of commerce to put onto the table other questions as well, of equal importance to those of the cooperatives, perhaps even more so, and which have been the object of discussion within the commercial sector for some time.[36]

L'Esercente's description of the issue of cooperative privileges as an unimportant trifle underlines the declining importance of the issue. Even more revealing were the matters which the newspaper regarded as of similar importance: the old chestnut of *commercio girovago*, the increasing invasion of producers into the area of retailing, and the lack of money in circulation in the economy because it was tied up in a large savings organisations. The newspaper appeared to be casting around for an issue on which small traders could unite.

[35] Ibid. The Federation leaders confirmed their opposition to the use of closures at the Annual General Meeting of the association held in early April. 'L'Assemblea Generale della Federazione', *L'Esercente*, 6 April 1902.
[36] 'Interessi degli esercenti', ibid., 27 April 1902.

12. *Labour relations and class politics*

The most notable change in the shopkeeping environment during the new century was that in the nature of the relations between employer and employee. Between 1878 and 1899 there were only two strikes involving workers in the *esercenti* sector in Milan, that of the bakery workers in 1886, and a one-day affair involving barbers' apprentices in 1893. Almost every *esercenti* profession witnessed some form of disruption around the 1900s, however, with a strike of confectionery workers in 1899, bakery workers in 1900 and 1901, poulterers' assistants in 1901, the waiters and bar staff of the *esercizi pubblici* in 1902 and 1903, and butchers, dairymen and hairdressers in 1903.

This strike wave undermined the paternalistic concept of labour relations that the proprietors held dear and had profound implications for the development of *esercenti* identity. This chapter analyses the development of labour relations within the *esercenti* sector at the beginning of the twentieth century. Chapter 13 examines the effect of these changes on the political strategy of the *esercenti* movement.

Milan was at the forefront of the Italian labour movement, as might be expected given the city's leading role in the industrial sector. The first worker associations, the Mutue, were friendly societies devoted to providing assistance to their membership, rather than industrial and political activity. In the 1890s, however, *leghe di resistenza* (leagues of resistance) began to develop amongst the most 'advanced' areas of manufacturing, such as the metallurgical sectors, organising strikes and forcing negotiations with management. The repression of 1898 gave added impetus to the development of the leagues, and the eventual recognition of the right to strike in 1901 sparked a new period of industrial conflict as workers attempted to win some of the benefits of the economic upturn for themselves.[1]

Coordinating the activities of these leagues was the Camera di Lavoro (Chamber of Labour). This was originally set up in 1892 as a strictly non-political labour exchange subsidised by the Municipio, but it developed into the central institution of organised working-class politics. As a labour exchange it was not as effective as might have been supposed: in 1903 a census of nearly half the workers in Milan found that only 3% of workers used the labour exchange provided for them in the Camera to search for work, although the figure was much higher for the best organised workers, such as the printers, whose exchange at the Camera had a monopoly on all vacancies in the profession.[2]

The importance of the Camera di Lavoro, however, was that it offered a physical centre for the labour movement in which information exchange and tactical planning and organisation could take place. Meetings of the labour force were held there, 'experts' were on hand to help with the resolution of problems (including representation of the workforce during negotiations), and at times it even provided accommodation for bodies of strikers to ensure that nobody left the building to go strike-breaking.

Within the *esercenti* sector, industrial relations were dominated by the idea of apprenticeship, and the close proximity that existed between worker and employer. Terms of employment were largely determined on an individual level except for certain piece rates which had been established across the whole of a profession. These were usually determined by shopkeeper associations, notably those of the bakers and *salumieri*, which also helped with the development of apprentices through the institution of competitions and prizes. They even assisted in the establishment of friendly societies among the workers, lending their own premises and, on occasion, funds, for the purpose. The benefit to the proprietors was that these worker groupings then acquiesced in the continuation of the paternalistic framework of relations.

Some groups of shopworkers were comparatively well organised

---

[1] On the Mutue see Merli, *Proletariato di fabbrica*, pp. 582–625; Tilly, 'The working class of Milan', pp. 335–46, 397; Tilly, 'I fatti di maggio', p. 153.

[2] These figures come from Società Umanitaria, *Le condizioni generali della classe operaia in Milano*, p. 116. On the Camera di Lavoro see also Merli, *Proletariato di fabbrica*, pp. 778–84; Tilly, 'The working class of Milan', pp. 345–52.

even at the beginning of our period. In 1885 the Consolato Operaio, a federation of worker associations, already included friendly societies of bakers, confectioners, butchers and hairdressers amongst its adherents. During the 1880s the hairdressers agitated somewhat ineffectively for reduced hours and the recognition of the Christmas Day holiday, whilst the better-organised bakery workers engaged in a series of actions, including strikes, in an attempt to win a monthly day off, administration of their own labour exchange and an end to night work. During a strike of 1886 *Il Secolo* claimed that of 1,900 bakery workers, 900 (47%) were members of the Mutuo Lavoranti Fornai, whilst a police survey of twenty-eight bakeries in the Corso Ticinese zone found that thirty-seven out of seventy workers (53%) were members. Membership was concentrated in the larger bakeries and amongst the unemployed.[3]

Between 1889 and 1899, however, hardly any labour agitation was recorded amongst the *esercenti* trades.[4] This reflected the severity of the depression and the willingness of the workforce to acquiesce in the conventions of paternalism. The Friendly Society of Grocers' Assistants for example, which was founded in 1896 with financial support from the Grocery Proprietors' Association, decided not to join the Camera di Lavoro because of its political tendencies. Workers also differentiated amongst themselves, as shown by the conduct of the Società di Mutuo Sussidi dei Commessi dei Negozianti di Milano which held itself aloof from the Consolato Operaio and refused to accept assistants into its ranks if their duties only encompassed across-the-counter sales.[5]

Why, then, the upsurge in unrest at the beginning of the twentieth century? One part of the explanation was economic. During the depression, shop labour had concentrated on preserving its position

[3] The *Guida di Milano*, publ. Savallo, 1885, lists the members of the Consolato Oreraio. On the hairdresser disputes see ASM, fond. Questura, c. 43, f. 1, b. 5; 'Cronaca', *Il Secolo*, 25/26/27 December 1880; 'Cronaca milanese: il riposo dei parrucchieri', ibid., 27/28 August 1886. The figures on membership of the Mutuo Lavoranti Fornai are quoted in 'Cronaca milanese: la questione dei fornai', ibid., 3/4 August 1886, whilst the police lists can be found in ASM, fond. Questura, c. 45, f. 1, which contains a considerable amount of information on the strike. See also the articles in *Il Secolo* between 31 July and 7 August 1886.

[4] No strikes are mentioned in the *esercenti* sector between 1886 and 1889 in either the Questura archives or *L'Esercente*; nor any significant agitation between 1889 and 1899.

[5] 'Il nuovo sodalizio dei Commessi e Facchini Droghieri', *L'Esercente*, 30 July 1896. *Statuti della Società di Mutuo Sussidi dei Commessi dei Negozianti in Milano* 1880, Art. 9, p. 4.

rather than on improving on it, so resentments were suppressed beneath the struggle to make ends meet. The upturn in *esercenti* fortunes allowed their workers to become more ambitious. This accords with the general pattern of labour activity in Milan. Of a total of 461 strikes in the city between 1879 and 1903, 229 occurred in the last three years of the period, and these involved 73% of all those who went on strike during the period. In 1901 alone, eighty-eight strikes involved 37.8% of the city's workforce.[6]

Furthermore, the justification of the paternalistic system offered by the employers was beginning to lose credibility. Proprietors took on young boys as apprentices, and usually provided them with food and lodging on the premises or within the proprietors' own home.[7] These types of arrangements often continued throughout a worker's career, particularly if, like bakery workers, they needed to be on the premises at night. By providing lodgings on the premises (and, not infrequently, by locking workers into the premises), the proprietors were able to guarantee that they did not 'abscond' to the bar. Employers were able to justify paying low wages to their employees because they provided them with these benefits, and, most importantly, with the opportunity to acquire a trade as a preparation to establishing a business of their own.

Now, however, the profession was becoming more commercial and the simple skills acquired in the shop would not suffice in order to set up in many businesses. The technical innovations in food production meant that much more capital was necessary to acquire the machines used for kneading, baking and simply taking the money. In addition, a higher level of education was vital in order to appreciate the art of bookkeeping.

Thus the barriers to entry into many trades were greater, and the gulf between employers successful enough to afford to hire several hands and those whom they hired was widening. Workers might break into business at the periphery, but they were unlikely ever to reach the level of those who employed them. Trades, such as hairdressing, where the costs of entry remained low were still domi-

---

[6] Società Umanitaria, *Scioperi, serrate*, pp. 8–10. On the escalation of strike activity in Milan in 1901 see Tilly, 'The working class of Milan', p. 179.

[7] Occasionally youths from the provincia would advertise for openings. The following insertion appeared in *L'Esercente* on 11 June 1903: 'Butcher's boy offers himself to important butchers' shops, without any wage request, apart from domestic board and lodging. Write to Luigi Allievi, S. Pietro Seveso (Prov. di Milano).'

nated by ex-employees, but the growth of *rivenditori* in trades such as baking may partly be explained by the much greater capital resources required to become a full-scale producer.[8]

Paternalism was disintegrating. In 1901, at a meeting of young *salumieri* held in a room made available by the proprietors, one apprentice maintained that Perego, the president of the proprietors' association, should be forced to leave the gathering. When Perego spoke he argued that the *giovani* would swiftly become *padroni* and ought not to rock the boat too much. None the less the youths decided to call for a reduction of weekend working hours.[9]

The attractions of the Camera di Lavoro grew as the likelihood of workers breaking into business on their own appeared to diminish. It was more sensible for workers to conduct themselves as such within their industrial relationships. The Camera was able to offer them advice on tactics and practical help such as the provision of accommodation during disputes in trades in which the worker usually resided at the premises of his employer. The influence of the Camera was evident in the manifesto issued by striking bakery workers in 1901 which stressed the need to behave like true members of the working class.[10]

At first the *esercenti* were taken aback by the increasing virulency of labour demands and tended to be conciliatory in their approach. This was a consequence of over-reaction to the change in relations and over-estimation of the power and determination of the workforce. The Società Umanitaria recorded that strikes amongst the food trades in 1901 were much more successful in achieving their aims than in other manufacturing sectors. As in all industries, however, these successes declined significantly in 1902–3, not least as *esercenti* positions hardened and they realised that they were no weaker than their employees.[11]

Retailers and food producers were relatively flexible over wage

[8] Former workers accounted for 80% of barber shop proprietors in 1903. Società Umanitaria, *Scioperi, serrate*, p. 108.

[9] 'Riunione dei giovani salumieri', *L'Esercente*, 9 June 1901.

[10] The bakery workers issued a statement to the citizens of Milan describing the 'brutalising' indignities of night work and the hiring or workers by agents who ran their operations from notorious bars. They declared that these disgraces had to be eliminated from the so-called moral capital of Italy, and to achieve this the bakery workers would have to raise themselves to the level of a true working class. 'I Panettieri Milanesi alla Cittadinanza' a manifesto issued by Il Comitato Direttivo on 21 September 1901 and reproduced in *L'Esercente* on 26 September 1901.

[11] Società Umanitaria, *Scioperi, serrate*, p. 20.

demands. For them, as for the workers, the real issue was the power to hire and fire, as exemplified in disputes over who should administer the *uffici di collocamento* (labour exchanges) and whether use of these institutions should be compulsory. This helps explain the decrease in the proportion of successful strikes in the period 1902–3. Amongst workers involved in food production, the proportion of strikers whose demands involved *uffici di collocamento* was as follows: 1879–1900, 88.7%; 1901, 90.5%; 1902, 96.6% and 1903, 93.8%. A declining proportion of strikers was involved in wage disputes; the percentages were 11.3% in 1879–1900, 9.5% in 1901, 3.1% in 1902 and 0.8% in 1903. In other industries in the city there was a similar increase in the percentage of strikers involved in disputes over *uffici di collocamento*, though the issue was not nearly so intense as in the food production sector. The percentages were: 1879–1900, 3.5%; 1901, 8.6%; 1902, 21.1% and 1903, 18.5%.[12]

The pattern within each *esercenti* trade was for workers' demands to become progressively more focused on issues concerning recruitment until they reached the 'bottom-line' position from which the proprietors would not budge. Claims over wages and conditions were relatively easily negotiated, whilst the institutions of *riposo festivo* (early closing on Sundays) and *riposo di turno* (individual holiday days) gained legitimacy during the period. Recognition of *uffici di collocamento* run by workers' associations, even part funding of these, gradually came to be acceptable. The sticking point was always reached when there was a demand that required proprietors to abide by certain operating principles, rather than manage their own enterprises as they wished. Such propositions usually involved either the imposition of a *riposo di turno* or a policy of only recruiting staff from the *uffici di collocamento* run by the Leagues.

The difficulty with the *riposo festivo* was insuring the adherence of all *esercenti* to the accord. Failure to comply hit not only the workers themselves but also those proprietors who did close early and then saw their trade disappear to someone else. Associations which came to an agreement with the workers had to work on propaganda campaigns to convince their members to adopt the measures, or, failing that, abuse them in the press – as was done to a

---

[12] In 1902 and 1903 strike action in solidarity with other workers was undertaken, accounting for 0.3% of strikers in 1902 and 5.4% in 1903. Ibid., pp. 14, 40.

grocer who refused to close on time. Workers sometimes took matters into their own hands. In 1901, the young *salumieri* succeeded in getting the pork butchers to agree to close at 16.00 on Sundays: when two proprietors refused to observe the accord, the apprentices demonstrated outside their premises.[13]

Initially it required strikes to have the *riposo festivo* considered – for example confectionery workers won Sunday afternoon off as a result of their strike in 1899.[14] The concept of *riposo festivo* was regarded as progressive, however, by much of influential public opinion, and in later years arrangements were more often arrived at by negotiation. The 1903 congress of trade associations endorsed the principle, and many shopkeeper associations introduced a form of *riposo* maintaining, like the fuel sellers, that 'modern needs required it'.[15]

The *riposo di turno* was more controversial. The principle was fairly well accepted – after all it worked well in England – but the administrative details, notably those of who was responsible for replacing the worker, and at whose expense was the day off, were often the cause of dispute. In 1904, the Socialist, Cabrini, introduced a very confused bill which sought to make both the *riposo festivo*, and some form of *riposo di turno*, obligatory. This was opposed by *L'Esercente* which argued that Sunday was an important day for many businesses and that it was wrong to 'impose relaxation' upon someone. In fact the provisions of the bill would have left local authorities to come to arrangements with the *esercenti* over this issue, but, in any case, the bill was defeated by a secret vote, after each of its articles had been passed.[16] By 1906, however, the Consiglio Superiore del Lavoro of the Italian parliament was at work on a new bill dividing shops into three categories that would either shut, open until midday, or open as usual but with the employees receiving a day's *riposo di turno* elsewhere in the week. A

[13] 'Il riposo festivo', *L'Esercente*, 11 July 1901.
[14] ASM fond. Questura. c. 59, f. 1899, contains details of the strike and its outcome.
[15] The extraordinary assembly of the Consorzio Commercianti in Combustibili at which this motion was passed in reported in 'Il riposo festivo dei sostrai', *L'Esercente*, 16 May 1902. The Congress stated that the '*riposo festivo* should be promptly accepted and ratified by legislation'. 'I lavori del congresso fra Commercianti ed Industriali a Roma', ibid., 12 June 1903.
[16] 'La legge sul riposo festivo alla Camera', *L'Esercente*, 4 March 1904; 'Il riposo festivo e gli esercenti', ibid., 13 March 1904; 'I responsabili del trionfo della viltà', ibid., 17 March 1904.

law enforcing a one-day-a-week holiday, the *riposo settimanale*, was eventually passed in 1912.[17]

The *esercenti* movement came to accept the principle of *riposo*, though maintaining that the decision as to whether or not it was granted should be left to the individual proprietor. The strongest objections were not to the concept of time off, but the linkage made between this and acceptance of temporary hands supplied by the *ufficio di collocamento* of the relevant shopworker organisation. The development of these *uffici* demonstrated the shopkeepers' willingness to work in harmony with organised labour, until any threat of limiting the prerogative of the individual proprietor arose.

The usual method for employers to recruit workers was through an agent or mediator. Some proprietors, however, found, that intermediaries could not be relied upon to provide suitable hands, especially for skilled jobs. Consequently various *esercenti* associations established their own *uffici di collocamento*, the *salsamentari* as early as 1872.[18] Workers, too, faced difficulties with intermediaries who charged high fees and were often perceived as corrupt. Private agencies could also be rough as disputes broke out, fuelled by alcohol consumed in the *bettole* from which many were run. Many workers' associations were first established in an attempt to take control of the labour market through the creation of their own *uffici*.[19]

This could leave the owners' and workers' *uffici* in direct competition. Proprietors ran these agencies in their own interests and employees in theirs. The workers often demanded the right to either joint or exclusive management of a single exchange. As early as 1887, the bakery workers, the best organised of the *esercenti* employees, gained joint control over their labour exchange following an impressive strike. In contrast, hairdressers, some of the poorest and least organised workers, had to wait until 1903 before a strike succeeded in closing down the owners' *ufficio*. Even then proprietors resumed using agents once the strike was over.[20]

---

[17] 'La legge sul riposo festivo o settimanale', ibid., 14 January 1906; Tilly, 'The working class of Milan', p. 263.

[18] Società Proprietari Salsamentari, *Venti anni di vita sociale*, pp. 36–8; Società Proprietari Salsamentari, *Regolamento per l'ufficio di collocamento del personale salariato*.

[19] This was one of the first aims of the Friendly Society of Grocers' Assistants which was founded in 1896. 'Il nuovo sodalizio dei Commessi ed Facchini Droghieri', *L'Esercente*, 30 July 1896.

[20] 'Società Proprietari Forni', *L'Esercente*, 18 November 1888; Società Umanitaria, *Scioperi, serrate*, pp. 111–14.

Many societies were willing to concede the running of an *ufficio di collocamento* to the workers, provided they were not obliged to use it. The grocers and confectioners both did so, while the *salumieri* and restaurateurs were prepared to run such an organisation jointly with their employees. What they would not do was recruit from it. In 1903, 84.7% of those employed in *esercizi pubblici* and 50.3% of those in food production had used private agencies or direct contact to get work, whilst most people involved in the other retail trades had found their position through contacts or relatives.[21]

It was the employees' demands that their *uffici* be granted a monopoly over the supply of labour to the employers that led to the most bitterly contested disputes between worker and proprietor in the first years of the twentieth century. In 1901 the Mutua Proprietari Forno, in an attempt to avoid a strike, agreed to urge its members to make use of the *ufficio di collocamento* run by the workers at the Camera di Lavoro, but individual employers continued to recruit from other sources and a strike was called. Despite this and much subsequent agitation, the proprietors refused to concede, and in 1903 the arbitration board ruled that the agreement between the proprietor and worker associations did not require employers to use the union's labour exchange.[22]

The chief cause of tension was that the *uffici* organised by the Camera di Lavoro automatically sent replacement workers to a proprietor whose regular employee was taking his *riposo di turno*. Employers refused to accept them, arguing that they had a right to select who came on to their premises and into their employment. They believed these substitutes were likely to be unskilled and might prove to be 'troublemakers'. The leagues, however, realised that they could only be of any value to their members if they succeeded in securing them a job. They used the system of substitutes to provide work for those members who had no permanent employment. Operating this type of closed shop made the leagues attractive to workers and gave them the bargaining power they needed against management.

The issue of the *turno* could be counter-productive, however. In 1902 a strike organised by the friendly society for restaurant and bar

[21] Società Umanitaria, *Le condizioni generali della classa operaia in Milano*, pp. 116–19.
[22] 'L'importante adunanza di ieri della Mutua Proprietari Forno', *L'Esercente*, 10 October 1901; 'Importante sentenza sul turno di riposo', ibid., 8 January 1903.

staff forced proprietors to agree to recruit only from the *ufficio di collocamento* at the Camera di Lavoro. Proprietors refused to employ some workers sent to them as substitutes for workers on leave, however, as it was apparent that many were not waiters or cooks, but merely members of the unemployed. When the friendly society, itself headed by an ex-hairdresser, called a meeting to discuss renewed strike action, this degenerated into a slanging match between those in work and those out of it, with the former being scathing about the lack of qualifications of the latter. No stoppage took place.[23]

The growth of worker agitation conducted across trades rather than within individual units, the battles over the *ufficio di collocamento* and the right of individual proprietors to hire whom they liked, the frequent resort to institutionalised arbitration; these were all indicative of the growing importance of collectivism in employer–employee relations. Even in defending the right of individual proprietors to conduct themselves as they chose, the *esercenti* associations were engaged in a form of collective negotiation more frequently associated with modern industry than the paternalistic system previously found within the food trades. Although, as small traders were keen to point out, employers were still frequently working side-by-side with their employees, relations between the two were now conducted on what was effectively a class basis.

Evidence of the new climate can be seen in the increasing use of the arbitration mechanisms. The law governing these institutions was passed in 1893 but lack of interest meant none was set up in Milan until 1898. There were three parts to each *collegio dei probiviri* (arbitration board); the *plenario* (the board itself), the *ufficio di conciliazione* (conciliation office), and the *giuria* (jury). The conciliation office and the jury were both made up of an equal number of members elected by the employers and workers, and a President appointed by Royal Decree. Anyone of either sex over 21 years of age and associated with the relevant industry for more than one year could vote, and it was the responsibility of the Municipio to draw up the electoral lists – though this was often passed on to the Camera di Commercio and the Camera di Lavoro.[24]

---

[23] 'La tumultuosa assemblea generale dei camerieri, cuochi ed affini', *L'Esercente*, 23 April 1903.
[24] The plenary body was essentially concerned with the administration of the institution and the reporting of its views to government (a function somewhat akin

The *esercenti* movement took little notice of the *probiviri* until 1900 when a jury ruled that a bakery worker had been unfairly dismissed for agitating for a return to the terms of the defunct 1884 contract between bakery workers and their employers. Although the board also ruled that the 1884 concordat had fallen into disuse and was therefore not a valid basis for a wage claim, the *esercenti* were angered by the former decision and the movement began to play a much bigger role in promoting candidates for election to the relevant *collegio dei probiviri*: that dealing with the *industrie alimentari* or food trades. Thereafter the Federation ran lists of recommended candidates who were duly returned.[25]

Recourse to arbitration increased rapidly during the first few years of the century, as shown in Table 12.1. In 1903 the Mutuo Proprietari Forno went as far as to set up an *ufficio di citazione* to advise bakers due to appear before the board.[26] *L'Esercente* urged its subscribers to participate in elections to the board, in the same manner they had once urged them to register for the vote itself. The importance the newspaper attributed to these elections was indicative of the changing nature of workplace relations. Whereas disputes had previously been settled directly between the individual employer and employee concerned, they now formed part of a wider arena of collective industrial politics.

Small traders recognised the efficacy of the Camera di Lavoro in building working-class consciousness, and argued that the *esercenti* needed a similar institution. *A palazzo degli esercenti* was once again mooted as a home for all *esercenti* operations, and this time, owing to the greater prosperity of the movement and the sector

to that of the Camera di Commercio). The conciliation office met both sides to any sort of industrial dispute in private, and if this failed to resolve the issue it then went to the industrial jury which had jurisdiction in all matters up to a limit of L. 200. If both sides agreed, however, the jury could sit as an arbitration board to deal with matters which were beyond its competence. A full description of the functioning of the arbitration services can be found in a series of five articles on 'L'Istituto dei Probiviei' published in *L'Esercente* between 14 March and 6 April 1901. A lecture delivered by Avv. Alessandro Crosti to the Federation on the subject 'I probiviri ed il contratto di lavoro' was reproduced by *L'Esercente* on 7 and 10 April 1903.

[25] 'Pei soci della "Mutua Proprietari Forno": una sentenza assurda per non dir peggio!', *L'Esercente*, 12 April 1900; 'L'Istituto dei Probiviri', ibid., 25 November 1900.

[26] 'Ai soci della "Mutua Proprietari Forno"', *L'Esercente*, 1 May 1903.

236   THE POLITICAL ECONOMY OF SHOPKEEPING IN MILAN

Table 12.1. *Cases taken to the 'collegio dei probiviri: industrie alimentari', 1898–1903*

	1898	1899	1900	1901	1902	1903
Requests for conciliation						
Arrived during year	143	264	351	985	975	544
Pending from previous year		2	13	39	125	148
Total	143	266	364	1024	1100	692
Disputes resolved						
Ufficio di conciliazione	46	126	143	287	157	122
Giuria	23	39	42	150	247	216
Abandoned/resolved elsewhere	72	88	140	462	548	332
Unresolved at end of year	2	13	39	125	148	22
Cases brought by:						
Manager/proprietor	0	9	16	93	63	94
Worker	143	255	335	931	1037	598

Source: Atti della Camera di Commercio di Milano 1905 'Controversie sottoposte ai 17 Collegi di Probiviri del Distretto dal primo anno di funzionamento (1898) a tutto il 1903' (unnumbered page in Appendix).

generally, sufficient funds were raised for the project to go ahead.[27] That it was felt that a rival institution was needed was indicative of the unpalatable truth that in class politics, proprietor and worker were on opposite sides.

City politics were also now effectively class based. The inexorable growth of the franchise, and with it the working-class vote, meant that other elements within society had to determine their political positions in relation to this bloc. They might choose to work in alliance with it, or against it, but arithmetic made clear that there would only ever be room for two contesting alliances; the weight of numbers of the working class would triumph against any divided opposition. This did not preclude some classes from cooperating with the Socialists and incorporating them into a larger bloc, but there could be no major clashes of interest within such alliances.

The 'liberal' professionals and the white-collar and clerical workers were still able to contemplate such arrangements for their centre-left Radical and Republican parties. The 'reformist' Socialists were glad of the respectability such alliances afforded them, and were prepared to allow these other parties to have far more councill-

[27] See 'L'importante assemblea dei delegati della Federazione generale fra Esercenti e Commercianti', *L'Esercente*, 31 May 1901; 'La "Casa" degli Esercenti', ibid., 31 March 1901; 'Palazzo degli Esercenti', ibid., 27 October 1901.

ors and administrative positions than their grass-roots support merited.

What about small traders? The fact that proprietors worked alongside their employees, and that many had themselves passed through the apprenticeship system, contributed to the *esercenti*'s perception of themselves as workers, and their sympathetic sentiments towards the working class. This was reflected in the identification of shopkeepers with the Democratic bloc in Milanese politics, a bloc of those who perceived themselves as excluded from the centres of political and economic power. The extension of the *dazio* belt to the disadvantage of suburban shopkeepers had reinforced this perception, leading the Federation, though not *L'Esercente*, to renew the alliance with the Democrats in 1899.

This alliance was not suited to the circumstances of the new century, however. Part of the price demanded by the Socialists for their continued support of the Democrat administration, for example, was the retention of the subsidy to the Camera di Lavoro. *Esercenti* representatives on the Council were forced to vote in favour of this, even though most traders were hostile to the organisation. Socialist ideology favoured the interests of the worker and consumer over those of the employer and retailer no matter what the size or status of the latter. The logic of the situation forced shopkeepers to look to the centre-right for allies, irrespective of their gut feelings. Conversely it was now very much in the establishment's interest to bring the *esercenti* into their coalition as a bulwark against the workers and socialists. Behind the growing acceptance of the *esercenti* as a legitimate interest group within the echelons of commerce, examined in chapter 11, lay a simple political imperative.

The days in which shopkeepers could picture themselves as outsiders, closer to their employees than to the city establishment, were past. The replacement of zonal politics by class politics dictated a shift in shopkeeper identity. We can now analyse the course of events which led the *esercenti* representatives in the Democratic administration of 1899 to help bring it down in 1904.

13. *The* esercenti *and the centre-left administration, 1900–1905*

The political contest within Milan during the first years of the new century was fundamentally different from that which had preceded it. The most obvious sign of this was the Giunta itself, the first to be drawn from the Democrat bloc, made up of what were referred to as the *partiti popolari*. The change of administration was an indication of the progress of democratisation in Milanese politics. The process was an evolutionary one, but the period at the beginning of the twentieth century marked a significant step in the development of mass politics.

The key to this was the switch from wealth to literacy as the basis of the franchise.[1] This change had been instituted in 1882 for national elections, and in 1889 for local ones, and it effectively insured a gradual change in electoral calculations. As educational levels improved, particularly amongst those who laboured in the better-organised and better-rewarded industries to which Milan played host, so the number of voters rose. By 1904 there were 59,418 voters on the municipal rolls of whom 20,914 were designated as workers, whilst 8,933 were given as *esercenti*. The political rolls contained 20,370 workers and 7,851 *esercenti* amongst the 52,773 registered. Office workers made up around 12,000–13,000 voters, professional some 5,500–7,000.[2]

These figures underline the importance of the working-class vote in the city, and help explain the success of the Milanese Socialist party. Far from all members of the working class were Socialists, of course, and a considerable number of Socialist leaders were not members of the working class, but by 1899 the Milanese Socialists had built an impressive power base in the city, demonstrated when

[1] Membership of the male sex remained the primary qualification, however.
[2] Figures from 'La grande lotta politico-elettorale', *L'Esercente*, 27 October 1904.

the party leader, Turati, won two by-elections to the Chamber of Deputies after twice being disqualified from sitting in the house on account of his conviction by a military court following the 'May events' of the previous year.[3] This electoral base was particularly significant when considered in relation to the structure of the Democratic alliance, as the other *partiti popolari* represented more restricted social constituencies whose importance would inevitably decrease as literacy and political awareness rose amongst the working class.[4]

At the turn of the century, however, neither the Socialists nor the *partiti popolari* were strong enough to win power on their own, but together they commanded enough votes to overthrow the Moderates and their allies. The Socialists provided the bulk of these votes, but realised that, to fringe voters, they were also the most off-putting element in the alliance. They were therefore prepared to let the leaders of the other *partiti popolari* make the running both in the elections themselves, and in the subsequent administration, contributing only twelve members of the *consiglio comunale*, none of whom sat on the Giunta. This also reflected the concerns within the party with regard to participation in 'bourgeois' administrations – one of the causes of the divisions between 'revolutionaries' and 'reformists' in the party.

All the members of the Giunta were drawn from the Radical party, including Baroni, President of both the Federation and the Bakers' Association. Nonetheless, the Municipio headed by the new mayor, Mussi, was bound to reflect the concerns of the Socialists who, in electoral terms, underwrote its programmes. The 'reformist' Socialists were anxious to demonstrate that access to political power could be used to improve the conditions of working-class life despite the claims of their 'revolutionary' colleagues to the contrary. Within a year two *assessori* of finance had left the administration, following conflicts with the Socialists over policy: the first because he opposed the municipalisation of the sewage system, the second because of his

[3] The chamber twice disqualified Turati in February and June 1899, and he was re-elected on 26 March and 13 August of that year. See Punzo, *Socialisti e Radicali*, pp. 29–30, 48.
[4] One reason *L'Esercente* was so hostile to the Council's commitment to subsidise the Camera di Lavoro, was that the Chamber laid on intensive writing courses which, the newspaper claimed, enabled the illiterate to qualify to vote Socialist. 'All'Italia del popolo', *L'Esercente*, 31 December 1902; 'Scuotiamoci', ibid., 5 December 1903.

disinclination to substitute a family tax for that on *valor locativo* and his preference for a privately administered school meals service. In November 1900 Arturo Stabilini became the new City Treasurer, the first Republican to join the Giunta and the second figure from the *esercenti* movement to enter the administration. The fate of his predecessors, however, was indicative of the difficulties inherent in any alliance between commerce and socialism in the new century.[5]

Nonetheless, the leaders of the Federation continued to advocate participation in the Democrat alliance as the most effective way of promoting small traders' concerns, not to mention their own political careers. *L'Esercente*, however, persisted in maintaining that this alliance was inevitably inimical to *esercenti* interests. The Socialists' desire to improve the quality of life of the working-class consumer would lead to increased intervention and regulation in the small-business sector, whilst there was a possibility that the *esercenti*, as employers, might be compromised in an alliance which was primarily concerned with improving workers' conditions and rights. This divergence of opinion over participation in the new administration dominated the politics of the *esercenti* movement for the next four years.

Barely a month after assuming office, Baroni found himself at the centre of the first of many conflicts of interest which plagued the shopkeepers' representative within the administration. Bakery workers demanded a return to the piece rates of the 1884 concordat between workers and proprietors (L. 4 for every 100 kg of flour worked in the *interno* and L. 3.75 in the *esterno* with 80 cents automatically deducted for food and lodging), with the *interno* rate to be paid throughout the extended *dazio* belt. In addition, the workers wanted the proprietors to contribute half the running costs of a worker-run *ufficio di collocamento*, pay a fee for each worker hired from the *ufficio*, and guarantee that employers' proprietors would only recruit from those on the books of the *ufficio*.[6]

Baroni and the executive of the Mutua Proprietari Forno negotiated an accord with the workers that met with most of their demands, but at an extraordinary general meeting the members rejected this. They acknowledged the necessity for an even wage rate

---

[5] Punzo, *Socialisti e Radicali*, pp. 121–9.
[6] The 1884 concordat was reproduced by *L'Esercente* on 11 March 1900 in the article 'La quistione [sic] fra proprietari e lavoranti fornai'. On the workers' demands see Punzo, *Socialisti e Radicali*, p. 92.

across the city and welcomed the idea of sharing the funding of the *ufficio di collocamento*, but they were not prepared to give any guarantees that they would use it. Why should the workers deny them the right to choose the best labour they could find?[7]

Baroni was severely attacked from both sides. The Socialist journal *La Lotta* described him as 'the standard bearer of all the selfishness of the employers' and called for his resignation from the Giunta.[8] Meanwhile *L'Esercente* was not slow to point out that the dispute demonstrated the impossibility of working within the Democratic alliance, and suggested that whilst the Federation was hamstrung, the Associazione fra Commercianti, Esercenti ed Industriali should take over the defence of *esercenti* interests. Prominent members of the Mutua wondered if Baroni had too many jobs to attend to.[9]

The Giunta could ill afford such a dispute so soon after assuming power, however. Consequently the Socialists urged workers to tone down their demands and Caldara, a Socialist councillor, used the council chamber to request that Mussi act as mediator. When the mayor offered his services if both sides agreed, Baroni seized on the lifeline and railroaded acceptance through a meeting of the Mutua Proprietari Forno, provoking further misgivings about his conduct and positions.[10]

The eventual outcome of this mediation was an agreement to return to the old concordat of 1884 with the piece rate of L. 4 applied throughout the city. Workers would receive their board-and-lodgings payment deductions in cash if they did not make use of the proprietors' facilities. The employers also agreed to contribute a sum towards the running of the *ufficio di collocamento* and to make use of it 'whenever it gave assurance of good service'. The settlement established what was to become the common pattern of proprietors giving way on salary demands, perhaps indicative of

---

[7] 'La grave questione dei fornai', *L'Esercente*, 21 January 1900; 'La quistione fra proprietari e lavoranti fornai', ibid., 11 March 1900; 'Intorno alla vertenza dei fornai', ibid., 22 March 1900.

[8] The article from *La Lotta* was published in *L'Esercente* under the title 'Quei cari alleati' on 8 March 1900.

[9] 'La quistione fra proprietari e lavoranti fornai: lettera aperta al Cav. Dott. Ettore Candiani', *L'Esercente*, 11 March 1900; 'La vertenza dei fornai', ibid., 18 March 1900.

[10] On the politics of this see Punzo, *Socialisti e Radicali*, p. 92 and 'L'imponente assemblea dei proprietari forno di mercoledì', *L'Esercente*, 15–16 March 1900.

improving market conditions, in order to retain control over hiring, hence the vague language of the promise to make use of the *ufficio*.[11]

This was not how *L'Esercente* represented the conflict. The journal dismissed *La Lotta*'s argument that the dispute was over whether or not it was right for workers to improve their conditions as inconsiderate; the heart of the issue was whether or not the proprietors could afford to better the workers' conditions. Did *La Lotta* consider it the duty of the proprietors to improve workers' conditions even at the expense of their own well-being? When many employers' standards of living were no better than those of their workers, was it any surprise that the latter were sometimes paid less than the rates set down in the concordat?[12] The failure of the workers and Socialists to appreciate any of this and their repeated characterisations of the *esercenti* as *ladri* (cheats and thieves) were what riled the proprietors, and *L'Esercente* was in no doubt that this disrespect had been given a substantial boost by the arrival of the *partiti popolari* in the city hall.

L'Esercente was keen to re-establish its political credibility within the movement following the 1899 elections in which the majority of shopkeepers had appeared to support the Federation's line over the newspaper's; but, though it reflected the proprietors' misgivings over Baroni's position, its emphasis on the workers' salary demands sat oddly with the fact that the members of the Mutuo Proprietari Forno had accepted these, even whilst rejecting Baroni's initial accord. So too did the newspaper's repeated attempts to link in the issue of cooperatives – whether as competitors forcing the bakers to reduce their profit margins, or as allies of the Socialists to whom the Federation were also linked within the Democratic bloc. *L'Esercente* even published an article 'dedicated to the Federazione Esercenti and the Mutua Forni' which recounted how the Belgian Socialist party intended to break with its Radical and Republican

---

[11] 'Definizione della vertenza tra proprietari e lavoranti fornai', *L'Esercente*, 30 September 1900.

[12] The paper argued that 1884 had been a prosperous time when profits had been in the order of L. 3 per 100 kg. Since then the depression of the 1890s and increased competition, particularly from the cooperatives, had driven profits down to L. 2 per 100 kg and necessitated lower pay scales. 'Intorno alla vertenza dei fornai', *L'Esercente*, 22 March 1900. According to Baroni, two-thirds of the proprietors worked alongside their employees, and four-fifths of them had a taxable income under L. 1,000, as shown in the *ricchezza mobile* returns. 'L'imponente assemblea dei proprietari forno di mercoledì', ibid., 15–16 March 1900.

allies at the first opportunity, attributing this unprincipled behaviour to the party's advocacy of the cooperative principle.[13]

L'Esercente gained a notable success when its list for the elections to the Council of the Mutua Proprietari Forno triumphed over Baroni's in March 1900. For Baroni, President since 1885, and the driving force behind the association's success, this was an unprecedented rebuke. Antonio Cardani, director of the successful *esercenti* commercial venture, the Bakers' Cooperative for the Manufacture of Luxury Bread, replaced Baroni as President.[14] Baroni regained office in the following year, but the first indication that the 'ordinary' *esercenti* would not grant unlimited political licence to their leaders had been given.

Over the course of the rest of 1900 and 1901, however, the political balance within the *esercenti* movement swung back towards the Federation and Baroni. The resounding victory of the *partiti popolari* in all six Milanese constituencies in the parliamentary elections of June 1900 indicated that the Democratic administration was going to last. The Federation policy of constructive engagement therefore gained credibility in that its fundamental premise was that the *esercenti* could best protect themselves by having a share in the exercise of political power. It was further strengthened by the award of the school lunches contract to the bakers and *salsamentari* associations in November 1900, an outcome which was at least partly attributable to the presence of Baroni and the other Federation representatives amongst the Democratic majority.[15]

Tadini's alternative strategy appeared somewhat dated. A congratulatory note sent to the new Milanese Giunta by the Lega Nazional delle Cooperative, along with Turati's comments in *Critica Sociale* that one course he hoped to convince the new Giunta to adopt was to support the cooperative movement, had initially suggested Tadini's fears would prove justified.[16] The new administration's attempts to favour cooperatives foundered on the laws

---

[13] 'Dedicato alla Federazione Esercenti ed alla "Mutua Forni"', ibid., 21 January 1900.

[14] 'La Mutua Proprietari Forno', ibid., 25 March 1900; 'Il nuovo consiglio e la caduta del Cav. Baroni', ibid., 25 March 1900; 'Il lavoro delle Associazioni Milanesi: società M. C. fra i proprietari forno', ibid., 29 March 1900.

[15] See pp. 213–14.

[16] Tadini, G., 'Ci siamo', *L'Esercente*, 18 January 1903; 'La grave questione dei fornai', ibid., 21 January 1903.

restricting municipal contracts to cooperatives composed entirely of 'needy' members, however, whilst the *esercenti* were now scoring clear successes in open competition against the consumer cooperatives.[17]

Tadini's advocacy of the Associazione fra Commercianti, Industriali ed Esercenti proved misguided. Its elitist image proved unacceptable to small shopkeepers, rendering it incapable of intervening effectively in disputes over issues such as the founding of the factory-based Cooperative Pirelli in May 1900.[18] The *esercenti* of the surrounding quarter of San Gioacchimo became caught up in a battle between the Federation and the Association over who should represent them in their fight against the cooperative, but is is clear even from *L'Esercente*'s account of the proceedings, that the Federation were more successful in presenting themselves as the friends of the small shopkeepers, whilst the Association's representatives were mocked for their titles and their overdeveloped sense of decorum. Indeed some shopkeepers declared themselves to be Socialist, despite their vehement opposition to privileged cooperatives, and spent much time attacking the political positions of the Association and *L'Esercente*.[19] Their reactions are indicative that small-scale shopkeepers located in the periphery of the city still distrusted the 'establishment', an echo of the zonal identity that favoured the Federation.

The Association was even denounced by influential critics of Baroni within the Federation and the Mutua Proprietari Forno, who regarded it as a Moderate organisation, and alleged that the Association paid Tadini to publicise it in his columns. Tadini denied both accusations, but it proved impossible to refute the charge of elitism, confirmed by the Associations' refusal to carry Appiani, a baker, on its list for the elections to the Camera di Commercio in December 1900. As Appiani was a known Moderate, even *L'Esercente* was forced to conclude that this was not a politically motivated exclusion, but the result of 'caste' objections.[20]

In the light of this, Tadini was forced into a *riavvicinamento* with

---

[17] See pp. 214–15.   [18] See pp. 215–16.

[19] 'Gli esercenti contro la cooperativa Pirelli', *L'Esercente*, 16 May 1900; 'Ancora gli esercenti e la cooperativa Pirelli', ibid., 17 May 1900; 'Gli esercenti del quartiere di San Gioacchimo all'Associazione fra Commercianti, Esercenti ed Industriali', ibid., 17 May 1900.

[20] '"L'Esercente" e l'Associazione di via Orefici', *L'Esercente*, 17 May 1900; 'Le elezioni commerciali', ibid., 2 December 1900.

the Federation, obliging him to rescind some of his criticisms of Baroni. In April 1901, he admitted he had misread the political situation in October 1899, and should have remained neutral during the elections instead of opposing the Federation. Whatever one thought of the Federation's politics, he argued, it was clear that it was an economic force for good and had succeeded in making the voice of commerce better heard within the Municipio.[21]

Baroni's position was further improved by the outcome of the bakery workers' strike in October 1901. The workers had presented an aggressive set of demands, mainly for new pay scales, but also harking on the issues of the *ufficio di collocamento*, night work and the obligation to undertake home deliveries. Again the proprietors showed themselves quite willing to consider certain proposals and set up a committee to study the technical feasibility of abandoning night work (this was to investigate how dough, worked the night before, could be kept fresh for baking in the morning). They were prepared to accept an *ufficio di collocamento* at the Camera di Lavoro, eight-day notice periods, weekly payment and Christmas Day off, as well as considering, though from a sceptical viewpoint, higher rates of pay. Even so, the workers ignored their leaders' recommendations and voted for industrial action.[22]

The strike marked a new phase in the employer–employee relationship in the *esercenti* sector. Mass meetings of over a thousand workers were held at the Arena. These adopted manifestos referring to a 'holy struggle' which, when won, would bring 'great honour not only to the bakers, but to all citizens and the entire Milanese proletariat'.[23] Assertions like these led *L'Esercente* to believe that the workers were being used by the Socialists as a means of attacking the class of proprietors. The bakers particularly resented the way in which workers courted public sympathy by emphasising in their manifestos their desire for improved conditions, rather than their fundamental demand for better pay which would inevitably lead to higher bread prices.[24]

[21] '"L'Esercente" e la Federazione', ibid., 7 April 1901; '"L'Esercente" e la Federazione', ibid., 14 April 1901.
[22] 'Intorno all'abolizione del lavoro notturno dei fornai', *L'Esercente*, 18 July 1901; 'Le pretese dei lavoranti fornai', ibid., 4 August 1901; 'Lo sciopero generale dei lavoranti fornai', ibid., 11 October 1901.
[23] 'I panattieri milanesi alla Cittadinanza', ibid., 26 September 1901.
[24] 'Il grande comizio dei lavoranti fornai all'Arena', ibid., 12 September 1901; 'La lotta tra lavoranti e proprietari fornai', ibid., 26 September 1901; 'La risposta dei proprietari fornai al memoriale dei loro lavoranti', ibid., 28 September 1901.

The proprietors were undoubtedly frightened, as was evidenced by the high attendance rates at meetings of the Mutua Proprietari Forno.[25] After sitting out the strike for ten days, however, the employers were able to negotiate an agreement in which they conceded very little to the workers. There would be a day off a month at the workers' expense, all workers bar the head baker would perform home deliveries, and 5 *centesimi* less would be deducted for food and lodgings. On wages, however, there was no word at all, whilst the proprietors again agreed to recommend their members to use the *ufficio di collocamento* at the Camera di Lavoro, but not to compel them to so do.[26] Although the strike hit the bakers hard (as the annual report of the Banca degli Esercenti confirmed), there was a general sense of elation that the proprietors had 'won' – an assessment with which the Socialist journal *Avanti* concurred. Baroni was regarded as the hero of the hour for leading the resistance to the employees' demands, enabling the issues raised by his membership of the Giunta to be ignored.[27]

This was a strictly temporary phenomenon, however. After 1901, the Federation's position was progressively weakened as relations between employers and employees deteriorated, in line with the general trend towards industrial discord in the city outlined in chapter 12. In June 1902 a dispute amongst hotel, restaurant and bar staff broke out over the issue of the *ufficio di collocamento*. Waiters sought to run the labour exchange by themselves, under the umbrella of the Camera di Lavoro, whilst the proprietors wanted a jointly administered *ufficio*. A mass meeting of 3,000 staff led to a five-day strike which demonstrated the ability of the employees to

[25] One of the reasons for setting up the Commission to investigate the *lavoro notturno* was the feeling expressed at meetings of the Mutua Proprietari Forno that a positive step towards abolition might improve relations between the employers and a workforce which was preparing to exercise its strength. See Zocchi's remarks, reported in 'Intorno all'abolizione del lavoro notturno dei fornai: la relazione Zocchi', *L'Esercente*, 18 July 1901. In the critical period of negotiation leading up to the strike there were at least two meetings of the Mutua Proprietari Forno attended by over 400 bakers (according to *L'Esercente* that is). 'L'adunanza della Mutua Proprietari Forno', *L'Esercente*, 28 September 1901; 'L'importante adunanze di ieri della Mutua Proprietari Forno', ibid., 10 October 1901.

[26] 'La fine dello sciopero dei lavoranti fornai e la ripresa del lavoro', ibid., 20 October 1901.

[27] 'L'imponente assemblea delle Mutua Proprietari Forno per la ratifica del concordato', ibid., 24 October 1901; 'La stampa socialista milanese e di Roma e lo sciopero dei panattieri', ibid., 24 October 1901; 'L'Assemblea Generale degli Azionisti della Banca degli Esercenti', ibid., 16 February 1902.

organise across many individual enterprises. In this they were assisted by the Camera di Lavoro, whose director, the Socialist Scaramuccia, also played a part in negotiating the agreement that ended the dispute.[28] This provided for a single exchange run by a committee of both sides, one day's rest in every fortnight, and a commitment that employers would give preference to workers who came from this *ufficio*, without being obliged to do so.

Their employers had again got the better of the deal, but the strike marked a further development in labour relations in that it involved both large and small enterprises within the sector. Not only were the workers taking collective action, the proprietors were also forced to do so, suggesting a community of interests between such diverse professions as hoteliers and small restaurateurs, even though the smallest businesses were probably less affected by the strike, and were exempted from some of the provisions of the settlement.[29] The divisions between employer and employee were becoming ever starker, however, as exemplified in the spate of disputes between individual proprietors and workers which were referred to the arbitration board. These cases usually concerned use of an *ufficio di collocamento* and were often sponsored by the Camera di Lavoro. The owners felt that the Socialists were goading on the workforce to challenge their right to manage: it was the threat to their independence of action, rather than higher wage claims, that irked the *esercenti*.[30]

This applied in fields other than industrial relations. Giunta policy reflected contemporary concerns with improving the quality of life of the consumer, a particular concern of the Socialists who wanted to promote the welfare of the working classes. Adulteration of provisions and falsification of their quantities or qualities were regarded as outrages against the customer, making the *esercenti* sector a prime target for regulation. Baroni and his colleagues sought to influence the administration from within, but were hamstrung because of the importance of the issue to the Socialists. Open

[28] 'Il personale d'albergo, osteria e trattoria', ibid., 24 April 1900; 'Lo sciopero dei camerieri', ibid., 8 June 1902; 'La fine dello sciopero dei camerieri', ibid., 12 June 1902.

[29] The provision for one day's rest a fortnight did not apply to enterprises with less than five employees, for example. 'La fine dello sciopero dei camerieri', *L'Esercente*, 12 June 1902.

[30] Of course, both sides knew that workers recruited from sources other than the *ufficio di collocamento* were more likely to accept lower wage rates.

opposition was impossible, given the political situation, yet the public silence of the Federation's representatives fuelled doubts about the credibility of its position, both in *L'Esercente* and within the organisation itself.[31]

The new hygiene regulations (Nuovo Regolamento d'Igiene), which came into force in April 1902, confirmed the fears of many of the shopkeepers' movement.[32] The regulations extended into areas which had previously been unregulated, and it was felt that the standards which were set were far too stringent. In consequence there would be higher prices and reduced margins as businesses struggled to conform to the new requirements. These ramifications were probably of most concern to those *esercenti* who were least affected by the deterioration in industrial relations: that is the very small businesses which only utilised family labour.

Butchers were particularly aggrieved by the new regulations which divided them into two categories, the first selling only prime-quality types of beef and veal, whilst the other dealt in inferior animals such as old cows and bullocks. The intent of this division was to prevent the public from being misled over the quality of their purchases. Butchers, however, especially those in the second category, believed the regulations separating the two types of enterprise were too restrictive, and argued that the distinction should be abolished. The foundation of the Society of Butchers' Shop Proprietors in 1902, uniting a long-disorganised and fractured profession, was a direct consequence of the introduction of the Nuovo Regolamento d'Igiene.[33]

The manner of the enforcement of the new regulations also annoyed the *esercenti*. Under the new administration the sanitary inspectorate was considerably strengthened with the development of a service that went out to test at the scene of suspected contraventions, the foundation of separate biological and chemical laboratories and the setting up of teams of samplers to determine suitable levels of 'purity'.[34] Inspections of premises handling food

---

[31] 'Osservazioni', *L'Esercente*, 20 February 1902.

[32] *Regolamento d'Igiene pel Comune di Milano 1902*.

[33] 'La riorganizzazione generale dei macellai', *L'Esercente*, 9 February 1902; 'L'Assemblea Generale dei Macellai alla Federazione degli Esercenti', ibid., 20 February 1902.

[34] See the account of the functioning of the sanitary inspectorate in Bordoni-Uffreduzzi, *I servizi di igiene nel comune di Milano*, esp. pp. VIII, 165; Bordoni-Uffreduzzi, *I servizi di igiene nel quinquennio 1901–1905*, esp. pp. 195–206.

Table 13.1. *Inspections of food shops and warehouses by sanitary inspectors, 1898–1905*

Year	Number
1898	7
1899	6
1900	18
1901	27
1902	194
1903	989
1904	2,334
1905	1,570

Source: Bordoni-Uffreduzzi, *I servizi di igiene nel comune di Milani* 1903 p. 165. Bordoni-Uffreduzzi, *I servizi di igiene nel quinquennio 1901–1905*, pp. 196–204.

and drink increased dramatically in number as can be seen in Table 13.1.

In July 1902, the rotation elections to the city council were held. The *partiti popolari* again fielded a single list including the 'reformist' Socialists. *L'Esercente* declared that it could not support this because of the inevitable conflict of interests between the shopkeepers and the proletariat. The Moderates were much loathed in Milan, but at least they had never threatened to harm *esercenti* interests through the establishment of municipal bakeries and pharmacies. It therefore recommended a mixed list in which fourteen Moderate nominees replaced all the Socialist candidates on the Democratic list and also some other nominees (including most from the Federation), to leave sixteen Democrats.[35]

It was significant that *L'Esercente* chose to defend its choices by instancing two well-known Moderate businessmen, Cesare Consonni and Guido Campari. Both were proprietors of high-class restaurants and bars which one would not normally associate with the *esercenti* movement.[36] The universal nature of the strikes by the staff of the *esercizi pubblici*, however, meant that proprietors of a wide variety of establishments now had to make common cause in

[35] 'Per le elezioni amministrativi', *L'Esercente*, 29 June 1902; 'Le elezioni amministrative alla Federazione degli Esercenti', ibid., 13 July 1902; 'Le elezioni amministrative', ibid., 19 July 1902.

[36] Campari was the proprietor of a high-class eponymous watering hole, and Consonni of the well-known Orologio restaurant (recommended by Baedeker as 'good and moderate'), both in the vicinity of the Piazza Duomo. Baedeker, *Italy from the Alps to Naples*, p. 24.

order to deal with the workforce. This was one of the principal causes of the *rapprochement* between the commercial elite and the *esercenti*.

Meanwhile the Federation looked increasingly beleaguered amongst the *partiti popolari* who only offered it two positions, instead of the customary four, on the Democratic list.[37] The General Meeting of the Federation, held just prior to the election, expressed disquiet at the way the 'big currents' in the alliance had determined its direction, and recommended the constitution of a special group within the Democratic bloc to defend *esercenti* interests. *L'Esercente* mocked the numbers of lawyers on the lists, including the Federation's own nominees, and asked why there were not more politicians from a commercial background.[38]

The Democrats again won an impressive victory at the polls and both Baroni and Angelo Piazza, Vice-President of the Federation, were given places in the new Giunta. None the less it was noticeable that there was a gap of between 250 and 500 votes between those Federation nominees recommended by *L'Esercente* and those the journal did not carry. Of the eight Moderates returned to the Council, four had been supported by *L'Esercente*. There was now a significant split in the *esercenti* movement, a split so wide that the Federation, along with the *salsamentari* association, set up their own journal to counter the criticisms of *L'Esercente*.[39]

The year 1903 saw considerable labour unrest. Employers and employees assumed ever more entrenched positions with conflict focused on the control of the labour supply. Proprietors alleged that the *ufficio di collocamento* which had been set up after the strike in the *esercizi pubblici* was inefficient because the Union of Cooks and Waiters had admitted all kinds of unemployed workers and despatched them as replacements for workers taking their *riposo di turno*. They also complained that it was under the influence of the Camera di Lavoro and had been addressed by the well-known revolutionary Socialist, Lazzari.[40]

The owners reverted to using recruitment agents despite the fact

[37] Punzo, *Socialisti e Radicali*, p. 235.
[38] 'Le elezioni amministrative: la conferenza del rag. E. Chiesa', *L'Esercente*, 20 July 1902.
[39] 'Le gravi insidie contro "L'Esercente"', ibid., 18 November 1902.
[40] 'A proposito del servizio di turno dei lavoranti fornai', ibid., 23 November 1902; 'L'agitazione fra il personale d'alberghi, ristoranti, birrerie, tratorie, osterie, ecc.', ibid., 16 December 1902.

that this was in breach of the agreement reached at the end of the strike in 1902. The union's response was to threaten a strike in order to force acceptance of the fortnightly *turno* and the employment of substitutes from the *ufficio di collocamento*. The proprietors refused to meet union representatives, however, saying they would only negotiate with representatives of those in full-time work in the *esercizi pubblici* and who were themselves employed in the sector.[41]

This struck the union's weak point. The majority of those attending union meetings lived by substituting for workers on their *riposo di turno*, and many did indeed come from other professions. The union leader, Codevilla, for instance, was an ex-hairdresser. A meeting of 300 full-time waiters opposed the strike as damaging to their public standing. When the decisive union meeting was held there were attempts to divide up the audience into those in work and those out of it. Umbrellas were thrown at the speakers, and the full-time workers withdrew from the meeting, forcing Codevilla to concede that a strike was impossible.[42]

There was also widespread agitation amongst those in Codevilla's former profession, that of haircutting. On 22 September 1902 a petition signed by 700 workers was presented to the proprietors' association. All but two of the employees' demands were accepted by the employers, but the workers were keen to experiment with strike action as a way of bringing the class together. Although the Hairdressers' League only numbered 220 members, over 1,000 out of around 1,200 staff obeyed the strike call on 9 January 1903 (this date was chosen to insure that employees had received their Christmas and New Year bonuses). The Camera di Lavoro played host to the strikers and squads were organised to ensure the stoppage was total. Cooperative salons were set up and proved popular with workers in the city. Fearful these might become too successful and unable to sustain the losses arising from the dispute, the employers began negotiations after just four days, although the strike went on until the 21 January. The discussions centred on the issue of *uffici di collocamento*, with the proprietors eventually agreeing to close their own exchange in favour of one to be organised by the League at the Camera di Lavoro. A reduction in hours was also granted.

[41] 'La tumultuosa assemblea generale dei camerieri, cuochi ed affini', ibid., 23 April 1903.
[42] 'I camerieri occupati contrari allo sciopero', ibid., 17 April 1903; 'La tumultuosa assemblea generale dei camerieri, cuochi ed affini', ibid., 23 April 1903.

It appeared that the workers had won a significant victory but their success was short-lived. The League failed to consolidate its position once the dispute was over and of the 300 or more new members who joined during the strike, only five or six stayed on once the dispute was over. The list of the new members was lost and the League was divided by personal arguments. The principals were able to revert to using intermediaries for hiring labour, indeed the ex-director of the proprietor's *ufficio* set himself up as a recruitment agent.[43]

A third dispute over the functioning of an *ufficio di collocamento* involved the butchers' shop workers in April 1903. An initial petition from the workers had demanded the recognition and funding of an *ufficio* by the employers, an annual contract (intended to guarantee stable employment), reduced working hours, an increase in the number of holiday days and an evening meal for workers who had to stay late on Saturdays. The employers refused to negotiate, and on 9 April 1903 a decision to strike was taken at a meeting at the Camera di Lavoro. Immediately the doors were closed to prevent anyone leaving and vigilance squads were again sent out to enforce the action.

Initially 1,200 butchers' shop workers were involved in the dispute although this number later fell to just over 1,000. Of these, 213 were members of the workers' League. The squads were very active, arguing with proprietors who refused to allow them onto their property, and often coming to blows with the workers whom they found there. The proprietors were forced to use their relatives to keep the shops running, but there was never a shortage of meat in the shops.[44]

Eventually the workers abandoned their demands concerning the *ufficio di collocamento* and annual contracts, and were easily able to negotiate a package of reduced hours, more holidays and the re-employment of all strikers, leading to a return to work on 16 April. As in all the disputes, the proprietors had held firm and maintained total control over the labour supply within their enterprise. None the less, the increasing militancy of the workers was a fright to them, not least in the context of the now habitual involvement of the

---

[43] For a full description of the conditions of the *parrucchieri*, as well as the strike itself, see Società Umanitaria, *Scioperi, serrate*, pp. 110–14.

[44] For details on this strike, ibid., pp. 69–73.

Camera di Lavoro. The proximity of this institution to the Socialists highlighted the political discomfort of the Federation.

Indeed, at the general assembly of the Federation in early April, the annual report was passed by the votes of fewer than a third of the 300 or so members present, with the majority abstaining. The leadership was criticised for its aloofness and failure to address the real problems of the members. Its ties to the Giunta had prevented any action being taken over the problem of hygiene contraventions or the subsidy to the Camera di Lavoro; matters of 'class interest' (the term used) were merely referred to the *collegio dei probiviri*. Instead the Federation spent its time organising members' excursions to historic towns such as Vigevano. *L'Esercente*, meanwhile, showed how the delegate system at the Federation was used to create positions for favourites within the Federation.[45]

There were now clear signs of rebellion against the Federation's position, and these intensified later in the year, when the Municipio set up a Commission to examine setting up its own bakeries to supply municipal institutions such as hospitals and schools, and to provide an alternative source of cheap bread for the poor. Municipal bakeries had been advocated by the Milanese Socialists as early as 1897, in response to the rapid rise in prices that year, and were a subject of some discussion in the part as a whole; but the passage through parliament in 1903 of a law permitting municipalisation gave renewed impetus to the project.[46] The immediate inspiration, however, was the system instituted by the Socialist-dominated city council in Catania, which had already been the subject of considerable attack by the *esercenti* movement, and the object of hostile resolutions at the national congresses of commercial federations.[47]

[45] Leather dealers, for example, were represented by four delegates although there were probably no more than eight members who practised this trade. 'Per le elezioni dei delegati alla Federazione Esercenti', *L'Esercente*, 10 March 1903. See also 'L'imponente adunanza alla Federazione degli Esercenti avvenuta lunedì sera', ibid., 19 March 1903; 'La terza adunanza generale alla Federazione Esercenti', ibid., 5 April 1903.

[46] On municipalisation see Berselli *et al.*, eds., *La municipalizzazione*, and in particular the article by Meriggi, 'Il progetto di municipalizzazione del pane', pp. 427–58.

[47] The Municipio had decided to set up the commission in response to the passing of the *legge 29 marzo 1903, n. 103*, which regulated the ways in which *municipalizzazione* could be implemented. Giolitti's motives for passing this law were as much fiscal as ideological; it was hoped that the municipal services would make a positive contribution to local government finances. See Pozzana, *Tra pubblico e privato*, p. 6. For attacks on municipalisation see 'I lavori del Congresso fra

Baroni and his colleagues were extremely embarrassed. The fear that any Socialist-influenced Giunta would attempt some form of municipalisation had been one of the most persistent arguments used by *L'Esercente* against continuing in alliance with the Democrats in 1899/1900, and the apparent scotching of it by Mussi in 1901 had played an important part in the newspaper's reassessment of relations between itself and the Federation. Now such a proposal was actually on the table and, to compound his misfortune, Baroni was the Giunta member due to receive the Commission's report.[48] The creation of the Commission was itself a compromise between the Socialists, notably Caldara, who believed the proposed service should be a first step on the way to total municipalisation of the bakery sector, and the Radicals, including Mussi, who were hostile to any consideration of a service that served clients other than those already in the municipal sector.[49] The very fact of the setting up of such a commission appeared clear proof to the *esercenti* that Socialist demands were pushing the Giunta further to the left, however, whilst the length of time that the Commission sat served to increase speculation and disenchantment with the administration and the Federation's participation in it.

The Mutua Proprietari Forno produced a highly detailed pamphlet costing out the various options and demonstrating that it would be impossible to produce bread at a price lower than that at which it was supplied by the private bakers.[50] However, the argument was

Commercianti e Industriali a Roma', *L'Esercente*, 11 June 1903, and Buffoli, L., 'La municipalizzazione del pane a Catania', *L'Esercente*, 17 March 1903.

[48] 'La municipalizzazione del pane', *L'Esercente*, 10 July 1903.

[49] Meriggi, 'Il progetto di municipalizzazione', p. 440.

[50] At this time bakers were producing twenty-five types of *pane casalingo* (basic breads for workers) and thirty-six types of *pane di lusso* or *pane viennese* (high-quality breads). In addition they performed three to four home deliveries a day and frequently offered sales on credit (*il fido*). The proprietors argued that to compete with them the municipal bakeries would have to buy out the existing bakeries and turn them into *rivenditori* of the mass-produced bread, and use an inferior form of flour to make just one type of bread, in large-sized loaves only. Credit sales would have to be abandoned and families would no longer be able to use the local baker's oven or get heat from the ashes which were distributed amongst the poor in winter. Workers would no longer get the traditional Christmas and high-summer tips, and there would be far fewer of them in any case. This was due to the efficiency of large-scale production in reducing labour costs. In other areas, however, the ovens were less efficient, crucially in the making of bread itself, which tended to be burnt on the outside and undercooked within. This was because the amount of water vapour given off by the dough in a large coke-fired oven was sufficient to lower the temperature significantly in the latter part of

based on the assumption that municipalisation would be an attempt to suppress the private sector totally: undoubtedly the aspiration of some of its proponents, but not the design of the proposal itself.

According to the bakery proprietors, 1,500 workers would be made redundant, 600 bakers plus their families – roughly 1,800 persons in all – would be ruined, to save workers 1.5 to 3 *centisimi* a day on bread. Yet the past performance of mass-production bakeries in Milan had been lamentable as all three private bakeries, including the recent Panificio Milanese, founded with a capitalisation of over L. 1,000,000, had been forced to close, whilst the Unione Cooperative bakery had failed to make a significant impact on the market despite selling at 5 *centisimi* below the average price per kilo. The well-educated palate of the Milanese consumer, reared on the delights concocted by the private bakers, would never accept the lower standards of the factories.[51]

The Socialists disputed the proprietors' arguments. Giovanni Montemartini, the leading theoretician of municipalisation, and a reformist Socialist, asserted that because the bakery was intended solely to serve the working classes, its employees would never go on strike. If mechanisation was gathering pace within the industry, he asked, why did the proprietors assume that only the municipal bakeries would cause redundancies? And why shouldn't proprietors experience the same hardships as befell workers who were forced to learn other jobs? Above all, though, the project's supporters stressed the fact that, despite the forebodings of the proprietors, the

baking. Yet start the oven any higher and the bread came out burnt. The degree of uniformity in the bread was in inverse proportion to the size of the oven used. When using a small-scale wood-fired oven, however, the water vapour could be controlled by means of a coiled instrument called a *bollitore* which regulated its release. There would be no gains in hygiene as both ovens thoroughly sterilised the bread that they cooked, so that the greater the number of hands through which the baked bread passed before reaching the consumer, the greater the risk of it becoming noxious. Naturally the transport of bread from the municipal bakeries to the vendors would involve the greater degree of handling. Other factors to consider, according to the Mutua Proprietari Forno, were what would happen if either the bakery workers or the electricians went on strike, thus depriving the whole city of bread, and the amount of tax revenue which both the state (L. 50,000 in *ricchezza mobile* revenues) and the Comune (L. 27,490 from the *tassa esercizio* and other duties) would lose as a result. Where would the Municipio find the money for the upkeep of the bakeries? Società Mutua Proprietari Forno di Milano, *La panificazione privata e la panificazione municipalizzata.*

[51] Ibid., pp. 32–4.

service was not intended to replace the existing Milanese bakeries but to work alongside them.[52]

Answering this criticism, Tadini argued that any compromise measure, such as that in Catania, would inevitably lead to price-cutting and a drop in quality, as municipal and private bakeries attempted to win the custom of the working classes. Obstacles to free competition, such as a *calmiere* (official price control) would be bound to be introduced by the Municipio in an attempt to turn the battle their way. Consumers would lose out as the private bakers abandoned the production of other forms of bread and the home delivery service, in order to match the price of the municipal service.[53]

Baroni's position as a member of the administration, and President of the Federation and the Bakers' Association, was now untenable. He lost the presidency of the Mutua Proprietari Forno to Dott. Carlo Luraschi, who, like Baroni, was a proprietor of a large bakery rather than of a modest enterprise. None the less, it was clear that the membership intended to overturn Baroni's line. Luraschi carried the battle into the Federation by proposing a motion at the 1904 Annual General Meeting, calling for an *esercenti* programme with clearly defined goals to be incorporated into a new statute. Its aim would be to create an economic class consciousness which could form the basis for the construction of a political 'class programme'.

Luraschi argued that the Federation had failed to inculcate such a consciousness because membership of the Democratic alliance effectively prevented it from standing up to the Camera di Lavoro, the unions and the Socialists. Most of his speech concentrated on the 'abyss' of ideology separating the Socialists from the traditional Democrats, notably the principle of economic collectivity. Nothing demonstrated this better than the proposed municipalisation of the bakeries. Now a similar proposal to deal with pharmacies was already under discussion amongst the Socialists, whilst elsewhere in the country Socialists had already municipalised the bakeries of Catania, the slaughterhouses of Parma and the bakeries, mills, pharmacies and pasta plants of Reggio Emilia.

---

[52] See the article by Montemartini in *Il Tempo* of 20 August 1903, and reproduced in *L'Esercente* on 23 August 1903 under the title 'La panificazione private e la panificazione municipalizzata a Milano: ai signori socialisti'.

[53] Tadini, G., 'La panificazione privata e la panificazione municipalizzata a Milano: le nostre considerazioni', *L'Esercente*, 23 August 1903.

In Reggio, Luraschi argued, the *esercenti* had organised too late. In Milan they still had a chance. The starting point of a new programme had to be 'economic' action by and for the class itself. There should be propaganda campaigns in favour of technical schools and special courses in commercial subjects. The Federation should protect the *esercenti* against increases in taxes and rents, and from the attacks of the unions and the Camera di Lavoro. The action, however, had to extend from the economic to the political. Shopkeeper interests should be represented in both the city council and the national parliament. Hence Luraschi's call for a new '*partito economico*', which would confine itself solely to supporting the interests of small-scale commerce.[54]

Luraschi's prescription of a third party was the weakest part of his analysis. His main thrust, however, was that economic interests were the prevailing force in contemporary politics and that alliance with the Socialists was incompatible with this reality. The Federation, he argued, could not go on ignoring the arrival of class politics but should play the political game according to the new rules. The universality of this new situation was demonstrated by the fact that Luraschi was able to convince the national congress of small businesses to adopt a similar motion calling for a *partito economico*.[55]

Passing the measure at the Federation itself proved more difficult. Officials found excuses for putting off the vote until a later date, and then for cancelling this subsequent meeting because the hall was not large enough to hold the number of members (mostly supporters of Luraschi) who turned up. A month after the motion was proposed, it was passed by 200 votes to 15. The manœuvring in which the Federation officials had indulged served only to confirm Luraschi's portrayal of them as an undemocratic cabal, primarily concerned with satisfying their own political ambitions. Shortly afterwards the Mutua Proprietari Forno voted to withdraw from the Federation altogether by 102 votes to 3. It was followed by the butchers' and *salsamentari* associations.[56]

[54] 'Alla Federazione Esercenti: un nuovo indirizzo politico-economico?', *L'Esercente*, 17 April 1904.
[55] 'Il Congresso dei Commercianti ed Industriali Italiani a Napoli: I lavori I. Federazione nazionale', ibid., 9 June 1904. This report of the Congress was written by Luraschi himself, a sign of his favour with the newspaper.
[56] 'L'imponente Assemblea Generale di venerdì sera', ibid., 1 May 1904; 'Per l'indirizzo politico-economico alla Federazione', ibid., 17 May 1904; 'Assemblea

Hostility to the Socialists intensified as the party became more deeply enmeshed in the battle between the 'reformist' and 'revolutionary' tendencies within it. Speeches at the party's Bologna conference were used by Luraschi to demonstrate the contempt in which some members held the *petit bourgeois* classes. The 'revolutionaries' won control of the Milanese Camera di Lavoro, putting further pressure on the 'reformists' to obtain concrete benefits from their support of the Giunta. This intensified the pressure for a municipalisation programme, causing Mussi to resign in December 1903 in protest at the proposed municipalisation of electricity. The 'reformist' socialists were forced to join the Giunta to show their support for the new mayor, Barinetti.[57]

When the Giunta was reshuffled Baroni and Piazza lost their places, but other *esercenti* politicians, notably Stabilini, replaced them. All the shopkeeper representatives remained in the Democratic alliance, however, even though this had been clearly rejected by the Federation's members. After all these upheavals, the Commission examining the prospects for municipal bakeries rejected the scheme in March 1904, arguing that the project was too risky and might well meet with customer resistance, and suggesting that the best way to protect the consumer was through stricter hygiene regulations.[58]

Had the decision gone the other way, the shopkeeper representa-

Generale della Mutua Proprietari Forno', ibid., 16 June 1904; 'La crisi alla Federazione', ibid., 19 June 1904; 'Intorno alla crisi alla Federazione', ibid., 21 June 1904.

[57] See Punzo, 'Riformisti e politica comunale', p. 227; Punzo, *Socialisti e Radicali*, pp. 289–97, 314.

[58] An extensive summary of the Commission's report appeared in 'Gli studi per un forno consorziale del comune e delle Opera Pie a Milano', *L'Esercente*, 5, 8 May 1904. The main reasons for rejection were that the capacity used to produce bread for the schools could not suddenly be switched into production for the public during the holidays because there was no distribution network. Unione Cooperativa's failure to undercut the private bakers when bidding for the *refezione scolastica* contract was also taken into account, as was the fact that the necessary supplies of cheap flour could not be guaranteed unless, as in Palermo and Reggio Emilia, one instituted a municipal mill as well – something which was outside the commission's terms of reference (the Comune of Florence rejected a plan to municipalise its bakeries in 1905 for this reason: Pozzana, 'Nel panorama delle aziende pubbliche degli enti locali a Firenze', p. 7). Those cities such as Catania and Reggio which had set up municipal ovens had only kept their prices down by paying very low wages. Finally there was the question of *il fido*, which the public regarded as a right but which the municipal bakeries would not be able to administer except by appointing intermediaries to negotiate this, thereby increasing costs. See also Meriggi, 'Il progetto di municipalizzazione del pane', p. 440.

tives might have been forced to resign from the Council. As it was, they succeeded in holding on until the next major crisis, the General Strike of September 1904.

The strike was organised by the Camera di Lavoro as part of a general protest about the killings by police of peasants demonstrating at Castelluzzo on Sicily on 15 September. The strike had no defined aims or length and was merely intended as a political protest, yet it almost completely shut down Milan during its first two days. Shops were forced to close, either by gangs of youths who were roaming the streets or simply for lack of workers. The intimidatory violence destroyed any last illusions that shopkeepers may have had about their 'special' relationship with their own employees, or the working-class movement in general. It was clear that participants in the strike regarded the shopkeeper as merely another member of the repressive bourgeois establishment and treated him accordingly. Obviously the feelings of those actually involved in the strike were more extreme than those of all working-class organisations and their members, but the fact remained that the strike was called by the labour movement.[59]

The Federation reacted by putting out a manifesto which regretted the incident at Castelluzzo and accepted the legitimacy of a protest strike. At the same time it lamented the violence and intimidation and argued that the right to work was being denied its members. It ended with a call to its members to reopen their businesses, which many did. A similar manifesto deploring the violence was issued by the Associazione fra Commercianti, Industriali ed Esercenti, significantly acting in conjunction with the Mutua Proprietari Forno. This stated that the strike had proven the need for better organisation amongst the *esercenti* in order to deal with the acts of vandalism which had closed down the city. *L'Esercente*, which, like all newspapers, did not appear during the strike, regarded the protest as 'the triumph of the revolution'.[60]

Luraschi welcomed the Federation manifesto, but argued that the strike was merely a further proof of the need for the *esercenti* to organise in defence of their own class interests, arguing that,

just as one should draw lessons and salutary admonitions from the great social movements, from historical events, from political

---

[59] On the nature of the General Strike in Milan see Punzo, *Socialisti e Radicali*, pp. 306–35.

[60] 'Il trionfo della rivoluzione', *L'Esercente*, 18/20/22 September 1904.

changes, from all that which constitutes, in an extremely concise but philosophically profound expression, the evolution of humanity, so shopkeepers, traders and industrialists should admit that this general strike, whether one wishes to call it a tempest, a triumph of hooliganism or whatever, was a great lesson to them ...

We had not expected acts of unheard of violence, nor to have waited behind the shop shutters, revolver in hand, for the invasion of the hooligans, nor the breakage of shop windows, nor the shutting-down of the engine which powered mixing machine for salami and other products, but as early as last April we spoke these very words at the full General Assembly of the *esercenti*.

'Finally the programme should be extended to defend the *esercenti* class against high-handedness and oppression from whichever quarter it comes' ...

When we spoke very frankly, not against individuals but in favour of an ideal – the organisation of the *esercenti* – we were called utopianists, day-dreamers, reactionaries, clowns, both within the Federation and outside it. Today we are very happy to note that the course we adopted was the only one, the correct one, to follow and if the storm of the last days finally serves to create the organisation of all the commercial and industrial classes of Milan we will bless it as it is our conviction, as it was yesterday and will be always, that the creation in Italy, and above all in our city, of a commercial party with modern ideas could do much for the country, particularly our Milan which has so much need of the participation of all honest individuals to achieve the high purpose to which it is destined.[61]

The tenor of the comments made at the delegate meeting of the Federation which followed the strike was much the same. The manifesto that had been issued was widely praised, except by Piazza who resigned both his office of Vice-President and his membership of the Federation itself. Two other members of the Federation executive called for a distancing from the Democratic administration, however. They were primarily influenced by the strike, but also took into account Socialist calls for the transfer of the school lunches contract to a cooperative now that the law

---

[61] Luraschi, C., 'Una grande lezione', *L'Esercente*, 23 September 1904.

permitting cooperatives to tender for all municipal projects was about to come into effect.[62]

A few days later the Giunta passed a motion declaring its support for the strike and its aims. Three Federation councillors, including Baroni, resigned their seats forthwith, whilst three others, including Stabilini, followed Piazza's lead in preferring to relinquish their association with the Federation than that with the Democrats.[63] Their actions leant further weight to Luraschi's charge that the Federation had been hijacked by politicians posing as *esercenti*. The Giunta was doomed, however, as the Moderates realised that if they resigned their seats as well the effect would be to force a partial election, because of an insufficient number of council seats being occupied. This they duly did, precipitating the partial elections of November 1904 which in turn led to the fall of the Democratic administration.[64]

Between November 1904 and January 1905 three sets of elections were held in Milan: a parliamentary election caused by the defeat of the government in early November, partial elections to the Council in late November and full Council elections in January. The Federation did not run candidates in any of these; indeed, Baroni declined the offer of a seat at the parliamentary elections because of the Democrats' continued alliance with Socialists.[65] During the national elections, the Federation issued a 'class programme' similar to that proposed by Luraschi. *L'Esercente*, in keeping with its normal practice, supported Democrats but not Socialists; although the newspaper also argued that the Moderates had done more for the *esercenti* than any other party, and lamented the occasions at which Radicals and Conservatives were involved in runoffs against each other rather than in opposition to Socialists or Catholic extremists.[66]

[62] 'Contro lo sciopero generale', *L'Esercente*, 7 October 1904; 'Le opinioni del Cav. V. Aliprandi' ibid., 9 October 1904; 'L'assemblea dei delegati di venerdì sera alla Federazione', ibid., 9 October 1904; 'La refezione scolastica', ibid., 11 October 1904. See also Punzo, *Socialisti e Radicali*, pp. 335–7.
[63] 'I consiglieri comunali degli esercenti si dimettono', *L'Esercente*, 11 October 1904; 'La defezione di alcuni consiglieri comunali degli esercenti', ibid., 11 October 1904.
[64] See Punzo, *Socialisti e Radicali*, pp. 338–9.
[65] Baroni also declined the offer to fight the same seat for the Moderates! Ibid., p. 346. See also 'La candidatura del Cav. Luigi Baroni al VI° Collegio', *L'Esercente*, 23 October 1904; 'Gli esercenti alle urne', ibid., 30 October 1904.
[66] 'La lotta politico-elettorale: i nostri candidati', ibid., 3 November 1904; 'I risultati dei ballottaggi', ibid., 15 November 1904.

In the partial elections to the city council, the Federation again preferred not to run its own candidates, but to concentrate on a propaganda campaign to register *esercenti* voters. The individual shopkeeper associations, however, those representing the butchers, the *salsamentari*, and the *esercizi pubblici* proprietors, all joined *L'Esercente* and the Associazione fra Commercianti, Industriali ed Esercenti in supporting the Moderate list. *L'Esercente* explained that a Moderate victory would precipitate a full council election in which *partito economico* candidates, of the type recommended by Luraschi, could participate. The Moderates duly won these elections, with most of the press attributing this to the *esercenti* vote. A disgruntled article in *Il Tempo*, a Socialist newspaper, claimed society would be none the poorer if all the *esercenti* went out of business.[67]

In the full elections of 1905 the Federation, though not running its own candidates, did decide upon a list composed of both Moderates and Democrats considered favourable to commerce. This became the Unione Commerciale Progressiva list, recalling Luraschi's dream of a third party, but the majority of *esercenti* organisations did not support it, arguing there was no room for such a distraction. *L'Esercente*, the bakers, the butchers, the grocers, the *salsamentari* and the *esercizi pubblici* proprietors all joined with the Associazione in supporting the Moderate list. Again the names of candidates such as Giuseppe Spatz, proprietor of the high-class Hotel Milan were highlighted; men with whom the average *esercenti* had previously had little in common but with whom they now shared the status of victims of strike action.[68]

The overall result of the 1905 elections was a clear win for the Moderates who won fifty-two seats (ten of them held by Catholics) as opposed to twenty-eight won by the Democrats (all Radicals). This was a rare split result as, of the sixty-four seats reserved for the

[67] 'Le elezioni amministrative: un'importantissma adunanza alla Federazione Esercenti', ibid., 20 November 1904; Tadini, G., 'L'Assemblea Generale alla Federazione Esercenti: un po' di considerazioni', ibid., 23 November 1904; 'Le elezioni parziali amministrative', ibid., 24 November 1904; 'Il trionfo delle classi commerciali e industriali nelle elezioni amministrative di Milano', ibid., 27 November 1904. See also Punzo, *Socialisti e Radicali*, pp. 357–61.

[68] 'Per le prossime elezioni amministrative: l'adunanza dei delegati alla Federazione', *L'Esercente*, 8 January 1905; 'L'assemblea dei soci alla Federazione', ibid., 15 January 1905; 'Le elezioni generali amministrative e la Federazione Esercenti', ibid., 18 January 1905; 'Le prossime elezioni generali amministrative: la lotta elettorale. Il partito commerciale', ibid., 27 January 1905.

majority list, thirty-six were taken by Moderates who were supported by both their own organisation and the Unione Commerciale Progressiva, and twenty-eight went to the Radicals supported by the Unione, the Federazione Socialista and their own party. The sixteen posts reserved for the minority list all went to Catholics and Moderates, whilst six Radicals failed to be elected because, although backed by the Unione, they lacked the approval of the revolutionary Socialists.[69] Even so, the importance of the Unione to the overall result should not be underestimated.

The course of the Democratic administration between 1900 and 1905 had made clear that the *esercenti* could no longer operate within that political alliance. The essential division in Milan was no longer one between the city and the suburbs, but that between proprietors and workers. The Federation's policy of alignment with the Democrats dated back to the *dazio* division within the city, but *L'Esercente* was right to assert that in the new century the aims of the Socialists and the interests of small traders would prove incompatible.

The two events which did most to persuade shopkeepers of this were the proposals for the municipalisation of bread in 1903 and the General Strike of 1904, but both were indicative of broader trends within the period. The campaign for municipalisation was indicative of the interventionist intent of the reformist Socialists, intended to favour the interests of the working-class consumer. This inevitably led to the increased regulation of small commerce, and disaffection amongst the *esercenti*. This resentment was probably greatest amongst the smallest operators, who had fewer resources to devote to meeting the higher standards, and most to lose from competition for working-class custom from the Municipio.

Those traders who were also employers learnt from the labour disputes of the 1900s that the paternalistic and individualistic relationship between proprietor and worker was a thing of the past. Increasingly they found they had more in common with proprietors of larger enterprises. In September 1904, the strikers lumped all the *esercenti* in the same class as the rest of the commercial and political establishment. The small traders did not just form the opposition in an economic struggle, they were to be classified as such in

[69] Punzo, *Socialisti e Radicali*, pp. 368–70.

the political one. As Luraschi's analysis made clear, a form of 'class politics' had arrived.

It was hardly surprising therefore that the *esercenti* should look to political alliances with the centre-right to defend them from their persecutors, just as they had once sought defenders on the left when their interests were threatened by the policies of the old city establishment. The suburban shopkeepers had belonged on the 'left' side of the city's geographical division, but they, along with all the *esercenti*, could only operate on the other side of the class division that replaced it.

The process was not one of incorporation into the conventional right, however. The success of the Unione Commerciale Progressiva demonstrated the continuing political autonomy with the *esercenti* sector, with many traders preferring to back this mixed list, rather than simply defect to the Moderates. There was a willingness to deal with the establishment, but not to identify with it: something which had been made clear by the failure of Tadini's attempts to transfer the allegiance of his readers to the Associazione fra Commercianti, Industriali ed Esercenti in 1900 and 1901.

Furthermore, the 'ordinary' *esercenti* again demonstrated that they were capable of pursuing courses of action independently of their 'leadership'. They refused to follow Tadini in 1900, the bakers' association overthrew Baroni in 1901 and 1904, whilst Federation members voted down their executive's strategy in the same year. The political course followed by the *esercenti* movement between 1900 and 1905 was one determined by the membership, rather than the leadership, and did not involve incorporation into the conservative mainstream: rather it was a recognition of the incompatibility of the interests of small commerce and municipal Socialism as practised in the city.

14. *Shopkeepers and Socialists 1905–1922*

This book has presented an analysis of the *esercenti* movement in the twenty years between 1886 and 1905 within the context of shopkeeping in the city. The reasons for starting in 1886 are self-evident; it was in this year that Rusca founded *L'Esercente*, providing both the impetus for a shopkeeper movement, and a record of its activities for future historians. Finishing in 1905 neatly concludes a twenty-year period which coincides with one complete turn of the business cycle of depression and growth. Also, 1905 marked the end of a key moment in the politics of the movement with the effective closure of the strategy of a left alliance following the experience of the shopkeeper during the period of *partiti popolari* administration between 1900 and 1904. The purpose of this chapter, in which much context is left out for the sake of brevity, is to show how the politics of the movement in its subsequent years developed along lines that evolved in the first twenty.

By 1905 three key strands in the political development of the small-trader movement could be observed. There was no longer a sufficient basis for alliances involving the Socialists, with their consumer-orientated interventionist strategies, and shopkeepers who sought a minimum of interference in their own trades. Aside from this restriction, however, the *esercenti* were prepared to seek deals with parties across the rest of the spectrum in order to achieve their aims. This autonomy did not mean that the constraints imposed by the shape of the political system could be avoided, however – the movement had to operate with due regard to its size and was therefore forced to choose sides in the electoral contest, rather than strike out on its own.

This restriction was demonstrated after the 1905 local elections. The Unione Commerciale Progressiva had shown that mixed lists could have an influence on the outcome of elections, but that an independent third party could not succeed. At most the list had attracted some 1,000 votes. The nearest thing to a shopkeeper representative on the new Moderate Giunta was Candiani, the industrialist who led the Associazione fra Commercianti, Industriali ed Esercenti. Politics were still dominated by two rival blocs. The best that the *esercenti* could do was act as an interest group, maximising their influence within whichever electoral bloc offered them the most.

As the episode of the Unione demonstrated, there was no sudden swing to the right amongst the *esercenti*; indeed, there was considerable reluctance to acknowledge that the political divisions within Milanese society were so drawn as to make their own presence amongst the Moderate bloc inescapable. In the partial elections to the council held in 1906 both *L'Esercente* and the Federation, including President Baroni, supported the Liberal-Moderate bloc; but the newspaper was swift to assert that this was because the *esercenti* remained true democrats who now found that Ettore Ponti, the liberal leader of the new Giunta, was closer to their thinking than the *partiti popolari*.[1] Both the Federation's honorary president, Rosio, and its vice-president, Carabelli, stood on the Moderate list and were duly elected.

This was far from a case of absorption into the Moderates, however, as events of the succeeding year showed. In 1907 a sharp turndown in the business cycle across all sectors of the economy left small traders protesting that their access to credit had been severely curtailed. In October there was a general strike in the city, once again a protest against the shooting of demonstrating pickets. Ponti showed the strikers considerable sympathy, as he also did bakery workers by proposing that night working should be abolished. The mayor's stances reflected his commitment to what he saw as modern, managerial-style administration, but they lost him friends amongst the *esercenti*.[2]

The need to fight their own corner was now apparent, and a new organisation was formed to fight the corner of commerce generally. The Partito Economico (Economic party) came into being in November 1907, endorsed by Baroni on behalf of the Federation,

---

[1] 'Le elezioni amministrativi', *L'Esercente*, 24 June 1906.
[2] Punzo, 'Riformista e politica comunale', p. 249. On Ponti's style of administration see Porro, 'Assimistrazione e potere locale' pp. 1791–841.

Candiani for the Association, and Tadini in the columns of *L'Eser-cente*. The party's programme stated that its aim was to protect the interests of the 'bourgeoisie of labour', that is to say the *esercenti* and the peasantry, who suffered at the hands of 'cumbersome bureaucracy' and 'workers in perennial agitation'. The party's principal economic concerns were opposition to excessive taxation, the promotion of professional training and the protection of 'honest' commerce, whilst its political activity was to consist of attracting representatives of all the tendencies within the liberal and democratic parties to it, and lending support in elections to those who had endorsed the party's programme, or the principles behind it. It was hoped that the party would inspire similar initiatives all over the country, although one of its statutes excluded all those whose religion influenced their political thinking, i.e. Catholic conservatives, from joining.[3]

The language of the Economic party was that of class politics. *L'Esercente* saw the party as performing the equivalent function for the 'bourgeoisie of labour' that the Camera de Lavoro performed for the working classes. It was through organisation that 'the unknowing proletarian masses, who most of the time yield to the will of leaders intent on exploiting them' had imposed injustices on the *esercenti*, and it was through organisation that these could be overturned, not, of course, for the good of the class itself but for that of the whole of the country.[4]

In practice, however, the Economic party was not a political party of its own, but an interest lobby. It brought together representatives of the various commercial organisations in campaigns over specific issues, but at elections its approach of endorsing candidates belonging to other parties was no different from that of other *esercenti* organisations. Although it was no doubt intended to coordinate these choices, disputes soon occurred.

In the partial elections of June 1908, for instance, the Economic party, along with *L'Esercente*, decided to back the Liberal-Moderates under Ponti once again. The Federation, however, rightly protested that the Economic party had not undertaken any consultation with its membership, and declined to support the Moderate list on the basis that it included Catholic conservatives, a political grouping specifically excluded from the ranks of the Partito

[3] The programme was published in *L'Esercente*, 7 November 1907.
[4] 'Gli scopi che prefigge il Partito Economico', *L'Esercente*, 7 November 1907.

Economico. Disillusioned by Ponti's conciliatory attitude towards workers, especially bakery workers, and his high-spending administration, they instead endorsed a list put forward by the Radical and Republican parties, who had now split away from the Socialists. The largest organisation within the *esercenti* movement moved back towards the political centre.

For the rest of 1908 and on into 1909, Ponti continued to give offence to both the *esercenti* and the traditional conservatives within his own bloc. In December 1908 the Giunta introduced a proposal to substitute the tax on rentable values (*valor locativo*) with a family tax – a move towards a more progressive system of taxation that provoked a right-wing backlash led by Emanuele Greppi culminating in the fall of Ponti in May 1909, and his replacement by another liberal, Bassano Gabba.

Ponti's search for additional financial resources also brought him into conflict with the *esercenti*, whose premises were exempt from the *valor locativo*. It was the considerable increases in taxes on the occupation of 'public space' and on signs and insignia, adopted in October 1908, that were most resented by small traders, however; and this struggle continued under Gabba. Shopkeepers who wished to utilise the area beyond the front of their premises, for displays of merchandise or pavement tables for example, had to obtain an annual licence from the Comune in accordance with a law of 1874, which also specified norms for awnings, signs or other insignia.[5] The 1908 regulations appeared to tighten the definition of public space even further, applying it to the entirety of the space between buildings, rather than just the ground area, and therefore measuring the resultant occupation of this space in three, as opposed to two, dimensions. Licence fees rocketed, whilst the *esercenti* claimed that the new methods of assessment contravened the norms laid down in the law of 1874.

When the first demands were issued in November 1909, the matter came to a head. At a meeting of the city council, Candiani proposed a motion supported by Rosio and Carabelli calling for the suspension of the tax. This was defeated by fifty-one votes to eleven, with nine abstentions, but the breakdown of the voting showed how divisive the issue had become. Those against were drawn from all sectors of the *esercenti* movement; as well as the representatives of

[5] *Il Prontuario*, pp. 15–16.

the Association and the Federation named above, they included Perego, the conservative councillor from the Società Salumieri, and Rossi, a Moderate elected as part of the Unione Commerciale Progressiva in 1905. Greppi also opposed the tax as did others on the right, whilst the abstentions were recorded amongst the radicals of the democratic tendency. The tax was supported by a combination of the Liberal Moderates and the Socialists.[6] Political space for *esercenti* interests appeared to exist both on the right and in the centre.

With the tax confirmed by the council, the *esercenti* took their protests elsewhere. Rossi called on the provincial administration to strike it down as unconstitutional, whilst the Federation took its protests to the Chamber of Commerce and the Prefect. In the interim it announced that it would urge shopkeepers not to pay, and would call for a shutdown of shops at the first sign of coercive action by the council. Candiani, a member of the city Giunta, resigned. The Municipio admitted that its first assessments were inaccurate – the Federation claimed these charged for the pulls on the end of electric doorbells, rating them at one square metre – but even the new assessments were rejected by the Federation as arbitrary and excessive.[7] Eventually, at the end of the year, Gabba conceded to the *esercenti*, setting up a committee to examine the tax, a four-month extension on payments, and the waiving of fines imposed for non-payment up until that point.[8]

The opposition amongst the conservative Moderates to Gabba's allegedly high-spending, high-taxing Giunta culminated in a decision not to carry the mayor and two other Giunta members who became eligible for re-election in the partial elections of 1910. The *esercenti* movement had to decide whether to support this list, which represented Moderates who had condemned the tax on public areas, or that of Radicals and Republicans who had abstained from supporting the tax and represented the democratic tendency to which many *esercenti* still claimed allegiance. A split ensued with *L'Esercente* and the Association again supporting the

---

[6] 'Interessi cittadini: la tasse sull'ocupazione delle aree pubbliche in Consiglio Comunale', *L'Esercente*, 5 November 1909; Nasi, 'Da Mussi a Mangiagalli', p. 57.
[7] 'L'agitazione degli esercenti milanesi per l'aggravio di tassa sull'occupazione spazi ed aree pubbliche', *L'Esercente*, 3 December 1909; 'L'agitazione degli esercenti milanesi: le ragioni esposto in un ricorso all'on. Giunta Provinciale Amministrativa', ibid., 15 December 1909.
[8] 'Interessi cittadini: la fine degli agitazione degli esercenti', ibid., 2 January 1910.

Clerico-Moderate list, whilst the Federation opted for the Democrats. Surprisingly the Economic party also made advances to the Democrats, employing the slogan 'Neither with the Clericals, nor with the Socialists'.[9] The Democrats rejected this approach, however, refusing to deal with the same Partito Economico that had previously done deals with the Catholic conservatives in spite of its own constitution. This refusal led to the Economic party and the Federation fielding their own candidates in a list entitled 'The Electoral Union of Democratic and Liberal Commercial Associations'.

The list of twenty-five included six figures who were prominent in the *esercenti* movement, including Baroni and Carabelli, whilst there were no more than two candidates on the Moderate list who could claim to have contacts with the world of small commerce. *L'Esercente*, however, denounced the Federation as masons whose conduct would only rebound to the detriment of small traders by splitting the anti-Socialist vote. This duly proved to be the case, with the Socialists polling around 10,500 votes and winning twenty-five seats, the Moderates some 7,500 and six seats, the Democrats about 4,000 votes and the Federation/Economic party list about 1,900 votes.

The affair of the tax on public spaces and the elections of 1910 were suggestive of the range of options available to the small-trader movement, as much as the divisions within it. All the *esercenti* associations were opposed to the tax and had worked together to defeat it – come the election, however, they had to choose between the two political blocs that had offered them assistance to do this. That the Association, led by the conservative councillor Candiani, should line up with the Moderates was inevitable, whilst it was only slightly less so that the Federation, with its leadership still linked to the Radicals and its roots amongst the smallest shopkeepers, should first line up with the Democrats. *L'Esercente*'s contention that the real enemies of commerce remained, by the logic of their own ideology, the Socialists, was decisive in determining its own stance, and its disparagement of the Economic party's performance.[10] Clearly a good number of the five thousand or so members of the Federation, and the roughly two thousand strong Partito Economico, did not back the list, but when one considers that this

---

[9] 'La lotta elettorale amministrativa', ibid., 17 June 1910; Punzo, 'Riformisti e politica comunale', pp. 264–5.
[10] 'L'esito delle elezioni parziali', *L'Esercente*, 21/22 June 1910.

was an election in which only about a third of all electors bothered to cast their votes, it is the number that did back the list which is impressive. Right, centre and independent political strategies all had significant numbers of supporters amongst the *esercenti*.[11]

It was the divisions within the Clerico-Moderate bloc itself, however, that cost it the election, and the result led to the toppling of Gabba as Greppi's tendency won the battle for control within the party. Full elections were held in January 1911 from which the Moderates emerged victorious with Greppi taking over the mayoral duties. It appears that the Partito Economico this time courted the Moderates, but with such limited success that Tadini declared he could not support a list that contained just two *esercenti* representatives in comparison with seventeen lawyers. *L'Esercente* suggested that, from the point of view of small traders, there was little to choose between the Moderates and the Democrats, and largely abstained from participation in the campaign.[12] An increase in Democrat votes was suggestive that most *esercenti* support went in that direction, however.[13]

L'Esercente could afford its lukewarm attitude to political activity at this time, because its chief nightmare, a resurrection of the Democrat-Socialist bloc, was not on the cards. In 1912, however, Giolitti introduced virtual universal suffrage, resulting in a doubling of the Milanese local electorate from 70,000 to 140,000 in 1913, and creating the opportunity for the Socialists to win power without recourse to alliances.[14] After breaking with the Democrats the reformist Socialists had continued to advocate a consumer-orientated programme that was intended to broaden their electoral appeal. This featured much municipal intervention, often predicated on an attraction to the 'modern' management techniques of large-scale private enterprises which operated through economies of scale. Whilst the left attacked this programme as no more than managing capitalism, the reformists believed it offered benign administration to the advantage of the citizen.

[11] Membership figures are based on those available for 1914. According to this source, the Association had 1,000 members at that time. Comune di Milano, *Annuario storico statistico 1914*, p. 280.

[12] Tadini, G., 'Le elezioni amministrative', *L'Esercente*, 19 January 1911; 'Agli esercenti e commercianti: a proposito della lotta elettorale', ibid., 22 January 1911.

[13] Punzo, 'Riformisti e politica communale', p. 267.

[14] Nasi, 'Da Mussi a Mangiagalli', p. 71.

For the *esercenti*, however, such a programme spelt disaster. A small-scale inefficient sector that dealt in the distribution of such primary wants as food and fuel was ripe for intervention. When full council elections were held in 1914, the majority of the *esercenti* organisations argued that the key task was to stop the Socialists. Given the nature of the new franchise, it seemed imperative that the *esercenti* organisations line up behind the leading anti-Socialist list, that of the Associazione Liberali uniting liberals, moderates and Catholic conservatives. The Association, the Economic party and *L'Esercente* duly did so, but the Federation executive instead cast its lot in with the Radicals. At a general meeting to discuss the executive's action, opponents claimed a fix, and the meeting was abandoned without a vote being taken.[15] The Federation's decision was widely condemned, with *L'Esercente* again recalling the disastrous episode of the Radical-Socialist administration of 1900–4, and arguing that whatever the democratic sentiments of the *esercenti*, any post-election alliance between men of such widely different sentiments could only lead rapidly to 'the organisation of disorder, financial today, political tomorrow'.[16] Many trade associations, including those for bakers, pork butchers and tobacconists, disassociated themselves from the Federation, and endorsed the Liberal list.

The vote was tight, with the Socialists picking up 34,596 votes and sixty-four seats, and the Associazione Liberali list 32,117 votes and the sixteen seats reserved for the minority. There were 8,736 seats for the Radicals and 2,077 for the Republicans. With so few votes separating the first two lists, it was not unreasonable for *L'Esercente* to argue that the Federation was guilty of splitting the anti-Socialist vote and thereby facilitating the victory of the enemies of small traders it was supposed to represent. Indeed, the paper argued, the Federation had promoted indolence and apathy amongst the *esercenti* and had let down all those who looked to the movement to provide a clear lead during a moment of danger.[17]

The new Socialist administration, led by Emilio Caldara, was given an opportunity to practise interventionism on a much greater scale than would otherwise have been the case by the outbreak of

---

[15] 'Interessi cittadini: in prossimità delle elezioni amministrative', *L'Esercente*, 7 June 1914.
[16] 'Le elezioni amministrative odierne', ibid., 14 June 1914.
[17] 'La vittoria dei socialisti', ibid., 16/17 June 1914.

war in Europe in 1914, and Italy's entry into the conflict the following year. On 27 July 1914, before hostilities had even begun, the Giunta introduced a maximum price for bread, and this was extended on 6 August to other goods such as rice, sugar, coffee and pasta: something Caldara claimed would have been done even under normal circumstances. Initially there were complaints by small traders at the prices imposed, most notably about the calculations on which the price for bread was based, but these were reviewed on a weekly basis and the *esercenti* organisations appear to have cooperated in this.[18]

The Giunta's policy of direct intervention in the market through the direct purchasing of provisions proved more controversial. The food provisioning department was upgraded and commenced grain purchases in August 1914, whilst in December a mill was rented in which the corn was ground. The resultant flour was passed to the Milanese Federation of Consumer Cooperatives which baked bread for the Comune that was then supplied to charitable institutions, hospitals, housing associations and consumer cooperatives, including Unione Cooperativa.[19] This pattern of distribution was reproduced when the municipality moved into the purchase of other necessities such as potatoes, pasta and beans. The justification behind the policy was that the availability of low-priced commodities in the cooperatives was the most effective way of restraining prices and eliminating the opportunity for speculative hoarding.

This offended those small traders who were deemed to need controlling. *L'Esercente* demonstrated that the first two purchases of grain made by the Comune were at prices that were actually higher than those prevailing on the open market, and argued that sufficient stocks were available in September 1914 to avoid the need for panic buying.[20] The involvement of the cooperatives was hardly calculated to appeal to shopkeepers either, particularly when Caldara argued that this system protected the poor from falling into the use of *il fido*, which he saw as a form of usury that enabled them to drink in the *osteria* whilst running up chronic debts.[21]

---

[18] 'Il calmiere nel pane', *Città di Milano*, July 1914, p. 24; 'I contraccolpi della guerra e i provvedimenti per attenuare gli effetti', ibid., August 1914, pp. 6–8; Punzo, *La giunta Caldara*, p. 61.

[19] Nejrotti, 'L'amministrazione comunale di Milano e i consumi popolari', pp. 461–2.

[20] 'Interessi cittadini: acquisto del grano', *L'Esercente*, 15/16 September 1914.

[21] Punzo, *La giunta Caldara*, p. 129.

This was indicative of the Socialists' attitude towards the *esercenti* sector. *Città di Milano*, the Comune's official magazine, published a series of articles dealing with the various provisioning trades in the city. The bakery trade was described as 'backward', because of the large number of small-scale concerns and the increasingly low ratio of inhabitants per bakery: out of the twenty-six provincial capitals in northern Italy, Milan (with 871) was one of only six that had fewer than a thousand inhabitants per bakery, and bread was more expensive in these cities than in the others.[22] The same ratio for the number of outlets where alcoholic drinks could be consumed was one for every ninety-six inhabitants, instead of the supposedly desirable one to five hundred. *Città di Milano* maintained that stores such as dairies, tobacconists, ice-cream parlours and grocers that stocked drinks were particularly responsible for promoting the scourge of alcoholism as women and children regularly entered their premises.[23] In another article attacking the 'irrationality' of the fruit and vegetable trade, the magazine argued that the 'inorganic' nature of the retailing sector indicated that it was still 'in the period of infancy'.[24]

This was contrasted with the 'modern' organisation of retailing in foreign cities such as Berlin, London and Paris. There the prevalence of department stores and multiple retailers meant that the role of the intermediary had been restricted to the point that the retailer was the agent of the producer. There was a logical distribution of stores; their high volumes and the elimination of *il fido* guaranteed the public low prices and quality brands. By contrast in Milan there were only sixteen retail stores with more than five branches.[25]

Whilst the Socialists might not sympathise with the profit motive driving such operations, they were impressed by their ability to deliver low prices to the consumer and sought to import similar modernity to Milan. In December 1915 the Giunta produced a plan to institute municipal bakeries capable of producing healthy bread at a lower price than that in the private sector. This was to be achieved in an integrated operation from milling through to retailing, taking advantage of the economies of scale offered by the use of large ovens, bulk buying and a more rational distribution network.

---

[22] 'Il pane', *Città di Milano*, July 1914, pp. 3–5.
[23] 'Il commercio delle bevande alcooliche in Milano', ibid., September 1913, pp. 2–4.
[24] 'Come si approvvigiona il Verziere di Milano', ibid., August 1914, pp. 2–3.
[25] Ibid.

Much stress was laid on the allegedly healthier bread that would be produced, and the inadequacies of the existing industry. Veratti, the Giunta member in charge of hygiene, stated: 'We can't allow an industry in this condition to survive.'[26]

It was clear that the Socialists intended that the bakeries established would outlast the war, and eventually supplant the private sector to the point of extinction. The understandable hostility of the *esercenti* to this was shared by the liberal opposition, which, though it had shown itself prepared to tolerate interventionism during wartime, objected to the idea that the Giunta should suppress private economic activity and expose itself directly to the risks inherent in commercial activity. In May 1916 the Provincial Giunta ruled that because the project was intended to create a permanent institution, it would have to pass through the long sequence of stages laid down for the formal municipalisation of a utility in Giolitti's law of 1903, effectively condemning it to the scrapheap.[27]

During 1916, the government assumed much greater control over price-fixing and the purchasing of essential commodities, particularly imports. Although this meant a reduction in the Giunta's powers in these areas, however, the government also passed legislation enabling local administrations to set up autonomous agencies for the provision of consumer goods to non-profit organisations such as cooperatives and charities, in order to exercise a restraint on prices. The legislation specified, however, that these agencies were to be closed within six months of the end of the war.

Milan moved swiftly to establish such an agency, known as the Azienda Consorziale dei Consumi, which had the aim of 'acquiring and producing commodities of widespread consumption to sell them to all consumers in the best possible condition and without any intent of speculation'.[28] The agency had a much wider intent than the government legislation provided for, as the lack of reference to any date for closure in its constitution made clear. The facilities and personnel of the council food-provisioning service were transferred to the Azienda as was the central provisioning agency of the cooperatives belonging to the Socialist-sympathising League of Cooperatives. Sixty-eight charitable institutions and sixty-one consumer cooperatives participated in the Azienda, which also set up its own retail outlets.

---

[26] Punzo, *La giunta Caldara*, p. 124.   [27] Ibid., pp. 124–5.
[28] Nejrotti, 'L'amministrazione communale di Milano', p. 463.

From the beginning the *esercenti* and the Liberal opposition were opposed to the Azienda, recognising in it an attempt to suppress the role of middlemen in commerce.[29] Their opposition became yet more intense when, after the war, the Azienda showed no sign of ceasing its activities, but rather expanded into new areas such as shoe and clothing production, in addition to the production of bread (in ovens belonging to the cooperatives), butter, cheese and firewood and the processing of various kinds of meat. The Azienda was in charge of the distribution of all the produce directly purchased by the state, including the decision as to how much should be allotted to each *esercente*, whilst many other commodities were bought in a wholesale operation that served both the cooperatives and over fifty outlets that the Azienda opened itself.[30]

Increasing reliance on the Azienda was the Socialists' response to the rising cost of living in the city during 1919 and 1920. This problem became acute after crowds took to the streets on the morning of Sunday 6 July, breaking into shops and looting them of their contents, in imitation of riots that had already taken place in other Italian cities. In many cases shopkeepers were forced to sell their goods to the crowds at much-reduced prices, but these rituals often degenerated into the simple violence and looting that was recorded elsewhere. Disorders broke out in both the centre and the suburbs, though activity was naturally more pronounced in less well-off-areas. Twenty-five branches of the Unione Cooperativa were attacked, and it, and many other shopkeepers, protested about the lack of protection by the police.[31]

Socialists, shopkeepers and other observers all concurred in the conviction that the government's economic programmes lay at the heart of the problem, though their criticism of such programmes differed widely. To the Socialists, the problem was that the government had moved too quickly in eliminating rationing of many goods, and removing price controls in an attempt to return the country to a freer market. The *esercenti* on the other hand believed

---

[29] Punzo, *La giunta Caldara*, p. 134.
[30] Nejrotti, 'L'amministrazione comunale di Milano', p. 464.
[31] Accounts of the lootings by some of the shopkeepers affected can be found in ASW, Gab. Prefettura, 296, Reclami di esercenti e negozianti saccheggiati il 6 luglio 1919. See also the press coverage of events in *Avanti!*, *Corriere della Sera*, and *Il Popolo d'Italia*.

that the lack of free trade in commodities exacerbated food short-
ages and prevented a return to normality.[32]

Immediately after the riots, the Comune imposed price reductions
of around 40 to 50% on basic provisions whilst the government
produced new regulations for the constitution of committees to
establish prices based on the cost of production, but with an 'equitable' margin for the retailer. As the Socialists found the price-fixing
committees unable to prevent further price rises, they concentrated
their efforts into the expansion of the Azienda, hoping to manœuvre
the market in favour of the consumer.[33]

Although both the Giunta and the Camera di Lavoro denounced
the violence, they wasted little sympathy on the *esercenti*. *Avanti*, the
Socialist daily, claimed that in the city:

Although there was a widespread conviction that certain excesses
could have been avoided, one notes a sense of satisfaction ...
There was too much repressed anger in the soul of the people,
against the big and little starvation-mongers, for it not to break
out. For four years, shopkeepers, merchants and intermediaries
have pocketed money by speculating on the need of the population, and for four years one had to tolerate their provocative
heightened arrogance. Behind his counter the shopkeeper considered himself as a sort of dictator. The law, the fixed prices, the
threats of prosecution were risible things, regarded by the shopkeeper with contempt. The goods at fixed prices were always of
poor quality. 'If you want the good stuff' – said the shopkeeper
with mocking irony – 'you pay for it at the price that I fix.' If the
customer dared to make a timid protest, the shopkeeper
responded, 'You go and protest to *your* mayor' and out came
curses and swear words against Caldara, against the Socialists
and even against the Government.[34]

Not surprisingly the *esercenti* movement had little time for the
labour movement. *L'Esercente* pondered the morality of the

[32] See Argo, 'Cronaca di Milanoa: la sommossa annonaria milanese', *Avanti!*, 7 July
1919; Tadini, G., 'L'agitazione contro il caro-viveri', *L'Esercente*, 8 July 1919. For
other interpretations of government culpability see Mussolini, B., 'Rimedi eroici
ed urgente per la crisi: decimare le ricchezze', *Il Popolo d'Italia*, 6 July 1919;
Einaudi, L., 'La politica dell'organizzazione per gli approvvigionamenti. Le
difficoltà della situazione e il programma del governo', *Corriere della Sera*, 8 July
1919. A useful recent analysis of this period of Milanese history is Foot, 'Alliances
and socialist theory'.
[33] Punzo, *La giunta Caldara*, pp. 87–8.
[34] 'Cronaca di Milano: giornata calma e sacheggio legale', *Avanti!*, 8 July 1919.

Camera di Lavoro promoting demonstrations against the cost of living and then lamenting that these had got out of control.[35] It increasingly made reference to the famine in Russia as a demonstration of the inadequacies of the Socialists' strategy for provisioning, and regularly ran scare stories about Bolshevism, requisitioning and the abolition of private property. The government, however, had acted no better in introducing such swingeing price cuts. *L'Esercente* protested vigorously that small traders had been sacrificed by the government in order to appease public opinion, suggesting to people that a terrestrial paradise could be established through looting and rioting.[36] The state had failed in its duty to protect private property during the riots, and refused to compensate the *esercenti* for their losses in spite of claims, championed by the Economic party, that the lack of intervention by the forces of public order amounted to dereliction of duty on the part of the authorities.[37] Moreover, the government had not made any equivalent attempt to deal with the rapid rise in shop rents.

The *esercenti* were equally unhappy with the radical right. On 23 March 1919 the Fascist movement was founded in Milan, following a meeting held at the Palazzo degli Esercenti in Piazza San Sepolcro, in rooms hired out by the Circolo per gli Interessi Industriali, Commerciali e Agricolo, the commercial association that contested elections to the Chamber of Commerce. This did not imply an endorsement on either side, however. Rooms were hired out to a variety of organisations, including those of a political character, whilst the edition of *Il Popolo d'Italia*, the Fascist newspaper, that covered the foundation meeting also reported the denunciation of fishmongers selling overpriced cod by the Milanese Azienda Consorziale dei Consumi under the headline 'Thieves! Thieves! Thieves!'[38] During the cost-of-living riots the newspaper openly sympathised with the crowd, and, on the day after the Milanese riots, Mussolini stated that blame resided with the 'commercial

[35] 'Fatti e realtà', *L'Esercente*, 13 July 1919.
[36] 'Il pericolo', ibid., 10 July 1919.
[37] ASM, Gab. Prefettura, 296, Reclami di esercenti e negozianti saccheggiati. See the telegram of 20 July 1919 from the President of the Partito Economico Italiano, Somasco, to the Ministero dell'Interno, and Ministero dell'Interno Direzione Generale della Pubblica Sicurezza, Div. IV, sez.1, n.10071.38, risposta a nota del 20.7.1919, n.6112/6165.
[38] '23 marzo. La Nostra adunata', *Il Popolo d'Italia*, 18 March 1919; 'Cronaca milanese: Ladri! Ladri! Ladri!', ibid., 24 March 1919.

bourgeoisie' as well as the Socialists and the government. He claimed that provisioning and price-fixing policies had never been applied seriously, enabling hoarding and speculation to take place, whilst many shopkeepers and wholesalers had guilty consciences about the exploitation they had practised during both the war and the armistice.[39] After the price reductions were reduced the paper turned to denouncing enterprises it alleged had infringed the new regulations. In at least one instance this proved not to be the case.[40]

Given these circumstances, the key political choice facing the *esercenti* movement appeared to be that of whom they should attempt to keep out of power, rather than which bloc would do them most favours. At the parliamentary elections of November 1919, the Federation and the Economic party cast their lot in with an alliance of both Liberals and Democrats known as the Fascio Patriottico, in an attempt to prevent the installation of a dictatorship of the proletariat in the country. The Federation leadership argued that participation in the bloc was necessary in order to avert a general political crisis within the country, and that this had to take precedence over the resolution of the particular problems confronting small traders. *L'Esercente* also supported the alliance, but later revealed its unhappiness with such tactics. The newspapers argued that the Liberals had done the *esercenti* few favours in government, whilst the Federation had not even obtained a promise for legislation that would abolish institutions such as the Azienda. Once the election was over, Tadini made clear that his own preference would have been to exploit the new electoral system of proportional representation within multimember constituencies by fielding independent *esercenti* candidates as happened in Genoa and Turin.[41]

Disagreements within the movement over the strategy to be followed at parliamentary elections were not mirrored at city level. Here the imperative was simple – get the Socialists out. The victory

---

[39] Mussolini, B., 'Triplice lezione', *Il Popolo d'Italia*, 7 July 1919.

[40] ASM, Gab. Prefettura, 296, Reclami vari per l'aumento dei prezzi, contains a letter of 16 August 1919 from 'one of the many victims of protected usury' denouncing a trattoria for overcharging on the basis of a letter published in *Il Popolo d'Italia*. Investigation by the Questura found this was not the case. R. Questura di Milano, n.70962, Div. 3a, 4 September 1919.

[41] 'Alla vigilia delle elezioni politiche', *L'Esercente*, 9 November 1919; 'La risposta del Cav. Edoardo Piovella, Presidente della Federazione degli Esercenti', ibid., 20 February 1920; 'Gli esercenti e commercianti di fronte alle elezioni', ibid., 24 April 1921.

of the left-wing 'maximalists' within the Milanese Socialist party, isolating Caldara and his colleagues in the Comune, further fuelled *esercenti* fears, and by the time of the administrative elections held in November 1920 the language was essentially that of class struggle and civil war. *L'Esercente* called on its readers to halt the tide of Bolshevism, and remember that:

> Russia was one of the best granaries in the world ... Today famine and desolation reign in Russia. The maximalists ... want to reduce Italy to the same conditions ... Bolshevism would be the ruin of you. Remind yourself that you have the duty to defend your city because with it you defend your existence and that of your family.[42]

The newspaper urged its readers to wrap themselves in the flag of the fatherland and published a poem (by a lawyer) urging the *esercenti* to oppose the plebeian mob.[43]

The election was a straight two-party fight between the Socialist list and that of the Blocco d'Azione e Difesa Sociale (Bloc of Action and Social Defence) which comprised all the other major political groupings. The Federation was able to obtain seven slots on the Blocco list, and Piazza San Sepolcro was used as the location of the bloc's secretariat. A 74% turnout suggested to *L'Esercente* that the commercial classes were finally playing their role in city politics, but even this was unable to prevent the Socialists' victory by 73,020 votes to 70,926.[44]

With the maximalists in the town hall, the Azienda, government import controls and the fixed-price regime still operating, and inflation, notably that of shop rents, continuing apace, it was no wonder that the sense of abandonment and hostility amongst the *esercenti* movement persisted. In October 1920, Tadini blamed the parliamentary system for failing to produce the strong man who could right Italy's wrongs, and suggested that it might be necessary to use extra-legal measures to overthrow the government's restrictive provisioning regime.[45] After the local elections, *L'Esercente*

---

[42] 'L'imminente battaglia elettorale per l'amministrazione cittadina', ibid., 4 November 1920.
[43] Palmegiano, Avv. M., 'Il grido dell'esercente', *L'Esercente*, 7 November 1920.
[44] 'L'odierna battaglia elettorale', *L'Esercente*, 7 November 1920; 'Ciò che si è fatto e ciò che si può fare', ibid., 21 November 1920.
[45] 'Delitti senza nome', ibid., 28 October 1920.

pronounced that 'the moment has arrived in which inertia represents the major danger'.[46]

Although much of Tadini's rhetoric contained the kind of radical nationalism associated with the Fascists, there was no attempt on his part to move small traders towards a party which, in Milan, in any case still focused its efforts on building a base amongst dissident workers. In April 1921, when a new set of parliamentary elections were held, the newspaper was again adamant that the *esercenti* movement should take advantage of the system of proportional representation to field candidates of its own, anticipating that two or three might be elected. Advancing this proposition Tadini argued that the Liberals had not delivered in government, whilst many *esercenti* would find it difficult to choose between the lay democratic parties, and the new Catholic mass party, the Popolare. There was no mention of the Fascists in this discussion, although they formed part of the alliance of lay parties known as the Blocco Nazionale.[47]

L'Esercente published a political programme for the elections that embraced most of the movement's demands. The guiding principle was the protection of public order and private property, with the guarantee of a right to work. In economic policy, the programme called for the encouragement of private enterprise, the reduction of state involvement in the economy to a minimum and the suppression of 'all the interferences born with the war'. There should be no more experiments in taxation or industrial reform, decentralisation, a reduction of state bureaucracy and free trade in all products except those required for national defence.[48]

Once again the newspaper failed to convince the *esercenti* organisations of its case. The Federation signed up with the Blocco Nazionale, and its president, Viganò, was found a place on the alliance's list. *L'Esercente* grudgingly accepted this, arguing that primary importance had to be given to the task of defeating the Socialists, and paying tribute to the larger number of candidates from commercial backgrounds on the list. In the event the Blocco won seven seats to the Socialist's fifteen, with the Popolare taking five and the Communists one. Mussolini received over 40,000 votes more than any other candidate on the Blocco list, whilst Viganò just failed to be elected. Tadini argued that the results highlighted the

[46] 'Ciò che si è fatto e ciò che si può fare', ibid., 21 November 1920.
[47] 'Gli esercenti e commercianti di fronte alle elezioni', ibid., 24 April 1921.
[48] 'Programma economico', ibid., 17 April 1921.

difficulties of a proportional system in which candidates from the same list ended up fighting each other, creating opportunities for political chicanery within an alliance. He refrained from openly accusing Mussolini of this, but pointed out that if the Communists were able to win a seat on the basis of 21,000 votes, then the *esercenti* would have stood an excellent chance of securing the election of some candidates had they run a list of their own.[49]

For the *esercenti*, the remainder of 1921 and most of 1922 were dominated by a long-running dispute over what time in the morning bakery workers should begin work. An accord was reached between the executive of the Mutua Proprietari Forno and the workers' union, but this was rejected by a more militant faction within the proprietors' association, who subsequently overthrew the executive. A violent dispute ensued, notable for the murder of the vice-president of the Mutua Proprietari Forno, Angelo Bocchiola, on 25 May 1922, a crime the proprietors' association was swift to blame on the union. A further motive for the attack was that Bocchiola had started to recruit his own workers from an alternative *ufficio di collocamento* set up by workers hostile to the union, which had attached itself to the Fascist syndicate. Fascist squads took to beating up members of the original, Socialist, union; and by agreeing terms with the breakaway organisation in August the proprietors were able to break the strike without making concessions to the majority of workers. Although it was clear that the Fascists' main aim remained the organisation of dissident workers, the proprietors still had reason to be grateful to them.[50]

In August 1922, reacting to a general strike called to protest against political violence, the Fascists invaded the Milanese town hall, leading the Prefect to dismiss the Socialist administration in a bid to restore order. In October came the march on Rome and the appointment of Mussolini as Prime Minister. There was relatively little coverage of these events in *L'Esercente*, although Tadini welcomed the arrival of Mussolini because he promised to be a leader rather than a minister, praising what it believed were his intentions of reducing state interference in the economy and returning func-

---

[49] 'La valorizzazione delle forze commerciale nelle prossime elezioni', ibid., 8 May 1921; 'Proseguire!', ibid., 22 May 1921.
[50] For an account of the strike see Granata, *La nascita del sindacato fascista*, pp. 197–200.

tions to the private sector.[51] In 1923 some of these hopes seemed rewarded when the statutory controls on the opening hours of *esercizi pubblici* were abolished, but it was the introduction of a new decree on shop leases in 1924, instituting a new procedure for reviews and extensions, that won the approval of the Federation, the Association and *L'Esercente*. Mussolini's peremptory dismissal of the landlords' protest – 'the government must understand and balance the interests of the totality of the citizenry' – was much appreciated.[52] In the same year price controls on bread were finally removed, but the Fascists' popularity waned as they continued to promote the Azienda as a device for controlling prices, introduced changes in local taxation and promoted an anti-inflationary atmosphere that, in 1926, led *L'Esercente* to write of a 'denigratory campaign against small commerce'.[53]

This brief survey of the history of the next twenty years of the *esercenti* movement in Milan is suggestive of many changes in the nature of shopkeeper politics, but also of continuities between this period and its predecessor. All small-trader strategies were founded on the impossibility of an alliance between the Socialists and the *esercenti* following the disaster of the centre-left administration at the turn of the century. The period of Socialist rule in the Comune between 1914 and 1922 confirmed this, with the introduction of a series of municipal initiatives, most notably the Azienda Consorziale dei Consumi. Attitudes towards the Socialists hardened, and the gap between worker and proprietor widened as the movement learnt to talk the language of class politics. Opposition to intervention, be it by state or local authority, became the touchstone of *esercenti* politics.

The most effective way of mounting this opposition was the continual subject of debate within the movement, however. Political autonomy was accompanied by strategic plurality. The *esercenti* were quite prepared to switch their votes from one grouping to another if they thought this was in their interests, and the various

---

[51] 'Necessità di governo', *L'Esercente*, 9 November 1922.
[52] 'Dopo il decreto sui fitti dei negozi (ovvero: la ligua batte dove il dente duole)', ibid., 28 February 1924. On opening hours see 'Il trionfo della logica', ibid., 8 November 1923.
[53] 'La campagna denigratoria contro il piccolo commercio', ibid., 5 September 1926. See also 'Basta colle utopie! (Ancora in tema di caro-viveri)', ibid., 4 January 1925; 'Insegnamenti di ricordare (a proposito di consorzi)', ibid., 15 November 1925; Nejrotti, 'L'amministrazione comunale di Milano', pp. 465–8.

organisations changed their endorsements frequently. Rarely, however, did they all concur over which political bloc best represented their interests. Centre, right and independent strategies were all supported by strands within the movement at the same election.

This was true of both the pre- and post-war periods, but in the latter choices were constrained by the fact that an effective opposition to the Socialists had to embrace both Liberals and Democrats in one political alliance, thus merging the centre and right alternatives. In the heightened political atmosphere generated at a time when revolution was undoubtedly thought to be on the cards, *L'Esercente*'s independent strategy, though logical, was rejected as offering no solution to the general crisis. Milanese politics became a left–right struggle, with the administrative elections of 1920 and 1922 witnessing a straightforward contest between the Socialists and a single bloc representing all other parties. Inevitably the *esercenti* supported the latter, and celebrated its victory in the elections that followed Mussolini's attainment of power.[54] It was the bloc's success, not the black shirts', however, that was celebrated, even though some small traders were undoubtedly involved with the latter. The *esercenti* movement dealt with the Fascists as it did with other political parties, applauding actions of which it approved and decrying those of which it did not, and continued to do so within the increasing constraints imposed after 1922.

[54] 'Insegnamenti', *L'Esercente*, 14 December 1992.

Conclusion: identity and autonomy

The *esercenti* movement in Milan was much concerned with the need to develop a distinctive shopkeeper identity that would, in turn, sustain the movement. Each component part of the movement tried to mould this identity into line with its own outlook, leaving the historian the difficult task of untangling the various strategies proposed by different factions within the movement, and assessing the relative appeal of these to the *esercenti*. It would be foolish to imagine that a definitive history of the development of a shopkeeper consciousness could ever be written, but analysis of the Milanese movement does provide a concrete context in which the questions raised about shopkeeper history and politics in the Introduction can be addressed.

Throughout the 1880s and 1890s the division of Milan into two different *dazio consumo* zones dominated commercial, industrial and political life in the city. The origins of the shopkeeper movement reflected this division very clearly. It was the *micca* affair and the continuing efforts of the city administration to raise more revenue from the suburbs that created the circumstances in which *L'Esercente* and the Federation were able to establish themselves. Their constituency was the proprietors of those stores which would be most affected by changes in the application of the *dazio consumo*: those provisioners of staple goods – such as bakers, pork butchers and grocers – who formed the greatest part of the retail community in the suburban districts. These shopkeepers' political identity was primarily zonal rather than occupational, and they tended to see themselves as spokesmen for those suburban residents who were excluded from participation in city politics, instead of associating with city-centre shopkeepers who had a very different view of the *dazio* division.

The importance of the local commercial environment in deter-mining shopkeeper behaviour recalls the recent stress that historians of the *petite bourgeoisie* have laid on the importance of analysing the shopkeepers' position within the neighbourhood. Shopkeepers in both the *interno* and *esterno* generally shared the same political outlook as the other residents in their community. This empathy, though, was based on shopkeepers' commercial interests. The *eser-centi* movement's close ties to the Democrats, political champions of the suburbs and of those who felt themselves excluded from the Milanese establishment, should be understood in this context.

During the depression years of the early 1890s the focus of shopkeeper grievances shifted from the Moderates' revenue-raising policies to the issue of 'unfair' competition. As small traders suc-cumbed to the depression they blamed their customers for demand-ing such archaic benefits as *il fido* and the *regali natalizi*, and for deserting them in favour of such allegedly 'privileged' competitors as pedlars, *negozi di liquidazione* and consumer cooperatives. This was indicative of the weak nature of the much-vaunted affinity between shopkeepers and their clientele, and implied an important change in emphasis within the nature of *esercenti* identity. It was now shopkeepers, rather than suburbanites, who were the 'out-siders' in the face of a political and social consensus in favour of cooperation.

This presented the *esercenti* movement with an opportunity to increase its appeal to small traders throughout the city. At a practi-cal level, shopkeeper organisations were able to offer some advice and assistance on how to cope with the commercial crisis, whilst the battle against cooperative privilege demanded that shopkeepers agitate as an interest group within the political process – precisely the kind of collective activity that the movement promoted. The campaign against consumer cooperatives played a crucial role in developing an *esercente* consciousness because it involved an occu-pational grievance, common to shopkeepers throughout the city, yet one not shared by the other residents of the zone in which a proprietor's business was located.

The two sets of elections held in 1895 gave notice of the extent of these changes when the *esercenti* followed Rusca's advice to vote for mixed lists of candidates, rather than support the 'cooperators' and Socialists on the Democrat list that was endorsed by the Federation. This entailed a shift to the right, but it was neither inevitable nor irreversible, and should not be overstated. The starting point for the mixed list was the Democrat list from which unacceptable names were then removed and replaced by those of small traders with other political persuasions. The crucial point was that occupational self-interest determined the way the *esercenti* cast their votes.

Between 1895 and 1899 the *allargamento* debate again divided the *esercenti* on zonal lines, as suburban traders recognised that changes to the *dazio* system posed a far greater threat to their commercial viability than the challenges of the consumer cooperatives, whilst shopkeepers in the central area were presented with the opportunity to overcome the competition of the *frontisti*. It was hardly surprising that the shopkeeper movement should splinter along the lines dictated by commercial geography in these years, with the appearance of a spate of breakaway associations and newspapers. Whilst there was undoubtedly a return to zonal identification, with much propaganda about the links between the *esercento* and his neighbourhood, it should be remembered that this was primarily explained by the suburban shopkeepers' need to defend their most critical trading advantage within the Milanese commercial environment.

The process of social differentiation, by which the *esercenti* came to regard themselves as forming a distinct occupational grouping, continued during these years. The shopkeepers' role of neighbourhood spokesmen had been eroded by the expansion of the local franchise in 1889 which had enabled the lower classes, particularly educated workers, to make their own voices heard in the political arena, often through Socialist representatives. These politicians supported cooperative privileges, suggesting disloyalty among the *esercenti* clientele. It was white-collar employees who patronised the most successful consumer cooperatives in the city, however, leading small traders to draw sharp distinctions between the precariousness of their own position and the security of that of the *impiegati*. The *esercenti* were also disturbed by the ideas expressed within the newly emerging labour organisations, and regarded 1898 as a warning about the persuasiveness of such dangerous notions. *L'Esercente*'s appeals to workers to respect the social hierarchy in the aftermath of the May events, and Baroni's endorsement of the actions of Bava Beccaris, suggested that proprietors were now conscious of a considerable social distance between their own interests and aspirations, and those of their clientele.

In the elections of the following year, however, suburban traders demonstrated that their primary concern was the undermining of their commercial position by the *allargamento*, and, in contrast to 1895, they rallied behind the Federation and the Democrat list, despite its inclusion of the Socialists. To this extent zonal interests and identity still ruled. The Federation's representatives joined the centre-left executive but the logic behind such an alliance collapsed when the administration conceded that there could be no reversal of the *allargamento*. A new commercial environment encompassing the whole city was established, one in which shopkeepers' occupational concerns were of greater importance than those which arose from their location. In political terms these translated into opposition to the Socialists and their policies of municipal interventionism, culminating in the resignation of Federation representatives from the council as a result of pressure from the ordinary membership. In the social sphere the penetration of labour activity into the *esercenti* sector itself led to a much clearer demarcation between shop-worker and proprietor.

Conversely, there was now a greater community of interest between the *esercenti* and other groups of proprietors. The admission of hoteliers into the ranks of professions that were regarded as linked to, if not part of, the *esercenti* movement, occasioned by an industrial dispute across both sectors, was one notable indication of this shift. The *esercenti* associations now played a significant role in the Chamber of Commerce from which they had once been excluded, and they were even rewarded by government concessions, such as the alteration of the bankruptcy laws in 1903.

It was the *esercenti* who brought themselves into this system, however, rather than Giolitti or the Milanese bourgeoisie calling them forth. The collective forms of association and activity that characterised the small-trader movement in Milan reflected the development of a specific occupational identity, albeit one that tolerated several different forms, reflecting the heterogeneity of the sector. The movement was notably wary of the attempts of organisations such as the Associazione Commercianti, Industriali ed Esercenti to incorporate the *esercenti* into broader class politics, particularly when it was realised that the *esercenti* were expected to form part of the lowest cast within such larger blocs. The respect for property and the social order, through which the *esercenti* distinguished themselves from the working class, did not demand an uncritical acceptance of the bourgeoisie. Those concessions won at local and national level came about as the result of successful participation in the political contest; not an elite programme of social protection.

Such qualifications also apply to any attempt to interpret the *esercenti* political experience as merely a progression from left to right. In 1905 the shopkeeper movement was united in its support of the Moderate list against that of the Democrats and Socialists. It seems clear that by this juncture the 'left' option, as represented by the Socialists, was closed. The party stood for interventionist policies that were clearly contrary to shopkeeper interests, and shopkeepers believed that its ideology encouraged attacks on private property such as those witnessed during the General Strike of 1904. It was impossible to make any case for shopkeepers voting Socialist in their own self-interest. As a result the *esercenti* were effectively shunted into the only other option available to them, that of the right.

There are two important points to be made here, however. The first is that the progress of the movement until that point was not simply a trek across the political spectrum. The bulk of the movement had supported the Democrats in the 1880s, had moved towards the centre by 1895, turned back to the Democrat-Socialist alliance by 1899, and in 1905 rejected this in favour of the Moderates. The second is that 1905 was not the end of the story. When the Democrats separated from the Socialists, they won back the support of a significant section of the movement, including that of the Federation. In this sense the Milanese case is a vindication of the model of shopkeeper political autonomy, with changes in political direction best explained by reference to local circumstance.

Indeed the Milanese movement was notable for the diversity of political positions it embraced. It was only on rare occasions, such as that of 1905, that all the component parts of the movement could agree over electoral strategy to follow. This serves as a warning not to develop too constricting a concept of *esercenti* political identity – shopkeepers were prepared to support a variety of political strategies. It also points to a further form of autonomy amongst the Milanese movement in that adherents to the movement were able to influence its direction by siding with one leadership faction rather than another. The eventual resignation of the Federation counsellors in 1904 was a good example of this.

Whilst these demonstrations of autonomy echo those found in other studies of shopkeeper movements, it is difficult to make close comparisons between Milan and other cities because of the unique nature of the *dazio* division that arose as a result of the incorporation of the Corpi Santi into the city in 1873. In 1909 Turin extended its *cinta daziaria*, provoking anger amongst its suburban shopkeepers; but the population of the affected area was only one-seventh that of the city, whereas in Milan the two zones were of almost equal size.[1]

A more telling comparison is that between the fates of the centre-left administrations that ruled over otherwise very different cities in Italy in the early 1900s. These often put forward consumer-orientated projects of the kind advocated by the reformist Socialists in Milan, including the establishment of municipal bakeries: a project that came to fruition in Catania as well as several smaller *comuni*. The municipalising *municipii* of Bologna, Catania, Parma and Reggio Emilia were all dismissed in elections around the middle of the decade as a result of anti-interventionist alliances in which small traders played a significant role.[2]

The Milanese experience, then, when viewed in this comparative perspective, would seem to suggest an important corrective to the model of shopkeeper behaviour that stresses the strata's political autonomy. The strategy of alliances with the 'left' was ruled out after 1905. This was an important limit on the options available to the *esercenti*. Thus, if as in 1905 the electoral choice confronting them was support of one of two lists, one of which contained Socialist candidates, then the movement had no real options at all.

This suggests some ways of reconciling the stress that advocates of *petit-bourgeois* political autonomy have laid upon the importance of politics, ideology and local circumstances in determining the directions pursued by shopkeeper movements with the objections of those who point out that nearly all such movements end up on the right. Politics and ideology did matter in Milan: political structures and local circumstances combined in 1905 to mean that only two choices were available to the shopkeeper movement, but the pro-

[1] Einaudi, 'La riforma tributaria di una grande città' in *Cronache economiche e politiche*, Vol. 2, p. 649.

[2] Meriggi, 'Il projetto di municipalizzazione del pane', pp. 438–52; Gianolio, 'La municipalizzazione a Reggio Emilia', pp. 370–6; Taddei, 'La municipalizzazione dei servizi a Parma', pp. 664–72.

consumer, interventionist ideology of the Socialists ruled out one of the two choices. These were important limitations on the political autonomy of the *esercenti*.

This was not, however, a simple case of another shopkeeper movement ending up on the right: after 1905 plurality returned to the movement when both centre and right strategies again became available. The Democrats and the right-wing Moderates both attracted support within the movement because of their opposition to the taxation policies of liberal Moderates such as Ponti, confirming that the *esercenti* had not been incorporated into any broad-based conservative bloc but continued to approach politics on the basis of ocupational self-interest.

The expansion of the franchise in 1912 made it much easier for Socialists to take control of local municipalities, whilst the war and its aftermath gave them the chance to extend interventionism far deeper. After 1914 anti-Socialism again dominated *esercenti* politics in Milan, in response to the new administration's repeated interventions into the market and its avowed intent to modernise the small-retail sector. Again there are parallels with other municipalities. In Bologna, the Socialist administration instituted a system of price controls and sold its own bread and fruit, leading to shopkeeper attacks on *comune bottegaio*; in Florence, the local Unione Esercenti participated in a Moderate-Nationalist-Liberal bloc as early as 1915. Following the cost-of-living riots the post-war Socialist administrations in Bologna and Ferrara decreed severe price cuts in addition to those imposed by the government, a further echo of the Milanese case. Whenever municipalities attempted to intervene in the food-provisioning sector they inevitably came into conflict with the *esercenti*, and the zealousness with which the Socialists denounced the small-retail sector brought forth a reciprocal response of anti-Socialist activity.[3]

It is necessary to distinguish between anti-Socialism and support for the right. In the post-war period in Milan, the *esercenti* movement supported a series of blocs which encompassed parties of both the centre and the right, and both these elements were attractive to significant sections of the movmeent – more so than the Fascists. The debate about running *esercenti* candidates in parliamentary

[3] Spini and Casali, *Firenze*, p. 107; Cavazza, 'Bologna dall'età napoleonica al primo Novecento', pp. 338–9; Corner, *Fasciam in Ferrara*, pp. 62–6; Sapelli, 'La municipalizzazione: socialist, cattolici e liberisti a confronto', pp. 174–7.

elections in order to exploit the introduction of proportional representation emphasised that no political party was automatically considered capable of adequately representing small-trader interests. What appeared to be imperative, however, was the defeat of the Socialists, given the record of the administration in Milan and the fear of what might happen should they assume power at the national level. Anti-Socialism, not right-wing extremism, characterised shopkeeper politics in Milan during the immediate post-war period.

The evidence from Milan is both of autonomy and of the limits to it. The *esercenti* movement did not move inexorably across the political spectrum from left to right, it was not incorporated into a broad conservative stratum, and it did not align itself with the extreme right in response to a *grand peur* resulting from a very real commercial and political crisis. The political responses of the movement reflected the *esercenti* identity that it had helped develop an occupational identity that differentiated between small traders and other social groupings, and whose primary characteristic was that of commercial self-interest. By 1905, however, it was clear that the ideology of the Milanese Socialists was in direct conflict with those interests, so precluding *esercenti* support for political options favouring the left. When circumstances dictated that only one bloc could effectively oppose the Socialists, as happened both in 1905 and in the post-war period, then the movement had no choice but to endorse it. Recognising these limitations does not invalidate the case for political autonomy amongst the *petite bourgeoisie*, but does explain why the *esercenti* movement should end up on the right of the political divide.

Bibliography

I ARCHIVES

Archivio della Camera di Commercio di Milano (ACC)
scat. 73, f.1 (street trading)
scat. 124, ff.1–4 (bankruptcy procedures)
scat. 125, f.6 (reform of bankruptcy laws)

Archivio dello Stato di Milano (ASM)
Fond. Questura
c.27 (carnival)
c.43 (strikes and disorders)
c.45 (strikes and disorders)
c.51 (strikes and disorders)
c.52 (strikes and disorders)
c.53 (strikes and disorders)
c.57 (extension of the *dazio* belt)
c.59 (strike statistics)
c.65 (milling and baking exhibition, firearms sales, prohibited games)
c.86 (rest days)
c.91 (bakers)
c.107 (associations and cooperatives)
c.108 (associations and cooperatives)
c.109 (associations)
c.113 (periodical publications)
c.116 (periodical publications)

Gabinetto Prefettura
295 (political unrest)
296 (political unrest)

II PRINTED WORKS

i Newspapers, periodicals and serial publications

Atti della Camera di Commercio di Milano
Atti Parlamentari
Avanti!
Bollettino Demografico-Sanitario-Igienico-Meteorologico a cura del Comune di Milano
Città di Milano. Bollettino Municipale Mensile di Cronaca Amministrativa e di Statistica a cura del Comune di Milano
Corriere della Sera
Dati statistici a corredo del resoconto dell'amministrazione comunale, Milan
L'Esercente, 1873
L'Esercente, a.k.a. *La Voce degli Esercenti*, a.k.a. *L'Esercente Italiano*
Guida di Milano, publ. Savallo
La Lombardia
Il Popola d'Italia
Il Secolo
Statistica giudiziaria civile commerciale e statistica notarile a cura della Direzione generale della statistica

ii Books

Adburgham, A., *Shops and shopping 1800–1914*, 3rd edn. London, 1989.
Alfani, A., *Battaglie e vittorie: nuovi esempi di volere è potere*. Florence, 1890.
Ansaldo, G., *Il ministro della buonvita*. 3rd edn. Milan, 1963.
Associazione fra gli Industriali ed i Commercianti della Città e Provincia di Bologna, *Relazione della commissione per gli studi sulla procedura dei fallimenti*. Bologna, 1901.
Atti del comitato esecutivo della esposizione internazionale di apparecchi di macinazione e panificazione in Milano: maggio–agosto 1887. Vol. 2. Milan, 1888.
Autori vari, *Vita milanese*. Milan, 1889.
Baedeker, K., *Italy from the Alps to Naples*. Leipzig, London and New York, 1904.
Baglioni, G., *L'ideologia della borghesia industriale nell'Italia liberale*. Turin, 1974.
Ballini, P. L., *Le elezioni nella storia d'Italia dall'Unità al fascismo: profilo storico-statistico*. Bologna, 1988.
Barbadoro, I., ed., *La crisi di fine secolo (1880–1900)*. Storia dell Società Italiana, Vol. 19. Milan, 1980.
L'Italia di Giolotti. Storia della Società Italiana, Vol. 20. Milan 1981.
Barberis, Avv. M., *Sulla ditta, insegna e nome commerciale*. Milan, 1911.
Bardeaux, C. L., *Catalogo delle guide di Milano preceduto da un breve saggio storico sulle guide stesse*. Estratto da 'Archivio Storico Lombardo' 1938–1943. Milan, 1969.
Bartoccini, F., *Roma nell'Ottocento: il tramonto della 'Città Santa', nascita di un capitale*. Bologna, 1985.

Bechhofer F. and Elliot B., eds., *The petite bourgeoisie: comparative studies of an uneasy stratum.* London, 1981.
Berselli, A., Della Peruta, F. and Varni, A., eds., *La municipalizzazione in area padana.* Milan, 1988.
Blackbourn, D., *Class, religion and local politics in Wilhelmine Germany: the Centre Party in Württemberg before 1914.* New Haven, 1980.
Blackbourn, D. and Eley, G., *The peculiarities of Germany history.* Oxford, 1984.
Bordoni-Uffreduzzi, G., *I servizi di igiene nel comune di Milano. Relazione al Sindaco.* Milan, 1903.
I servizi di igiene nel quinquennio 1901–1905. Milan, 1906.
Bradford, M. G. and Kent, W. A., *Human geography: theories and their applications.* Science in Geography Series, No. 5. Oxford, 1977.
Briganti, W., ed., *Il movimento cooperativo in Italia 1854–1925. Scritti e documenti.* Rome and Bologna, 1976.
Buffoli, L., *Le società cooperative di consumo.* Milan, 1885.
L'organizzazione delle società cooperative. Milan, 1886.
Lo sviluppo della cooperazione in Europa. Milan, 1904.
Camera di Commercio ed Arti di Roma, *Testo del progetto di legge sul concordato preventivo approvato e relazione della commissione camerale.* Rome, 1897.
Canavero, A., *Milano e la crisi di fine secolo (1896–1900).* Milan, 1976.
Candeloro, G., *Storia dell'Italia moderna.* Vol. 7. *La crisi di fine secolo e l'età giolittiana.* Milan, 1974.
Carocci, G., *Giolitti e l'età giolittiana.* Turin, 1961.
Caroleo, A., *Le banche cattoliche dalla prima guerra mondiale al fascismo.* Milan, 1976.
Cattaneo, C., *L'insurrezione di Milan nel 1848 e la successiva guerra* (ed. G. Macaggi), Castello, 1921.
Scritti economici. 3 vols. (ed. A. Bertolino). Florence, 1956.
Ceriani, P., *Il Comune di Milano. Presente ed avvenire.* Milan, 1896.
Clark, M., *Modern Italy 1871–1982.* Harlow, 1984.
Il comitato centrale contro l'allargamento della cinta daziaria alla Onerevole Giunta Municipale di Milano in confutazione della proposte di modificazioni nell'ordinamento Tributario del Comune presentate all'Onerevole Consiglio Comunale. Milan, 1895.
Comune di Milano, *Annuario storico statistico 1914.* Milan, 1915.
Relazione sulla refezione scolastica distribuita nelle scuole comunali negli anni 1900–1 e 1901–2. Milan, 1903.
Regolamento municipale per l'applicazione della tassa sul valore locativo. Milan, 1902.
Reparto Dazio Consumo, *Giurisprudenza amministrativa per controversie daziarie trattate dalla giunta municipale di Milano dal 1 settembre 1898–31 dicembre 1901.* Milan, 1902.
Conferenze tenute all'esposizione internazionale di apparecchi di macinazione e panificazione in Milano, maggio–agosto 1887. Milan, 1888.
Convenzione fra il Municipio di Milano e la Società del Pubblico Macello. Milan, 1887.

Corner, P., *Fascism in Ferrara 1915–1925*. London, 1975.

Crossick, G., ed., *The lower middle class in Britain 1870–1914*. London, 1977.

Crossick, G. and Haupt, H. G., eds., *Shopkeepers and master artisans in nineteenth-century Europe*. London, 1984.

Davis, J. A., *Conflict and control: law and order in nineteenth-century Italy*. Basingstoke, 1988.

Decastro, Cav. N., *La tassa di esercizio e rivendita*. Como, 1903.

Della Peruta, F., *Società e classi popolari nell'Italia dell'Ottocento*. Palermo, 1985.

Della Peruta, F., Leydi, R. and Stella, A., eds., *Milano e il suo territorio*. Mondo Popolare in Lombardia series, No. 13, 2 vols. Milan, 1985.

Dizionario biografico degli Italiani. Istituto dell'Enciclopedia Italiana fondato da Giovanni Treccani: Vol. 11, Rome, 1969; Vol. 15, Rome, 1972.

Dompè, Rag. C., *Manuale del commerciante ad uso della gente di commercio e degli istituti d'istruzione commerciale*. Milan, 1903.

Einaudi, L., *Cronache economiche e politiche di un trentennio 1893–1925*. 2 vols. Turin, 1959.

Eley, G., *Reshaping the German right: radical nationalism and political change after Bismarck*. New Haven, 1980.

Fantoni, U., *Agli esercenti*. Milan, 1896.

Federazione Italiana delle Società di Mutuo Soccorso, *Il consulente legale delle Società di Mutuo Soccorso. Almanacco dei previdenti pel 1903*. Como, 1902.

Federazione Socialista Milanista, *Numero unico: pane a buon mercato*. Milan, 1897.

Ferri, A. and Rovesi, G., eds., *Storia di Bologna*. Bologna, 1978.

Fiocca, G., ed., *Borghesi e imprenditori a Milano dall'Unità alla prima guerra mondiale*. Bari, 1984.

Fonzi, F., *Crispi e lo 'Stato di Milano'*. 2nd edn. Milan, 1972.

Franzina, E., *Venezia*. Bari, 1986.

Fraser, D. and Sutcliffe A., eds., *The pursuit of urban history*. London, 1983.

Frisoni, G., *Corrispondenza commerciale italiana*. 7th edn. Milan, 1921.

Gandolfi, L., *Botteghe milanesi dell'Ottocento nella loro pubblicità epistolare*. Milan, 1980.

Gellately, R., *The politics of economic despair: shopkeepers and German politics 1890–1914*. London, 1974.

Gerschenkron, A., *Continuity in history*. Cambridge, Mass., 1968.
Economic backwardness in historical perspective. New York, 1962.

Gobbi, U., *Il nuovo progetto di legge sui dazi comunali e la riforma tributaria milanese*. Milan, 1898.

Granata, I., *La nascita del sindacato fascista. L'esperienza di Milano*. Movimento Operaio, No. 66. Bari, 1981.

Hunecke, V., *Classe operaia e rivoluzione industriale a Milano 1859–1892*. Bologna, 1982.

King, B. and Okey, T., *Italy today*. London, 1909.

Koshar, R., ed., *Splintered classes: politics and the lower middle classes in interwar Europe*. New York, 1990.

Lega Nazionale della Cooperative Italiane, *Statistica delle Società Cooperative Italiane esistenti nel 1902*. Milan, 1903.

Legge n.197 sul concordato preventivo nei fallimenti pubblicata in data 24 maggio 1903. Milan, 1903.

Malacarne, I., *Manuale del commerciante ossia trattato dei materiali primi di commercio*. Milan, 1853.

Mandel, E., *Long waves of capitalist development: the marxist interpretation*. Cambridge, 1980.

Manighetti, L., *Commercianti all'Erta! Ovvero anzichè procedere, regalate*. Milan, 1892.

Mantegazza, P., *Almanacco igienico popolare: l'arte di conservare gli alimenti e le bevande*. Milan, 1887.

Mellini, C., *Storia dell'Unione Cooperativa*. Milan, 1905.

Melpa, C., *Come si fa il commerciante*. Bologna, 1911.

Merli, S., *Proletariato di fabbrica e capitalismo industriale: il caso italiano 1880–1900*. Florence, 1972.

Milla, P.E., *Commercio e commercianti*. Milan, 1912.

Commessi di commercio. Milan, 1912.

Ministero dell'Agricoltura, Industria e Commercio (MAIC), *Statistica degli scioperi avvenuti nell'industria e nell'agricoltura durante gli anni dal 1884 al 1891*, Rome, 1892.

Statistica degli scioperi avvenuti nell'industria e nell'agricoltura durante gli anni 1892 e 1893. Rome, 1894.

Mori, G., *Il capitalismo industriale in Italia*. Rome, 1977.

Mozzarelli, C., ed., *Economia e corporazioni: il governo degli interessi nella storia d'Italia dal medioevo all'età contemporanea*. Milan, 1988.

Mozzarelli, C. and Pavoni, R., eds., *Milano fin de siècle e il caso Bagatti Valsecchi. Memoria e progetto per la metropoli italiana*. Milan, 1991.

Nord, P. G., *Paris shopkeepers and the politics of resentment*. Princeton, 1986.

Numero Unico della Società Anonima Cooperativa di Consumo fra gli addetti allo stabilimento Pirelli e C.. Milan, 1906.

Poggiali, C., *Ferdinando Bocconi: Mercurio in finanziera*. Milan, 1945.

La popolazione di Milano secondo il censimento 31 dicembre 1881. Milan, 1883.

La popolazione di Milano secondo il censimento eseguito il 9 febbraio 1901. Milan, 1903.

La popolazione di Milano secondo il censimento eseguito il 10 giugno 1911. Milan, 1915.

Pozzano, G., *Tra pubblico e privato. Storia della centrale del latte di Firenze e Pistoia*. Florence, 1985.

Il Prontuario: guida practica per gli esercenti. Edito per cura del Giornale Amministrazione Commerciale ed Industriale 'L'Esercente'. Milan, 1890.

Punzo, M., *La giunta Caldara. L'amministrazione comunale e Milano negli anni 1914–1920*. Bari, 1986.

Socialisti e Radicali a Milano: cinque anni di amministrazione democratica 1899–1904. Florence, 1979.

La Rappresentanza de' Macellai di Milano, *I macellai di Milano al pubblico.* Milan, 1874.

Regolamento d'igiene pel Comune di Milano 1902. Milan, 1902.

Resoconto morale della giunta municipale del Comune nelle annate 1892–1894. Milan, 1896.

Riosa, A., ed., *Il socialismo riformista a Milano agli inizi del secolo.* Milan, 1981.

Romanelli, R., *Sulle carte interminate. Un ceto di impiegati tra privato e pubblico: i segretari comunali in Italia, 1860–1915.* Bologna, 1989.

Rosa, G., *Il mito della capitale morale.* Milan, 1982.

Rota, G., *Ragioneria della cooperative di consumo.* Milan, 1920.

Sabbatini, L., *Notizie suelle condizioni industriali della provincia di Milano.* Milan, 1893.

Sapelli, G., ed., *Il movimento cooperativa in Italia.* Turin, 1981.

Sapelli, G. and Degl'Innocenti, M., eds., *Cooperative in Lombardia dal 1886.* Renate (Provincia di Milano), 1986.

Schneider, J. and Schneider, P., *Culture and political economy in western Sicily.* New York, 1976.

Snider, A., *Calcoli e commenti sulla attendibilità delle previsioni Ferrario circa il maggior gettito del dazio consumo attesto dall'allargamento della cinta daziaria.* Milan, 1895.

Società Anonima Cooperativa di Consumo fra Impiegati e Professionisti, *Cenni storico-statistico e statuto.* Milan, 1906.

Società Anonima Cooperativa Suburbana di Consumo fra gli Agenti delle Strade Ferrate con sede in Milano, *Cenni storici e statistici raccolti ed ordinati per A. Dalla Cola.* Milan, 1890.

Storia e sviluppo della Società. Milan, 1907.

Società Mutua Proprietari Forno di Milano, *La panificazione privata e la panificazione municipalizzata a Milano (studiato dal punto di vista finanziario, igienico ed economico-sociale).* Milan, 1903.

Società Proprietari Salsamentari, *Regolamento per l'ufficio di collocamento del personale salariato.* Milan, 1889.

Venti anni di vita sociale 1869–1889. Milan, 1889.

Società Umanitaria, *Le condizioni generali della classe operaia in Milano: salari, giornate di lavoro, reddito ecc. risultati di un'inchiesta compiuta il 1 luglio 1903.* Milan, 1907.

Società Umanitaria: Ufficio del Lavoro, *Scioperi, serrate e vertenze fra capitale e lavoro in Milano nel 1903.* Milan, 1904.

Soresina, M., *Mezzemaniche e signorine. Gli impiegati privati a Milano,* Milan, (1880–1992).

Spini, G. and Casali, A., *Firenze.* Bari, 1986.

Statuto della Associazione Cattolica degli Esercenti in Milano. Milan, 1895.

Statuto della Società di Mutuo Sussidi dei Commessi dei Negozianti in Milano. Milan, 1880.

Statuto organico della Società Cooperativa Alimentari fra gli impiegati civili

governativi ed i pensionati governativi civili e militari residenti in Milano.
Milan, 1881.
Storia di Milano. Vols. 15, 16. *A cura della fondazione Treccani degli Alfieri per la storia di Milano.* Milan, 1962.
Torquato, C. G., *Disposizione sul concordato preventivo e sulla procedura dei piccoli fallimenti: riflessioni sopra un disegno di legge.* Rome, 1902.
Unione Cooperativa di Milano, *Catalogo estate 1906.* Milan, 1906.
Vallardi, P., *Milano può abolire la cinta daziaria?* Milan, 1898.
Volkov, S., *The rise of popular anti-modernism in Germany: the urban master artisans 1873–1896.* Princeton, 1978.
Zaninelli, S., *I consumi a Milano nell'Ottocento.* Rome, 1974.
Zezzos, R., *Milano e il suo commercio.* Milan, 1966.
Storia dei macellai milanesi. Rome, 1938.
Vita della bottega (guida sentimentale del commercio). Milan, 1942.
Zoni, G. C., *Il giovane commerciante.* Milan, 1889.

iii Articles

Adami, R. and Ago, L., 'I fenomeni di trasformazione urbana e il ruolo del ceto imprenditoriale', in Fiocca, ed., *Borghesi e imprenditori a Milano,* pp. 291–363.
Antonelli L., 'Le Camere di Commercio napoleoniche. La Repubblica e il Regno d'Italia', in Mozzarelli, ed., *Economia e corporazioni,* pp. 193–236.
Bachi, R., 'Storia della Cassa di Risparmio delle Provincie Lombarde 1823–1923', in *La Cassa di Risparmio delle Provincie Lombarde nella evoluzione economica della regione 1823–1923.* Milan, 1923, pp. 3–321.
Bechhofer, F. and Elliot, B., 'Pretty property: the survival of a moral economy', in Bechhofer and Elliot, eds., *The petite bourgeoisie,* pp. 182–200.
Berezin, M., 'Created constituencies: the Italian middle classes and fascism', in Koshar, ed., *Splintered classes,* pp. 1–30.
Berger, S., 'The uses of the traditional sector in Italy: why declining classes survive', in Bechhofer and Elliot, eds., *The petite bourgeoisie,* pp. 71–89.
Bigatti, G., 'Commercianti e imprenditori nella Milano postunitaria. Le origini della Riva', *Storia e Società,* 39 (1988), 86–95.
Blackbourn, D., 'Between resignation and volatility: the German *petite bourgeoisie* in the nineteenth century', in Crossick and Haupt, eds., *Shopkeepers and master artisans,* pp. 35–61.
'Economic crisis and the *petite bourgeoisie* in Europe during the 19th and 20th centuries', *Social History,* 10, 1 (1985), 95–104.
'The *Mittelstand* in German society and politics, 1871–1914', *Social History,* 3, 4 (1977), 409–33.
Bonfante, G., 'La legislazione cooperativistica in Italia dall'Unità a Oggi', in Sapelli, ed., *Il movimento cooperativa,* pp. 191–252.
Caroleo, A., 'L'Unione Cooperativa di Luigi Buffoli', in Sapelli and Degl'Innocenti, eds., *Cooperative in Lombardia,* pp. 199–215.

Catalono, F., 'Vita politica e questioni sociali 1859–1900', in *Storia di Milano*, Vol. 15, pp. 37–316.

'Milano tra liberalismo e nazionalismo', in *Storia di Milano*, Vol. 16, pp. 51–123.

Cavazza, G., 'Bologna dall'età napoleonica al primo Novecento', in Ferri and Rovesi, eds., *Storia di Bologna*, pp. 283–391.

Childers, T., 'Interest and ideology: anti-system politics in the era of stabilization 1924–1928', in Feldman, G. D., ed., *Die Nachwirkungen der Inflation auf die deutsche Gesichte 1924–1928*. Munich, 1985, pp. 1–20.

Cocucci Deretta, A., 'I cappellai monzesi dall'avvento della grande industria meccanica alla costituzione della Federazione Nazionale', *Classe*, 1972, 155–80.

Cova, A., 'Interessi economici e impegni istituzionali delle corporazioni Milanesi nel Seicento', in Mozzarelli, ed., *Economica e corporazioni*, pp. 109–32.

Cristofili, M. C. and Degrada, L., 'L'archivio della cancelleria delle società commerciali di Milano', in *La storia contemporanea negli archivi lombardi: Un indagine campione*. Publ. Regione Lombardia Assessorato alla cultura e agli enti locali, Milan, 1977, pp. 32–3.

'L'archivio generale del Tribunale di Milano (sezione fallimentari)', in *La storia contemporanea negli archivi lombardi: un'indagine campione*. publ. Regione Lombardia Assessorato alla cultura e agli enti locali, Milan, 1977, pp. 37–8.

Crossick, G., 'Shopkeepers and the state in Britain 1870–1914', in Crossick and Haupt, eds., *Shopkeepers and master artisans*, pp. 239–69.

Crossick, G. and Haupt, H. G., 'Shopkeepers, masters artisans and the historian: the *petite bourgeoisie* in comparative focus', in Crossick and Haupt, eds., *Shopkeepers and master artisans*, pp. 3–31.

Dalla Volta, R., 'Il dazio consumo in Italia', *La Riforma Sociale*, 2 (1894), 994–1001.

D'Angiolini, P., 'Il moderatismo lombardo e la politica italiana: dall'Unità al periodo crispino', *Rivista Storica del Socialismo*, 5, 15/16 (1962), 83–134.

Degl'Innocenti, M., 'La cooperazione lombarda dalla fondazione della Lega all'avvento del fascismo' in Sapelli and Degl'Innocenti, eds., *Cooperative in Lombardia*, p. 21–83.

'Geografia e strutture della cooperazione in Italia', in Sapelli, ed., *Il movimento cooperativo*, pp. 3–87.

Della Peruta, F., 'La società lombarda e la cooperazione dall'Unità alla prima guerra mondiale', in Sapelli and Degl'Innocenti, eds., *Cooperative in Lombardia*, pp. 11–20.

'Lavoro e fabbrica a Milano dall'Unità alla prima guerra mondiale', in Della Peruta *et al*, eds., *Milano e il suo territorio*, Vol. 1, pp. 231–342.

Dotti, A., 'Gli istituti di credito in Milano: gli istituti di credito nel primo trentennio unitario', in *Storia di Milano*, Vol. 15, pp. 977–1002.

Fenoaltea, S., 'Decollo, ciclo e intervento dello Stato', in Caracciolo, A., ed., *La formazione dell'Italia industriale*. Bari, 1969, pp. 95–113.

Fontana, F., 'La vita di strada', in Autori vari, *Vita milanese*, pp. 130–56.

Ganci, S. M., 'L'opposizione democratico-borghese. Republicani e radicali', in Barbadoro, ed., *La crisi di fine secolo*, pp. 213–14.
Gerschenkron, A. and Romeo, R., 'The industrial development of Italy: a
debate', in Gerschenkron, *Continuity in history*, pp. 98–124.
Gianolio, A. 'La municipalizzazione a Reggio Emilia fra progresso e
reazione', in Berselli *et al.*, eds., *La municipalizzazione*, pp. 370–84.
Gozzazini, G., 'Borghesie italiane dell'Ottocento', *Italia Contemporanea*, 78
(1990), 117–26.
Haupt, H. G., 'The *petite bourgeoisie* in France 1850–1914: in search of the
juste milieu?', in Crossick and Haupt, eds., *Shopkeepers and master
artisans*, pp. 95–119.
Kurgan-van Hentenryk, G., 'A forgotten class: the *petite bourgeoisie* in
Belgium 1850–1914', in Crossick and Haupt, eds., *Shopkeepers and
master artisans*, London, 1984, pp. 120–33.
Levi Pisetzky, R., 'La vita e le vesti dei Milanesi nella seconda metà
dell'Ottocento', in *Storia di Milano*, Vol. 15, pp. 721–854.
   'La vita e le vesti dei Milanesi all'inizio del nuovo secolo', *Storia di
Milano*, Vol. 16, pp. 977–1002.
Lodolini, E., 'Le ultime corporazioni di arti e mestieri (sec XIX)' in Autori
vari, *Problemi economici dall'antichità ad oggi: studi in onore del Prof.
Vittorio Franchini*. Milan, 1959, pp. 278–319.
Lonardi, G., 'Scompariranno centomila negozi', *La Repubblica*, 2 Novem-
ber 1985, 50.
Lyttleton, A., 'Milan 1880–1922: the city of industrial capitalism', in
Brucker, G., ed., *Peoples and communities in the western world*, Vol. 2.
Homeward, IL, 1979, pp. 250–88.
Mainoni, P., 'La camera dei mercanti di Milano tra economia e politica alla
fine del medioevo', in Mozzarelli, ed., *Economia e corporazioni*,
pp. 57–80.
Mayer, A. J., 'The lower middle class as a historical problem', *Journal of
Modern History*, 47, 3 (1975), pp. 409–37.
Meriggi, M., 'La borghesia italiana', in Kocka, J., ed., *Borghesie Europee
dell'Ottocento*. Venice, 1989, pp. 161–86.
   'Vita di circolo e rappresentanza civica nella Milano liberale', in Moz-
zarelli and Pavoni, eds., *Milano fin de siècle*, pp. 141–62.
   'Dalla rappresentanza degli interessi alla legittimazione costituzionale.
Le Camere di Commercio in Lombardia dal 1814 at 1859', in Moz-
zarelli, ed., *Economia e corporazioni*, pp. 237–72.
Meriggi, M. G., 'Il progetto di municipalizzazione del pane. Giuseppe
Garibotti e l'utopia del "pane municipale"', in Berselli *et al.*, eds., *La
municipalizzazione*, pp. 427–58.
Minervini, E., 'Il carnevale di Milano tra istituzione e spontaneità', in Della
Peruta *et al.*, eds., *Milano e il suo territorio*, Vol. 2, pp. 439–51.
Morris, J., 'I bottegai e il mondo dei Bagatti Valsecchi' in Mozzarelli and
Pavoni, eds., *Milano fin de siècle*, pp. 377–85.
Mozzarelli, C., 'La riforma politica del 1786 e la nascita delle Camere di
Commercio in Lombardia', in Mozzarelli, ed., *Economia e corpora-
zioni*, pp. 163–92.

Nasi, F., '1860–1899: Da Beretta a Vigoni: storia dell'amministrazione comunale', *Città di Milano*, 85, 5 (1968).

'1899–1926: Da Mussi a Mangiagalli: storia dell'amministrazione comunale', *Città di Milano*, 86, 6/7 (1969).

Nejrotti, M., 'L'amministrazione comunale di Milano e i consumi popolari tra guerra mondiale e fascismo', in Berselli *et al.*, eds., *La municipalizzazione*, pp. 459–72.

Pagani, G., 'Alcune notizie sulle antiche corporazioni milanesi d'arti e mestieri', *Archivio Storico Lombardo*, 19 (1892), 881–906.

Porro, A., 'Amministrazione e potere locale: il Comune di Milano', in ISAP, *L'amministrazione nella storia moderna*. Vol. 2, Milan, 1985, pp. 1791–849.

Punzo, M., 'Riformisti e politica communale', in Riosa, ed., *Il socialismo riformista*, pp. 201–74.

Romano, R., 'Gli inizi del capitalismo italiano', in Barbadoro, ed., *La crisi di fine secolo*, pp. 11–51.

'L'industrializzazione nell'età giolittiana', in Barbadoro, ed., *L'Italia di Giolitti*, pp. 225–81.

Rossi, A., 'Cereali e pane: conferenza tenuta dal Comm. Sen. Alessandro Rossi 16 luglio 1887', in *Conferenze tenute all'esposizione internazionale di apparecchi di macinazione e panificazione*, pp. 28–45.

'Macine e forni: conferenza tenuta dal Comm. Sen. Alessandro Rossi 15 luglio 1887', in *Conferenze tenute all'esposizione internazionale di apparecchi di macinazione e panificazione*, pp. 4–27.

Rumi, G., 'La vocazione politica di Milano', in Mozzarelli and Pavoni, eds., *Milano fin de siècle*, p. 17–22.

Sapelli, G., 'La municipalizzazione: socialisti, cattolici e liberisti a confronto nel primo quindicennio del XX secolo', in Berselli *et al.*, eds., *La municipalizzazione*, pp. 158–207.

Sapori, A., 'L'economia milanese dal 1860 al 1915', in *Storia di Milano*, Vol. 15, pp. 857–936.

Schettini, M., 'L'antiquariato a Milano', *Le Vie d'Italia*, 62, 8, (1956), 981–8.

Taddei, F., 'La municipalizzazione dei servizi a Parma nel periodo giolittiano: appunti per una ricerca', in Berselli *et al.*, eds., *La municipalizzazione padana*, pp. 665–77.

Tilly, L. A., 'I fatti di maggio: the working class of Milan and the rebellion of 1898', in Bezucha, R. J., ed., *Modern European social history*. Lexington, 1972, pp. 124–58.

Titta, A., 'Gli istituti di credito in Milano: gli istituti di credito in Milano durante il periodo 1890–1914', in *Storia di Milano*, Vol. 15, pp. 1005–26.

Trezzi, L., 'Governo del mercimonio e governo della città a Milano nella prima metà del XVIII secolo', in Mozzarelli, ed., *Economia e corporazioni*, pp. 133–53.

Ullrich H., 'Il declino del liberalismo lombardo nell'età giolittiana', *Archivo Storico Lombardo*, 10, 1 (1975), 199–250.

Vaccari, D., 'Ferdinando Bocconi', *Realtà Nuova*, 25, 3, 1960, 270–8.

Vecchio, G., 'La classa politica milanese nello stato liberale: i moderati (1870–1900)', in Mozzarelli and Pavoni, eds., *Milano fin de siècle*, pp. 273–90.

Vigne, T. and Howkins, A., 'The small shopkeeper in industrial and market towns', in Crossick , ed., *The lower middle class in Britain*, pp. 184–210.

Volkov, S., 'Review of Crossick and Haupt, eds., *Shopkeepers and master artisans*', *Social History*, 11, 2 (1986), 266–9.

Weiner, J. M., 'Marxism and the lower middle class: a response to Arno Mayer', *Journal of Modern History*, 48, 4 (1976), 66–71.

Winkler, H., 'From social protectionism to national socialism: the German small-business movement in comparative perspective', *Journal of Modern History*, 48, 1 (1976), 1–18.

II UNPUBLISHED MATERIAL

Foot, J., 'Alliances and socialist theory. Milan and Lombardy, 1914–21' (PhD thesis, University of Cambridge, 1991).

Morris J., 'The political economy of shopkeeping in Milan 1885–1905' (PhD thesis, University of Cambridge, 1989).

Pozzana, G., 'Nel panorama delle aziende pubbliche degli enti locali a Firenze l'esperienza di un'impresa degli ultima trent'anni: la Centrale del Latte' (Paper delivered to the conference 'L'uso pubblico dell'interesse privato: il caso della Centrale del Latte di Firenze e Pistoia', Florence, 8/9 November 1985).

Tilly, L. A., 'The working class of Milan 1881–1911' (PhD thesis, University of Toronto, 1974).

Index

Past and Present Publications

* Published also as a paperback
† Co-published with the Maison des Sciences de l'Homme, Paris

For EU product safety concerns, contact us at Calle de José Abascal, 56–1°, 28003 Madrid, Spain or eugpsr@cambridge.org.

www.ingramcontent.com/pod-product-compliance
Ingram Content Group UK Ltd.
Pitfield, Milton Keynes, MK11 3LW, UK
UKHW042316180425
457623UK00005B/11